Microsoft System Center 2012 Orchestrator Cookbook

Automate mission-critical tasks with this practical, real-world guide to System Center 2012 Orchestrator

Samuel Erskine (MCT)

Andreas Baumgarten (MVP)

Steve Beaumont

BIRMINGHAM - MUMBAI

Microsoft System Center 2012 Orchestrator Cookbook

First published: August 2013

Production Reference: 2210813

Published by Packt Publishing Ltd.
Livery Place
35 Livery Street
Birmingham B3 2PB, UK.

ISBN 978-1-84968-850-5

www.packtpub.com

Cover Image by Garson Shortt (garsonshortt@yahoo.com)

Credits

Authors
Samuel Erskine
Andreas Baumgarten
Steve Beaumont

Reviewers
Anders Asp
Robert Ryan

Acquisition Editor
Andrew Duckworth

Lead Technical Editor
Balaji Naidu

Technical Editors
Vrinda Nitesh Bhosale
Dipika Goankar
Kapil Hemnani

Project Coordinator
Wendell Palmer

Proofreader
Amy Guest

Indexer
Hemangini Bari

Graphics
Ronak Dhruv
Valentina D'Silva

Production Coordinator
Nilesh R. Mohite

Cover Work
Nilesh R. Mohite

About the Authors

Samuel Erskine (MCT) has over 15 years experience in a wide range of technologies and industries (public and private) including working for fortune 500 organizations. In 2009 he founded a consultancy practice organization in the United Kingdom focused on implementing Microsoft System Center systems management and IT Service management products. He merged the original United Kingdom organization with Syliance IT Services in 2012 and became the third member of the Syliance IT Services (`www.syliance.com`) global management team. He is a Computer Engineering graduate and holds various technology vendor/industry certifications. Apart from this book, Samuel is also the lead author for *Microsoft System Center 2012 Service Manager Cookbook* and one of the contributing authors to the System Center 2012 Configuration Manager Unleashed book. He is an active participant in the System Center community with a blog at `www.frameworktorealwork.com`.

I would like to thank Garson Shortt for the picture of the book cover. Garson can be found at `https://www.facebook.com/pages/Garson-Shortt-Photography/171621896321926`.

Thank you to Nasira Ismail for the great business process engineering insights and contributions.

I would like to acknowledge and thank Manoj Parvathaneni (The Dude) and Jeffrey Fanjoy (SCORCH MAC DADDY) for their deep product technical validation.

The book was only possible due to a great team. I would like to acknowledge and thank my co-authors Andreas Baumgarten and Steve Beaumont for delivering on my vision for this book.

Andreas Baumgarten (MVP), IT Architect with the German IT service provider H&D International Group, has worked as an IT pro for more than 20 years. He has always been interested in Microsoft technologies and he can also look back on 14 years of experience as a Microsoft Certified Trainer. Since 2008, he has been responsible for the field of System Center technology consulting and ever since he has taken part in SCSM 2010, 2012, 2012 SP1 and 2012 R2 and System Center Orchestrator 2012 Technology Adoption Program with H&D. With his deep inside technology know-how and his broad experience across the System Center product family and IT management, he now designs and develops private cloud solutions for customers System Center Orchestrator 2012, 2012 SP1 and 2012 R2. In October 2012, he was awarded the Microsoft Most Valuable Professional (MVP) title for System Center Cloud and Datacenter Management.

Steven Beaumont has been working in the IT field since 1998 and is a known authority on everything related to System Center. His career started with low-end system building and support, graduating to manage a crack team of enterprise class support specialists; with the release of Service Manager 2010, he ventured into customization and released some solutions to the community via the TechNet Gallery, helping to show how to extend the usage of the product.

Steve provides consultancy and designs specifically for System Center 2012 and Private Cloud solutions. He is the co-author of *Microsoft System Center Service Manager 2012 Cookbook*, which includes a host of tips and techniques to administer System Center, providing best practice advice and 'recipes' to get the most from Service Manager. He also runs his own blog (`http://systemscentre.blogspot.com`), which covers the full range of System Center components and areas related to desktop design, deployment, and optimization.

About the Reviewers

Anders Asp is a System Center specialist at Lumagate AB with a core focus on Service Manager and Orchestrator. He's also teaching the official Service Manager course at training centers in Scandinavia and has been talking at several large events.

Anders is very active on the official Service Manager forums at TechNet and is regularly blogging about the product on his own blog at `www.scsm.se`. In April 2012 Anders was awarded with the Microsoft Most Valuable Professional (MVP) title in the System Center Cloud and Datacenter Management area and recently got his MVP award renewed.

Robert Ryan is an IT professional with over 15 years industry experience. Working in both public and private sectors to provide 3rd line infrastructure support across global locations.

Robert is responsible for major technology projects which include server rationalization, virtualization and messaging. Currently he is focusing heavily on a private cloud deployment using the Microsoft System Centre Suite.

In my personal time I enjoy technology, film, and time with my wife Natalie and our five children.

I would like to thank the authors for giving me the opportunity to work on this publication.

---

www.PacktPub.com

Support files, eBooks, discount offers and more

You might want to visit www.PacktPub.com for support files and downloads related to your book.

Did you know that Packt offers eBook versions of every book published, with PDF and ePub files available? You can upgrade to the eBook version at www.PacktPub.com and as a print book customer, you are entitled to a discount on the eBook copy. Get in touch with us at service@packtpub.com for more details.

At www.PacktPub.com, you can also read a collection of free technical articles, sign up for a range of free newsletters and receive exclusive discounts and offers on Packt books and eBooks.

http://PacktLib.PacktPub.com

Do you need instant solutions to your IT questions? PacktLib is Packt's online digital book library. Here, you can access, read and search across Packt's entire library of books.

Why Subscribe?

- Fully searchable across every book published by Packt
- Copy and paste, print and bookmark content
- On demand and accessible via web browser

Free Access for Packt account holders

If you have an account with Packt at www.PacktPub.com, you can use this to access PacktLib today and view nine entirely free books. Simply use your login credentials for immediate access.

Instant Updates on New Packt Books

Get notified! Find out when new books are published by following @PacktEnterprise on Twitter, or the *Packt Enterprise* Facebook page.

Table of Contents

Preface

System Center 2012 Orchestrator is an improved version of Opalis, an acquisition of a well-established product by Microsoft. The Opalis product was acquired by Microsoft in 2009 and has seen continual feature updates to its core functionality as well as alignment to the System Center 2012 product feature offerings.

System Center 2012 Orchestrator (SCORCH) is a powerful and versatile process automation Information Technology (IT) toolset. SCORCH provides seamless interconnections between the multiple software products in use in typical IT management environments. This component of the System Center 2012 product uses a graphical workflow creation toolset, and a set of connectors between multiple vendor products known as Integration Packs (IP) to address its objectives.

The installation and post installation phases of SCORCH require you to plan and configure the product in a methodical sequence based on your requirements. The aim of the book is to address the challenges faced by many first time users of SCORCH on how to best plan, deploy, and more importantly automate the right processes in their respective organizations. The objective of the authors is to start the reader's journey of Orchestration by sharing valuable insight from real world scenarios.

The book is written in the Packt style which provides the reader with independent, task oriented steps to achieve specific SCORCH objectives. The authors recommend that you read the first three chapters as a background for subsequent chapters if you are new to SCORCH and process automation software products. The book may be read in the order of interest but where relevant the authors refer to dependent recipes in other chapters.

What this book covers

Chapter 1, Unpacking System Center 2012 Orchestrator, provides the steps required to install and configure SCORCH. This chapter contains recipes on the two installation scenario types for SCORCH; single server and multi-server deployments. The objective is to provide the reader with the steps required for installation of SCORCH in either scenario.

Chapter 2, Initial Configuration and Making SCORCH Highly Available, covers the initial configuration tasks a SCORCH administrator would need to perform after successfully installing the product. The chapter also delves into how SCORCH can be made highly available and the implementation of an example of configuring a security delegation model for SCORCH.

Chapter 3, Planning and Creating Runbook Designs, delves into the workflows (Runbooks) planning and designing process for SCORCH. The planning and designing of Runbooks is a prerequisite for successful value add automation using SCORCH. This chapter also provides a brief primer to the SCORCH.

Chapter 4, Creating Runbooks for Active Directory Tasks, helps SCORCH Administrators to create Runbooks to automate typical manual tasks performed in Active Directory. The recipes in this chapter are focused on the life cycle of user accounts in typical organizations.

Chapter 5, Creating Runbooks for System Center 2012 Configuration Manager Tasks, focuses on automating the manual parts of scenarios addressed with System Center Configuration Manager. The specific scenarios include; deploying software updates, deploying applications, deploying agents to workgroup devices, and gathering client deployment status.

Chapter 6, Creating Runbooks for System Center 2012 Operations Manager Tasks, focuses on automating real world scenarios addressed with System Center Operations Manager Integration Pack.

Chapter 7, Creating Runbooks for System Center 2012 Virtual Machine Manager Tasks, focuses on automating real world scenarios addressed with System Center Virtual Machine Manager Integration Pack. The specific scenarios include; removing attached ISO images from virtual machines, automating the remediation of host compliance and working with virtual machine snapshots.

Chapter 8, Creating Runbooks for System Center 2012 Service Manager Tasks, explains the use of the System Center Service Manager Integration Pack in the automation of example ITSM tasks.

Chapter 9, Using Advanced Techniques in Runbooks, provides the recipes on advance features of Runbooks, which includes creating child Runbooks, error handling, implementing logging, and creating Looping Runbooks.

Appendix, Useful Websites and Community Resources, contains useful resources for SCORCH. SCORCH similar to most Microsoft products, has an extended solutions partner community. SCORCH has an extensive active support base on the World Wide Web. This appendix lists some of the sites which provide ready-made solutions and extensive real-world dynamic content on SCORCH.

What you need for this book

In order to complete all the recipes in this book you will need a minimum of one server configured with System Center 2012 Orchestrator SP1 and the relevant interconnecting technologies discussed. Here are the list of technologies the recipes depend on and their relevant versions used for this book:

- Microsoft Active Directory (Windows Server 2008 R2 and above)
- System Center 2012 Configuration Manager SP1
- System Center 2012 Operations Manager SP1
- System Center 2012 Virtual Machine Manager SP1
- System Center 2012 Service Manager SP1

The required software and deployment guides of System Center 2012 Product can be found at the following official Microsoft website `http://www.microsoft.com/en-us/server-cloud/system-center/default.aspx`.

The authors recommend using the online Microsoft resource due to the frequency of updates to the products supported requirements. Also note that the dynamic nature of the internet may require you to search for updated links listed in this book.

Who this book is for

The target audience of this book is SCORCH administrators and process owners responsible for implementing the IT process automation in their respective organizations. The recipes in this book range from beginner level and touches on expert level SCORCH administration knowledge. The ultimate goal is to provide the reader with knowledge to start their SCORCH journey, enhance their existing skills, and more importantly to share real world experience from seasoned technology implementers.

Conventions

In this book, you will find a number of styles of text that distinguish between different kinds of information. Here are some examples of these styles, and an explanation of their meaning.

New terms and **important words** are shown in bold. Words that you see on the screen, in menus or dialog boxes for example, appear in the text like this: "On the **Select features to install wizard** page ensure all options are checked."

[Warnings or important notes appear in a box like this.]

[Tips and tricks appear like this.]

Reader feedback

Feedback from our readers is always welcome. Let us know what you think about this book—what you liked or may have disliked. Reader feedback is important for us to develop titles that you really get the most out of.

To send us general feedback, simply send an e-mail to `feedback@packtpub.com`, and mention the book title via the subject of your message.

If there is a topic that you have expertise in and you are interested in either writing or contributing to a book, see our author guide on `www.packtpub.com/authors`.

Customer support

Now that you are the proud owner of a Packt book, we have a number of things to help you to get the most from your purchase.

Downloading the example code

You can download the example code files for all Packt books you have purchased from your account at `http://www.packtpub.com`. If you purchased this book elsewhere, you can visit `http://www.packtpub.com/support` and register to have the files e-mailed directly to you.

Errata

Although we have taken every care to ensure the accuracy of our content, mistakes do happen. If you find a mistake in one of our books—maybe a mistake in the text or the code—we would be grateful if you would report this to us. By doing so, you can save other readers from frustration and help us improve subsequent versions of this book. If you find any errata, please report them by visiting `http://www.packtpub.com/support`, selecting your book, clicking on the **errata submission form** link, and entering the details of your errata. Once your errata are verified, your submission will be accepted and the errata will be uploaded on our website, or added to any list of existing errata, under the Errata section of that title. Any existing errata can be viewed by selecting your title from `http://www.packtpub.com/support`.

Piracy

Piracy of copyright material on the Internet is an ongoing problem across all media. At Packt, we take the protection of our copyright and licenses very seriously. If you come across any illegal copies of our works, in any form, on the Internet, please provide us with the location address or website name immediately so that we can pursue a remedy.

Please contact us at `copyright@packtpub.com` with a link to the suspected pirated material.

We appreciate your help in protecting our authors, and our ability to bring you valuable content.

Questions

You can contact us at `questions@packtpub.com` if you are having a problem with any aspect of the book, and we will do our best to address it.

1
Unpacking System Center 2012 Orchestrator

In this chapter we will cover the following recipes:

- Planning the Orchestrator deployment
- Installing a single-server deployment
- Installing the Management Server in a multiserver deployment
- Installing the Runbook Server in a multiserver deployment
- Installing the Orchestration Console and the Web Service server in a multiserver deployment
- Installing the Runbook Designer in a multiserver deployment

Introduction

Microsoft System Center 2012 Orchestrator (**SCORCH**) is a process automation and multi-technology product connection toolkit. It delivers the following two key challenges of an organization:

- Automation of manual repeatable tasks
- Connecting multiple IT vendor products

The first common IT challenge, "automation of manual repeatable tasks" when coupled with supporting organization policies can significantly improve IT value and efficiency. The second challenge "connecting multiple IT vendor products", provides organizations with a single logical product (SCORCH) to interconnect and coordinate the activities between the typical multi-vendor technology investments.

In order to deliver the capabilities of SCORCH we must unpack the product "our toolbox" by planning our deployment (what is the size, type, and contents of the toolbox), and installing the product based on our agreed deployment plan. This chapter focuses on the activities you must perform to have a fully functional SCORCH installation.

Understanding SCORCH deployment components

The SCORCH architecture is made up of six types of components. The basic automated activity delivered by SCORCH is called a **Runbook** which is commonly known as a workflow in other products. The six components which make up the SCORCH product are listed and described in the following table and illustrated in figure following the table:

SCORCH Component	Description
Runbook Designer	The Runbook Designer is the tool for creating and editing Runbooks. Runbooks are stored in the Orchestration database. A sub-component of the Runbook Designer is the Runbook Tester, which is used to validate the execution of Runbooks.
Orchestration Database	The Orchestration database is a Microsoft SQL Server database which stores Runbooks, the status of Runbooks and security delegation configuration. The database also stores the log files and configuration of the SCORCH deployment.
Management Server	The Management Server is the core communication component of the SCORCH architecture and is responsible for coordinating the communication between the Runbook Designer and the Orchestration database. There is only one Management Server per SCORCH deployment.
Runbook Server	The Runbook Server is responsible for executing instances of Runbooks. When a Runbook is invoked, a copy of the Runbook instance is sent to its assigned Runbook Server and then it is executed (by default, this is the first installed Runbook Server which is assigned the Primary role).
Orchestrator Web service	The Orchestrator Web Service is the interface that enables applications to connect to SCORCH. Typical tasks performed through the Web Service are Runbook status views, start, and stop actions.
Orchestrator Browser Console	Orchestrator Browser Console is a **Silverlight** supported web browser which uses the Orchestrator Web Service to communicate with SCORCH.

The six parts of SCORCH are illustrated in the following figure:

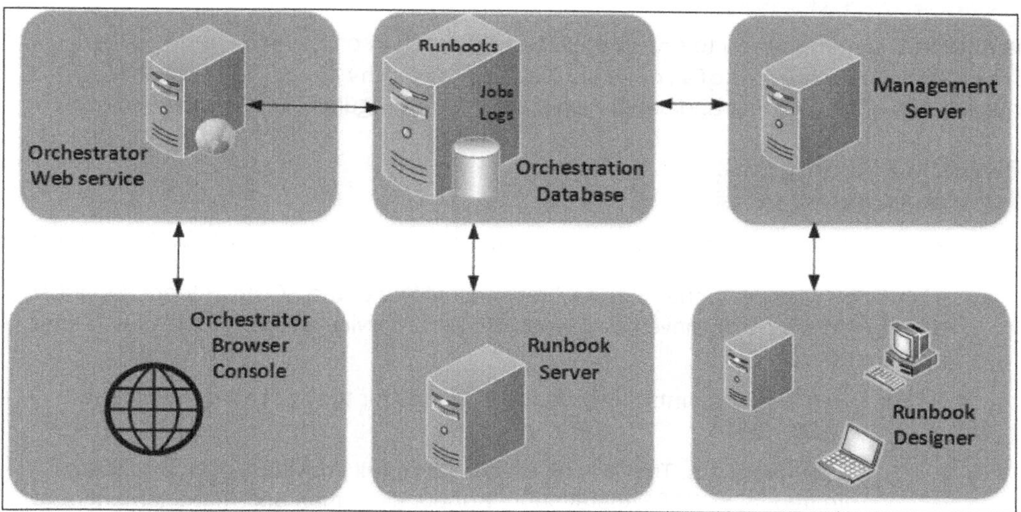

For the smallest implementation all the components can be deployed to one server (physical or virtual). You have the option to scale out the deployment by using multiple servers to host one or more components of SCORCH. The deployment choice is determined by the planning activities you perform before invoking the installation of the product. The *Planning the Orchestrator deployment* recipe discusses the factors you must consider to assist with the deployment choice.

About the Management Server

At the time of writing, the current version of SCORCH supports only one instance of a Management Server per deployment. You can deploy multiple instances of the other parts of the product with a note that we are still dealing with just one database per Management Server. The database instance can be made highly available.

Planning the Orchestrator deployment

The installation of SCORCH is simple. You must plan the deployment appropriately according to your needs. This recipe discusses and provides steps on common planning tasks to be performed before inserting the DVD or mounting the ISO for organizations who have successfully deployed SCORCH.

Getting ready

The authors recommend you to review the latest information on SCORCH at `http://technet.microsoft.com/en-us/library/hh420383.aspx` as the requirements of the product and supported platforms are regularly updated by Microsoft.

How to do it...

There are three planning categories, people, process, and the technology (SCORCH product).

1. Identify and agree on the roles and responsibilities of the SCORCH team. SCORCH deployments typically have three types of users; service accounts, Administrators, and operators.
    - Services accounts: They perform actions for the specific components of SCORCH
    - Administrators: They will typically perform all activities including, but not limited to, SCORCH installation, Runbook creation and management, and delegation of security to operators
    - Operators: They will typically use the SCORCH console and the Runbook Designer to create and manage Runbooks
2. Identify and document initial prototype processes to be used as the first candidate for automation and testing. The types of processes for this purpose should be simple repeatable tasks that fall into an organizations required standard service requests. Good candidates are service request which do not require authorization and approval. An additional example category is Windows operating system services that can be stopped and started as a part of trouble shooting.
3. Plan for the following technology requirements areas for SCORCH:
    - SCORCH deployment type

Deployment type	**Description**
single server	All SCORCH roles are installed on one physical or virtual machine. This scenario is typically implemented in test environments but is fully supported in production. This however becomes a single point of failure for highly automated environments.
multi-server	The SCORCH roles are separated and installed on one or more machines.

- Minimum hardware requirements for each SCORCH component

Component	Requirements
Management Server	▶ Operating system: Windows Server 2008 R2 or Windows Server 2012* ▶ 1 gigabyte (GB) of RAM, 2 GB or more recommended ▶ 200 megabytes (MB) of available hard disk space ▶ Dual-core Intel microprocessor, 2.1 gigahertz (GHz) or better ▶ Microsoft .NET Framework 3.5 Service Pack 1
Orchestration database	▶ Database: Microsoft SQL Server 2008 R2 or SQL Server 2012 ▶ Collation: SQL_Latin1_General_CP1_CI_AS ▶ Local or Remote (Basic Engine only)
Runbook Server	▶ Operating system: Windows Server 2008 R2 or Windows Server 2012* ▶ 1 gigabyte (GB) of RAM minimum, 2 GB or more recommended ▶ 200 megabytes (MB) of available hard disk space ▶ Dual-core Intel microprocessor, 2.1 gigabyte (GHz) or better ▶ Microsoft .NET Framework 3.5 Service Pack 1
Orchestrator Console/ Web Service	▶ Operating system: Windows Server 2008 R2 or Windows Server 2012* ▶ 1 gigabyte (GB) of RAM minimum, 2 GB or more recommended ▶ 200 megabytes (MB) of available hard disk space ▶ Dual-core Intel microprocessor, 2.1 gigahertz (GHz) or better ▶ Microsoft .NET Framework 3.5 Service Pack 1 ▶ Web Service: Internet Information Services (IIS) 7.0 and enabled IIS role ▶ Microsoft .NET Framework 3.5 Service Pack 1 ▶ Microsoft .NET Framework 4 ▶ Microsoft Silverlight 4**

Component	Requirements
Orchestrator Runbook Designer	▸ Operating system: Windows Server 2008 R2, Windows 7 (32/64 bit) or Windows Server 2012* ▸ 1 gigabyte (GB) of RAM minimum, 2 GB or more recommended ▸ 200 megabyte (MB) of available hard disk space ▸ Dual-core Intel microprocessor, 2.1 gigabyte (GHz) or better ▸ Microsoft .NET Framework 3.5 Service Pack 1

SCORCH 2012 SP1

It is required only for the computer running the console in its web browser but not the Web Service server.

- Services accounts and delegation groups

Account/Group	Type	Notes
Orchestrator management service	Service account	Create an Active Directory user account for this service. This is the main management server service account and it is granted log on as a service during the installation.
Orchestrator Runbook monitor service	Service account	Typically this is the same account as the Orchestrator Management Service.
Orchestrator Runbook service	Service account	Same user account as the Management and Runbook Server monitor service in a single deployment but can be different for multi-server deployments; Active Directory domain account recommended.
Runbook authors (`SCO_ADMINS`)	Group	Create an Active Directory group. This group will have the equivalent access of full administration to the SCORCH deployment.
Runbook operators (`SCO_CON_USERS`)	Group	Create an Active Directory group. This group will have the equivalent access of a Runbook operator to the SCORCH deployment.
Installation user	User	The user with full administrative rights on the SCORCH servers is required to perform the installation and configuration of the SCORCH deployment.

- Network Communication Ports

Source	Targeted computer	Default port	Configurable
Runbook Designer	Management Server	135, 1024-65535	Yes.
Management Server, Runbook Server, and Web Service	Orchestration database	1433	Yes; specified during the installation on the SCORCH supported version of Microsoft SQL Server. This is the case where the SQL Server instance is not using the default port.
Client browser	Orchestrator Web Service	81	Yes; during the SCORCH installation.
Client browser	Orchestration Console	82	Yes; during the SCORCH installation.

How it works...

The planning activities discussed are the minimum activities the authors recommend. The tasks performed at this stage will ensure that you ask for and plan for all your requirements before investing time in the actual installation. An additional benefit is identifying any people or budgetary risks before the deployment.

There's more...

There are two additional planning areas which are typically ignored in technology focused deployments. These areas are communication strategies and stakeholder management.

Communication strategy

One of the inaccurate myths of SCORCH is that it would automate the IT professional. SCORCH when implemented right would improve efficiency but will not replace people. On the contrary you need to communicate with the people who perform the manual tasks as they hold the key to how to best automate their efforts. Early engagement with all IT team members should be one of your key planning tasks.

Stakeholder management

Stakeholders are all users affected by the SCORCH deployment. An important category of stakeholders are the management team responsible for policy creation and enforcement. Automation without organization buy in may lead to conflicts at the political level of your organization. An example of such a scenario is the ability to create Active Directory user accounts with rights to specific organization areas and restricted resources.

Installing a single-server deployment

This recipe provides the steps required to install all the SCORCH roles on a single server. The single server deployment is appropriate for test and development environments. This deployment type will assist you with evaluation of the product, initial Runbook creation, and validation prior to deploying in your production environment. Though supported in production you must plan to implement the multi-server deployment to provide flexibility and availability.

Getting ready

You must plan to review the *Planning the Orchestrator deployment* recipe before performing the steps in this recipe. There are a number of dependencies discussed in the planning tasks which you must perform in order to be able to successfully complete the steps in this recipe.

The authors assume that you have access to all the installation media and the user account performing the installation, has administrative privileges on the server nominated for the SCORCH deployment.

How to do it...

The following figure provides a visual summary and order of the tasks you need to perform to complete this recipe:

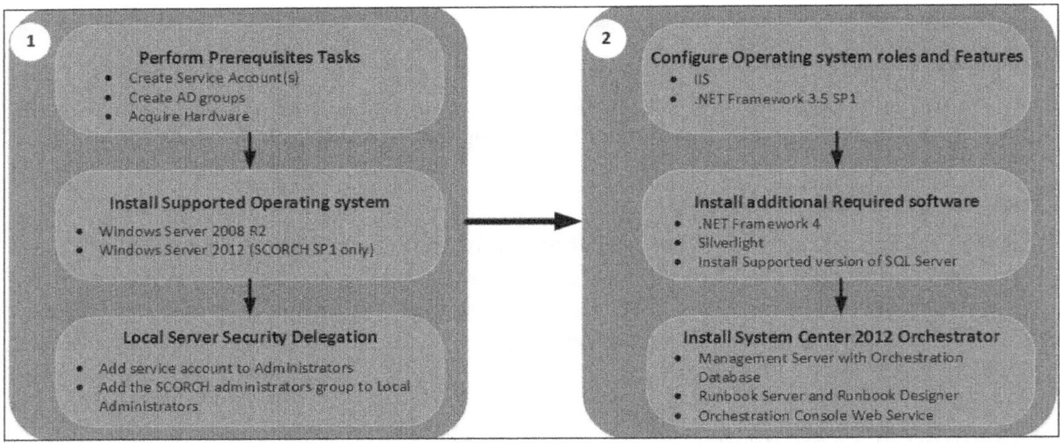

The deployment will be implemented in an Active Directory environment and with the Windows Server 2012 operating system. Perform the following steps to deploy SCORCH on a single machine:

1. In Active Directory create the required and recommended user accounts and groups. In this example we will create the following groups:

- Users: `SCO_MGTSVCA` and `SCO_RBSSVCA`
- Groups: `SCO_ADMINS` and `SCO_CON_USERS`

Name	Type	Description
SCO_RBSSVCA	User	SCORCH Runbook Server Service Account
SCO_MGTSVCA	User	SCORCH Management Server Service Account
SCO_CON_USERS	Security Group ...	SCORCH Console users
SCO_ADMINS	Security Group ...	SCORCH Administrators

2. Install a supported Windows Server operating system and join the server to the Active Directory domain in scope of the SCORCH deployment.
3. Add the two services accounts and the SCORCH Administrators group to the local Administrators group on the SCORCH server.
4. On the SCORCH server enable the following role and feature:
   - Role: **Web Server (IIS)** (default settings), note that the installation will enable this role for you if it is not found on the target server
   - Feature: **.NET Framework 3.5** SP1, you must specify a source file for .NET Framework 3.5 SP1 in the case of Windows Server 2012 and ensure that the DVD for Windows Server 2012 is loaded

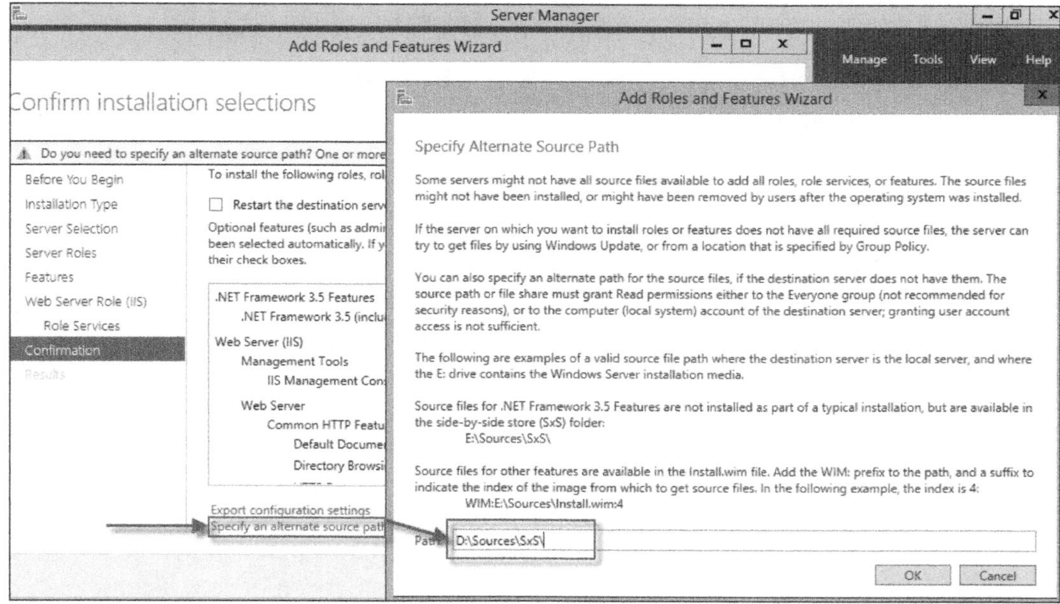

5. Install .NET Framework 4 if the operating system version is lower than Windows Server 2012 (.NET Framework 4x is already part of Windows Server 2012).

6. Optionally install Silverlight. After the SCORCH installation you will be prompted to install Silverlight if you run the console on the server.
7. Install a supported version of Microsoft SQL Server. In our example we will install Microsoft SQL Server 2012 standard edition with Service Pack 1. The following are the minimum options required for the installation:
    - Instance features: database engine services
    - Share features: Management Tools—Basic
    - Collation: SQL_Latin1_General_CP1_CI_AS
    - **Authentication Credentials**: **Windows Authentication** (recommended)
8. Insert or mount the SCORCH installation media on the server. Log on with a user account with administrative rights.
9. Launch the installation using the `SetupOrchestrator.exe` file. Click on **Install** under the **System Center 2012 Orchestrator Setup** section on wizard page.

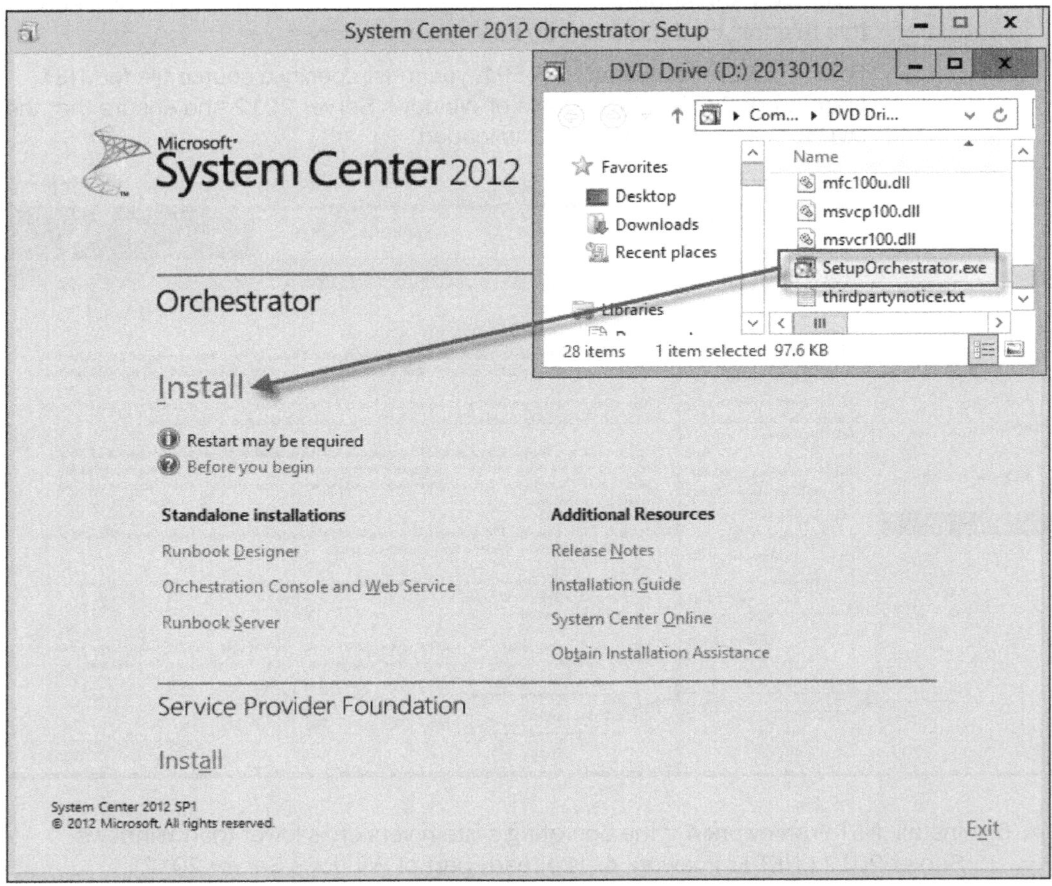

10. On the **Product Registration** page enter your organization details and the product Key (though the product key can be entered post installation, it is a best practice to enter this during the installation to reduce the risk of product evaluation expiry after the default 180 day period). Click on **Next**.
11. Review the **Please read this License Terms** page and accept to continue with the installation. Click on **Next**.
12. On the **Select features to install wizard** page ensure all options are checked. Click on **Next**.

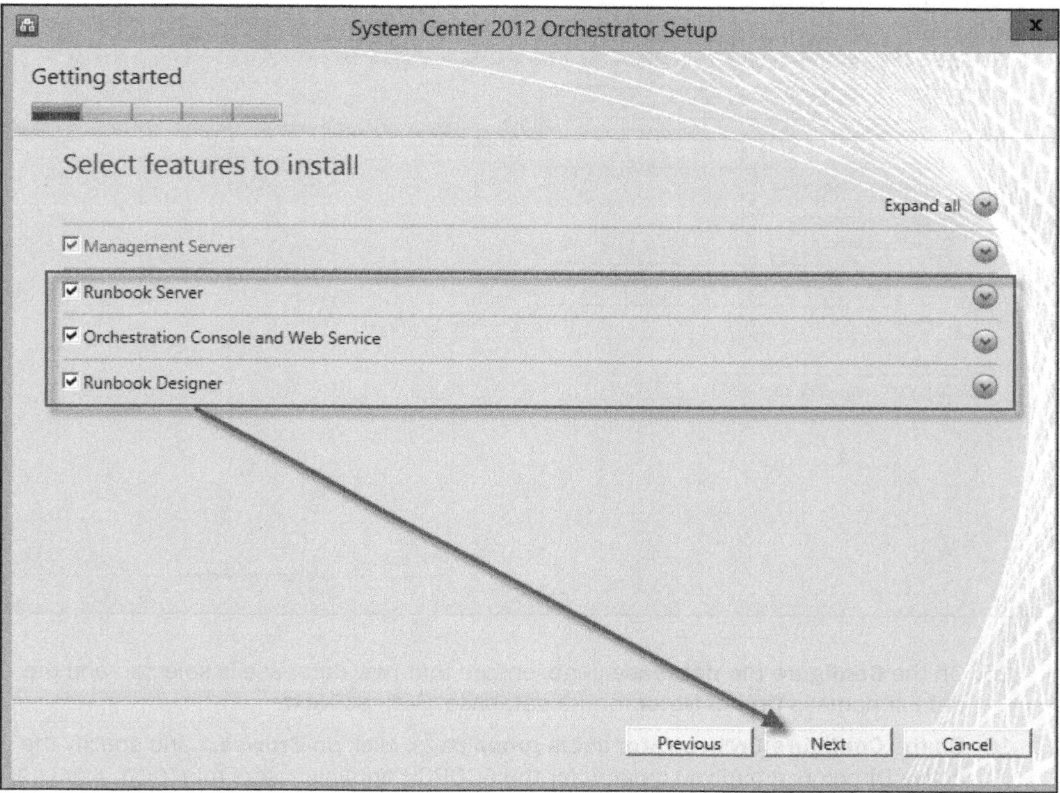

13. On the **Configure the service account** page type the user account you created for the management server service account and password. Click on **Test** to verify the details. Click on **Next**.

14. On the **Configure the database server** page type the server name and if applicable the instance of SQL where the Orchestration database will be created. Click on **Test** to verify the connection to the database server. Click on **Next**.

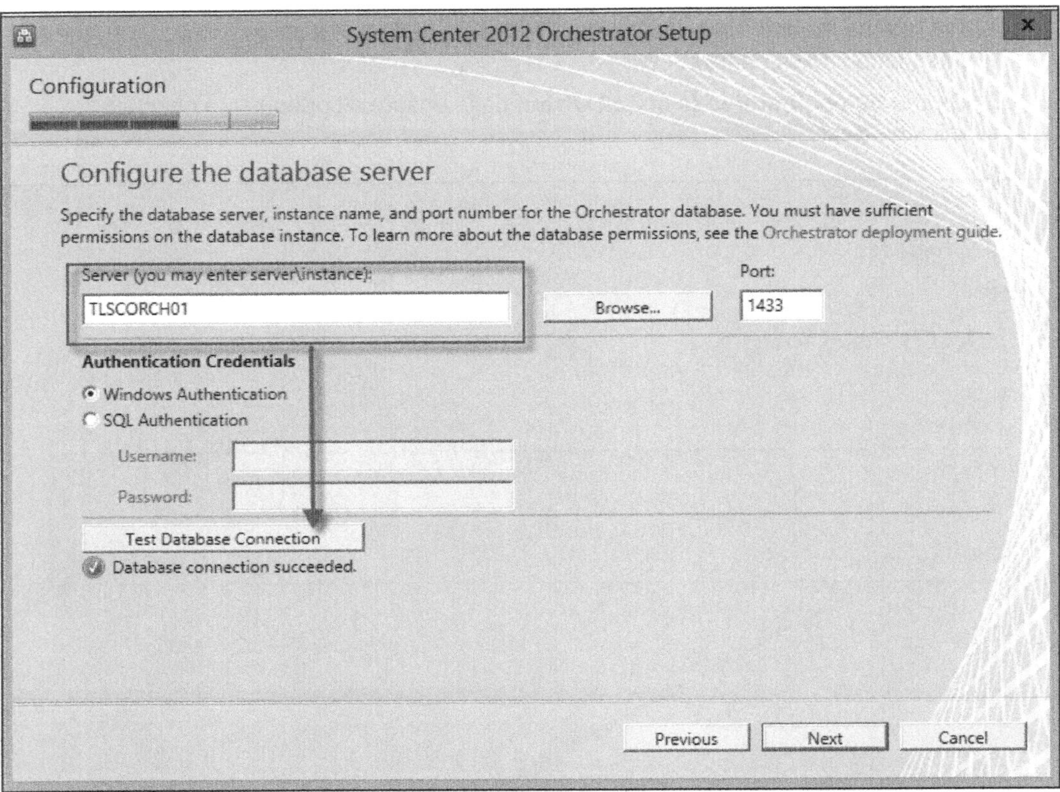

15. On the **Configure the database** page, ensure that new database is selected and the default name is **Orchestrator** for the database. Click on **Next**.
16. On the **Configure Orchestrator users group** page, click on **Browse...** and specify the Active Directory group you created for the SCORCH administrators role (`SCO_ADMINS` in our example). Click on **Next**.

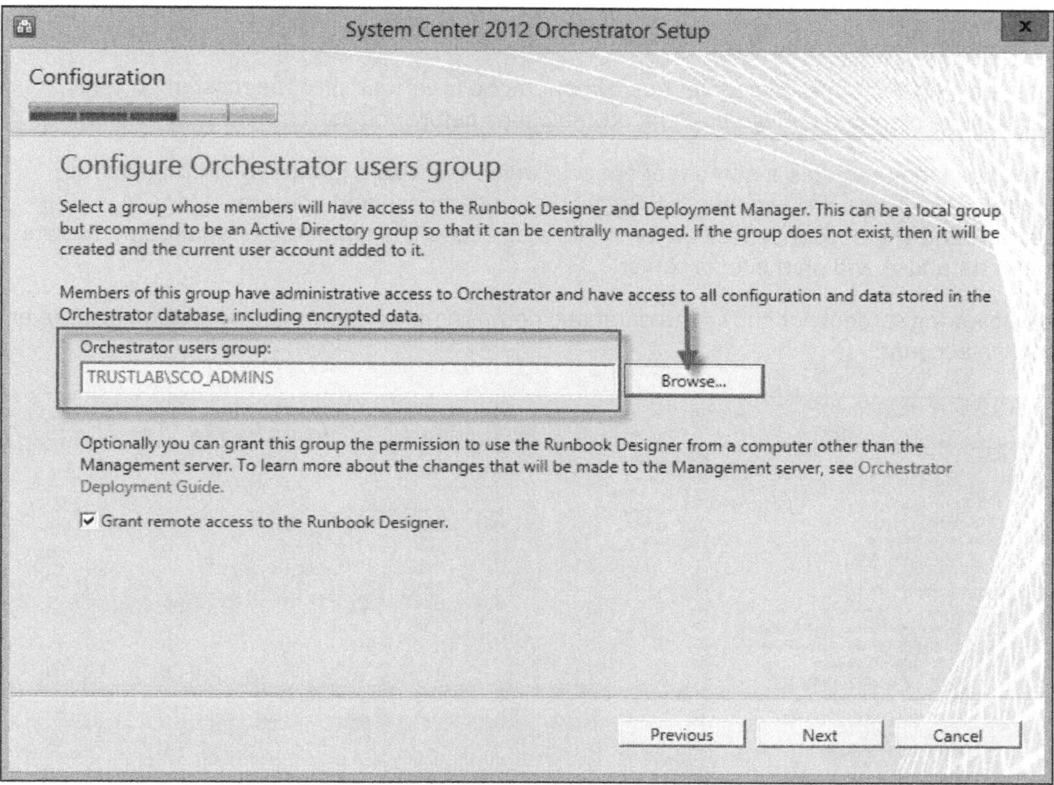

17. On the **Configure the ports for the web services** page leave the default options (81 and 82) or provide your custom options. Note that make sure you document the custom port if you change the default values. Click on **Next**.
18. On the **Select the installation location** page, accept the selected installation location or specify a custom location. Click on **Next**.
19. On the **Microsoft Update** page select your preferred option. Click on **Next**.
20. On the **Help improve Microsoft System Center Orchestrator** page select your preferred options. Click on **Next**.
21. Review the **Installation summary** page. Click on **Install** to start the installation.
22. On successful installation you are presented with final configuration options as follows:
    - **Launch Windows Update**
    - **Visit System Center Orchestrator Online**
    - **When Setup closes, start the Runbook Designer**

This completes the installation steps.

How it works...

Installing SCORCH in single server deployment mode is very simple. The most important aspect is to plan and configure all the prerequisites before you start the actual installation.

The installation requires a number of options, which the wizard guides you throughout the process. The installation creates the Orchestration database and prepares it for use in your deployment. The account specified for the service account is granted the required permission in the database and on the local server.

The following screenshot shows the database permissions granted to the management server service account:

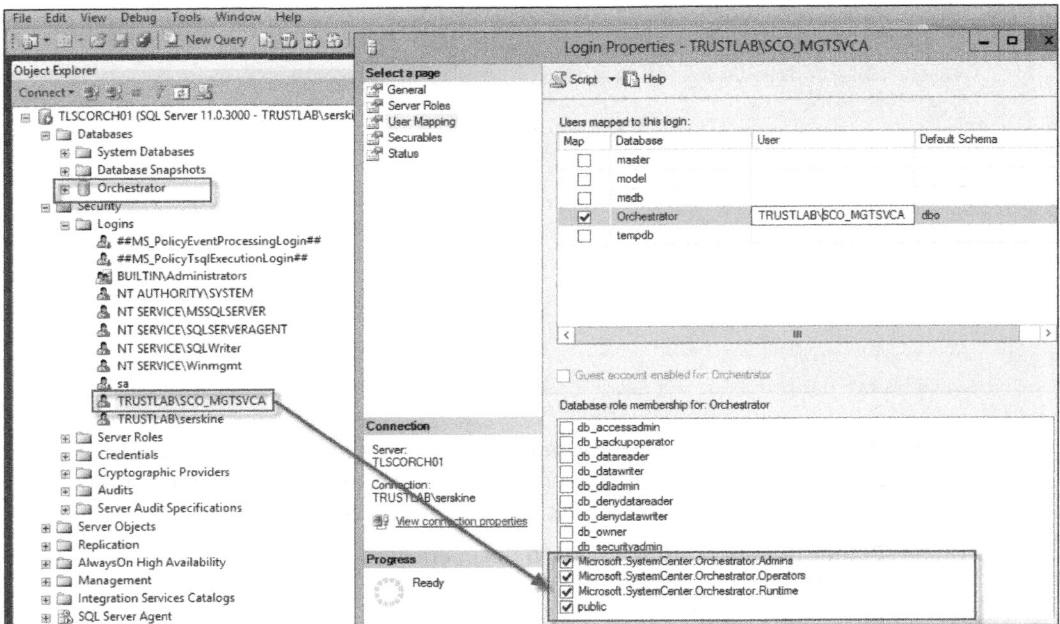

About service accounts

In our prerequisites we created two service accounts, one for the Management Service and the other for the Runbook service. In a single server deployment only one account is requested, which in our case is the management server service account. The Runbook Server service account will be used for additional Runbook Servers and is a best practice to separate the two accounts as they are granted different rights in the database. An additional benefit of using two or more accounts is to reduce the risk of a single point of failure for all service components.

There's more...

There is one additional configuration you must perform post installation on the Management Server.

Enabling network discovery is applicable to the Orchestrator database Runbook Designer role. Perform the following steps to enable network discovery:

1. In control panel navigate to **Network and Sharing** | **Change advanced sharing settings** | **Expand the Domain profile** | **Turn on network discovery**.
2. Click on **Save changes**.

Enabling network discovery enables auto-population of fields, which requires the selection of a computer name when creating Runbooks.

See also

The official online documentation is updated regularly and should be a point for reference at `http://technet.microsoft.com/en-us/library/hh420371.aspx`.

Installing the Management Server in a multiserver deployment

SCORCH features and components can be installed on a single server or across multiple servers. The multi-server deployment requires you to perform the installation in a specific order. The first server you must install is the Management Server which requires a supported instance of Microsoft SQL Server. This recipe provides the steps for installing the SCORCH Management Server.

Getting ready

You must plan to review the *Planning the Orchestrator deployment* recipe before performing the steps in this recipe. There are a number of dependencies in the *Planning the Orchestrator deployment* recipe, which you must perform in order to successfully complete the tasks in this recipe.

The authors assume that you have access to all the installation media and the user account performing the installation, has administrative privileges on the server nominated for the SCORCH deployment.

The example deployment in this recipe is based on the following configuration details:

- Management Server and database server `TLSCORCH01` on the same machine
- SCORCH SP1
- Microsoft SQL Server 2012
- Service account created in Active Directory: `SCO_MGTSVCA`
- Administrative users group created in Active Directory: `SCO_ADMINS`

How to do it...

The following figure provides a visual summary and order of the tasks you need to perform to complete this recipe:

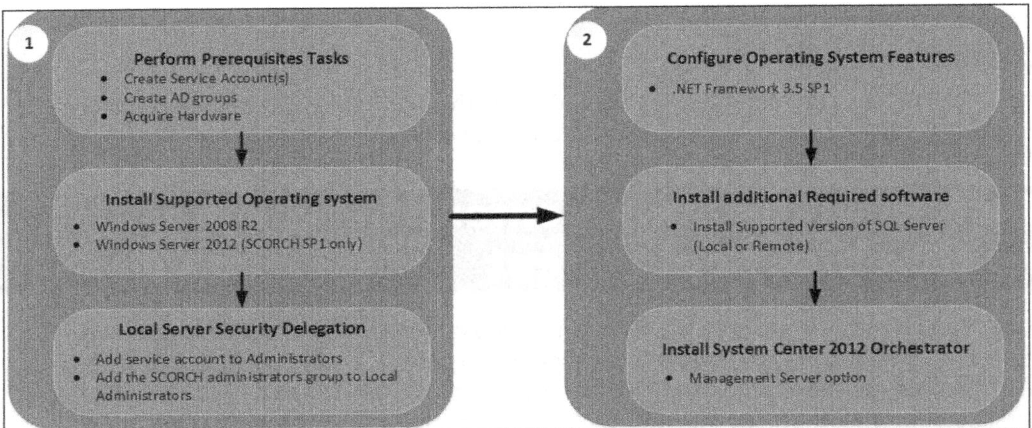

The deployment will be implemented in an Active Directory environment and with the Windows Server 2012 operating system. Perform the following steps to deploy a SCORCH Management Server in a multi-server deployment scenario:

1. Install a supported Windows Server operating system and join the server to the Active Directory domain in scope of the SCORCH deployment.
2. Add the service accounts and the SCORCH Administrators group to the local administrators group on the SCORCH server.
3. On the SCORCH server enable the following feature:
    - Feature: .NET Framework 3.5 SP1, you must specify a source files for .NET Framework 3.5 SP1 in the case of Windows Server 2012 ensure that the DVD for Windows Server 2012 is loaded
4. Install .NET Framework 4 if the operating system version is lower than Windows Server 2012 (.NET Framework 4x is already part of Windows Server 2012).

5. Install a supported version of Microsoft SQL Server. In our example we will install Microsoft SQL Server 2012 standard edition with Service Pack 1. The following are the minimum options required for the installation:
   - Instance features: Database engine services
   - Share Features: Management tools—Basic
   - Collation: SQL_Latin1_General_CP1_CI_AS
   - **Authentication Credentials**: **Windows Authentication** (recommended)
6. Insert or mount the SCORCH installation media on the server. Log on with a user account with administrative rights.
7. Launch the installation using the `SetupOrchestrator.exe` file.
8. On the splash screen under **Orchestrator** click on **Install** under the **System Center 2012 Orchestrator Setup** section on wizard page.

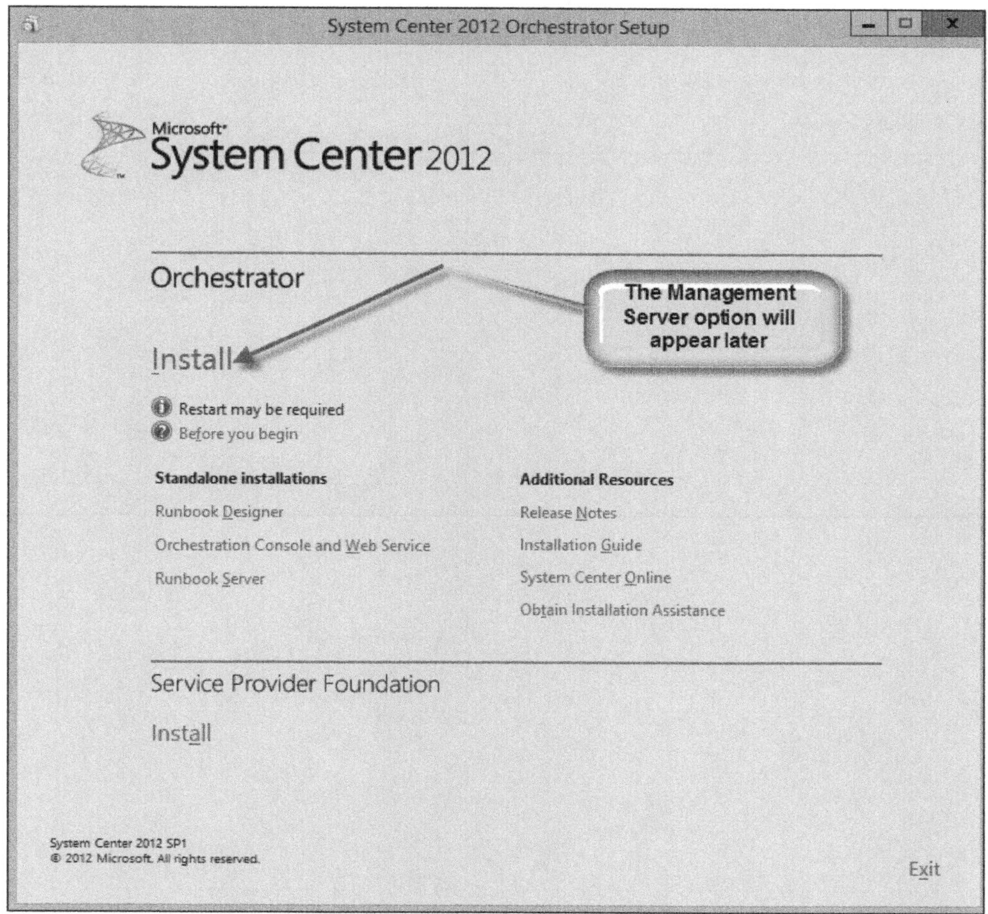

9. On the **Product Registration** page enter your organization details and the product key. Click on **Next**.
10. Review the **Please read this License Terms** page and accept to continue with the installation. Click on **Next**.
11. On the **Select features to install wizard** page uncheck all options (the only option checked should be the mandatory **Management Server**). Click on **Next**.

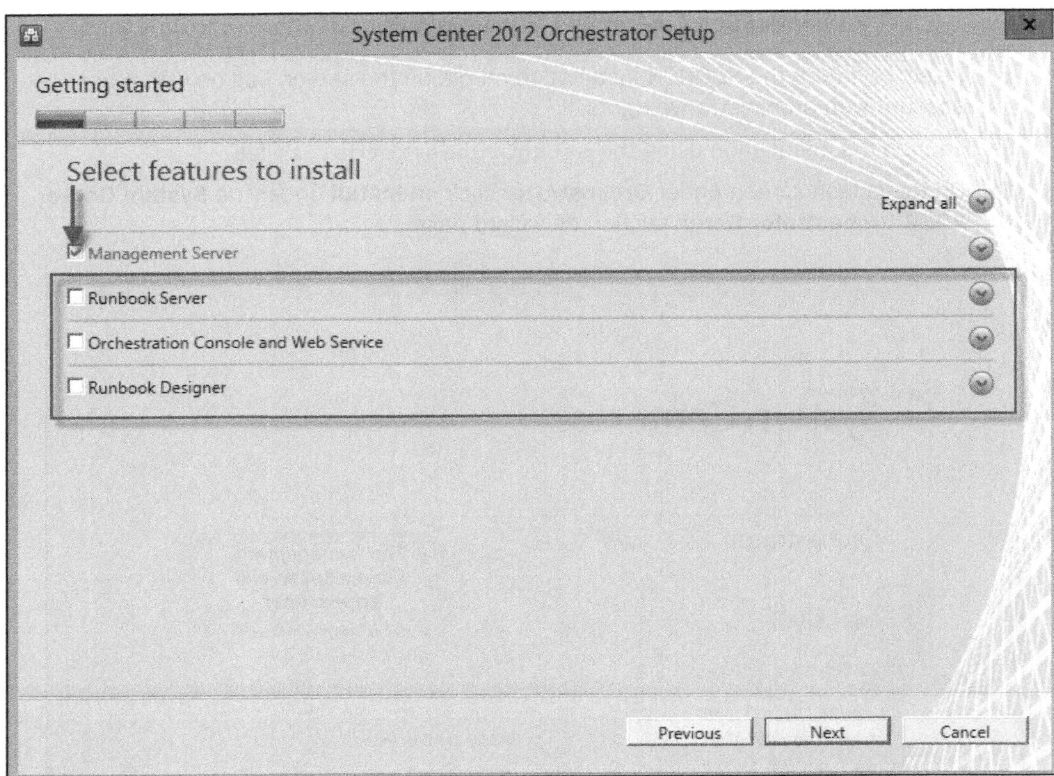

12. On the **Configure the service account** page type the user account you created for the management server service account and password. Click on **Test** to verify the details. Click on **Next**.

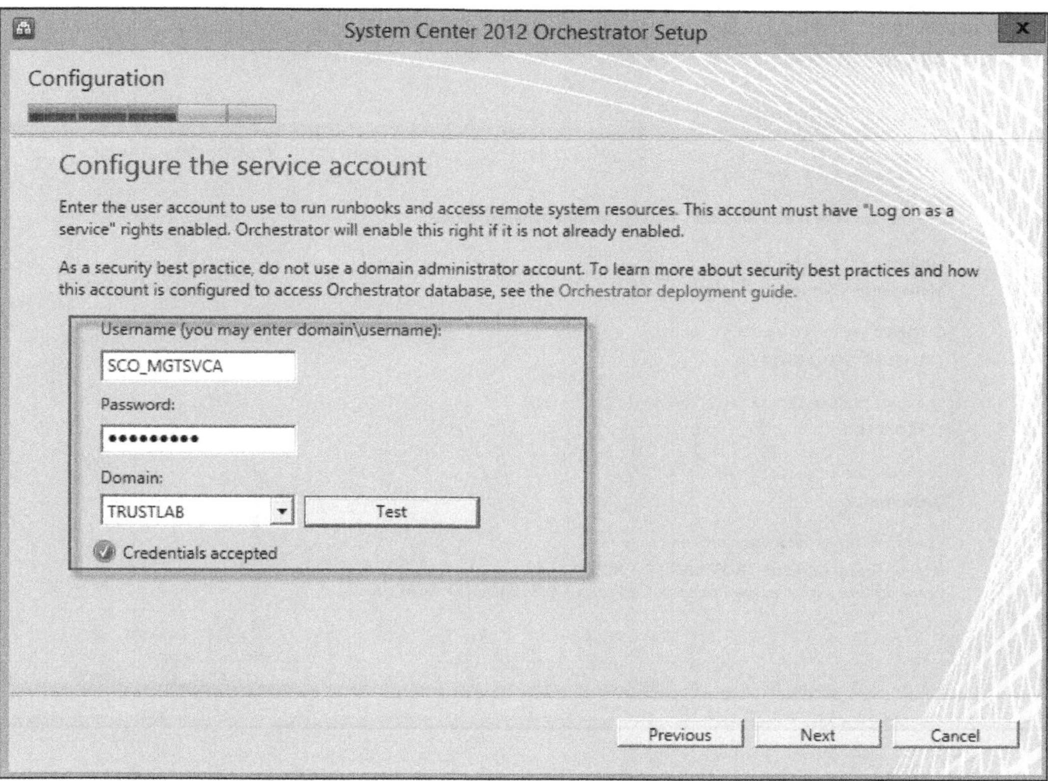

13. On the **Configure the database server** page type the server name and if applicable the instance of SQL where the Orchestration database will be created. Click on **Next**.
14. On the **Configure the database** page, ensure that new database is selected and the default name **Orchestrator** for the database. Click on **Next**.
15. On the **Configure Orchestrator users group** page, browse and specify the Active Directory group you created for the SCORCH administrators role. Click on **Next**.
16. On the **Select the installation location** page, accept the selected installation location or specify a custom location. Click on **Next**.
17. On the **Microsoft Update** page select your preferred option. Click on **Next**.
18. On the **Help improve Microsoft System Center Orchestrator** page select your preferred options. Click on **Next**.

19. Review the **Installation summary** page. Click on **Install** to start the installation.

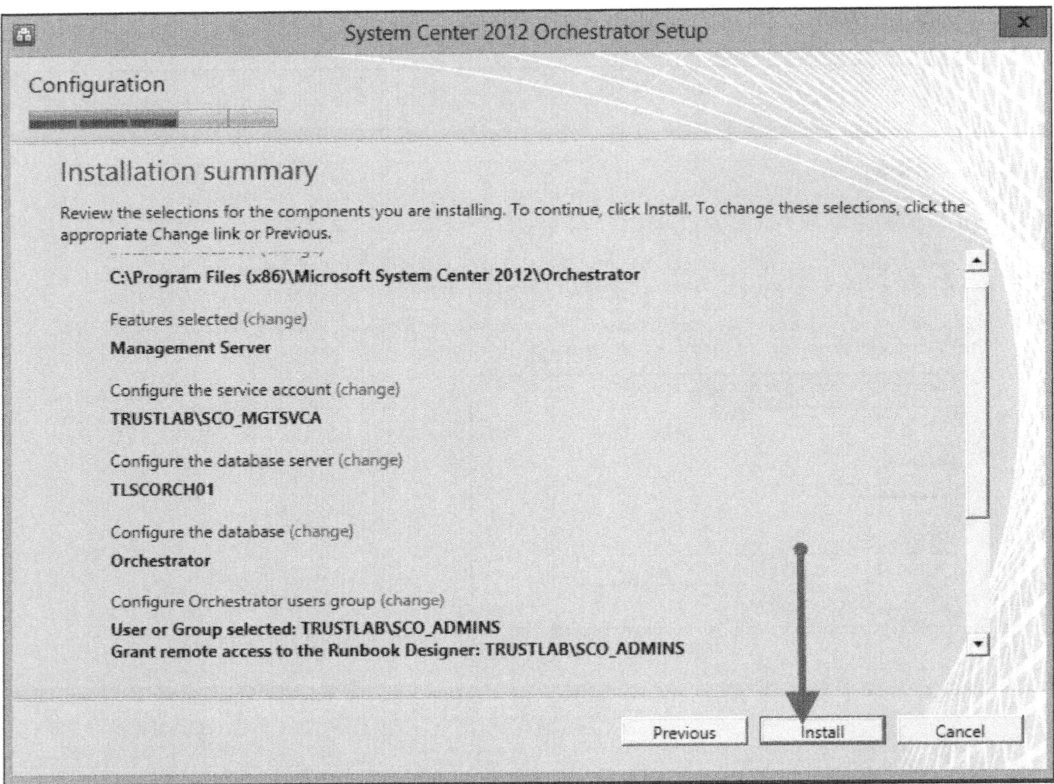

20. On successful installation you are presented with final configuration options as follows:

    - **Launch Windows Update**
    - **Visit System Center Orchestrator Online**

This completes the installation steps for the SCORCH Management Server in the multi-server deployment.

How it works...

The installation wizard guides you through the required settings. Once all the prerequisites are properly configured, the installation process creates the Orchestration database and installs the required program files for the Management Server feature.

The account specified for the service account is granted the required permission in the database. The following screenshot shows the database permissions granted to the management server service account:

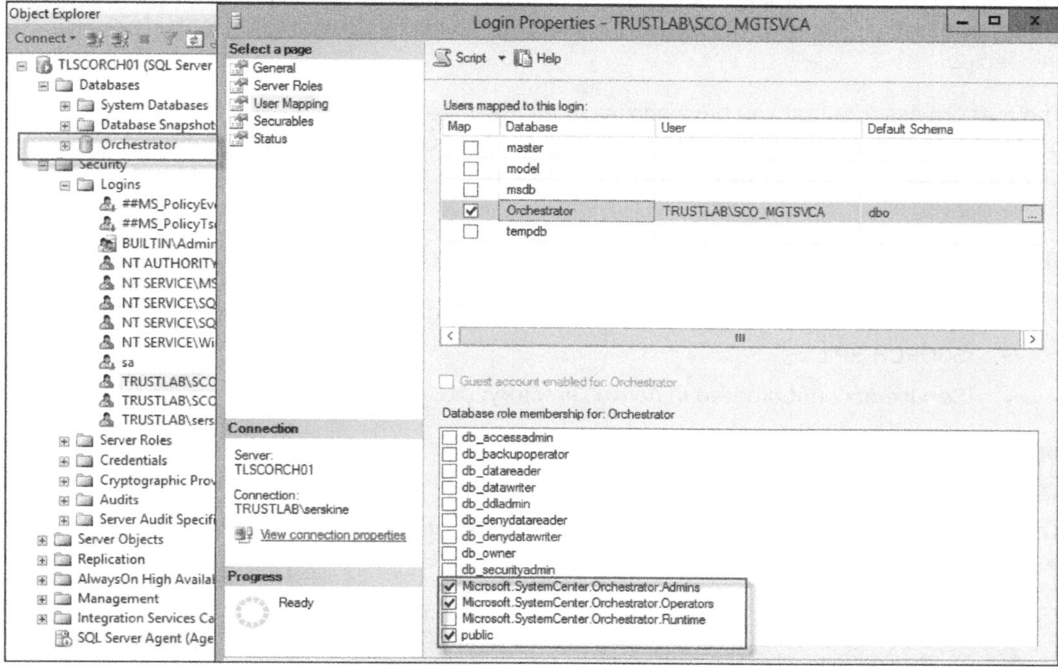

See also

The *How it works...* section of the *Installing a single server deployment* recipe.

Installing the Runbook Server in a multiserver deployment

SCORCH features and components can be installed on a single server or across multiple servers. The multi-server deployment requires you to perform the installation in a specific order. The first server you must install is the Management Server which requires a supported instance of Microsoft SQL Server. This recipe discusses installation of the Runbook Server component. You need at least one Runbook Server in a multi-server deployment.

Getting ready

You must plan to review the *Planning the Orchestrator deployment* recipe before performing the steps in this recipe. There are a number of dependencies in the *Planning the Orchestrator deployment* recipe, which you must perform in order to successfully complete the tasks in this recipe.

The authors assume that you have access to all the installation media and the user account performing the installation, has administrative privileges on the server nominated for the SCORCH deployment. You must also install a Management Server before you can install the Runbook Server.

The example deployment in this recipe is based on the following configuration details:

- Management Server and database server called `TLSCORCH01` is already installed
- SCORCH SP1
- Service account created in Active Directory: `SCO_RBSSVCA`

How to do it...

The following figure provides a visual summary and order of the tasks you need to perform to complete this recipe:

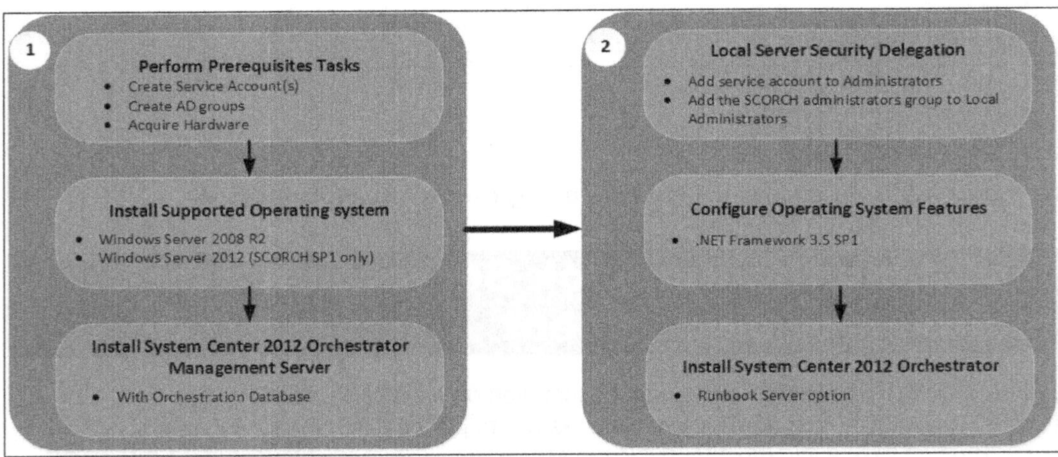

The deployment will be implemented in an Active Directory environment with the Windows Server 2012 operating system. Perform the following steps to deploy SCORCH Runbook Server in a multi-server deployment:

1. Install a supported windows server operating system and join the server to the Active Directory domain in scope of the SCORCH deployment.
2. Add the service accounts and SCORCH Administrators group to the local Administrators group on the SCORCH Runbook Server.
3. On the SCORCH server enable the following feature:
    - Feature: .NET Framework 3.5 SP1, you must specify a source files for .NET Framework 3.5 SP1 in the case of Windows server 2012 and ensure that the DVD for windows server 2012 is loaded
4. Install .NET Framework 4 if the operating system version is lower than Windows Server 2012 (.NET Framework 4x is already part of Windows Server 2012).
5. Insert or mount the SCORCH installation media on the Server. Log on with a user account with administrative rights.
6. Launch the installation using the `SetupOrchestrator.exe` file.
7. On the splash screen under **Standalone installations**. Click on **Runbook Server**.
8. On the **Product Registration** page enter your organization details and the product key. Click on **Next**.
9. Review the **Please read this License Terms** page and accept to continue with the installation. Click on **Next**.
10. On the **Configure the service account** page type the user account you created for the runbook server service account and password (In our scenario `SCO_RBSSVCA`). Click on **Test** to verify the details. Click on **Next**.
11. On the **Configure the database server** page type the server name and if applicable the instance of SQL where the Orchestration database is installed. Click on **Next**.
12. On the **Configure the database** page, ensure that existing database is selected and the default name **Orchestrator** or your custom name for the database is selected. Click on **Next**.
13. On the **Select the installation location** page, accept the selected installation location or specify a custom location. Click on **Next**.
14. On the **Microsoft Update** page select your preferred option. Click on **Next**.
15. On the **Help improve Microsoft System Center Orchestrator** page select your preferred options. Click on **Next**.

16. Review the **Installation summary** page. Click on **Install** to start the installation.

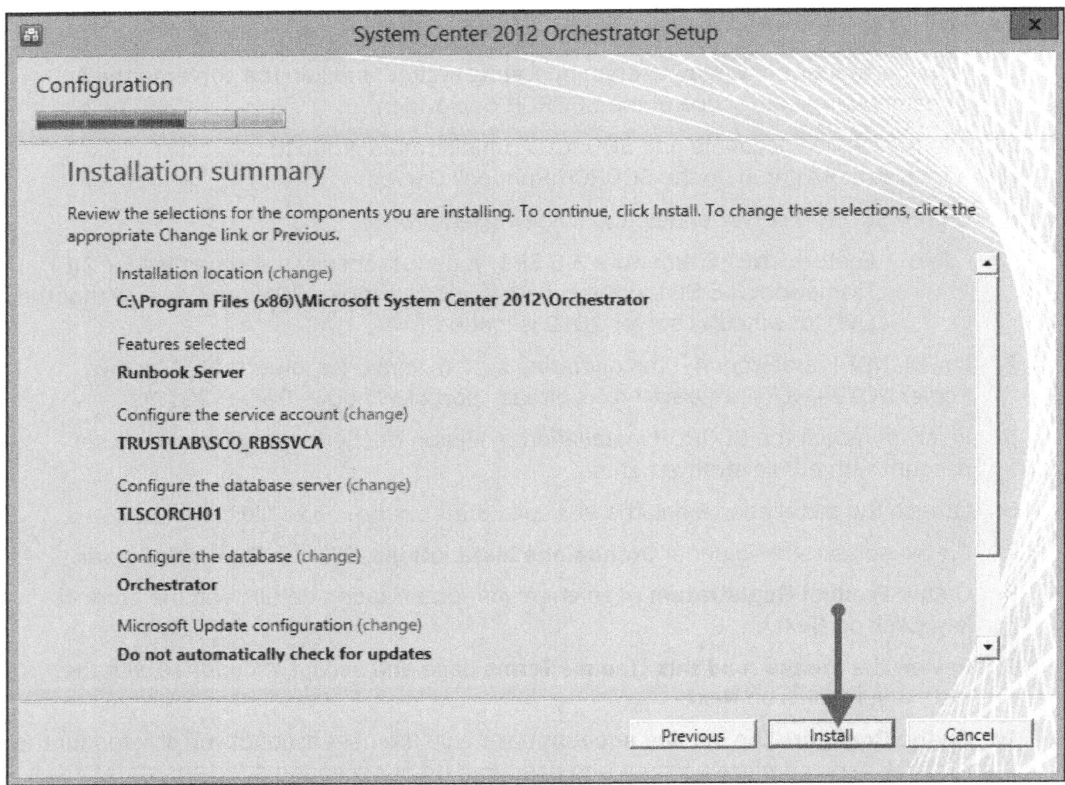

17. On successful installation you are presented with final configuration options as follows:

    - **Launch Windows Update**
    - **Visit System Center Orchestrator Online**

This completes the installation steps for the SCORCH Management Server in the multi-server deployment.

How it works...

The installation wizard guides you through the required settings. Once all the prerequisites are properly configured, the installation process installs the required program files for the Runbook Server feature.

The account specified for the service account is granted the required permission in the database. The following screenshot shows the database permissions granted to the runbook server service account:

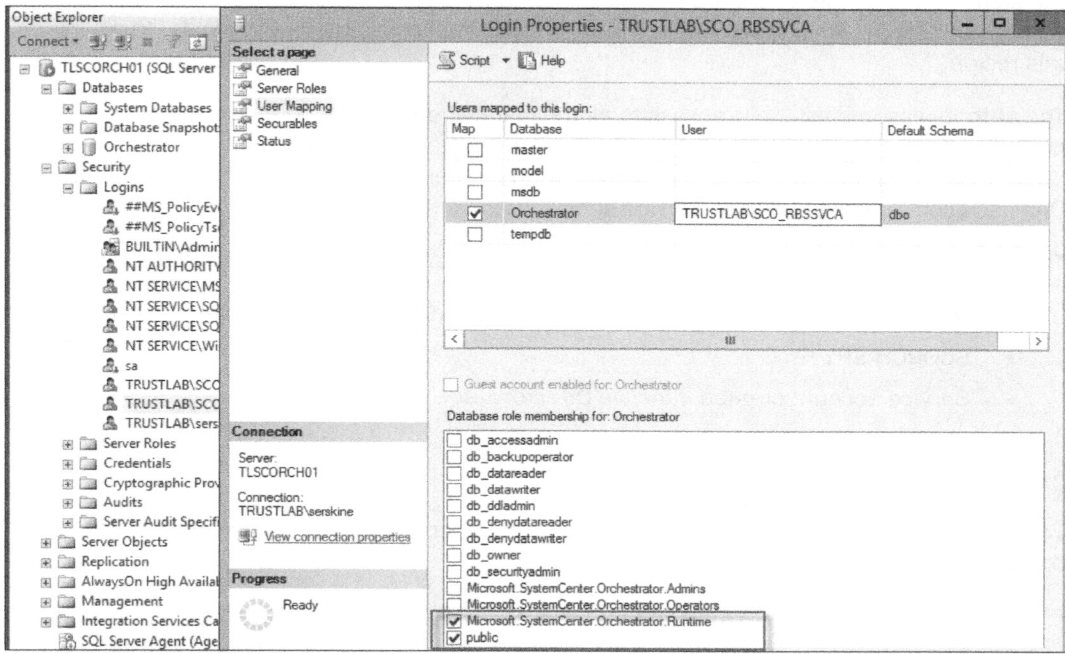

See also

The *How it works...* sections of the following recipes provide additional relevant information:

- The *Installing a single-server deployment* recipe
- The *Installing a Management Server in a multiserver deployment* recipe

Installing the Orchestration Console and the Web Service server in a multi server deployment

SCORCH features and components can be installed on a single server or across multiple servers. The multi-server deployment requires you to perform the installation in a specific order. The first server you must install is the Management Server which requires a supported instance of Microsoft SQL Server. This recipe discusses installation of the Orchestration Console and Web Service server component. You need at least one Orchestration Console and Web Service server in a multi-server deployment.

Getting ready

You must plan to review the *Planning the Orchestrator deployment* recipe before performing the steps in this recipe. There are a number of dependencies in the *Planning the Orchestrator deployment* recipe, which you must perform in order to successfully complete the tasks in this recipe.

The authors assume you have access to all the installation media and the user account performing the installation, has administrative privileges on the server nominated for the SCORCH deployment. You must also install a Management Server before you can install the Orchestration Console and Web Service server.

The example deployment in this recipe is based on the following configuration details:

- Management Server and database server called `TLSCORCH01` is already installed
- SCORCH SP1
- Service account created in Active Directory: `SCO_MGTSVCA`

How to do it...

The following figure provides a visual summary and order of the tasks you need to perform to complete this recipe:

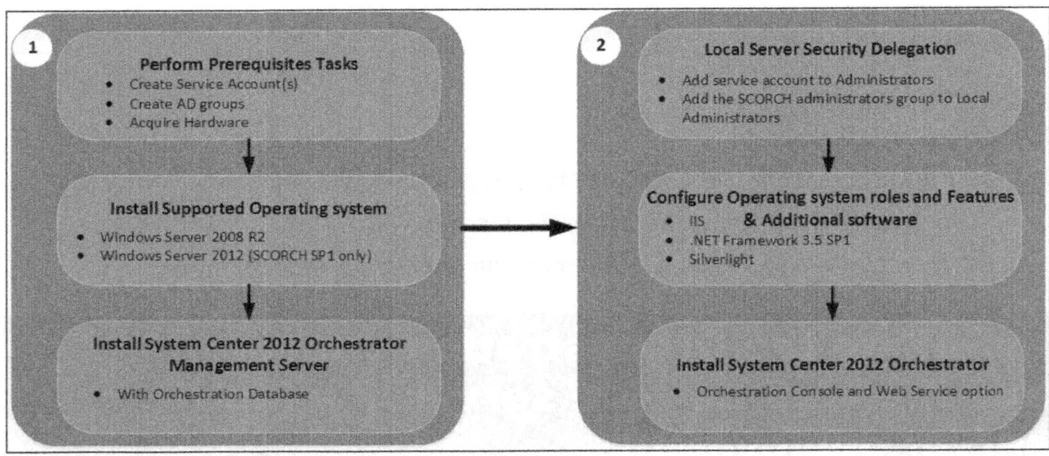

The deployment will be implemented in an Active Directory environment and with the Windows Server 2012 operating system. Perform the following steps to deploy the SCORCH Orchestration Console and Web Service in a multi-server deployment:

1. Install a supported windows server operating system and join the server to the Active Directory domain in scope of the SCORCH deployment.

2. Add the service accounts and SCORCH Administrators group to the local Administrators group on the SCORCH Orchestration Console and Web Service server.
3. On the SCORCH Orchestration Console and Web Service server enable the following role and feature:
    - Role: **Web Server (IIS)** (default settings)
    - Feature: .NET Framework 3.5 SP1, you must specify a source files for .NET Framework 3.5 SP1 in the case of Windows Server 2012 and ensure that the DVD for Windows Server 2012 is loaded
4. Install .NET Framework 4 if the operating system version is lower than Windows Server 2012 (.NET Framework 4x is already part of Windows Server 2012).
5. Optionally install Silverlight. After the SCORCH installation you will be prompted to install Silverlight if you run the console on the server.
6. Insert or mount the SCORCH installation media on the Server. Log on with a user account with administrative rights.
7. Launch the installation using the `SetupOrchestrator.exe` file.
8. On the splash screen under **Standalone installations** click on **Orchestration Console and Web Service**.
9. On the **Product Registration** page enter your organization details and the product key. Click on **Next**.
10. Review the **Please read this License Terms** page and accept to continue with the installation. Click on **Next**.
11. On the **Configure the service account** page type the user account you created for the management server service account and password (In our scenario `SCO_MGTSVCA`). Click on **Test** to verify the details. Click on **Next**.
12. On the **Configure the database server** page type the server name and if applicable, the instance of SQL where the Orchestration database is installed. Click on **Next**.
13. On the **Configure the database** page, ensure that existing database is selected and the default name **Orchestrator** or your custom name for the database is selected. Click on **Next**.
14. On the **Configure the ports for the web services** page leave the default options (81 and 82) or provide your custom options. Note that If you change these ports from their default, make sure you document the custom port options. Click on **Next**.
15. On the **Select the installation location** page, accept the selected installation location or specify a custom location. Click on **Next**.
16. On the **Microsoft Update** page select your preferred option. Click on **Next**.
17. On the **Help improve Microsoft System Center Orchestrator** page select your preferred options. Click on **Next**.

18. Review the **Installation summary** page. Click on **Install** to start the installation.
19. On successful installation you are presented with final configuration options as follows:
    - **Launch Windows Update**
    - **Visit System Center Orchestrator Online**

This completes the installation steps for the SCORCH Orchestration Console and Web Service server in the multi-server deployment.

How it works...

The installation wizard guides you through the required settings. Once all the prerequisites are properly configured, the installation process installs the required program files for the Orchestration Console and Web Service feature.

The account specified for the service account is used to connect the Orchestration Console and Web Service to the specified SCORCH database.

The installation creates and configures two websites and their required settings in the local installation of the Internet Information Services (IIS).The following screenshot shows the two sites created by the installation wizard:

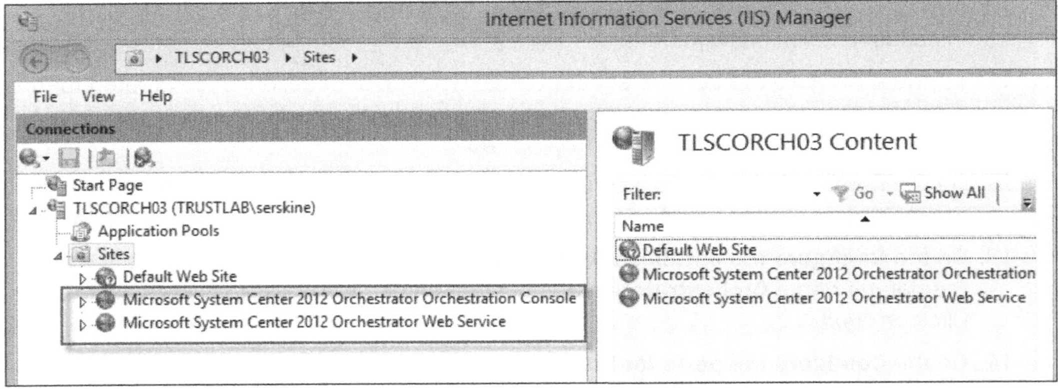

See also

The following recipes provide additional relevant information:

- The *Installing a single-server deployment* recipe
- The *Installing a Management Server in a multiserver deployment* recipe
- The *Installing a Runbook Server in a multiserver deployment* recipe

Installing the Runbook Designer in a multiserver deployment

SCORCH features and components can be installed on a single server or across multiple servers. The multi-server deployment requires you to perform the installation in a specific order. The first server you must install is the Management Server which requires a supported instance of Microsoft SQL Server. This recipe discusses installation of the Runbook Designer component. You need at least one Runbook Designer in order to create and manage Runbooks.

Getting ready

You must plan to review the *Planning the Orchestrator deployment* recipe before performing the steps in this recipe. There are a number of dependencies in the *Planning the Orchestrator deployment* recipe, which you must perform in order to successfully complete the tasks in this recipe.

The authors assume that you have access to all the installation media and the user account performing the installation, has administrative privileges on the server or client nominated for the SCORCH deployment.

You must also optionally install a Management Server before you install the Runbook Designer server. Though the Runbook Designer can be installed without a Management Server present, you won't be able to use the Runbook Designer for SCORCH until a Management Server with a corresponding database is installed.

The example deployment in this recipe is based on the following configuration details:

- Management Server and database server called `TLSCORCH01` is already installed
- **SCORCH SP1**
- Operating system for the Runbook Designer: **Windows 7**

How to do it...

The following figure provides a visual summary and order of the tasks you need to perform to complete this recipe:

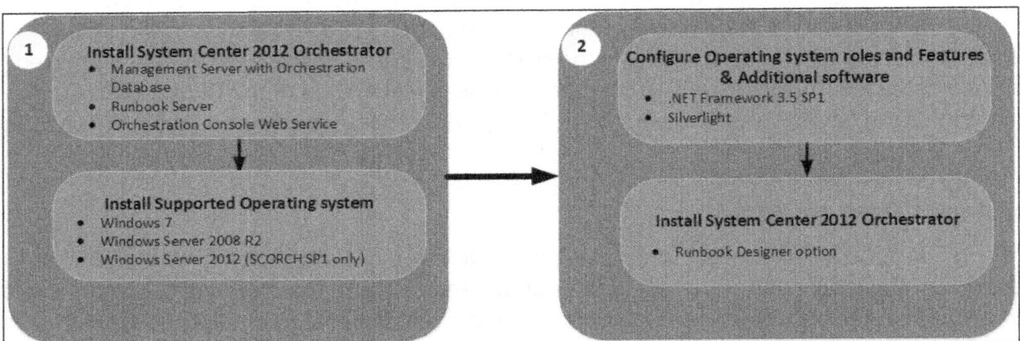

The deployment will be implemented in an Active Directory environment and with the Windows 7 operating system. Perform the following steps to deploy a SCORCH Runbook Designer in a multi-server deployment:

1. Install a supported Runbook Designer operating system and join the client to the Active Directory domain in scope of the SCORCH deployment.
2. On the SCORCH machine nominated for the Runbook Designer enable the following role and feature:
    - Feature: **.NET Framework 3.5 SP1**
3. Optionally install Silverlight. After the SCORCH installation you will be prompted to install Silverlight if you run the console.
4. Insert or mount the SCORCH installation media on the Runbook Designer nominated machine. Log on with a user account with administrative rights.
5. Launch the installation using the `SetupOrchestrator.exe` file.
6. On the splash screen under **Standalone installations**. Click on **Runbook Designer**.
7. On the **Product Registration** page enter your organization details and the product key. Click on **Next**.
8. Review the **Please read this License Terms** page and accept to continue with the installation. Click on **Next**.
9. Verify there are no errors on the **Prerequisites** page. Click on **Next**.

10. On the **Select the installation location** page, accept the selected installation location or specify a custom location. Click on **Next**.
11. On the **Microsoft Update** page select your preferred option. Click on **Next**.
12. On the **Help improve Microsoft System Center Orchestrator** page select your preferred options. Click on **Next**.
13. Review the **Installation summary** page. Click on **Install** to start the installation.
14. On successful installation you are presented with final configuration options as follows:
    - **Launch Windows Update**
    - **Visit System Center Orchestrator Online**

This completes the installation steps for the SCORCH Runbook Designer in the multi-server deployment.

How it works...

The installation wizard guides you through the required settings. Once all the prerequisites are properly configured, the installation process installs the required program files for the Runbook Designer.

The Runbook Designer is your interface to the SCORCH deployment for the purpose of creating and managing Runbooks.

There's more...

The Runbook Designer is similar to a standalone console and can be used to connect to any Management Server if the user running the designer has access rights delegated.

Connecting to the Management Server

When the Orchestrator Runbook Designer is launched for the first time, an attempt is made to connect to a Management Server on the machine. In our recipe we do not have the Management Server installed locally. To connect to the Management Server, for example `TLSCORCH01`, perform the following steps:

1. Navigate to **Start** | **All Programs** | **Microsoft System Center 2012** | **Orchestrator** | **Runbook Designer** (click on **OK** on the warning message if this is the first time you launch the **Runbook Designer**).

2. Select **Actions** from the menu bar and click on **Connect**.

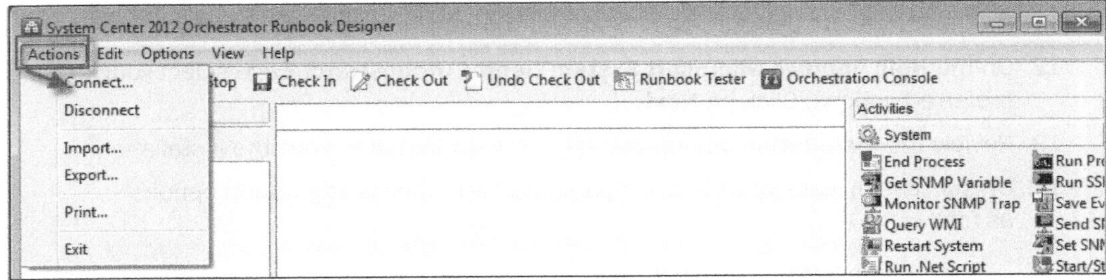

3. Type the Management Server name in the **Computer** field to connect to the Management Server of the multi- server deployment SCORCH environment in scope.

Orchestration Console URL

The **Runbook Designer** has a short-cut option to connect to and launch the Web Service server console. You must configure the correct URL for the console by performing the following steps:

1. Navigate to **Start** | **All Programs** | **Microsoft System Center 2012** | **Orchestrator** | **Runbook Designer**.
2. Select **Options** from the menu bar and click on **Orchestration Console Configure**. Type the **URL** of the web console with the port specified at the time of installation (port 82 by default).

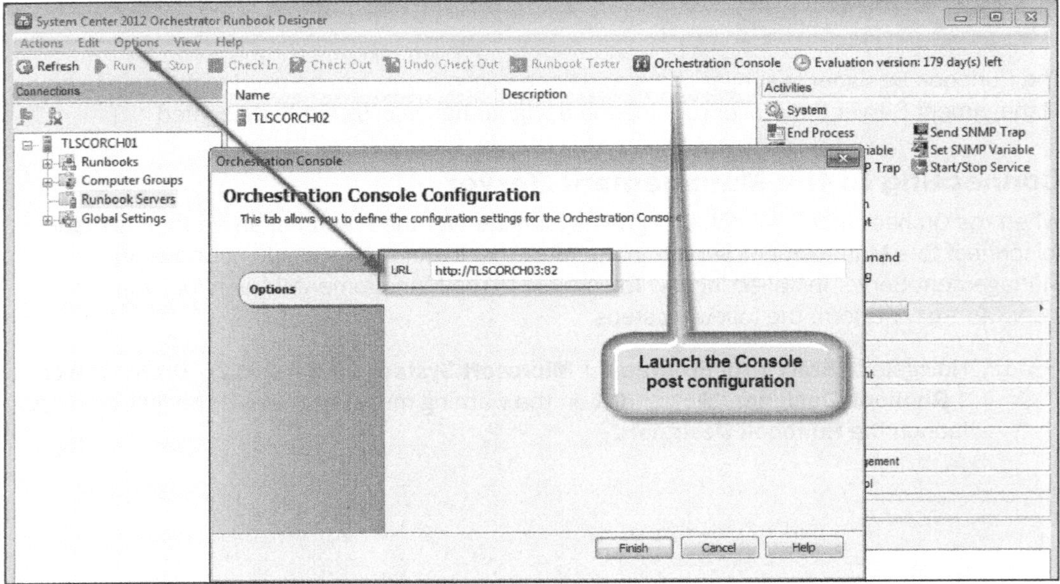

3. Test the console using the **Orchestrator Console** icon in the Runbook Designer console. Note that you will be prompted to install Silverlight if it is not already installed on the machine.

See also

The following recipes provide additional relevant information:

- The *Installing a single-server deployment* recipe
- The *Installing the Management Server in a multiserver deployment* recipe
- The *Installing the Runbook Server in a multiserver deployment* recipe
- The *Installing the Orchestration Console and the Web Service server in a multiserver deployment* recipe

2

Initial Configuration and Making SCORCH Highly Available

In this chapter, we will cover the following:

- Loading Integration Packs (IP)
- Configuring Integration Pack connections
- Deploying Runbook Servers and Designers with Deployment Manager
- Making your Runbooks highly available
- Creating and maintaining a security model for Orchestrator

Introduction

The recipes in *Chapter 1, Unpacking System Center 2012 Orchestrator*, discuss setting up the System Center 2012 Orchestrator environment. The environment can either be on a single machine or scaled out using multiple servers. The recipes in this chapter focus on some typical initial post deployment tasks. We will also discuss security configuration options and achieving SCORCH Runbook high availability.

Loading Integration Packs (IPs)

Microsoft System Center 2012 Orchestrator (**SCORCH**) automation is driven by process automation components.

These process automation components are similar in concept to a physical toolbox. In a toolbox you typically have different types of tools which enable you to build what you desire. In the context of SCORCH these tools are known as **Activities**.

Activities fall into two main categories:

- **Built-in Standard Activities**: These are the default activity categories available to you in the Runbook Designer. The standard activities on their own provide you with a set of components to create very powerful Runbooks.

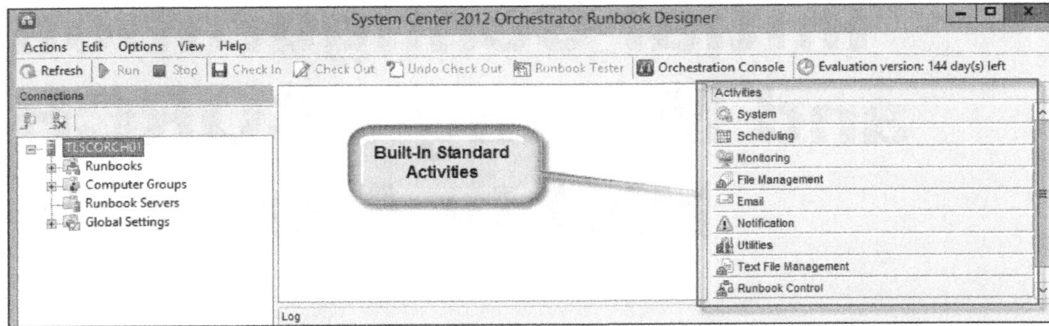

- **Integration Pack Activities**: Integration Pack Activities are provided either by Microsoft, the community, solution integration organizations, or are custom created by using the Orchestrator Integration Pack Toolkit. These activities provide you with the Runbook components to interface with the target environment of the IP. For example, the Active Directory IP has the activities you can perform in the target Active Directory environment.

This recipe provides the steps to load the second type of activities into your default implementation of SCORCH.

Getting ready

You must download the Integration Pack(s) you plan to deploy from the provider of the IP. In this example we will be deploying the Active Directory IP, which can be found at the following link `http://www.microsoft.com/en-us/download/details.aspx?id=34611`.

You must have deployed a System Center 2012 Orchestrator environment and have full administrative rights in the environment. Review *Chapter 1, Unpacking System Center 2012 Orchestrator*, if you have not deployed the SCORCH environment.

How to do it...

The following diagram provides a visual summary and order of the tasks you need to perform to complete this recipe.

We will deploy the Microsoft Active Directory (AD) integration pack (IP).

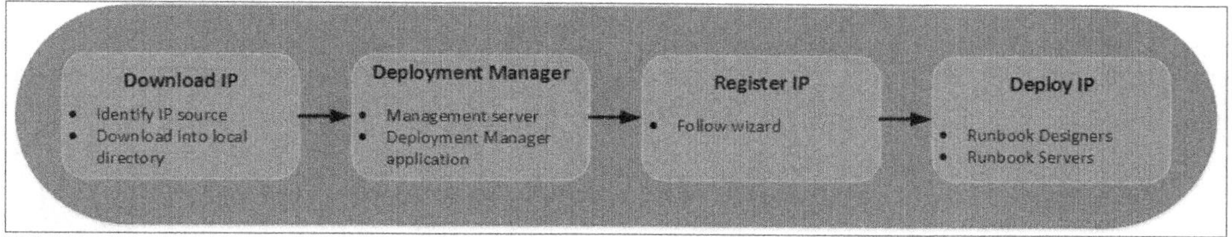

Integration pack organization

A good practice is to create a folder structure for your integration packs. The folders should reflect versions of the IPs for logical grouping and management. The version of the IP will be visible in the console and as such you must perform this step after you have performed the step to load the IP(s). This approach will aid in change management when updating IPs in multiple environments.

Follow these steps to deploy the Active Directory integration pack:

1. Identify the source location for the Integration Pack in scope (for example, the AD IP for SCO2012 SP1). Download the IP to a local directory on the Management Server or UNC share.
2. Log in to the SCORCH Management server. Launch the Deployment Manager.
3. Under **Orchestrator Management Server**, right-click on **Integration Packs**. Select **Register IP with the Orchestrator Management Server...**.

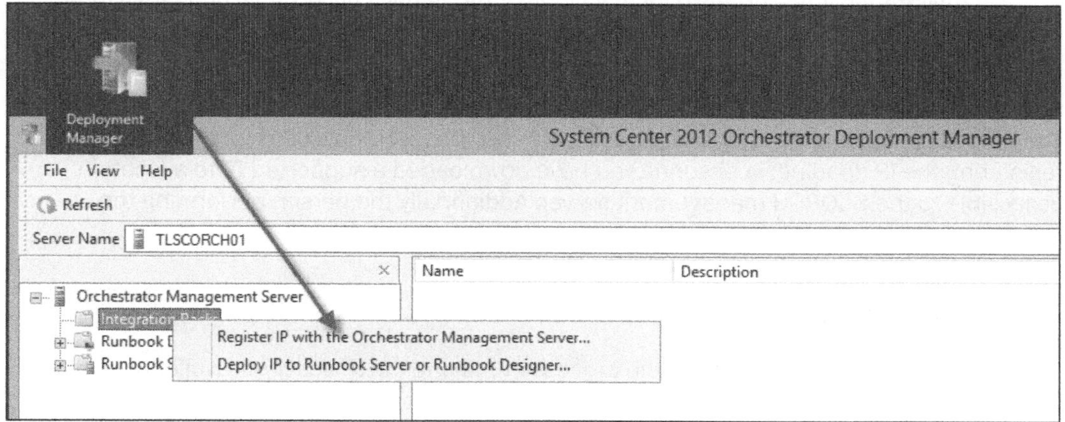

4. Click on **Next** on the welcome page. Click on **Add** on the Select Integration Packs or Hotfixes page. Navigate to the directory where the target IP is located, click on **Open**, and then click on **Next**.

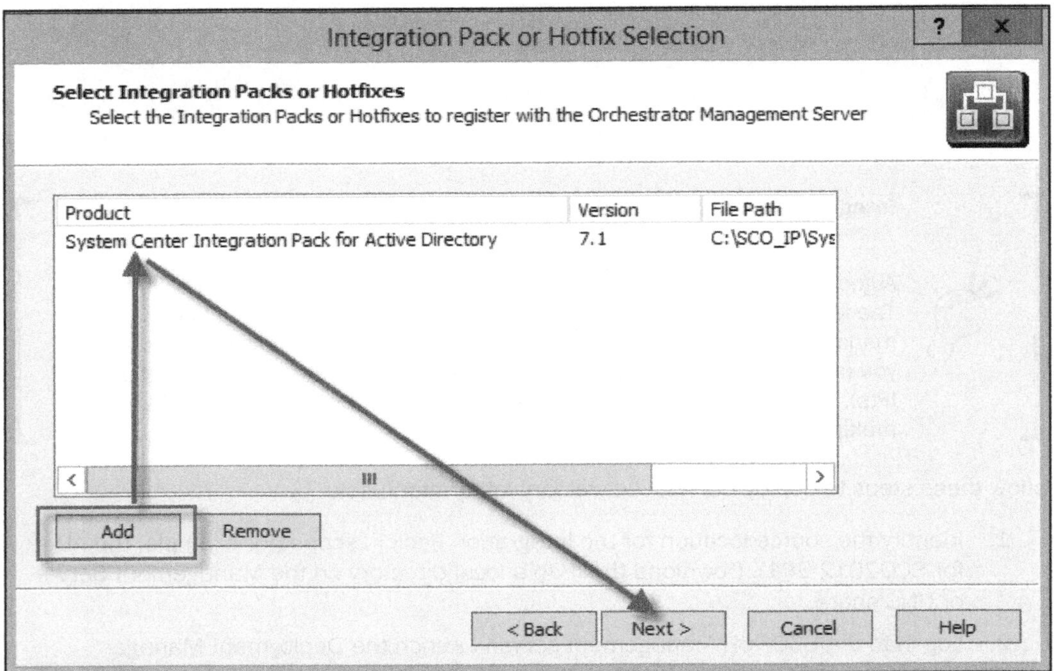

5. Click on **Finish**. Click on **Accept** on **End-User License Agreement** to complete the registration. Click on **Refresh** to validate if the IP has successfully been registered.

How it works...

The process of loading an integration pack is simple. The prerequisite for successfully registering the IP (loading) is ensuring you have downloaded a supported IP to a location accessible to the SCORCH management server. Additionally the person performing the registration must be a SCORCH administrator.

There's more...

Registering the IP is the first part of the process of making the IP activities available to Runbook designers and Runbook Servers.

Deploying the IP to Designers and Runbook Servers

Once the IP in scope (AD IP in our example) has successfully been registered, follow these steps to deploy it to the Runbook Designers and Runbook Servers.

1. Log in to the SCORCH Management server and launch Deployment Manager.
2. Under Orchestrator Management Server, right-click on the Integration Pack in scope and select **Deploy IP to Runbook Server or Runbook Designer...**.
3. Click on **Next** on the welcome page, select the IP you would like to deploy (in our example, `System Center Integration Pack for Active Directory`, and then click on **Next**.
4. On the computer Selection page. Type the name of the Runbook Server or designer in scope and click on **Add** (repeat for all servers in the scope).

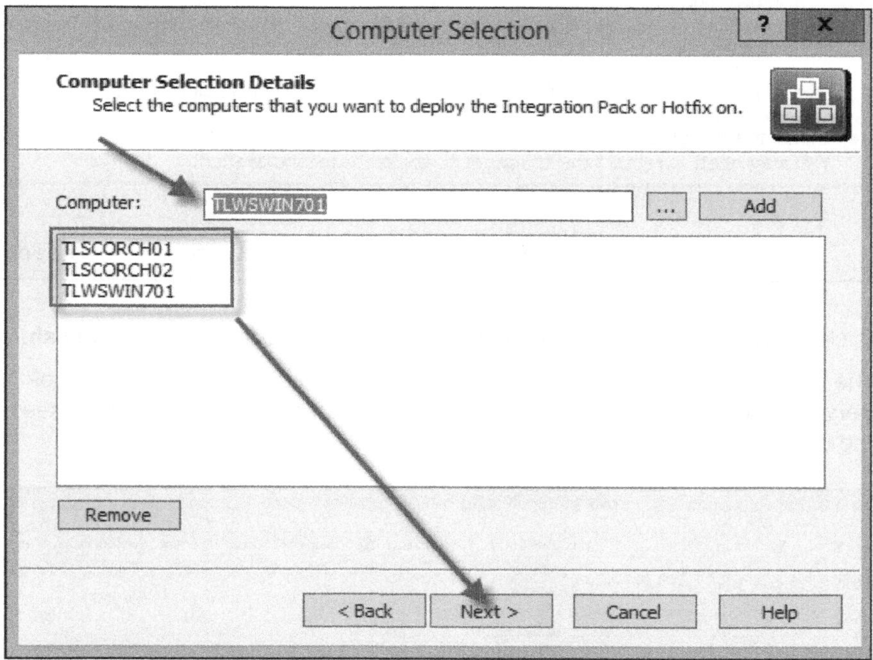

5. On the **Installation Options** page you have the following three options:
   - **Schedule the Installation:** select this option if you want to schedule the deployment for a specific time. You still have to select one of the next two options.
   - **Stop all running Runbooks before installing the Integration Packs or Hotfixes**: This option will as described stop all current Runbooks in the environment.

- **Install the Integration Packs or Hotfixes without stopping the running Runbooks**: This is the preferred option if you want to have a controlled deployment without impacting current jobs.

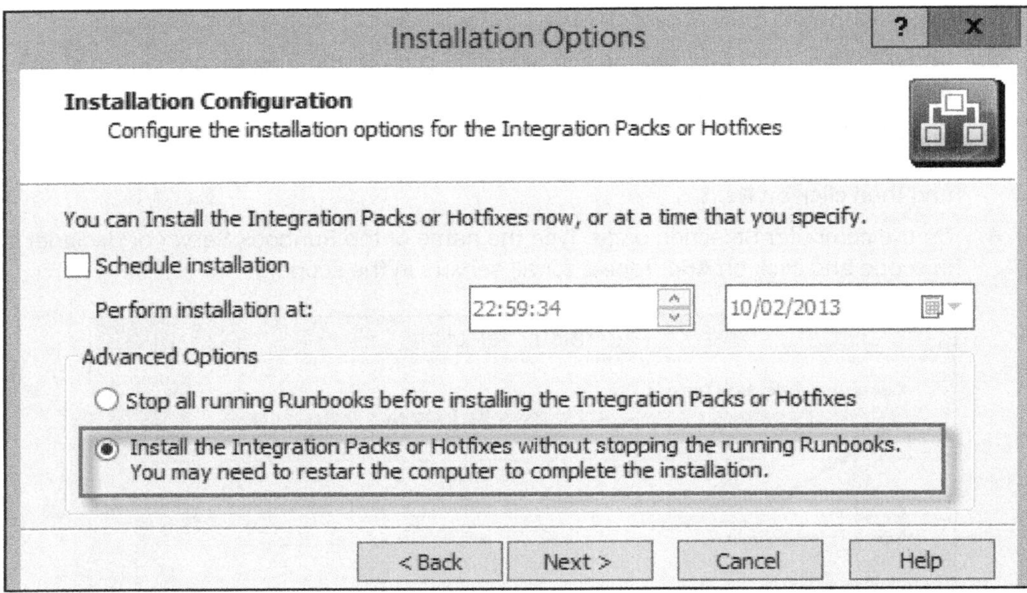

6. Click on **Next** after making your installation option selection. Click on **Finish**.
7. The integration pack will be deployed to all selected designers and Runbook Servers. You must close all Runbook designer consoles and re-launch to see the newly deployed Integration Pack.

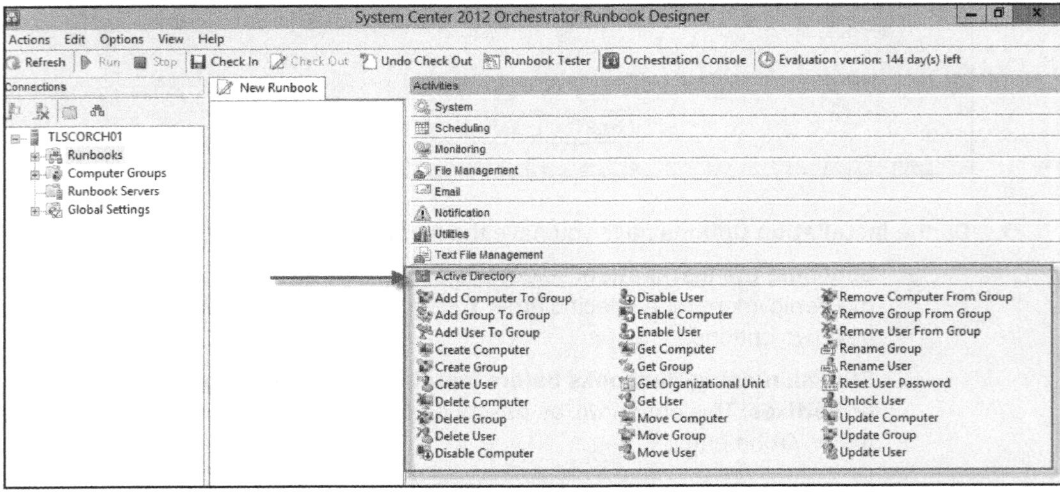

Configuring Integration Pack connections

This recipe provides the steps required to configure an integration pack for use once it has been successfully deployed to a Runbook Designer.

Getting ready

You must deploy an Orchestrator environment and also deploy the IP you plan to configure to a Runbook Designer before following the steps in this recipe.

The authors assume the user account performing the installation has administrative privileges on the server nominated for the SCORCH Runbook Designer.

How to do it...

Each integration pack serves as an interface to the actions SCORCH can perform in the target environment. In our example we will be focusing on the Active Directory connector. We will have two accounts under two categories of AD tasks in our scenario:

IP name	Category of actions	Account name
Active Directory	Domain Account Management	`SCOAD_ACCMGT`
Active Directory	Domain Administrator Management	`SCOAD_DOMADMIN`

The following diagram provides a visual summary and order of the tasks you need to perform to complete this recipe.

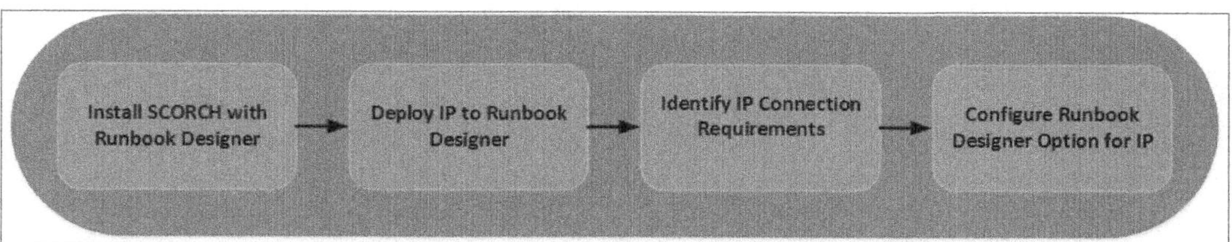

Follow these steps to complete the configuration of the Active Directory Integration Pack (IP) options in the Runbook Designer:

1. Create or identify an existing account for the IP tasks. In our example we are using two accounts to represent two personas of a typical active directory delegation model. `SCOAD_ACCMGT` is an account with the rights to perform account management tasks only and `SCOAD_DOMADMIN` is a domain admin account for elevated tasks in Active Directory.

2. Launch the Runbook Designer as a SCORCH administrator, select **Options** from the menu bar, and select the IP to configure (in our example, **Active Directory**).

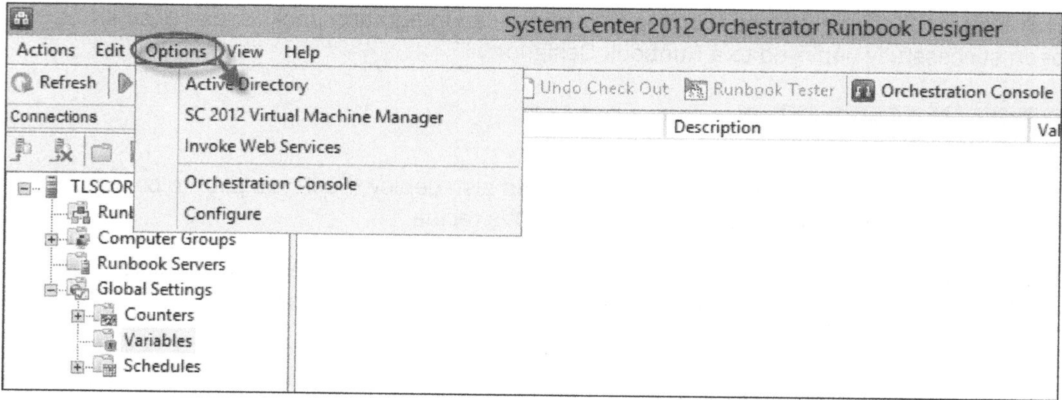

3. Click on **Add**, type `AD Account Management` in the **Name:** field, select **Microsoft Active Directory Domain Configuration** in the **Type** field by clicking on the **...**.
4. In the **Properties** section type the following:
    - **Configuration User Name**: `SCOAD_ACCMGT`
    - **Configuration Password**: Enter the password for `SCOAD_ACCMGT`
    - **Configuration Domain Controller Name (FQDN)**: The FQDN of an accessible domain controller in the target AD (In this example, `TLDC01.TRUSTLAB.LOCAL`).
    - **Configuration Default Parent Container**: This is an optional field. Leave it blank.

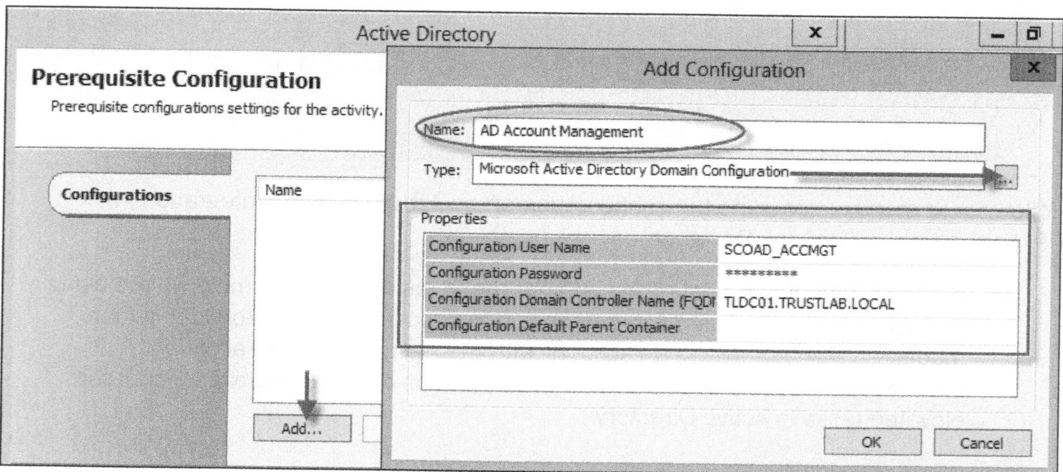

5. Click on **OK**. Repeat steps 3 and 4 for the Domain Admin account and click on finish to complete the configuration. The following screenshot illustrates the final configuration after completing the steps.

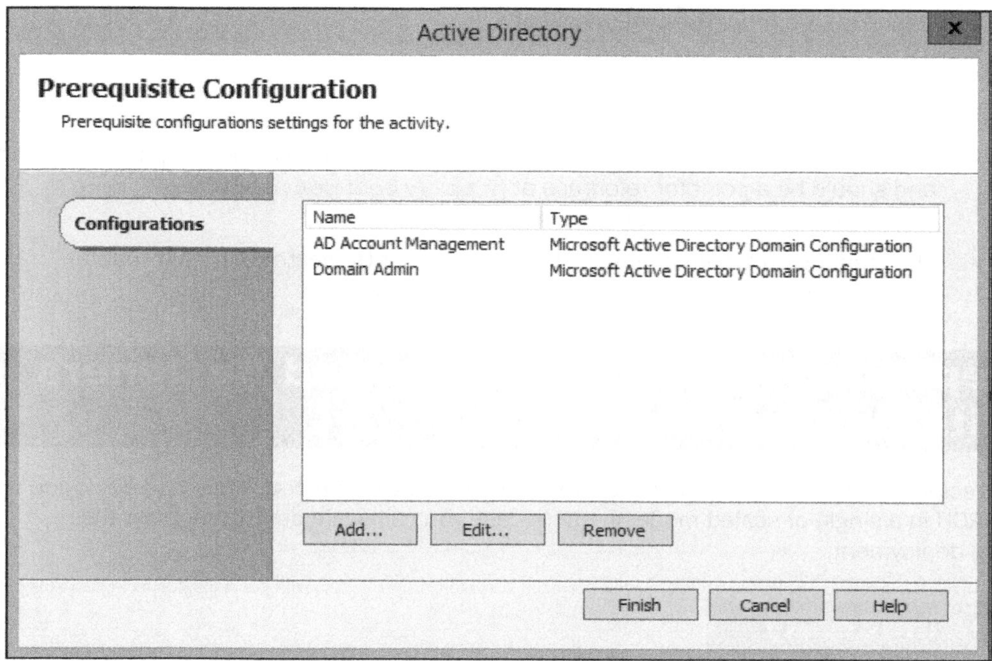

How it works...

The IP configuration is unique for each system environment SCORCH interfaces with for the tasks in scope of automation. The active directory IP configuration grants SCORCH the rights to perform the actions specified in the Runbook using the activities of the IP.

Typical Active Directory activities include, but are not limited to creating user and computer accounts, moving user and computer accounts into organizational units, or deleting user and computer accounts.

In our example we created two connection account configurations for the following reasons:

- Follow the guidance of scoping automation to the rights of the manual processes. If we use the example of a Runbook for creating user accounts we do not need domain admin access. A service desk user performing the same action manually would typically be granted only account management rights in AD.
- We have more flexibility with delegating management and access to Runbooks. Runbooks with elevated rights through the connection configuration can be separated from Runbooks with lower rights using folder security.

The configuration requires planning and understanding of its implication before implementing.

Each IP has its own unique options which you must specify before you create Runbooks using the specified IP. The default IPs that you can download from Microsoft include the documentation on the properties you must set.

See also

- The official online documentation for Microsoft Integration Packs is updated regularly and should be a point for reference at `http://technet.microsoft.com/en-us/library/hh295851.aspx`
- The creating and maintaining a security model for Orchestrator in this chapter expands further on the delegation model in SCORCH.

Deploying Runbook Servers and Designers with Deployment Manager

The recipes in *Chapter 1, Unpacking System Center 2012 Orchestrator*, discuss deploying SCORCH in a single or scaled mode. In either case you can scale out further after the initial deployment.

Getting ready

You must review the *Planning the Orchestrator deployment* recipe before performing the steps in this recipe. There are a number of dependencies in the planning recipe you must perform in order to successfully complete the tasks in this recipe.

You must install a Management server before you can install the additional Runbook Server(s) and Designers. The user account performing the installation has administrative privileges on the server nominated for the SCORCH deployment and must also be a member of **OrchestratorUsersGroup** or equivalent rights.

The example deployment in this recipe is based on the following configuration details:

- Management Server called `TLSCORCH01` with a remote database is already installed
- System Center 2012 Orchestrator 2012 SP1
- Service Account created in Active Directory: `SCO_RBSSVCA`

How to do it...

Deploying multiple Runbook Servers

In a SCORCH deployment you can configure multiple Runbook Servers for higher availability and load balancing. By default each Runbook Server can process 50 Runbook simultaneously; how well the Runbook Server handles this load depends on the actual Runbook activities.

The *Installing the Runbook Server in a multiserver deployment* recipe in *Chapter 1, Unpacking System Center 2012 Orchestrator*, discusses and provides steps for the individual server installation option.

Follow these steps to deploy an additional Runbook Server using the deployment manager:

1. Install a supported Windows Server operating system and join the server to the active directory domain in scope of the SCORCH deployment.
2. Add the service accounts and SCORCH administrators group to the local administrators group on the SCORCH Runbook Server.
3. On the nominated SCORCH Runbook Server enable the following feature:
    - NET Framework 3.5 SP1

   You must specify a source files for .NET Framework 3.5 SP1 in the case of Windows server 2012. Ensure the DVD for windows server 2012 is loaded.
4. Install .NET Framework 4 if the Operating System Version is lower than Windows Server 2012 (.NET Framework 4x is already part of Windows Server 2012)
5. Ensure you configure the allow ports and services if the local firewall is enabled for the domain profile. See the following link for details `http://technet.microsoft.com/en-us/library/hh420382.aspx`.
6. Log in to the SCORCH Management server with a user account with SCORCH administrative rights.
7. Launch System Center 2012 Orchestrator Deployment Manager. Right-click on **Runbook Servers** and select **Deploy new Runbook Server...**:

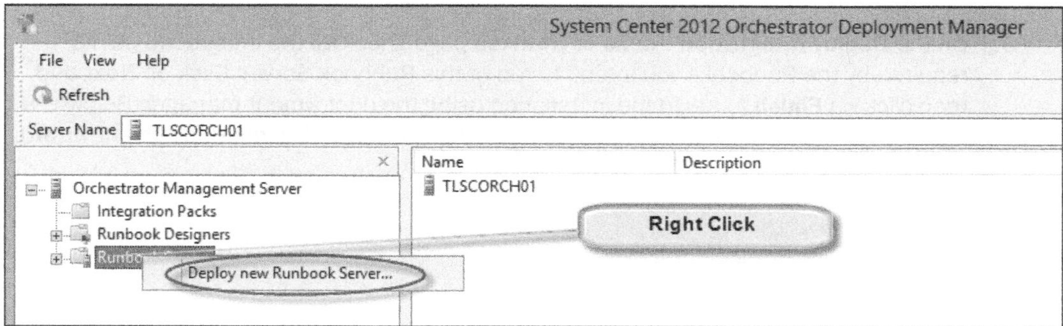

8. Click on **Next** on the welcome page, configure the following on the Service Information page, and click on **Next**:
    - **Computer**: Type the name of the new Runbook Server
    - **Description**: Optionally provide a description
    - **Account Information/User name**: Type the account nominated as the Runbook service account; for example, `SCO_RBSSVCA`
    - **Account Information/Password**: Type the password of the account nominated as the service account for this Runbook Server

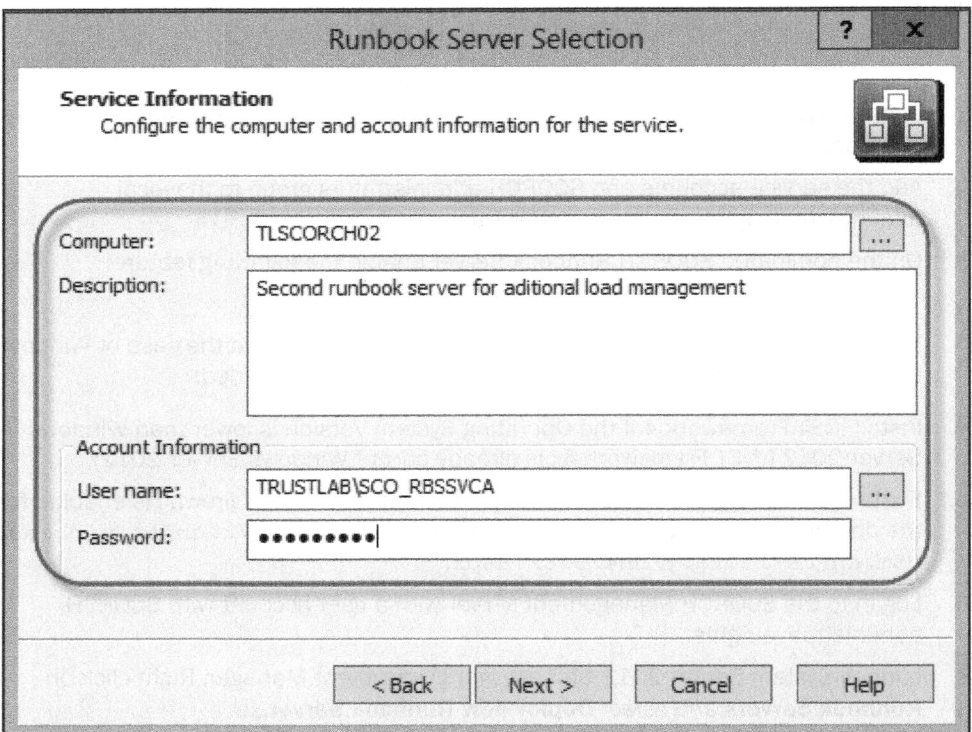

9. On the **Deploy Integration Packs or Hotfixes** page check all the integration packs required by the Runbooks you intend to run of this Runbook Server. Click on **Next** and then click on **Finish** to begin the installation using the deployment manager. Below is a summary of the successful status of the activities performed by the deployment wizard.

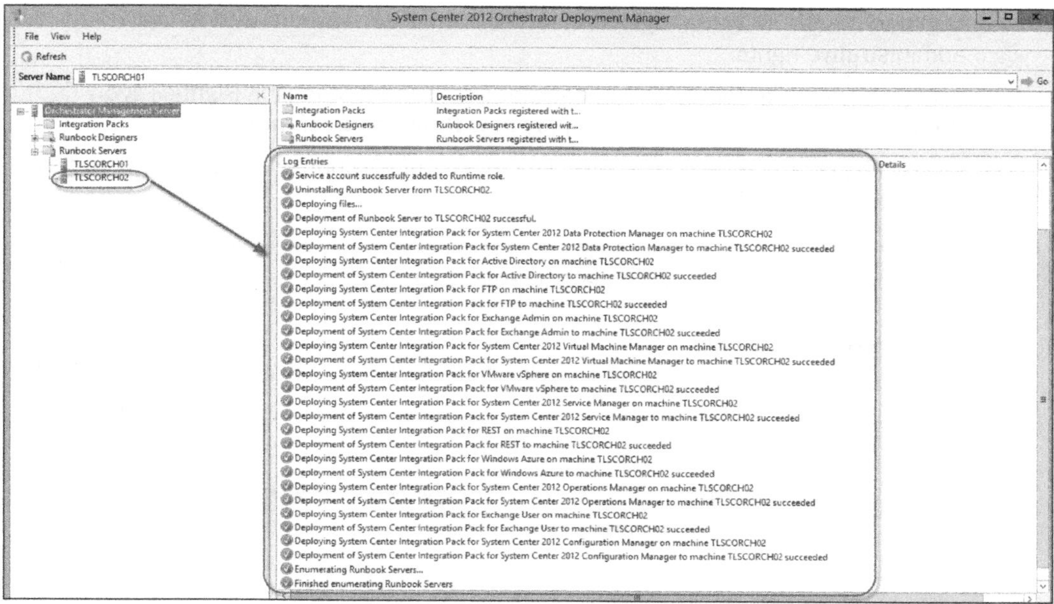

Deploying Runbook Designers using Deployment Manager

The **Runbook Designer** is used to build Runbooks using standard activities and or integration pack activities. The designer can be installed on either a server class operating system or a client class operating system.

The *Installing the Runbook Designer in a Multi-Server Deployment* recipe in *Chapter 1, Unpacking System Center 2012 Orchestrator*, discusses and provides steps for the installation using the SCORCH media.

Follow these steps to deploy an additional Runbook Designer using the deployment manager:

1. Install a supported operating system and join the active directory domain in scope of the SCORCH deployment. In this recipe the operating system is Windows 7.
2. On the nominated SCORCH Runbook Designer enable the following feature:
    - NET Framework 3.5 SP1 (enabled by default with Windows 7)

   You must specify a source files for .NET Framework 3.5 SP1 in the case of Windows server 2012. Ensure the DVD for windows server 2012 is loaded.

3. Ensure you configure the allowed ports and services if the local firewall is enabled for the domain profile. See the following link for details: `http://technet.microsoft.com/en-us/library/hh420382.aspx`.

4. Log in to the SCORCH Management server with a user account with SCORCH administrative rights.
5. Launch System Center 2012 Orchestrator Deployment Manager. Right-click on **Runbook Designers**, and select **Deploy new Runbook Designer...**.
6. Click on **Next** on the welcome page. Type the computer name in the **Computer:** field and click on **Add**. Click on **Next**:

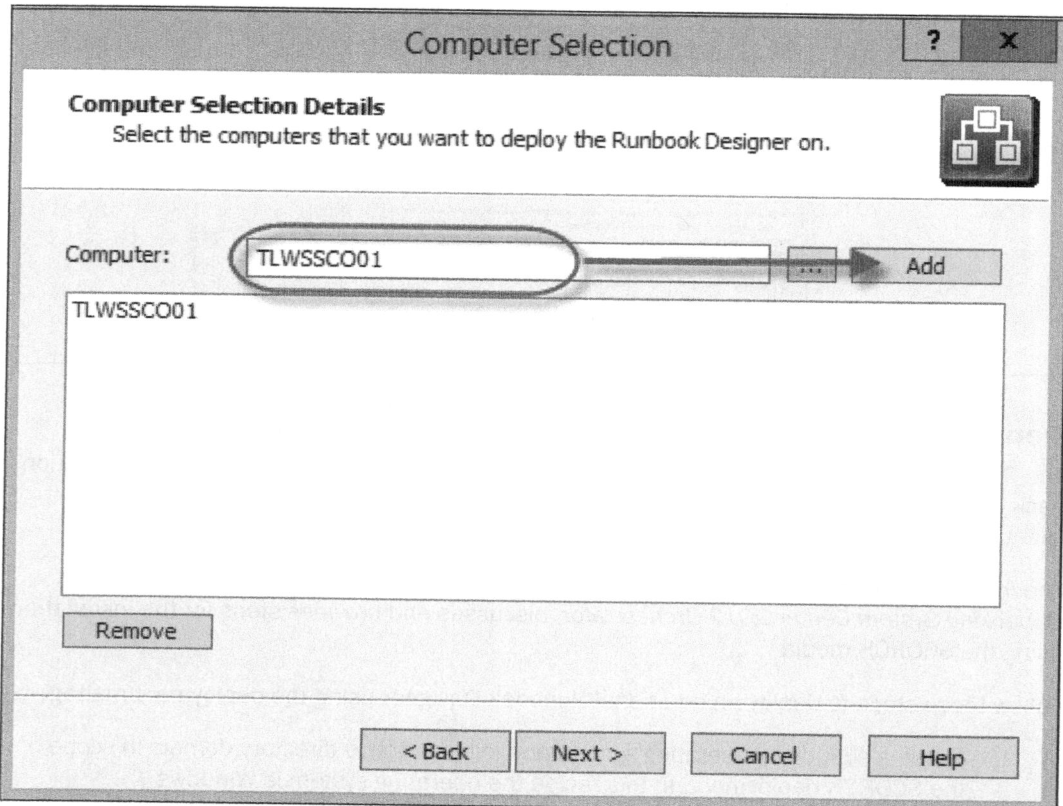

7. On the **Deploy Integration Packs or Hotfixes** page check all the integration packs required by the user of the Runbook Designer (for this example we will select the AD IP).

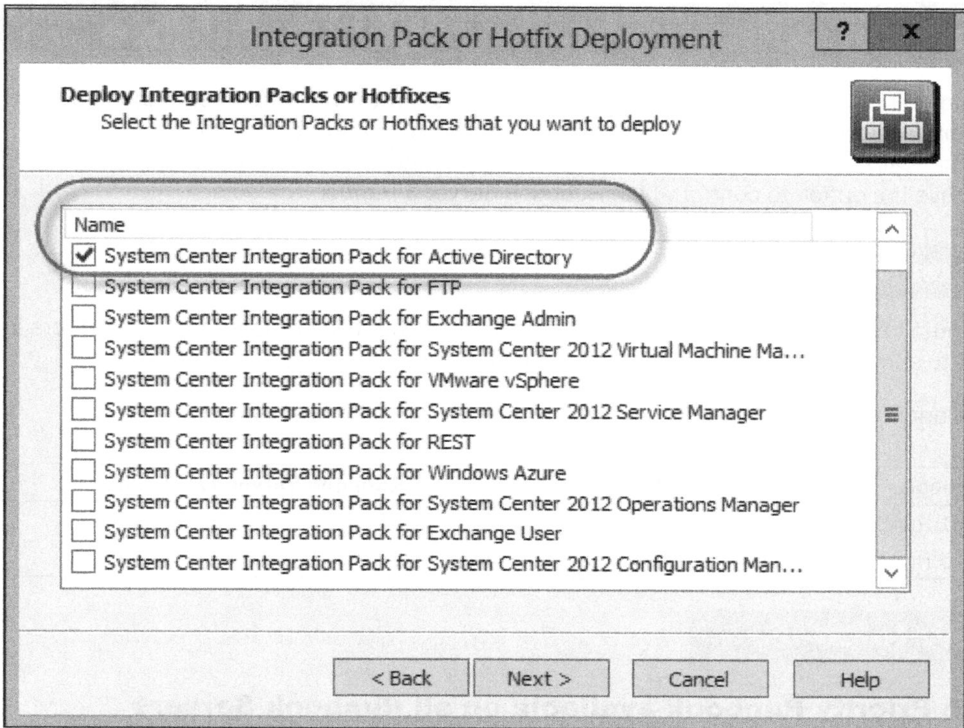

8. Click on **Next**. Click on **Finish** to begin the installation using the deployment manager.

How it works...

The Deployment Manager is a great option for scaling out your Runbook Servers and also for distributing the **Runbook Designer** without the need for the installation media. In both cases the **Deployment Manager** connects to the **Management Server** and the database server to configure the necessary settings. On the target system the deployment manager installs the required binaries and optionally deploys the integration packs selected.

Using the **Deployment Manager** provides a consistent and coordinated approach to scaling out the components of a SCORCH deployment.

See also

The following official web link is a great source of the most up to date information on SCORCH:

`http://technet.microsoft.com/en-us/library/hh237242.aspx`

Making your Runbooks highly available

The default installation of System Center 2012 orchestrator with multiple Runbook Servers automatically provides Runbook Server fault tolerance. The Runbooks you create will automatically run on an available Runbook Server if one of the multiple servers is unavailable. You have the option to control which Runbook Server a Runbook selects.

Getting ready

You must have a fully deployed SCORCH environment with two or more Runbook Servers in order to successfully complete the tasks in this recipe.

The planning criteria for this recipe is as detailed in the following table:

Runbook	Priority	Runbook Server availability
SLA 1 Runbook	High	All
SLA 5 Runbook	Low	1

How to do it...

High Priority Runbook available on all Runbook Servers

1. Log in to a SCORCH Runbook Designer computer with a user account with SCORCH administrative rights to the Runbooks in scope.
2. In the middle pane of the Runbook Designer, right-click on the Runbook in scope and select **Properties**. Click on the **Runbook Servers** tab.

3. Review **Override default Runbook Servers roles**. This setting must be unchecked to ensure the Runbook runs on a standby Runbook Server if the primary is unavailable.

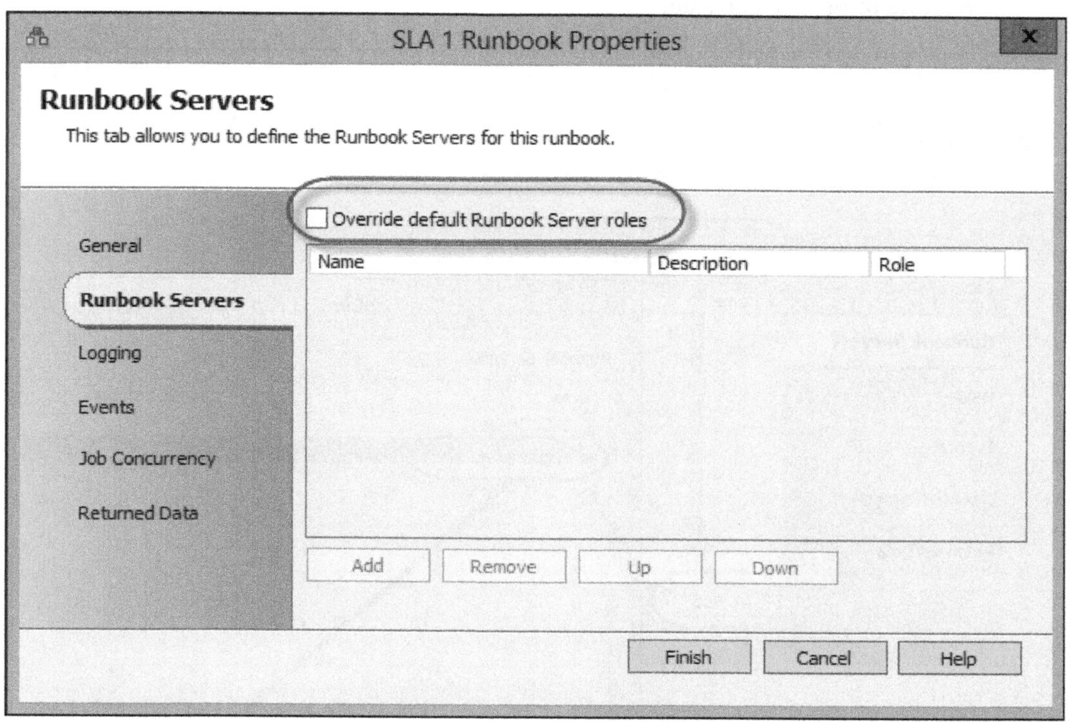

Low priority Runbook available on one Runbook Server

1. Log in to a SCORCH Runbook Designer computer with a user account with SCORCH administrative rights to the Runbooks in scope.

2. In the middle pane of the Runbook Designer, right-click on the Runbook in scope and select **Properties**. Select the **Runbook Servers** tab. Check **Override default Runbook Servers roles**. Click on **Add**.

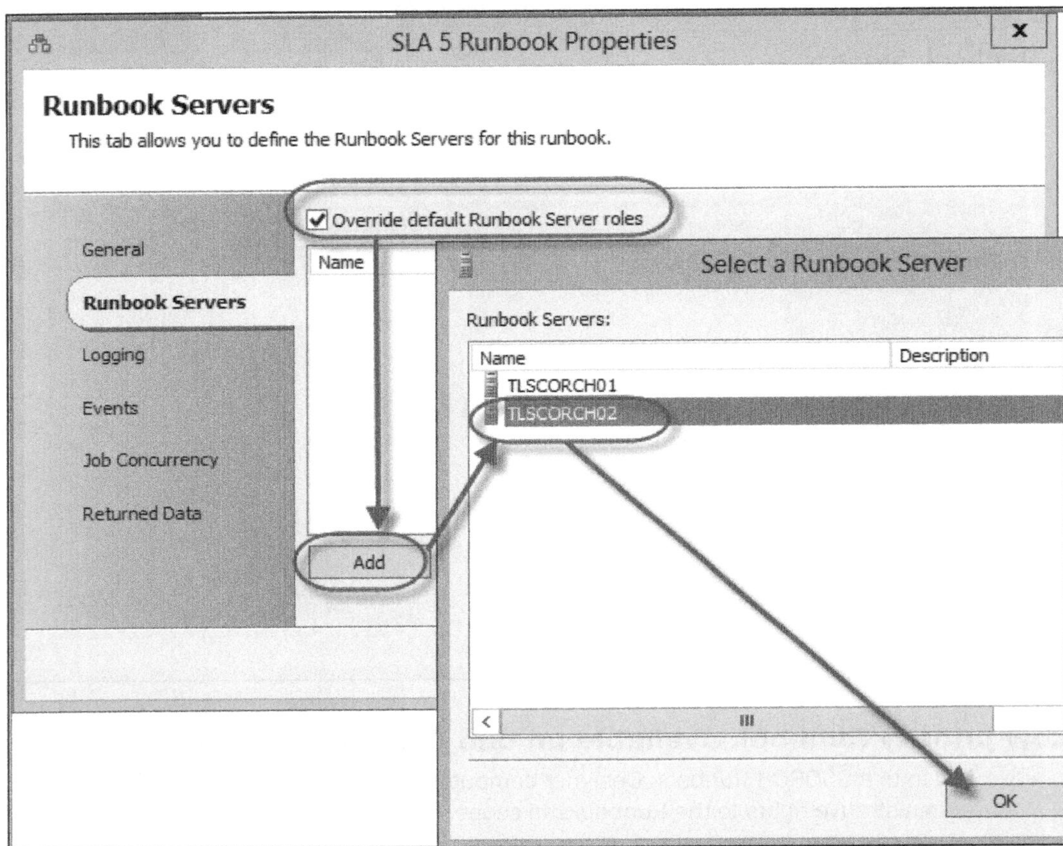

3. Click on **OK**. Click on **Finish** to complete the configuration. If prompted select **Yes** to check out the Runbook.

How it works...

The default option in the first scenario is the standard for ensuring that SCORCH automatically manages the availability of Runbook Servers. In the case of the default you are assured that your Runbook will be executed as long as at least one of the configured Runbooks is available.

The second option is useful for low priority Runbooks where you might want to control and limit the available Runbook Servers. It is recommended to leave the default setting for your premium Runbooks.

It might be beneficial to nominate a Runbook Server for testing purposes and in this case overriding the default setting may be a good option.

There's more...

You have the option to control the nominated primary Runbook Server setting globally for all Runbooks.

Promoting and demoting primary Runbook Servers

The first Runbook Server you install is nominated as the Primary Runbook Server for all Runbooks by default. If you add additional Runbook Servers you can also change the Primary globally by following these steps:

1. Log in to a SCORCH Runbook Designer computer with a user account with SCORCH administrative rights to the Runbooks in scope.
2. Select **Runbook Servers** in the middle pane of the Runbook Designer. Right-click on the Runbook Server in scope and either select **Promote to Primary**, **Promote**, or **Demote** to change the default system setting.

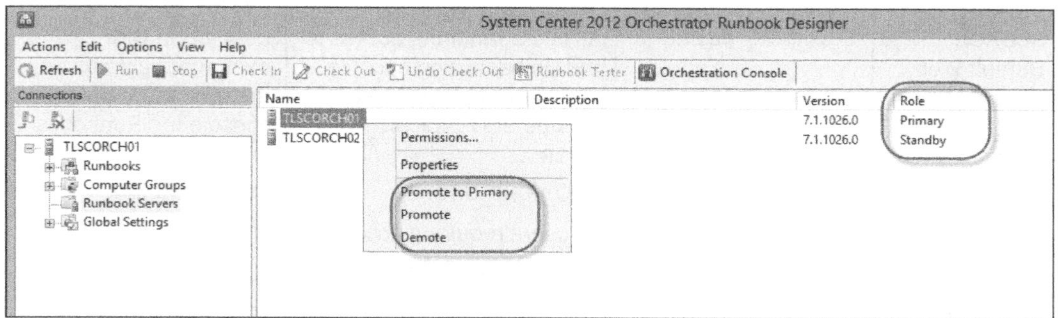

Creating and maintaining a security model for Orchestrator

Microsoft System Center 2012 Orchestrator provides you with the ability to delegate and secure components in its infrastructure. The process to create this security model differs from some of the other System Center family of products. In this recipe we will discuss and provide steps to configure a security model using a real world scenario.

Getting ready

You must have a fully deployed System Center 2012 Orchestrator environment in order to complete this recipe.

Security model scenario

In our example environment we have five roles in scope for our initial security configuration:

- SCORCH Full administrators
- SCORCH Default Web Console Users
- SCORCH Runbook Designer Users
- SCORCH Active Directory Runbook Designers
- SCORCH Active Directory Console Users

The following table describes the roles and their relevant assigned active directory groups:

Organization role	Active directory group	Members	Description
SCORCH Full administrators	SCORCH Admins	SCORCH infrastructure administrator users. Note that members will have elevated privileges via Runbooks.	Have access to all Runbooks and is the equivalent of an Active directory domain and enterprise admins roles.
SCORCH Default Web Console Users	`SCO_CON_USERS`	All users requiring access to the Orchestration console. In this example will also include `SCO_ADCON_USERS`.	User group with minimum rights to the Orchestration console (no Runbooks available).
SCORCH Runbook Designer Users	`SCO_RBD_USERS`	`SCO_RBD_USERS` All users requiring access to connect to the Management server with a Runbook designer in this example the group will also include `SCO_ADRBD_USERS`.	User group with minimum rights to connect the Runbook Designer to the management server.
SCORCH Active Directory Runbook Designers	`SCO_ADRBD_USERS`	Users nominated as AD Runbook designers.	Administrators with access to standard activities and the AD IP for Runbook creation and administration.
SCORCH Active Directory Activities Console Users	`SCO_ADCON_USERS`	Users nominated as AD Runbook executors and monitors with the Orchestration console.	Users with Access to run AD Runbooks using the Web Console.

How to do it...

The security model implementation will be split into five configuration categories:

- Prepare and Organize the environment
- Configure DCOM permissions
- Designer and Console Delegation
- Configure AD IP Runbook Permissions
- Restricting Options by Runbook Designer Integration Pack Deployment

The following diagram provides a visual summary and order of the tasks you need to perform to complete this recipe.

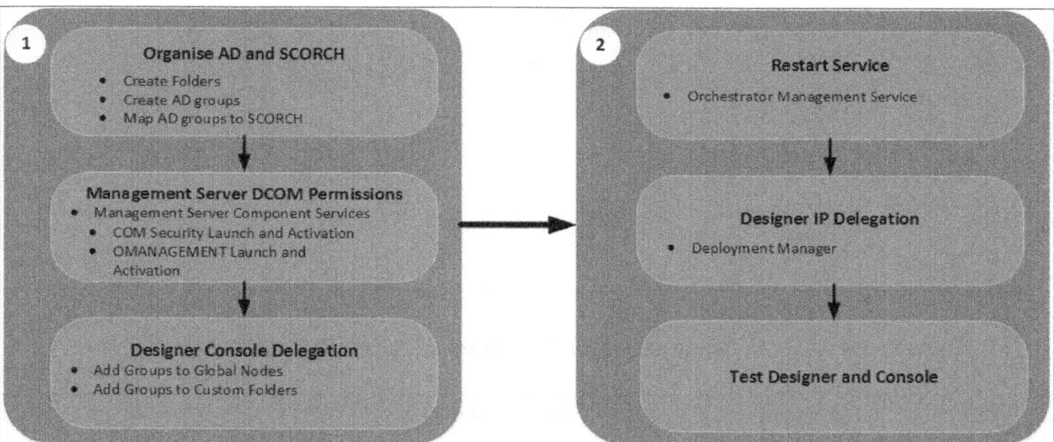

Preparing and organizing the environment

Consider the following table:

Node/sub node	Folder/sub folders	Description
Runbooks	`0.Root`	Create top-level global Runbooks here.
Runbooks	`Cookbook\Chapter 4`	Create AD Runbooks here.
Computer Groups	`0.Root`	Create top-level global computer groups here.
Global Settings\Counters	`0.Root`	Create top-level global Counters here.
Global Settings\Variables	`0.Root`	Create top-level global Variables here.
Global Settings\Schedules	`0.Root`	Create top-level global Schedules here.

We will follow these steps to create an initial folder structure for security delegation using the preceding table as our guide:

- Log in to a SCORCH Runbook Designer computer with a user account with SCORCH administrative rights and connect to the Management server.
- Select the Runbooks node. Right-click and select **New** | **Folder**. Type `0.Root` as the folder name.

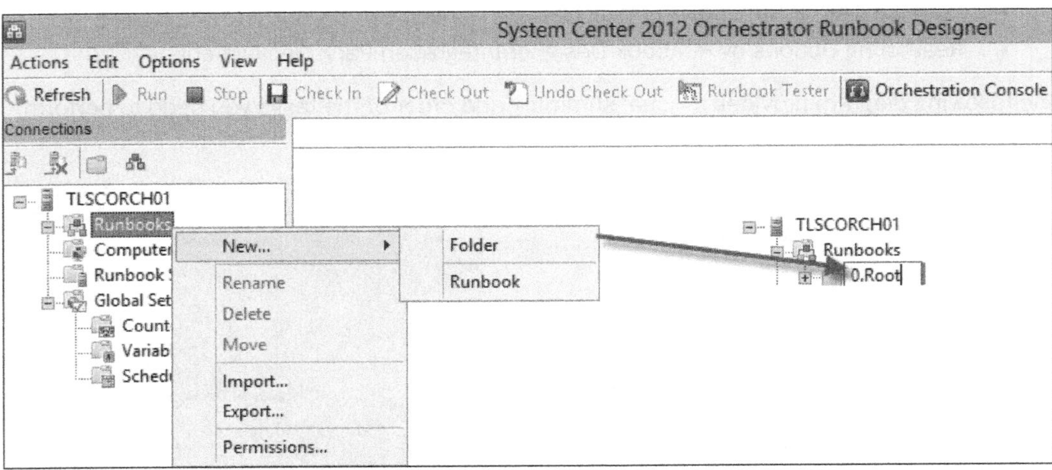

- Repeat the folder creation steps for the nodes specified in the table above.

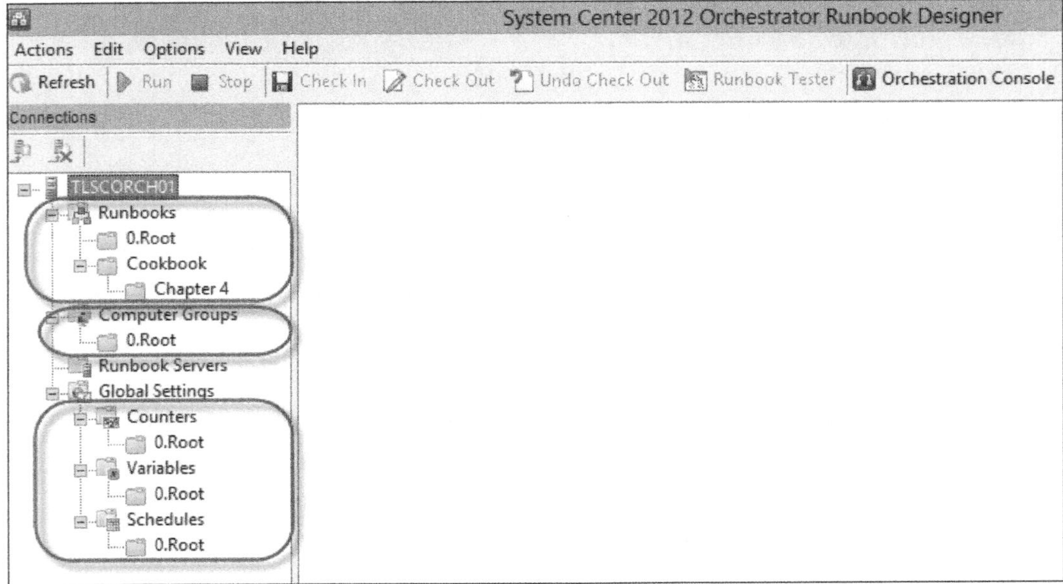

Configuring DCOM permissions

We will follow these steps to assign the DCOM security delegation using the security scenarios table. You must create the AD groups before you perform the steps in this recipe.

1. Log in to a SCORCH Management Server computer with a user account with SCORCH administrative rights.
2. Go to **Control Panel** | **Administrative Tool**. Launch Component Services. Expand the **Component Services** node and then expand **Computers**. Right-click on **My Computer** and select **Properties**:

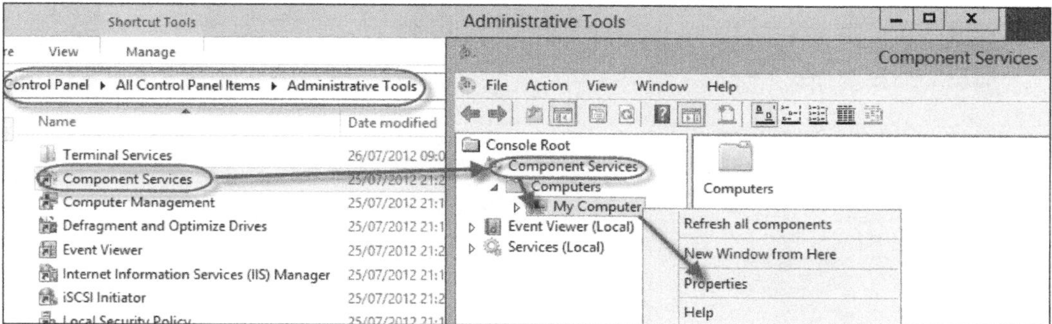

3. Select the **COM Security** tab. Under **Access Permissions**, click on **Edit Limits...**. Under **Group or user names:** box, click on **Add** and Select the AD groups nominated as general access for Console Users and Runbook Designers (In our example, `SCO_CON_USERS` and `SCO_RBD_USERS`). Click on **OK**.

4. Select the AD group you added and check **Local Access** and **Remote Access** in the **Allow** column. Click on **OK**.

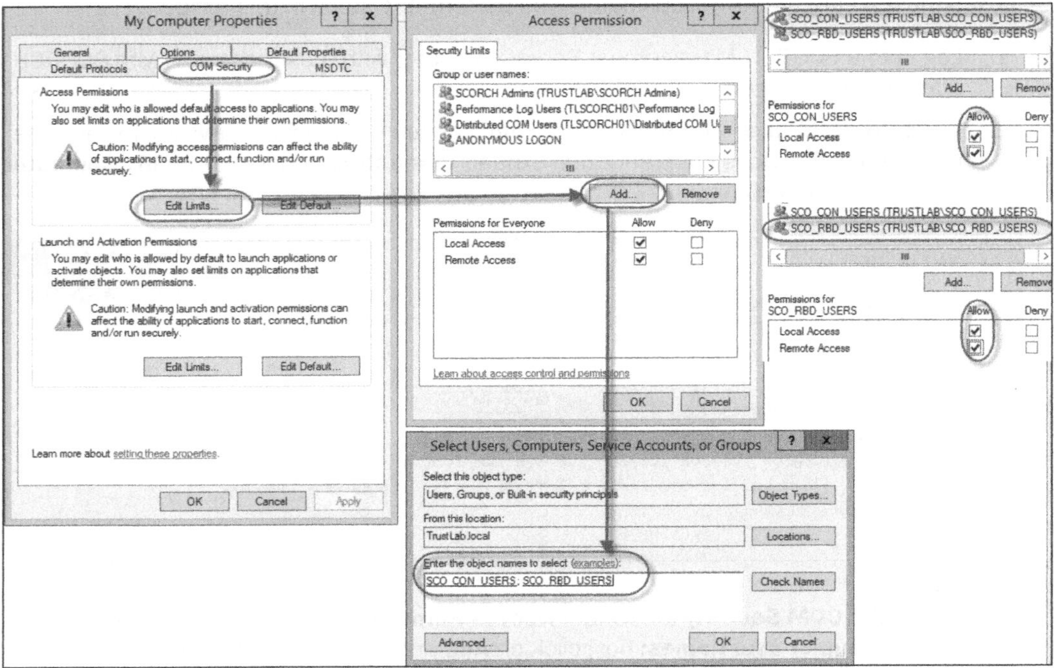

5. Ensure you are still on the **COM Security** tab. Under **Launch and Activation**, click on **Edit Limits...**. Under **Group or user names:** dialog box, click on **Add** and select the AD groups nominated as general access for Console Users and Runbook Designers (In our example, `SCO_CON_USERS` and `SCO_RBD_USERS`). Click on **OK**.
6. Select the AD groups in turn and check **Local Launch**, **Remote Launch** , **Local Activation** and **Remote Activation** options in the **Allow** column. Click on **OK** twice.

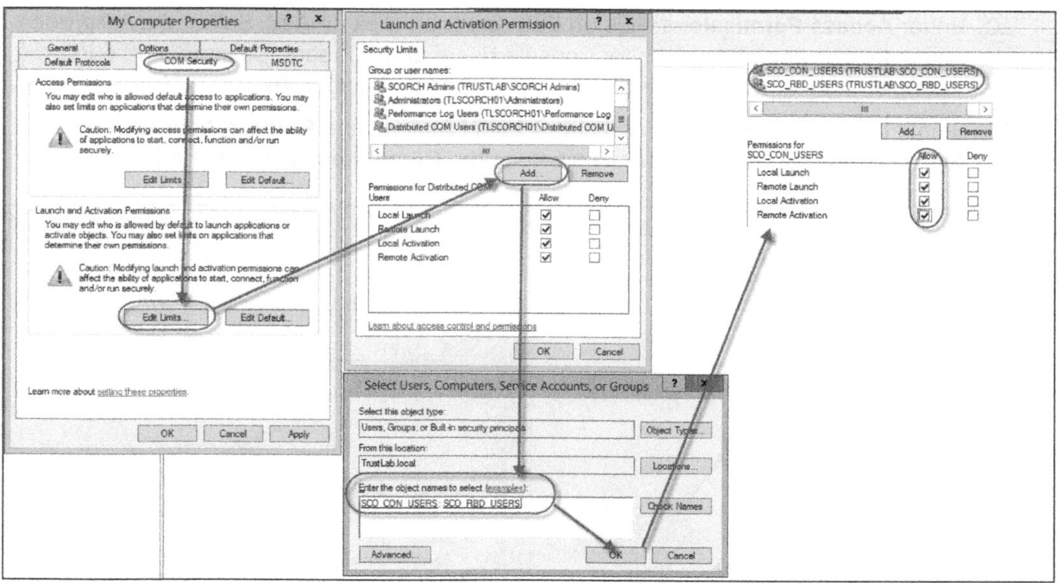

7. In the **Component Services** node, expand **Computers**. Go to **My Computer | DCOM Config**, scroll down to **omanagement**. Right-click on it and select **Properties**.
8. Click on **Security** tab. Under **Launch and Activation Permissions**, click on **Edit** and then click on **Add**. Select the AD groups nominated as general access for Console Users and Runbook Designers (In our example, `SCO_CON_USERS` and `SCO_RBD_USERS`). Click on **OK**.
9. Select the AD groups in turn and check **Local Launch**, **Remote Launch** , **Local Activation**, and **Remote Activation** in the **Allow** column, and click on **OK** twice.

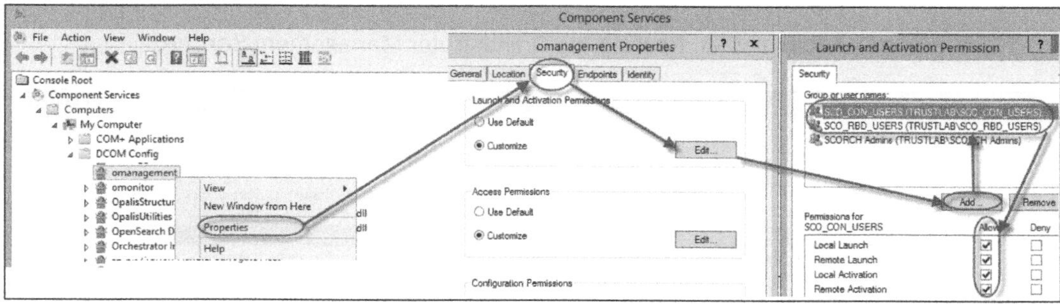

10. Under **Access Permissions** click on **Edit** and then click on **Add**. Select the AD groups nominated as general access for Console Users and Runbook Designers (In our example, `SCO_CON_USERS` and `SCO_RBD_USERS`). Click on **OK**.
11. Select the AD groups in turn and check **Local Access** and **Remote Access** in the **Allow** column. Click on **OK** twice and close the **Component services** node:

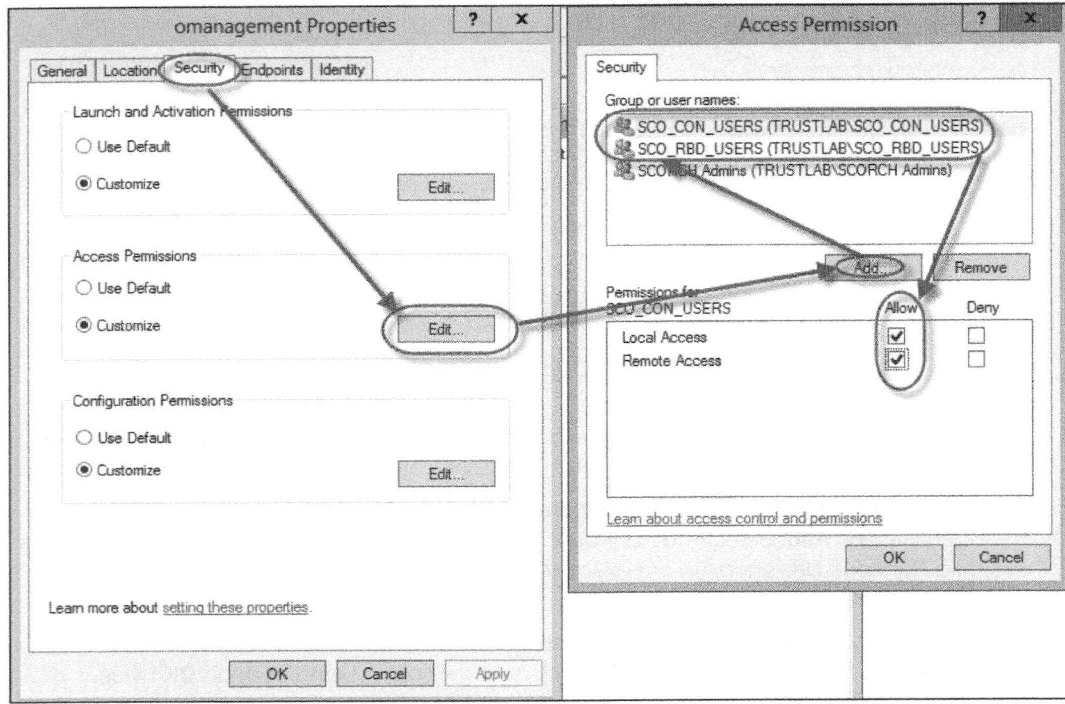

12. Run the **Services** applet. **Restart** the Orchestrator Management Service.

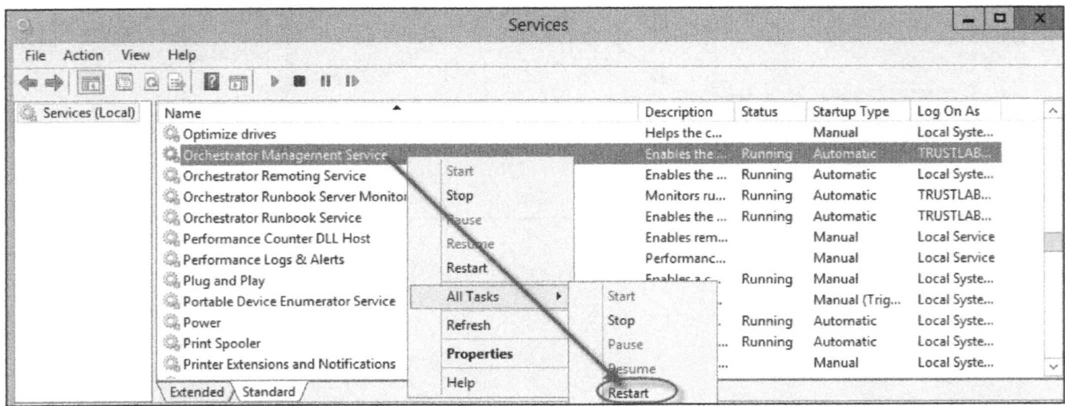

Designer and console delegation

Follow these steps to give general access to the Runbook Designer and Orchestration Console. In our example, we will grant the minimum access required to the two groups `SCO_CON_USERS` and `SCO_RBD_USERS`.

1. Log in to a SCORCH Runbook Designer computer with a user account with SCORCH administrative rights and connect to the Management server.
2. Select the **Runbooks** node. Right-click and select **Permissions**. Click on **Add...** Select the groups in scope; select each group in turn. Uncheck all permissions except **Read**. Click on **Advanced**. Select each of the groups you added in turn and click on **Edit**. In the **Applies to:** field, select **This object only**. Click on **OK** three times to apply the setting:

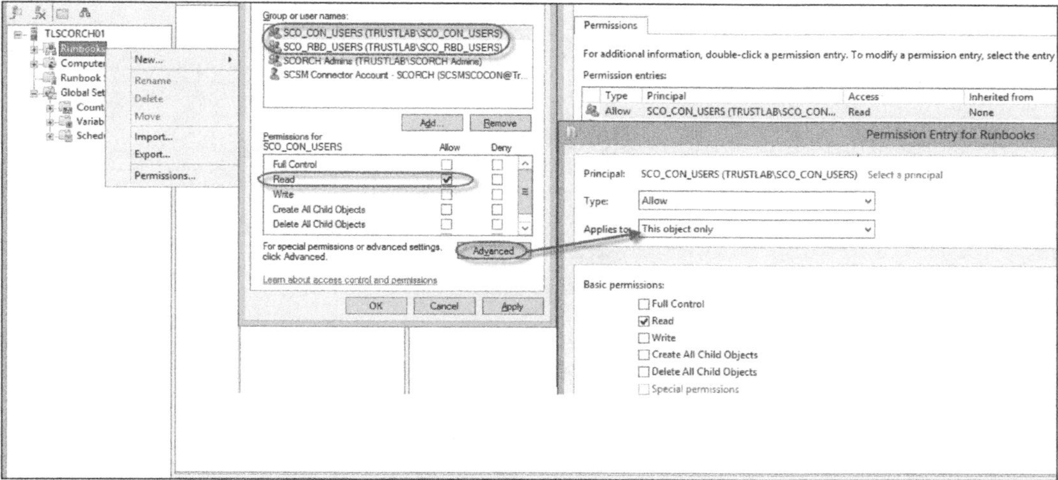

3. Repeat step 2 for the following node and sub-nodes:
   - **Computer Groups**
   - **Global Settings\Counters**
   - **Global Settings\Variables**
   - **Global Setting\Schedules**

4. Select the **Runbook Servers** node. Right-click and select **Permissions**. Click on **Add...**. Select the groups in scope. Select each group in turn. Uncheck all permissions except **Read**, and click on **OK**.

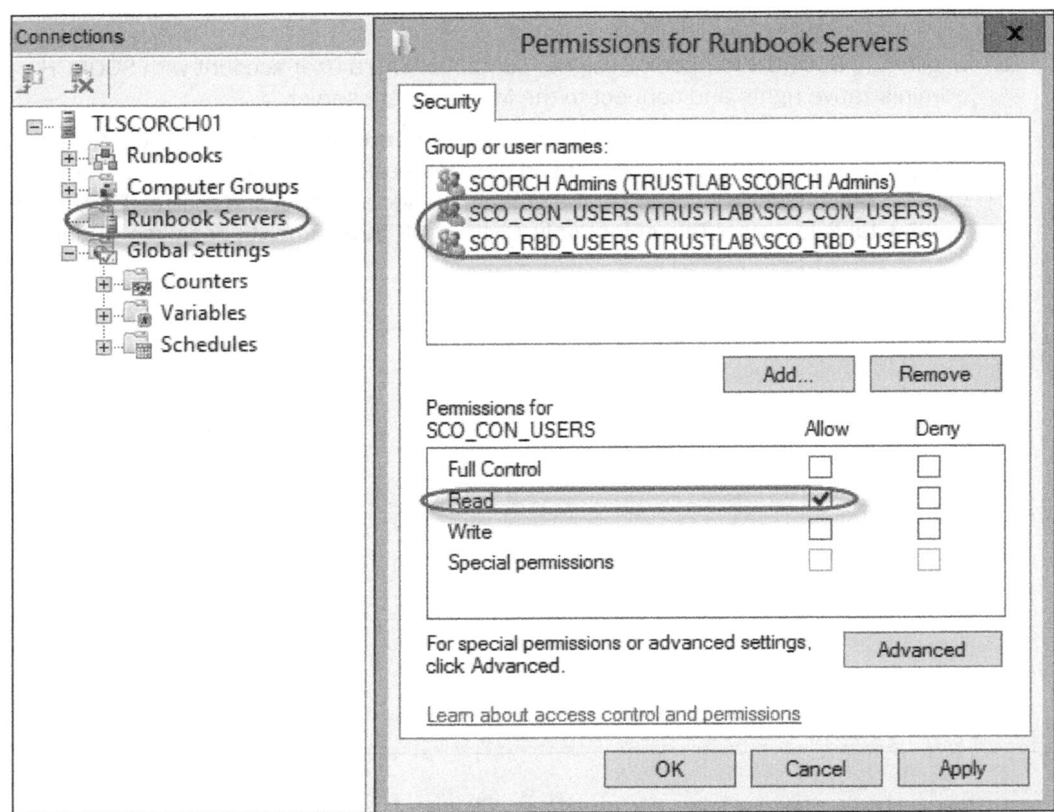

This completes the configuration for general access to the Designer and Orchestration console.

Configuring AD IP Runbook permissions

To grant access to a specific folder containing Runbooks. In our example `Cookbook/Chapter 4` contains our AD Runbooks, follow these steps:

1. Log in to a SCORCH Runbook Designer computer with a user account with SCORCH administrative rights and connect to the Management server.
2. Navigate to the Runbooks parent folder. Repeat the steps in the *Designer and Console Delegation* section to grant read only access to the Cookbook parent folder only in our example (select applies to **This object only** in the **Advanced** permissions).
3. Navigate to the folder or Sub-folder under the **Runbooks** node (Cookbook\Chapter 4 in our example). Right-click on the folder and select **Permissions**. Click on **Add** and select the Group nominated for the designer delegation (in our case SCO_ADRBD_USERS). Click **OK** and then click **Advanced**. Select the group you added and click **Edit** and then click **Show advanced permissions**, configure the permissions, and click **OK** when complete.

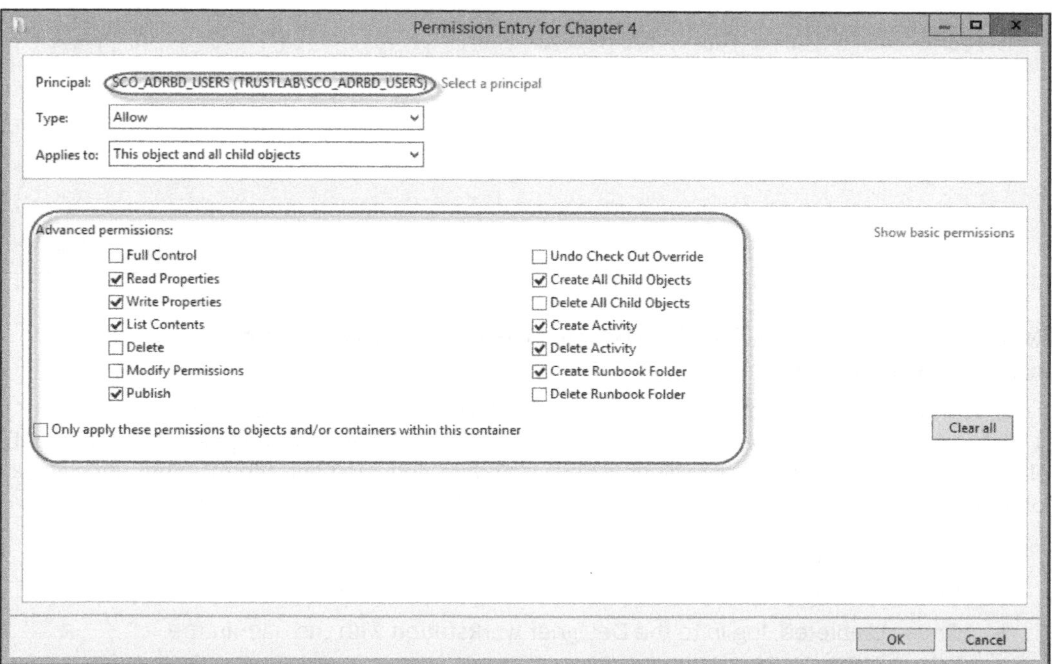

4. Repeat step 2 for the nominated Orchestration Console group (in our example SCO_ADCON_USERS but only select console required permissions (Read Properties, Write Properties, List Contents and Publish).

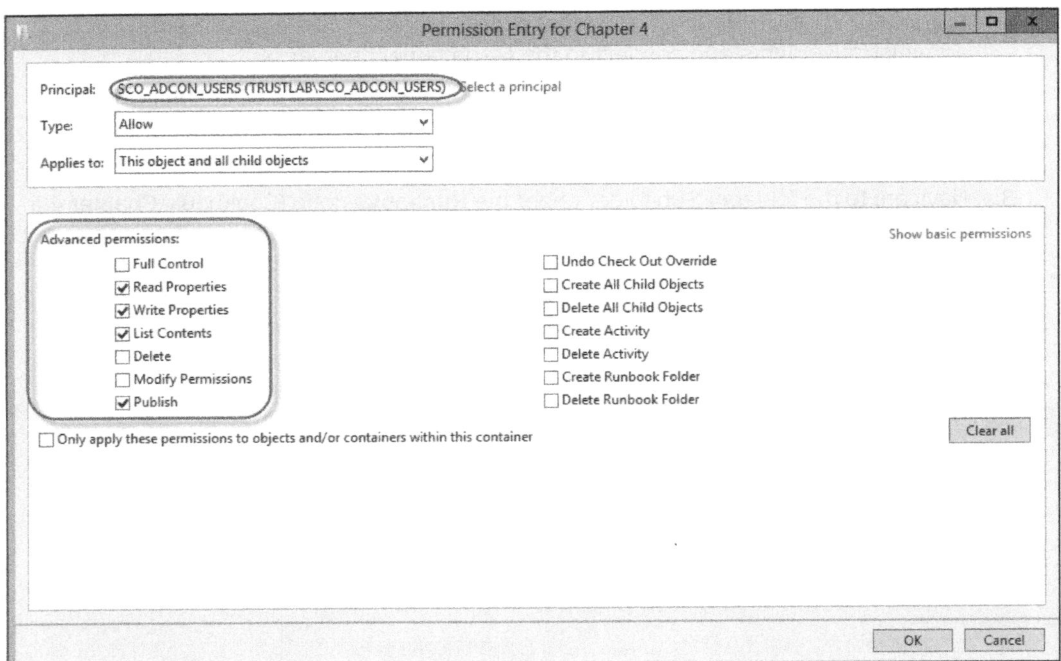

Restricting options by Runbook Designer Integration Pack Deployment

In our scenario we will install the SCORCH Runbook Designer on a workstation called `TLWSCO02` for a SCORCH delegated administrator responsible for creating and maintaining AD related Runbooks. The Designer will only have standard activities and the AD Integration Pack. Follow these steps to deploy a designer with the AD IP using Deployment Manager.

- Follow the steps in the recipe *Deploying Runbook Servers and Designers with the Deployment Manager*. Only select the AD IP for our workstation (`TLWSSCO02`).
- Once completed, log in to the Designer workstation with the user in the `SCO_ADRBD_USERS` group.

- Connect to the SCORCH Management Server using the Runbook Designer on `TLWSSCO02` and validate the user access to Runbooks and the options section.

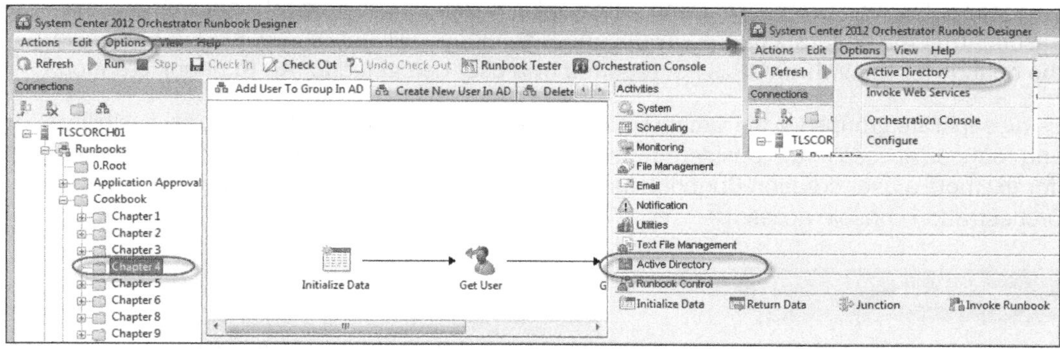

Note that all folders are visible but a user without permission to the folder will get an access denied message, as shown in the following screenshot:

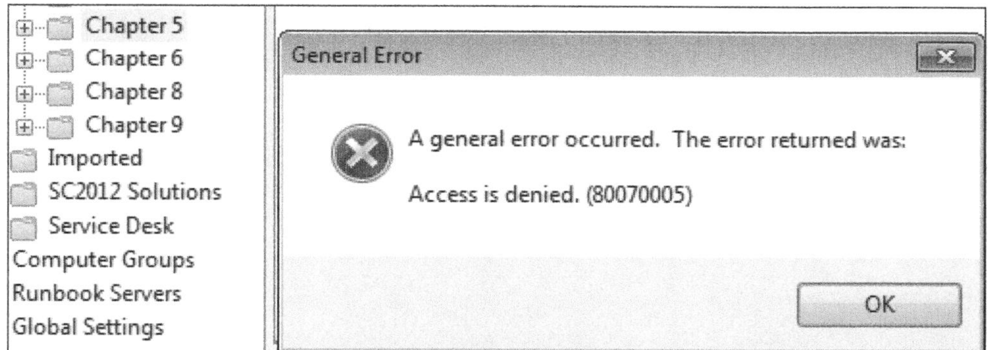

How it works...

The security framework in SCORCH requires that you grant access to the management server and the top-level folders or nodes before users can traverse to specific sub folders. The Runbook designer by default has four system nodes; **Runbooks**, **Computer Groups**, **Runbook Servers**, and **Global Settings**. We have the ability to manually create securable objects under the root of the **Runbooks**, **Computer Groups**, and **Global Settings**.

The recipe is split into four sections which you must plan to complete in order to grant the right level of access in an organized and maintainable manner.

Using top-level folders and default groups ensures that at minimum users can connect to the console and management server without the risk of executing or modifying existing Runbooks.

A further delegation using local Runbook Designers with only the IPs relevant to the users ensures that the general options which cannot be hidden will not be available (for example, the options for the VMware IP is not required by a user delegated for AD Runbook creation.)

Using separate groups for the Orchestration console provides you with additional flexibility and reduces access to the designer for administrators responsible for only executing Runbook (for example a user creation Runbook assigned to the service desk team will only require Orchestration console access).

See also

The following link provides additional information on SCORCH security delegation:

`http://technet.microsoft.com/en-us/library/hh420367.aspx`

3

Planning and Creating Runbook Designs

In this chapter we will cover the following recipes:

- Preparing Runbook scenarios
- Making Runbook scenarios automation ready
- Documenting Runbook designs
- Understanding the Orchestrator scenario building blocks

Introduction

Moving from manual processes to automation leads to the following questions:

- Is automation the root of all Information Technology (IT) evil?
- Is lack of automation the root of IT evil?

The answer to both questions is "it depends". In most circumstances we can say yes to either question. So 'evil' may sound a little strong for technology, however this is similar to the view of money. There is a definite fact that a lack of a well-defined and optimized process is the root of any automation evil. This chapter discusses steps we can take to ensure that the Runbooks (process workflows) we implement in Orchestrator, meet our needs as intended without the introduction of inefficient automation.

Preparing Runbook scenarios

Microsoft System Center 2012 Orchestrator (SCORCH) automation is implemented with what is known as Runbooks. Runbooks help us to implement manual tasks using a workflow approach.

This recipe provides example steps to identify candidates for SCORCH automation.

Getting ready

The key to a successful conversion of a manual process to a semi or fully automated process is a clear understanding of what you are trying to automate. A recognized method for describing the manual process is the use of stories better known as scenarios. Scenarios typically involve one or more stakeholders responsible for the ownership and execution of the process. You must plan to involve all stakeholders of the scenarios you plan to automate using SCORCH. At a minimum you must involve the owner of the process.

How to do it...

The following figure provides a visual summary and order of the tasks you need to perform to complete this recipe:

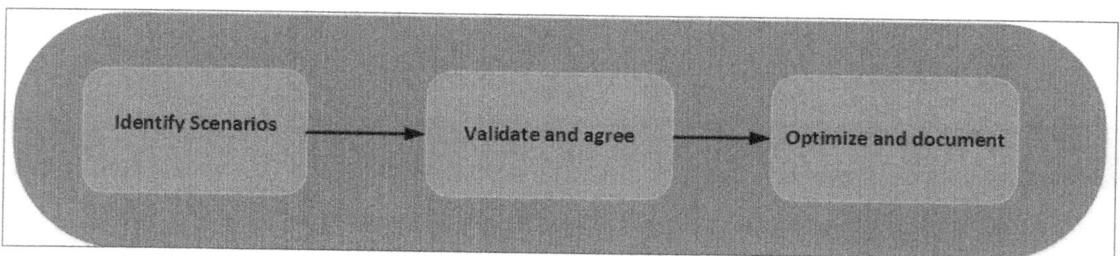

Here is an example of the steps you must perform to prepare for Runbook implementations:

1. Create a list of requested or identified manual repeatable tasks.
2. For each task, ask and document the answers to the following questions:
    - Who is the owner of the task?
    - How is the task done today?
    - Who is responsible for performing this task?
    - How long does it take to perform the task?
    - Is the task susceptible to errors/omissions?
    - Is the desired outcome consistent?
    - Does the task require input from another task(s)?
    - Do other tasks depend on the output of this task?

3. Identify and document all users and systems involved with the current manual task.
4. Discuss and agree on the tasks to be automated based on the information captured in the document.
5. The value of automation is a business and technological balance. Plan to involve the business decision makers in the selection of candidates for automation.

How it works...

Automation requires you to identify the right candidates of manual tasks based on actual need and value to your business. Typical scenarios may be identified as a result of business request for efficiency or may be even due to a proactive analysis of current processes and time taken to execute. The series of questions will help you to identify the right value and risks associated with automating the tasks.

These questions also capture the task owners and interfaces on which the task depends and/or which depends on the task.

The process will require formal and informal discussions. The outcome should be documented and agreed before proceeding to the SCORCH Runbook design.

A very important factor to understand is that Runbook designing; building, testing, and ongoing maintenance will also incur additional cost. A good candidate for automation should be able to positively offset the automated solution investment. An example of a bad candidate is a scenario similar to the insight from Anders Asp (MVP).

The task you plan to automate takes a manual effort from one person of 30 minutes per week. This equates to 26 hours a year (0.5 x 52 weeks). If the effort to create a Runbook to automate this task takes 80 hours to build, this scenario is not a good candidate as it would take more than 3 years to get a Return on Investment (ROI).

A good candidate for SCORCH is the following:

You plan to automate 8 manual tasks which take 15 minutes each to complete every week. If the effort to create a runbook to automate this task takes 5 hours to build, this scenario is a good candidate as it would provide an ROI after 2.5 months

Making Runbook scenarios automation ready

This recipe provides the steps required to prepare a manual process for automation.

Getting ready

You must plan to review and perform the steps in the *Preparing Runbook scenarios* recipe.

How to do it...

Perform the following steps to prepare each scenario for automation:

1. Create a flowchart of the steps to be executed in the scenario.
2. Identify tasks' steps which can be performed without requiring approval.
3. Identify tasks which require approval and categorize into two sections:
    - Pre-Approval by authorized requestor: The initial request is from an authorized source or person
    - Approval required at execution: A step requires approval before proceeding to execute
4. Split each manual task in the scenario into mini independent tasks.
5. The mini tasks should serve as the smallest unit of the blueprint for a Runbook.
6. Combine mini tasks in the sequence in which the overall scenario is executed. Stop the combination at the approval required steps.
7. Each approval step should be a check point to create a separate Runbook with the input from the current Runbook.
8. Separate event triggered inputs from human initiated inputs. Map the inputs to the mini tasks.

How it works...

The steps defined and discussed in the recipe provide a method to optimize a chosen scenario for automation. The objective you want to achieve is to remove the need for human intervention. If the task steps require human approval or input then you cannot achieve full automation with SCORCH. Your aim is to ensure that each Runbook can complete given expected set of inputs.

The final result should be similar to a specification with known inputs, processing steps, and expected outputs of each task.

Documenting Runbook designs

This recipe is a continuation of the first two recipes of this chapter. The *Preparing Runbook scenarios* recipe discusses identifying the right candidates for automation. The *Making Runbook scenarios automation ready* recipe provides steps on taking the scenario and optimizing it for the automation with SCORCH. This recipe completes the loop with a discussion and example on documenting a real scenario.

Getting ready

You must plan to review and perform the steps in the *Preparing Runbook scenarios* recipe and the *Making Runbook scenarios automation ready* recipe.

How to do it...

We will use the following scenario to discuss the steps in this recipe:

Scenario: You have a business requirement to automate the creation of new employee user accounts in Active Directory. Perform the following steps to document the design for the scenario:

1. Use a table to capture inputs, outputs, authorization, and notes on the process steps.

Scenario artifact	**Value**	**Additional notes**
Input	Human resources request	This can be a single user request or multiple requests using a text file.
Authorization and approval	Implied in the request	Standard domain account so authorization is in the request.
System/Technology for task execution	Active Directory	Permission right to create a user account.
Output	Enabled user account with initial random password	User account must be created with a flag to change password on first logon.
Output format	Print out of details	Print out details and provide to authorized new user.

2. Create a flowchart to represent the desired Runbook to implement the manual steps. The aim of the flow chart is to capture three core areas and their dependent parts as shown in the following figure (**Inputs**, **Processing,** and **Outputs**):

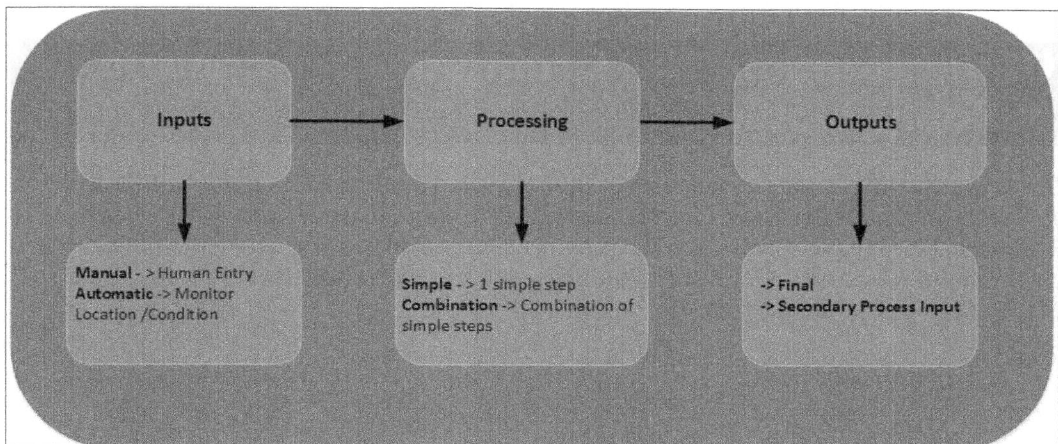

3. Using our scenario example and the preceding figure as a guide, the flowchart or your preferred documentation tool would have the following aspects:

    - **Inputs**: Provides required user details to the Orchestration Console or provide a file with a list of formatted user details within a specified accessible network location
    - **Processing**: This is an automated series of user creating steps (create user, set password, and enable)
    - **Outputs**: This send details to output channel(s) through console, e-mail or printer

How it works...

The documentation process approach discussed serves as a guideline and a high-level template. SCORCH is a very powerful tool which shares similar characteristics with software programming languages. Documenting the design will save you a great deal of time and frustration; you will have the opportunity to walk through the steps before investing time in the Runbook Designer console.

SCORCH Runbooks are self-documenting once created, but the logic and thoughts behind the final Runbook are not. This approach is similar to creating manual maps before converting to a satellite navigation system.

See also

- *Creating new users in Active Directory* in *Chapter 4, Creating Runbook for Active Directory Tasks*
- *Automating manual user creation service request fulfilment* in *Chapter 8, Creating IT Service Management Process Runbooks*

Understanding the Orchestrator scenario building blocks

This recipe provides a brief overview of SCORCH basics and serves as a primer for *Chapter 4, Creating Runbook for Active Directory Tasks* to *Chapter 9, Using Advanced Techniques in Runbooks*. Unlike other recipes, the focus of this recipe is on you understanding instead of performing. This recipe is however equally important as you will need an understanding of the SCORCH basics in order to create the recipes in the book.

Getting ready

You must have a fully deployed SCORCH environment. Your environment should have a database server, Management Server, Runbook Server, Runbook Designer, and an orchestration web console. The *Chapter 1, Unpacking System Center 2012 Orchestrator* discusses and provides steps on how to install and configure a typical SCORCH environment.

How to do it...

The basic terms you need to be familiar with and their description are as detailed in the following table:

Orchestration term	**Description**
Activities	These are the building blocks of an Orchestrator workflow which are known as Runbooks. There are two types, standard and custom activities.
Standard activities	These are the default installation activities visible in the Runbook Designer.
Custom activities	These are the activities you get from deploying an Integration Pack. An example is the Active Directory integration pack, which provides Active Directory activities such as create user or create computer.
Integration Pack (IP)	A bundle of activities for interfacing with the target environment/ technology. These can be vendor/3rd party solutions or you can create your own with the toolkit.
Runbook	This is a single unit of a process workflow in Orchestrator. The Runbook will have one starting point (input) and a series of steps with decision points and outputs.
Link (intelligent links)	Links connect two activities in a Runbook. Links are intelligent because they have configurable properties and conditional logic on how to proceed to the next step.
Monitors	An input activity which monitors a condition, for example, an event log entry type or a file location.
Trigger	Starting(input) a Runbook based on a monitored condition or as a result of the output of another Runbook
Counters	A global object you configure and use in Runbooks with looping activities (for example, you may create a counter to repeat a process for a fixed number of times before proceeding to the next step).

Orchestration term	Description
Schedules	Used to create a shared global date and time value for use in multiple Runbooks. For example, some activities may only be performed within defined maintenance windows.
Variables	Variables are similar in use to schedules. Variable are of a global nature, for example, defining a variable for shared drive or a computer name of a target environment.
Check out	This is the process of marking a Runbook for exclusive editing. You must check out the Runbook from the database before you edit it in the Runbook Designer.
Check in	This is the converse of check out. You check in the Runbook to save your changes to the Orchestration database and make it available for execution.
Published data	The properties of each activity either at runtime or generic is made available to other activities using what is known as a databus. These runtime or generic properties are known as published data.
Subscribe	The process of using information from either the Databus (published data) or global data like counters, variable, and schedules.
Databus	The Orchestration mechanism which hold data from activities. Subsequent activities or links may use the information from the databus as their inputs.
Job	A queue of jobs is created for Runbooks pending execution. Runbook Servers check this queue and execute the relevant job.
Instance	When a Runbook is executing on a Runbook Server it is known as an instance. More than one instance of the Runbook can be executed on the same Runbook Server or multiple Runbook Servers.
Pipelining	How you move from one activity to another based on the link conditions.

Plan to review the official online documentation for SCORCH which is continually updated by Microsoft for the latest information.

There's more...

The process of creating, testing, and running the automation of scenarios (Runbooks) is managed by three feature areas of SCORCH.

The three main feature areas you will typically be working within the SCORCH product are:

- The Runbook Designer console
- The Runbook Tester component
- The Orchestration web console

A tour of the Runbook Designer

Here are the basics of the Runbook Designer console showing the four main panes in the following screenshot:

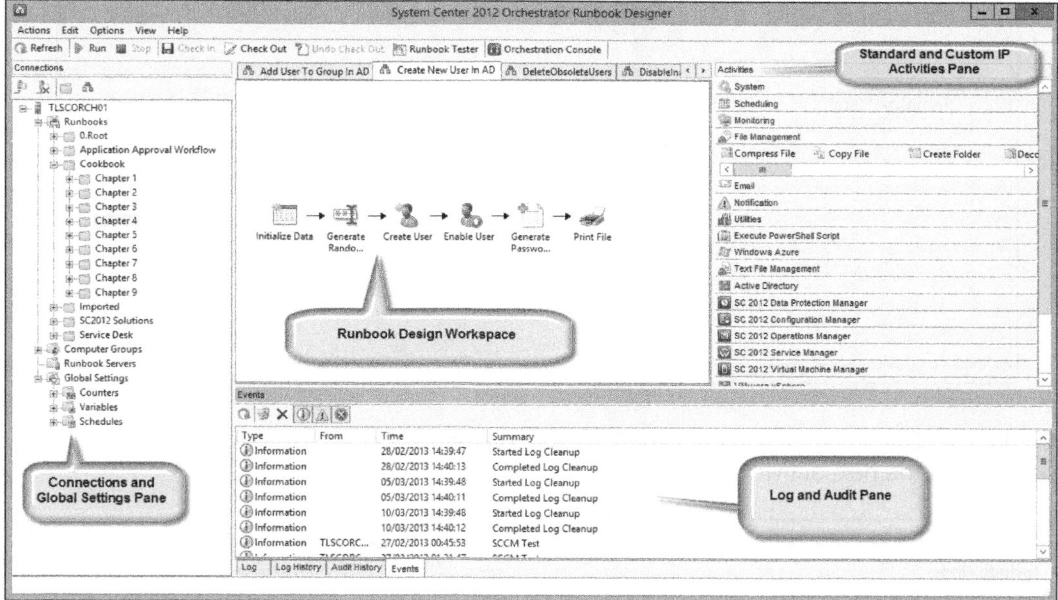

You drag the arrow from one activity to the other to create the link. Once the link is created (arrow headed line), you double-click on it to configure its properties. The following screenshot is as an example of a link:

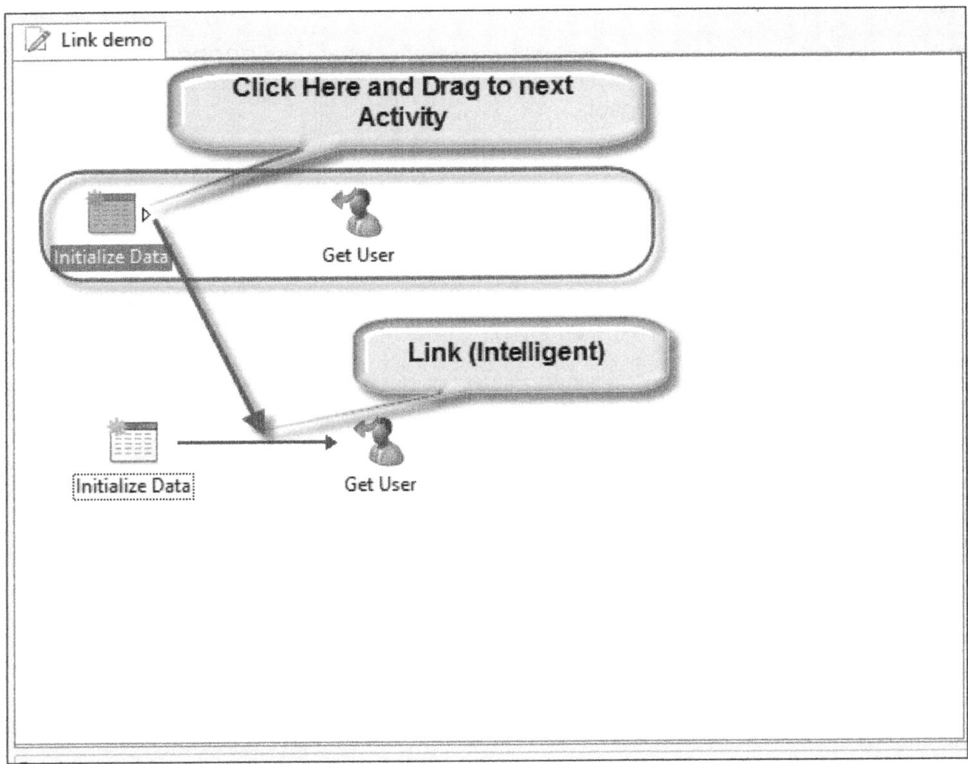

You double-click on the link to configure its properties and also see what published data is available for the next activity.

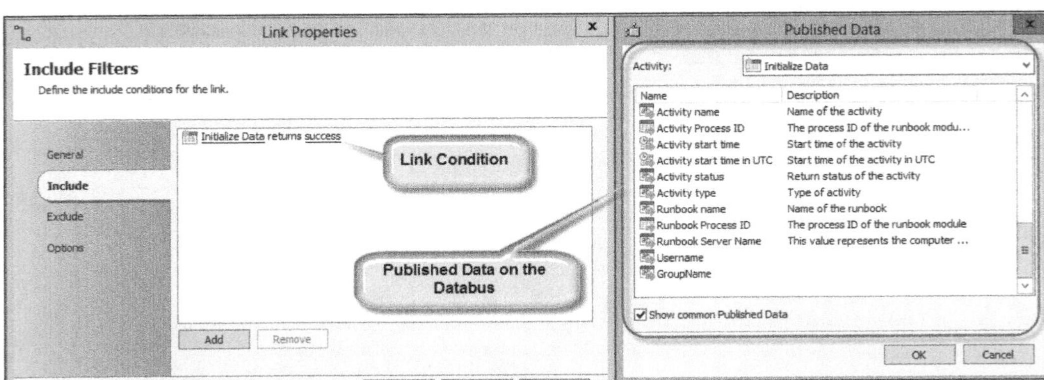

A tour of the Runbook Tester

You invoke the **Runbook Tester** component from the Runbook Designer console. You are prompted to check out the Runbook in scope if you have not done this already. Here are the basics of the **Runbook Tester** shown in the following screenshot:

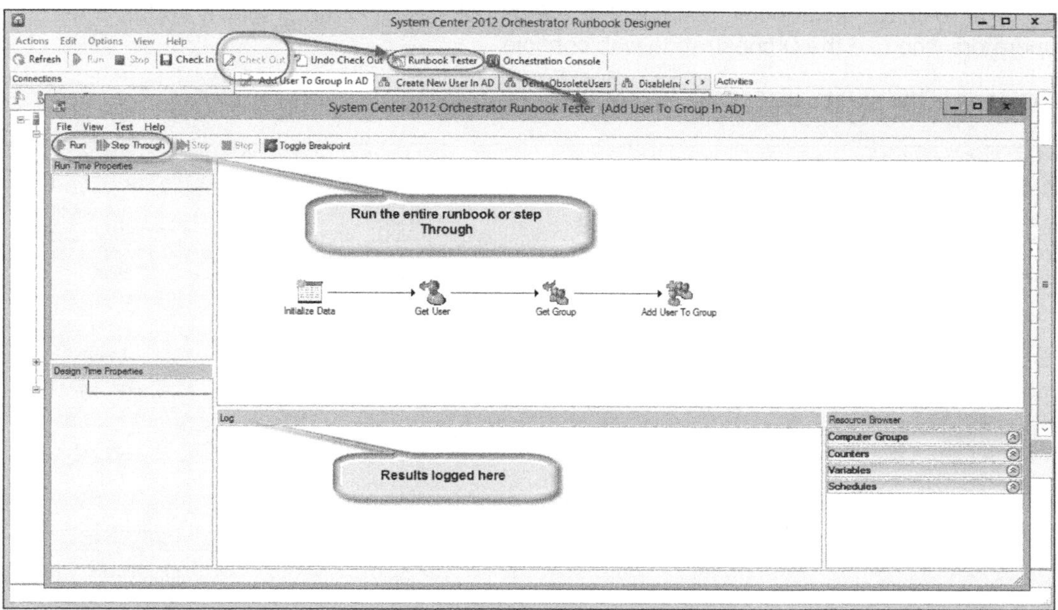

Runbooks run in the tester in most cases may run faster but it is important to validate the actual processing speed in normal operation.

Runbook Tester caution

The Runbook Tester is not a simulator. It would perform the actual activity in the Runbook. For example, if the Runbook deletes a user account then the action will be performed on the specified account. You use the tester to validate actual execution. In our example you will have to create a dummy account nominated for testing, in order not to impact a real account. A better practice is to test in a development environment and export your validated Runbooks into a production environment. Additionally the Runbook Tester executes in the context of the user who launched the tester. If your automation depends on a system/elevated account; then your tests will have to include a pre-production phase of letting the actual Runbook execute without the use of the tester (use the Web console).

The Orchestration web console

You use the orchestration web console to manually invoke Runbooks and monitor executing Runbooks.

This is effectively an Orchestrator operations role web console. An Administrator will use the designer to create a Runbook, test it with the Runbook Designer, and make it available to Operators who use the Orchestration web console.

Following is the screenshot of the Orchestration web console:

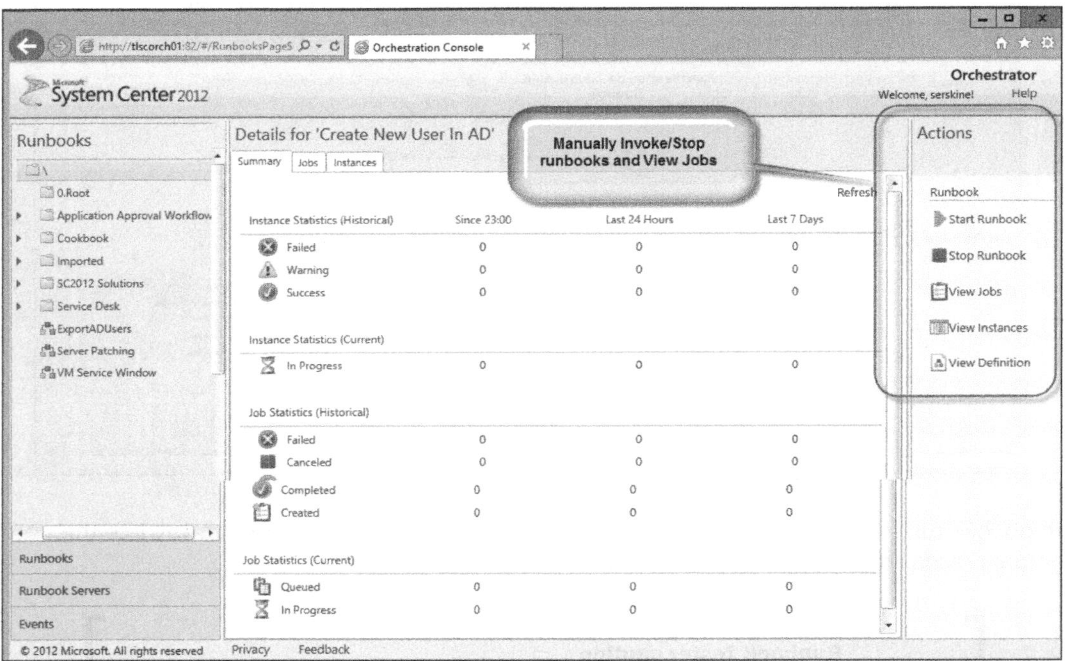

Runbook Designer standards and primer

This recipe provides you with introductory information on the Runbook Designer activities you must perform to create your Runbooks. The recipe also discusses current standard practices when working with the System Center 2012 Orchestrator component.

Getting ready

The requirements for this recipe is a fully deployed SCORCH environment and a user with administrative access to the Runbook Designer. The example provided uses the System Center Configuration Manager Integration Pack.

How to do it...

This recipe is categorized as follows:

- How to standardize your activity configuration
- Check In and check Out
- Working with custom and common published data bus parameters

How to standardize your activity configuration

Here are some general rules you can follow to standardize your SCORCH environment:

1. Create folder structures in the Runbook Designer. The structures must reflect how you intend to manage and delegate Runbooks. Examples are Runbook folders based on the automation process or the Integration Pack type.
2. Create a naming convention for your Runbooks and ensure you rename your activities.
3. The general rule for Runbook directions are from left to right. You can work from top to bottom and then left to right.
4. Color code the links between Runbooks. An example is to use green for successful actions and red for failures. The choice is yours but have a standard!
5. Create test Orchestrator Runbooks targeted at test environments.

Check-In and Check-Out

System Center 2012 Orchestrator Runbooks are stored in the Orchestration Database. When you edit Runbooks, you have to check out the Runbook. The check out is effectively taking a copy of the Runbook and marking the Runbook in the database as read only. No one can edit that specific Runbook until a check-In action is performed.

Here are the steps you must follow to check out a Runbook

1. In the Runbook Designer, select the Runbook (tab name) in the middle pane.
2. Right-click on the tab for the Runbook you want to check out and select **Check Out**.

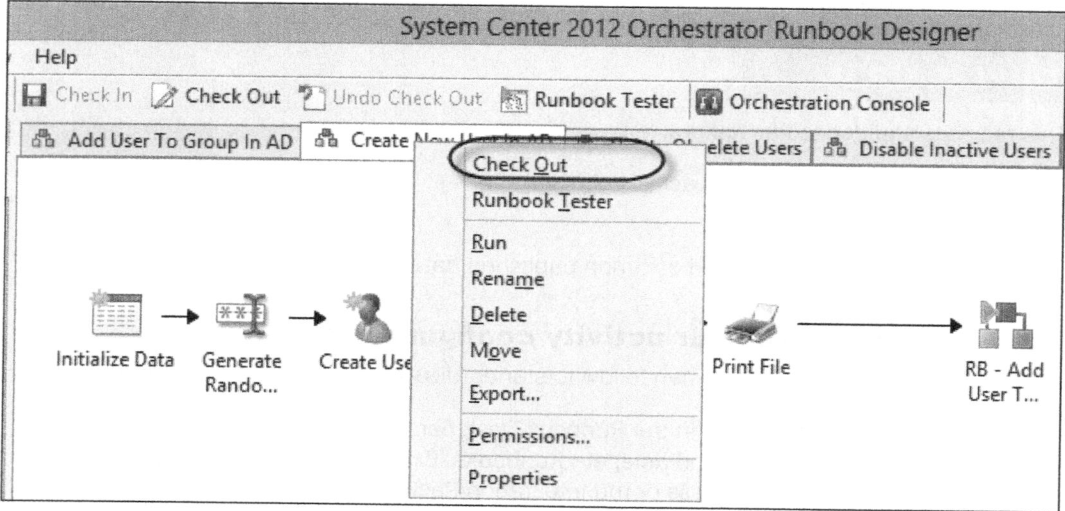

3. When you complete the Runbook configuration you must Check-In the Runbook. Here are the steps to Check-In the Runbook.
4. In the **Runbook Designer**, select the Runbook (tab name) in the middle pane.
5. Right-click on the tab for the Runbook you want to check In and select **Check In**.

Working with custom and data bus parameters

There are three common parameter types you will typically use in Runbooks:

- Basic custom parameter
- Parameters from previous activities
- Common Published Data

An example of configuring a basic parameter is the use of the **Initialize Data** activity. For example, if you need the user to provide a name for a collection that you intend to create with automation, follow the following steps:

1. Double-click on your **Initialize activity** and select the **Details** tab.
2. Click on **Add** and click on the underlined **Parameter 1** (this is the default value which you must rename).

3. Type your custom parameter name and click on **OK**.

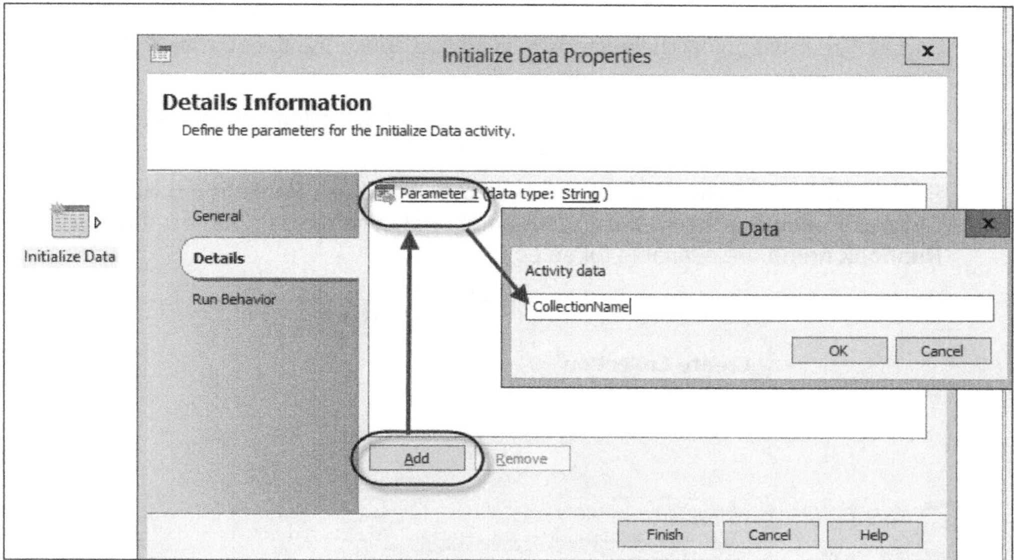

The second type of parameter is what you have available from the data bus from a previous activity. If you add a **Create Collection** activity from the Configuration Manager IP, you can use the **Subscribe to Published data** steps to access the first custom parameter as follows:

1. Double-click on the activity (for example**, Create Collection** activity), select the **Details** tab and select the **configuration** for ConfigMgr.
2. Right-click in the **Collection Name** field and select **Subscribe | Published Data | Initialize Activity**. Your parameter from the previous activity is available for selection:

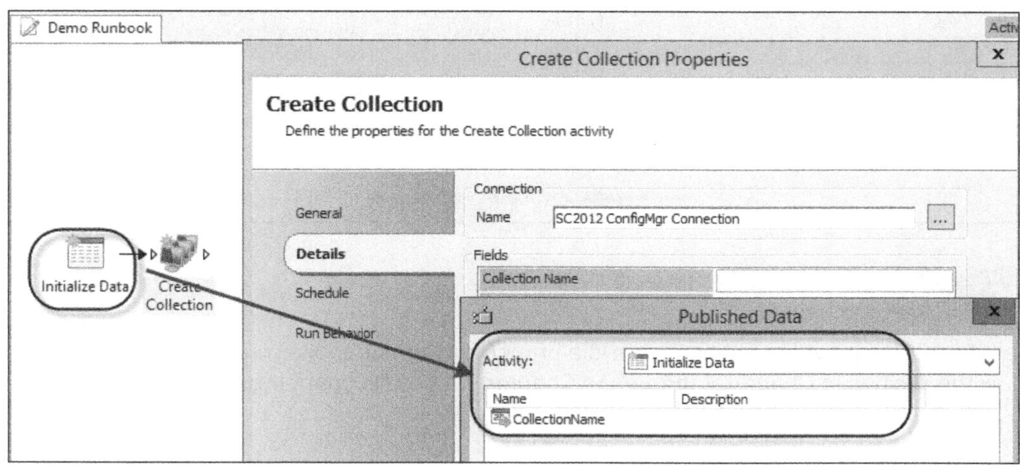

3. The third type of parameter is what you have generally from the data bus. These parameters are typically Runbook meta data information, for example the name of the Runbook. You may want to use this type of information in notifications (Runbook name). You must follow these steps to view and subscribe to common **Published Data** parameters.
4. Double-click on the **activity** (for example, **Create Collection** activity), select the **Details** tab. Select the configuration for ConfigMgr.
5. Right -click in the **Comment** field and select **Subscribe | Published Data** | check **Show common Published Data**. Here additional dynamic parameters such as **Runbook name** are available for selection.

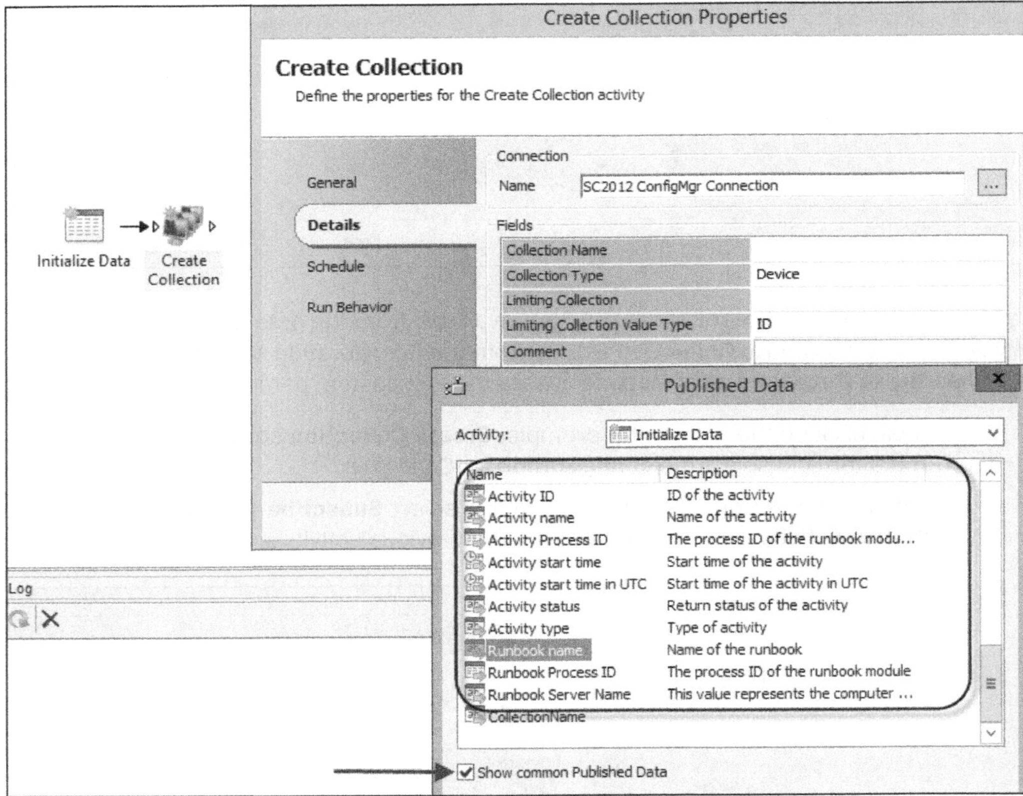

How it works...

The information provided in this recipe is a primer for the Runbooks you will create as you follow the recipes in *Chapter 4* through to *Chapter 9*. Use this chapter as a baseline guide and adjust to suit your specific environment.

There's more...

You have additional options to simply the process of configuring activities. One of the valuable options to be aware of is the expand field.

Expanding parameter fields

The fields in the Runbook designer can be expanded to provide a clearer view of the data you type or, data you subscribe to from the data bus. Simply right click in the field and select Expand to view all the data. The expand option is particularly useful when you must type scripts or, construct comments which span more than one line.

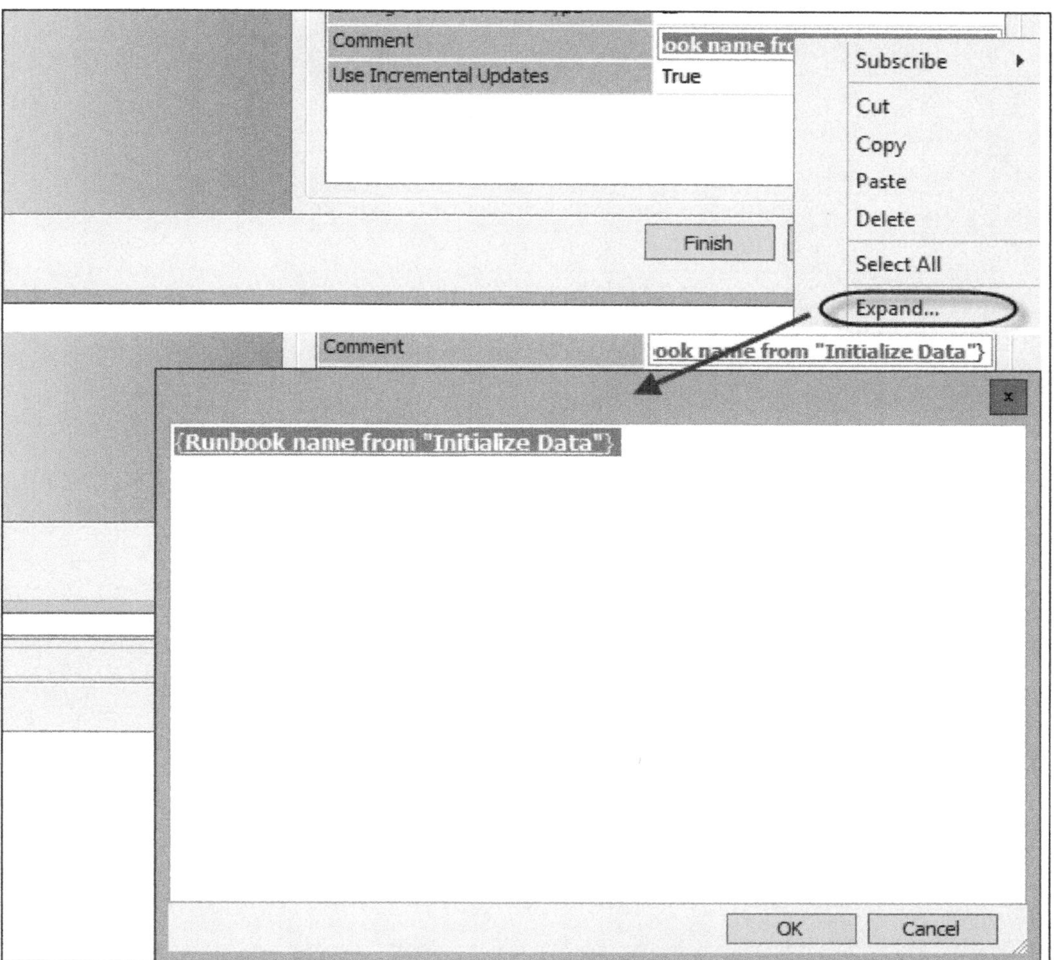

See also

The best and most up-to-date resource on Orchestrator basics is the following official Microsoft link for the product at `http://technet.microsoft.com/en-us/library/hh420344.aspx`.

4

Creating Runbooks for Active Directory Tasks

In this chapter we will be providing recipes on how to manage common Active Directory tasks using Runbooks in Microsoft System Center 2012 Orchestrator:

- Creating new users in Active Directory
- Adding users to groups in Active Directory
- Maintaining the organizational structure – moving accounts to new OUs
- Disabling user accounts in Active Directory
- Using SCORCH to remove obsolete user accounts

Introduction

Managing objects in Microsoft Active Directory is a repetitive daily activity in IT. These repetitive tasks offer a high potential for automation. The requirements to automate tasks are a definition of the user management process (or identity management process).The user management process described in the recipes of this chapter will cover the following scenarios:

- Creating new users in Active Directory
    - This is a typical on-demand daily request (on boarding of new employees)
- Adding users to groups in Active Directory
    - This is typical on-demand daily request (for access for resources; for example, shares, application, or printers)

- Maintaining organizational structure – moving accounts to new OUs
    - For example, employees changing departments
- Disabling user accounts in Active Directory
    - Automated detection of inactive accounts in directory service
    - May be started on a defined schedule (once a day or weekly)
    - Started on request (retiring employee)
- Using SCO to remove obsolete user accounts
    - Automated detection of obsolete, orphaned user accounts (disabled user accounts for a certain time)
    - May be started on a defined schedule

For all these user management tasks we will define a process with the required steps in each recipe.

For all recipes in this chapter the requirements are as follows:

- Installed and deployed Active Directory integration pack
    - For how to install integration packs in SCO, see the following recipes in *Chapter 2, Initial Configuration and Making SCORCH Highly Available*: *Loading Integration Packs (IP)* and *Configuring Integration Pack connections*.
- A user account with appropriate permissions in Active Directory to fulfill the tasks (create a user account, modify group membership, and move AD objects between OUs).

The following needs to be performed for all recipes in this chapter:

1. Create a connection in the SCORCH 2012 Runbook Designer to your Active Directory domain in scope.
2. Start the SCORCH 2012 Runbook Designer.
3. Choose **Options** from the menu and click on **Active Directory**.
4. Click on **Add**.
5. Provide a name of the configuration.
6. Select type, **Microsoft Active Directory Domain Configuration**.

7. Configure the settings using the information of the following table:

Setting	Description
Configuration User Name	User with appropriate permissions in AD
Configuration Password	Password of the user
Configuration Domain Controller Name (FQDN)	Full Qualified Domain Name of a domain controller
Configuration Default Parent Container	Distinguished name of a default OU in AD

8. Click on **OK**.
9. Click on **Finish**.

Creating new users in Active Directory

Creating new users in Active Directory is a repetitive task in most organizations. This user management process is common and often triggered by a new employee joining the company.

The following diagram shows the defined business process covered in this recipe:

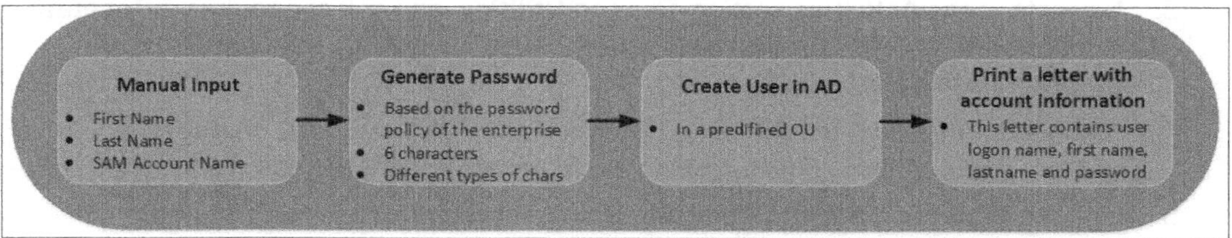

Getting ready

One of the steps in the process is to print a "password letter" for the newly created user. An installed and connected printer is required on the SCORCH 2012 server to fulfill the printing step of the process. This can be a local printer or a networked shared printer.

Perform the following steps in the Runbook Designer to prepare for the activity steps in this recipe:

1. In the Runbook Designer expand the connection to the SCORCH 2012 server.
2. Right-click on **Runbooks** and click on **New** (you can also right-click on a folder in Runbooks).
3. Right-click on the new created Runbook and rename it to `Create New User In AD` (Click on **Yes** to confirm the check out dialog box when prompted).

How to do it...

Follow the next steps to add and configure different activities in the Runbook to create a new user in Active Directory. A best practice is to start your activities from left to right in the design pane.

1. Navigate to the **Activities** section in the Runbook Designer. Click on **Runbook Control**, and select and drag an **Initialize Data** activity to the middle pane of the Runbook (start from the leftmost part of the pane and work to the right as you add additional activities).
2. Right-click on **Initialize Data | Properties**. Click on **Add** three times and use the following table to configure the three parameters in the **Details** section by clicking on each of the parameters in turn. Click on **Finish**.

Name of parameter	Data type	Contains information
`FirstName`	String	Contains the first name of the new user
`LastName`	String	Contains the last name of the new user
`SAMaccountName`	String	Contains the account name of the new user

3. Navigate to the **Activities** section. Click on **Utilities**, and select and drag a **Generate Random Text** activity into the middle pane of the Runbook to the right of the **Initialize Data** object.
4. Right-click and rename `Generate Random Text` to `Generate Random Password` by right-clicking and selecting **Rename** or mark the activity and press *F2*.
5. Link the **Initialize Data** and **Generate Random Password** activities. (See *the Understanding the Orchestrator scenario building blocks* recipe in *Chapter 3, Planning and Creating Runbook Designs*, for information on linking activities)
6. Double-click on the **Generate Random Password** activity and provide the information for the **Details** section using the following table and click on **Finish**:

Name of parameter	Value	Contains information
Text length	`7`	Password policy (length of passwords).
Lower-Case Characters	`1`	At least one lowercase character (complexity of passwords).
Upper-Case Characters	`1`	At least one uppercase character (complexity of passwords).
Numbers	`1`	At least one number character (complexity of passwords).
Symbols	Leave this option unchecked	Not required to meet the password policy in our example.

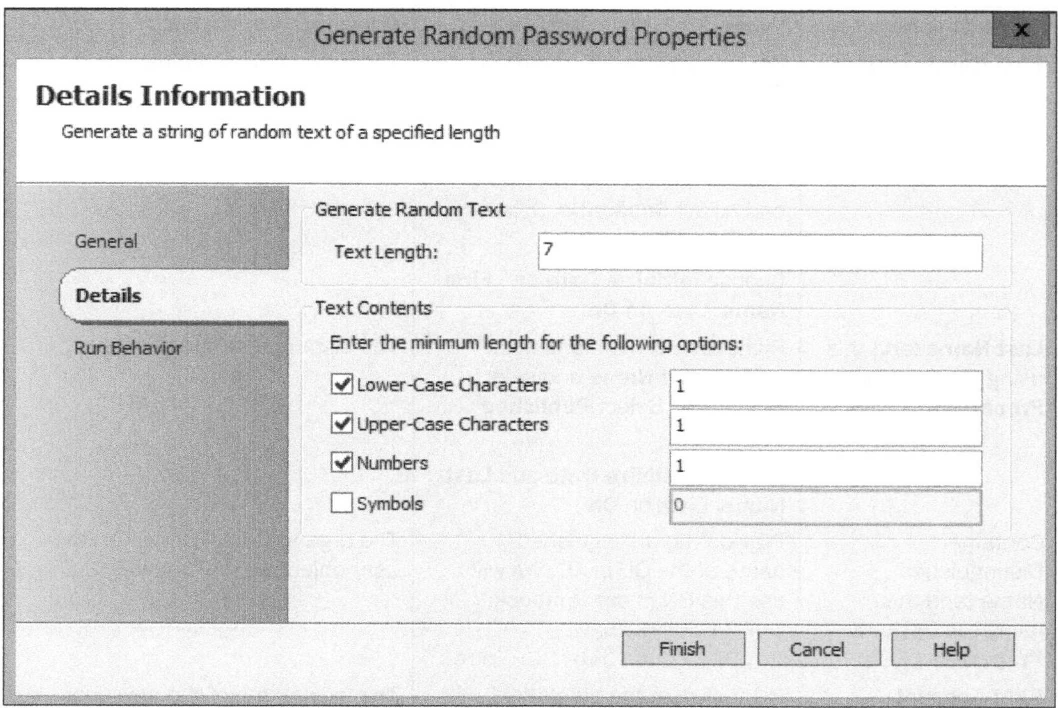

7. Navigate to the **Activities** section and click on **Active Directory**. Select and drag a **Create User** activity in the middle pane of Runbook next to the **Generate Random Password** activity.
8. Link the **Generate Random Password** activity to the **Create User** activity.
9. Double-click on the **Create User** activity and provide the following information in the **Properties** section:

Name of parameter	Value	Contains information
Configuration	Pick the configuration from the list **....**	The AD configuration we setup in the preparation of this chapter.
Common Name	Right-click in the blank field and select **Subscribe.** Click on **Published Data.** In the **Activity** field select **Initialize Data** and select **SAMAccountName.** Click on **OK.**	The username as part of the new distinguished name of the user object.

Name of parameter	Value	Contains information
First Name (add this using the **Optional Properties...**)	Click on **Optional Properties....** Select the **First Name** property from the **Available** section. Click on **OK**. Right-click in the blank field next to **First Name** and select **Subscribe**. Select **Published Data**. Choose **Initialize Data** and **First Name**. Click on **OK**.	The first name of the new user.
Last Name (add this using the **Optional Properties...**)	Right-click in the blank field next to **Last Name** and select **Subscribe**. Select **Published Data.** Choose **Initialize Data** and **Last Name**. Click on **OK**.	The last name of the new user.
Container Distinguished Name (add this using the **Optional Properties...**)	Provide the distinguished name of the OU in AD. We will use this DN in our Runbook: `OU=PACKT8505EN-04,DC=TrustLab,DC=local`	The organizational unit in AD the user object will be created.
SAM Account Name (add this using the **Optional Properties...**)	Right-click in the blank field next to **SAM Account Name** | **Subscribe** and select **Published Data.** Choose **Initialize Data** and **SAMAccountName**, and click on **OK**.	The login name of the new user.
Password (add this using the **Optional Properties...**)	Right-click in the blank field next to **Password**. Go to **Subscribe** | **Published Data**. Choose **Generate Random Password** and **Random Text**. Click on **OK** and then on **Finish**.	The random password.

10. Navigate to the **Activities** section. Click on **Active Directory** select and drag an **Enable User** activity into the middle pane of Runbook next to the **Create User** activity.
11. Link the **Create User** activity to the **Enable User** activity.

12. Double-click on the **Enable User** activity and provide the following information in the **Properties** section:

Name of parameter	Value	Contains information
Configuration	Pick the configuration from the list....	The AD configuration we setup in the preparation section of this chapter.
Distinguished Name	Right-click in the blank field next to **Distinguished Name** and select **Subscribe.** Click on **Published Data.** Choose **Create User** and select **Distinguished Name.** Click on **OK** and then click on **Finish.**	The Distinguished Name (DN) of the created user object.

13. Navigate to the **Activities** section and click on **Text File Management** select and drag a **Append Line** activity in the middle pane of Runbook next to the **Enable User** activity.
14. Right-click on the **Append Line** activity and rename the activity to `Generate Password Letter`.
15. Link the **Enable User** activity to the **Generate Password Letter** activity.
16. Double-click on the **Generate Password Letter** and provide the following information in the **Details** section:

Name of parameter	Value	Contains information

File	Click on **...** next to **File:**. Type the path of the file, for example:
	`C:\PACKT8505EN-Chapter04\`
	Right-click in the field just after \ of the file path. Select **Subscribe** and then select **Published Data**.
	Choose **Initialize Data** and select **SAMAccountName**. Type `.txt` and click on **OK** (the result should be similar to this:
	`C:\PACKT8585N-Chapter04\{SAMacountname from "Initialize Data"}.txt`
		The filename of the password letter.

File encoding	Unicode	Encoding of the file.

Name of parameter	Value	Contains information
Text	Right-click in the blank space next to **Text:**. Select **Expand** to provide an expanded field for ease of typing. Type the letter content. Use the **Subscribe published data** option to add information from the previous activities as shown in the earlier steps.	The text of the password letter. Use return button to introduce line breaks in your text.

The result might look like this:

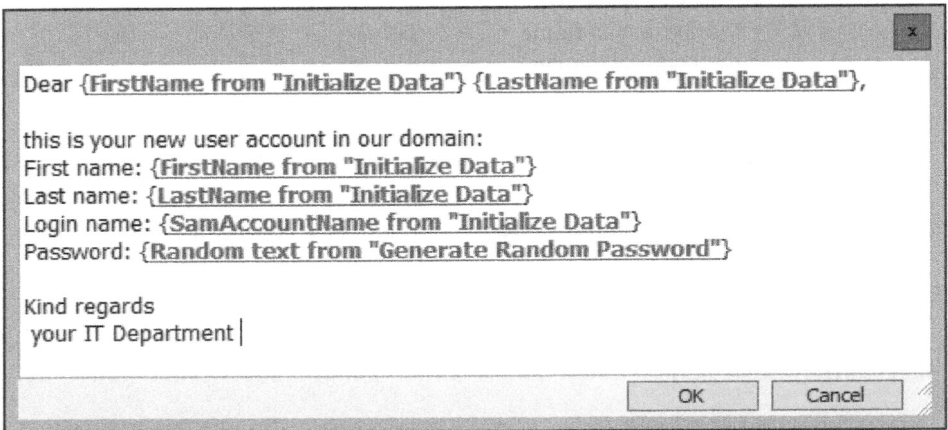

17. Navigate to the **Activities** section and click on **File Management**. Select and drag a **Print File** activity in the middle pane of Runbook next to the **Generate Password Letter** activity.
18. Link the **Generate Password Letter** activity to the **Print File** activity.
19. Double-click on the **Print File** activity and provide the information, given in the following table, in the **Details** section:

Name of parameter	Value	Contains information
File	Right-click in the blank field space next to **File:** | **Subscribe** | **Published Data**. Choose **Generate Password Letter** and double click **File path**.	The filename of the password letter.
Printer	Search and choose a printer.	The printer the password letter is sent to.
Filter	(no age filter)	Keep the default setting.

The final Runbook should look like this:

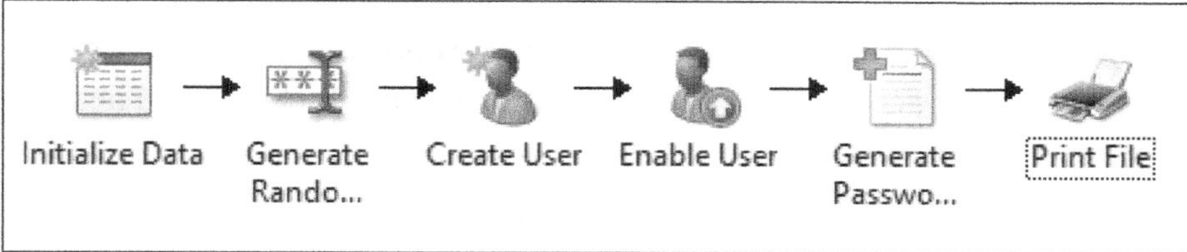

How it works...

When you start the Runbook in the Orchestrator Runbook Tester or using the **Orchestration Console** website you will be prompted for the three parameters: First Name, Last Name, and SAM Account Name (this is what we defined in the first activity of the Runbook, the **Initialize Data** activity).

After providing this information the next activity will be initiated and a random password is generated (the **Generate Password** activity). The password is generated by password policy of the organization which we specified as follows:

Length of password = 7, at least one lower-case character, at least one upper-case letter, and a number.

You must check the existing AD policy with your domain administration team, to ensure your Runbook settings are correct with regards to meeting the actual policy in use.

A user object will be created in the Active Directory in the OU specified in the Runbook activity—**Create User**.

The newly created user will be enabled (**Enable User** activity). This step is required because by default all newly created user objects are disabled.

A password letter will be created and stored in a folder (**Generate Password Letter** activity). This file is sent to a printer in the next step.

The password letter will be printed (**Print File** activity).

There's more...

Add additional properties to the newly created user

In this recipe we only provided the first name, the last name, the SAM account name, and the password of the new user.

You can add a lot more properties to the new user object if required.

Using Variables in different Runbook activities

Instead of manually typing the same text information each time, you can define variables for this in the Runbook Designer.

For instance we need the Distinguished Name (DN) of the domain a number of times in all Runbooks.

To add a variable follow these steps:

1. Expand the **Global Settings** | **Variables** section on the left-hand side of the Runbook Designer.
2. To organize your variables you can add folders below the **Variables** section. (This is optional but will aid with security delegation)
3. Create a new variable (right click **Variables** or a folder under **Variables** | **Variable**
4. Fill in the information and click on **Finish**.

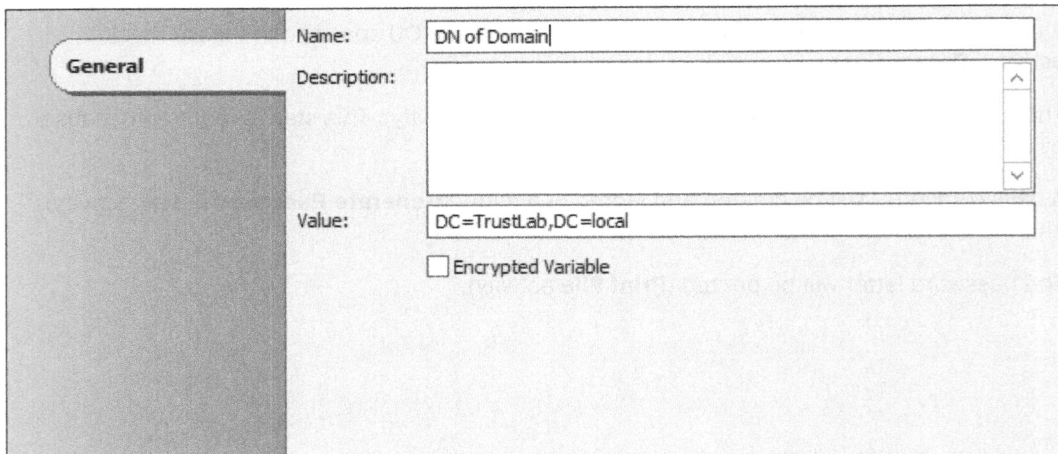

After this is done you can use this variable in different Runbooks by selecting **Subscribe | Variable**. Pick the variable you need from the available list of defined variables. For example the image below shows using the variable in the **Get Organization Unit** activity.

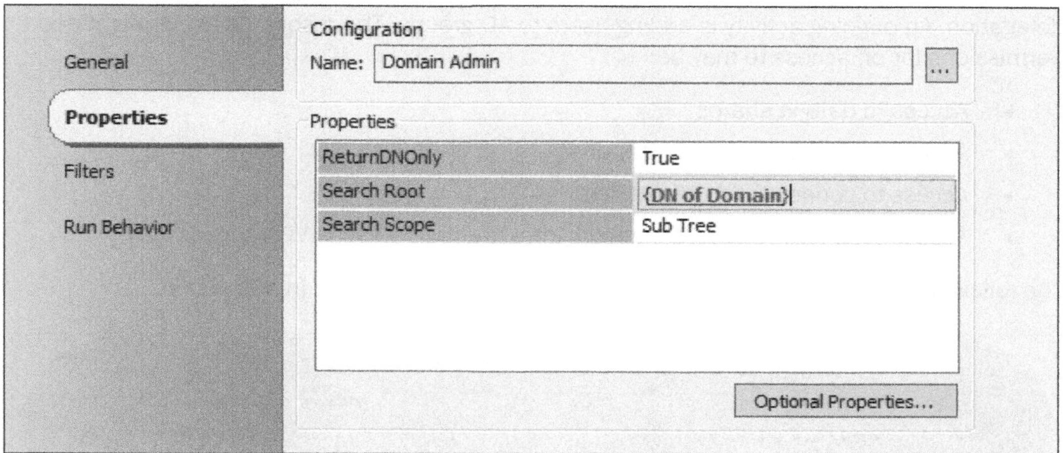

See also

Detailed information for the activities used in this Runbook can be found here at:

- Microsoft Technet – **Create User** activity: `http://technet.microsoft.com/en-us/library/hh553464.aspx`
- Microsoft Technet – **Enable User** activity: `http://technet.microsoft.com/en-us/library/hh553486.aspx`
- Microsoft Technet – **Generate Random Text** activity: `http://technet.microsoft.com/en-us/library/hh206114.aspx`
- Microsoft Technet – **Append Line** activity: `http://technet.microsoft.com/en-us/library/hh206072.aspx`
- Microsoft Technet – **Print File** activity: `http://technet.microsoft.com/en-us/library/hh206045.aspx`

Adding users to groups in Active Directory

Active Directory groups are typically used to grant access to resources or permission delegation. An ongoing activity is adding users to AD groups. The resources users might need permissions for or, access to may be:

- Access to data in shares
- Access to client/server applications
- Access to connect and use printers
- Access to different types of network infrastructure such as VPN access

The following diagram shows the defined business process covered in this recipe:

Getting ready

In addition to the preparation in the introduction of this chapter we need to create a new Runbook in the Runbook Designer.

1. In the Runbook Designer, expand the connection to the SCORCH 2012 server.
2. Right-click on **Runbooks** and click on **New** (you can also right-click on a folder in **Runbooks**).
3. Right-click on the newly created Runbook and rename it to `Add User To Group In AD`.

Though the business process looks simple (only two steps) the resulting Runbook needs some additional activities. The **Add User To Group** Runbook expects the full Distinguished Name (DN) of the user and group. We will add two additional activities to get this information. This provides the option to use the login name of the user (unique in the domain) and the name of the group (also unique in the domain). For instance login name = `PPan` and group name = `Marketing`.

How to do it...

The following steps and activities describe how to add a user to a group in Active Directory using SCORCH:

1. In the newly created Runbook navigate to **Activities**. Click on **Runbook Control**, select and drag an **Initialize Data** activity to the middle pane of the Runbook.
2. Add two parameters in this activity by double-clicking on the **Initialize Data** activity. Select the **Details** section, click on **Add**, and provide the details using the table:

Name of the parameter	Data type	Contains information
Username	string	Contains the login name of the user
Groupname	string	Contains the name of the group the user should be added to

3. Navigate to the **Activities** section and select **Active Directory**. Click and drag a **Get User** activity to the middle pane of the Runbook next to the **Initialize Data** activity.
4. Link the **Initialize Data** activity to the **Get User** activity.
5. Double-click on the **Get User** activity and provide the information in the following table on the **Properties** section:

Name of parameter	Value	Contains information
Configuration	Pick the configuration from the list.	AD configuration that we set up in the preparation of this chapter.
ReturnDNonly (add this using **Optional Properties**)	True (Click on **...** next to the **ReturnDNonly** to select this value).	We only need the DN of the user object.
SearchRoot	Type the Distinguished Name of the domain (you may also subscribe to a variable if this has been defined for this value).	For instance, `DC=TrustLab, DC=local`.
Search Scope	Sub tree (Use the **...** next to the **Search Scope** to select this value).	All OUs under Search Root will be enumerated.

6. On the **Filters** section of the **Get User** activity add the following filter using the **Add** button:

Name of parameter	Value	Contains information
Name	**SAM Account Name**	Property of the filter.
Relation	**Equals**	We need the specific user object in this case.
Value	Right-click in the field and select **Subscribe | Published Data**. Choose **Initialize Data** and select **Username | OK**. Click on **Finish.**	Username provided in the **Initialize Data** activity.

7. Navigate to the **Activities** section and select **Active Directory** select and drag a **Get Group** activity in the Runbook next to the **Get User** activity.
8. Link the **Get User** activity to the **Get Group** activity.
9. Double-click on the **Get Group** activity and provide the information in the following table under the **Properties** section:

Name of parameter	Value	Contains information
Configuration	Pick the configuration from the list.	AD configuration we setup in the preparation of this chapter
ReturnDNonly (add this using the **Optional Properties**)	True (Use the **...** next to the **ReturnDNonly** to select this value).	We only need the DN of the user object.
Search Root	Type the Distinguished Name of the domain (you may also subscribe to a variable if this has been defined for this value).	For instance, `DC=TrustLab, DC=local`.
Search Scope	Sub tree (Use the **...** next to the **Search Scope** to select this value).	All OUs under Search Root will be enumerated.

10. On the **Filters** section of the **Get Group** activity add the following filter using the **Add** button:

Name of parameter	Value	Contains information
Name	**SAM Account Name**	Property of the filter
Relation	**Equals**	We need exactly the user object in this case
Value	Right-click in the field | **Subscribe** | **Published Data** Choose **Initialize Data** and **Groupname**. Click on **OK** and then click on **Finish**.	Groupname provided in the Initialize Data activity

11. Navigate to the Activities section select **Active Directory**. Click and drag an **Add User To Group** activity into the middle pane of the Runbook next to the **Get Group** activity.
12. Link the **Get Group** activity to the **Add User To Group** activity.
13. Double-click on the **Add User To Group** activity and provide the information in the following table on the **Properties** section:

Name of parameter	Value	Contains information
Configuration	Pick the configuration from the list.	AD configuration we setup in the preparation of this chapter.
Group Distinguished Name	Right-click in the field and select **Subscribe** | **Published Data**. Choose **Get Group** and select **Distinguished Name** from the list of available published properties.	The Distinguished Name of the group.
User Distinguished Name	Right-click in the field and select **Subscribe** | **Published Data**. Choose **Get User** and select **Distinguished Name** from the list of available published properties.	The Distinguished Name of the user.

The Runbook should look like this now:

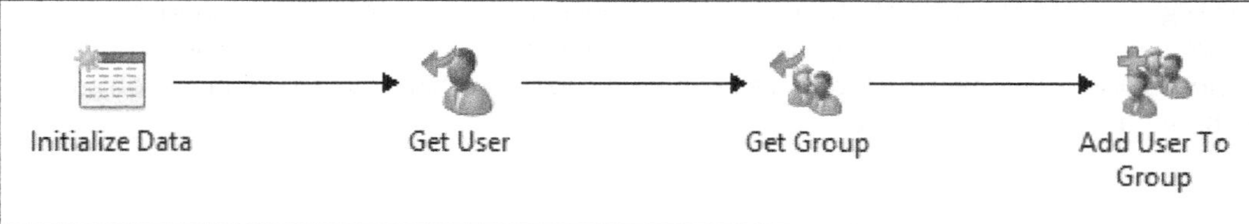

How it works...

When the Runbook is invoked in the Runbook designer or Orchestration Console website you will be prompted for a **user name** and a **group name**. (**Initialize Data** activity).

The **username** will be used as input for the **Get User** activity (Distinguished Name (DN) of the user object).The **groupname** will be used as input for the **Get Group** activity (Distinguished Name (DN) of the group object).

The user object will be made a member of the group object. Both objects are defined by the Distinguished Name in the **Add User To Group** activity.

There's more...

Removing a user from a group in Active Directory

To remove a user from an Active Directory group you can use the **Remove User From Group** activity in the **Active Directory** integration pack. The required parameters and information are the same as in the **Add User To Group** activity.

See also

Detailed information for the activities used in this Runbook are available here:

Microsoft Technet - **Get User** activity:`http://technet.microsoft.com/en-us/library/hh553476.aspx`

Microsoft Technet - **Get Group** activity: `http://technet.microsoft.com/en-us/library/hh553470.aspx`

Microsoft Technet - **Add User To Group** activity: `http://technet.microsoft.com/en-us/library/hh564142.aspx`

Maintaining the organizational structure – moving accounts to new OUs

In Active Directory, user accounts are usually moved to new or existing OUs to reflect business unit organization. This typically happens if employees move departments or locations; a corresponding move of the user account into a new OU is often required to reflect the business organizational structure. This recipe will show how this user maintenance job can be automated with SCORCH 2012.

The following diagram shows the defined business process covered in this recipe:

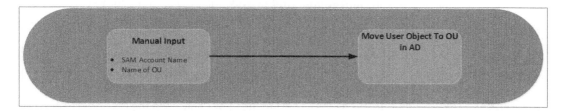

Getting ready

In addition to the preparation in the introduction of this chapter we need to create a new Runbook in the Runbook Designer.

1. In the Runbook Designer expand the connection to the SCORCH 2012 server.
2. Right-click on **Runbooks** and click on **New** (you can also right-click on a folder under **Runbooks**).
3. Right-click on the newly created Runbook and rename it to **Move User To OU**.

We will be using two more activities in the runbook than defined in the business process diagram. This is because the AD activity to move a user account to an OU requires the object names as **Distinguished Name** (DN). To keep the input simple we will use the **SAM account name** of the user and the name of the **OU**. We will query AD to get the DN of both objects.

How to do it...

The following steps and activities describe how to move a user to an OU in Active Directory using SCORCH 2012.

1. In the newly created Runbook navigate to Activities, click on **Runbook Control** under **Activities** select and drag a **Initialize Data** activity into the Runbook.
2. Add two parameters in this activity on the **Details** section by double-clicking the **Initialize Data** activity. Select the **Details** section and click on **Add** and provide the details using the following table:

Name of parameter	Data type	Contains information
Username	string	Contains the login name of the user.
OUname	string	Contains the name of the group the user should be added to.

3. Navigate to the **Activities** section and click on **Active Directory**. Click and drag a **Get Organizational Unit** activity into the Runbook next to the **Initialize Data** activity.

4. Link the **Initialize Data** activity to the **Get Organizational Unit** activity.
5. Double-click the **Get Organizational Unit** activity and provide the information specified in the following table on the **Properties** section:

Name of parameter	Value	Contains information
Configuration	Pick the configuration from the list.	AD configuration we set up in the preparation of this chapter.
ReturnDNonly (add this by the **Optional Properties**)	True (Use the **...** next to the **ReturnDNonly** to select this value).	We only need the DN of the user object.
Search Root	Type the Distinguished Name of the domain (you may also subscribe to a variable if this has been defined for this value).	For instance, `DC=TrustLab, DC=local`.
Search Scope	Sub Tree (Use the **...** next to the **Search Scope** to select this value).	All OUs under **Search Root** will be enumerated.

6. In the **Filters** section of the **Get Organizational Unit** activity add the following filter using the **Add** button:

Name of parameter	Value	Contains information
Name	Organization Unit	Property of the filter.
Relation	Equals	We need the specific Organization Unit object in this case.
Value	Right-click in the field and select **Subscribe** | **Published Data.** Choose **Initialize Data** and select **OUname** from the list of available properties.	Username provided in the **Initialize Data** activity.

7. Navigate to the **Activities** section in the Runbook and select **Active Directory**. Click and drag a **Get User** activity into the Runbook next to the **Get Organizational Unit** activity.
8. Link the **Get Organizational Unit** activity to the **Get User** activity.

9. Double-click on the **Get User** activity and provide the information in the following table on the **Properties** section:

Name of parameter	Value	Contains information
Configuration	Pick the configuration from the list.	AD configuration we setup in the preparation of this chapter.
ReturnDNonly (add this by the "**Optional Properties**")	True (Use the **...** next to the **ReturnDNonly** to select this value).	We only need the DN of the user object.
SearchRoot	Type the Distinguished Name of the domain (you may also subscribe to a variable if this has been defined for this value).	For instance, `DC=TrustLab, DC=local`
Search Scope	Sub tree (Use the **...** next to the **Search Scope** to select this value).	All OUs under Search Root will be enumerated.

10. On the **Filters** section of the **Get User** activity add the following filter using the **Add** button:

Name of parameter	Value	Contains information
Name	SAM Account Name	Property of the filter.
Relation	Equals	We need exactly the user object in this case.
Value	Right-click in the field | **Subscribe** | **Published Data**. Choose **Initialize Data** and select **Username**.	Username provided in the **Initialize Data** activity.

11. Navigate to the **Activities** section in the Runbook and select **Active Directory**. Click and drag a **Move User** activity into the Runbook next to the **Get Group** activity.
12. Link the **Get User** activity to the **Move User** activity.

13. Double-click on the **Move user** activity and provide the information in the following table on the **Properties** section:

Name of parameter	Value	Contains information
Configuration	Pick the configuration from the list	AD configuration we setup in the preparation of this chapter.
User Distinguished Name	Right-click in the field and select **Subscribe** | **Published Data**. Choose **Get User** and select **Distinguished Name**.	The Distinguished Name of the user.
New Container Distinguished Name (add this by using **Optional Properties**)	Right-click in the field and select **Subscribe** | **Published Data**. Choose **Get Organizational Unit** and select **Distinguished Name**.	The Distinguished Name of the new OU (Target OU).

The Runbook should look like this:

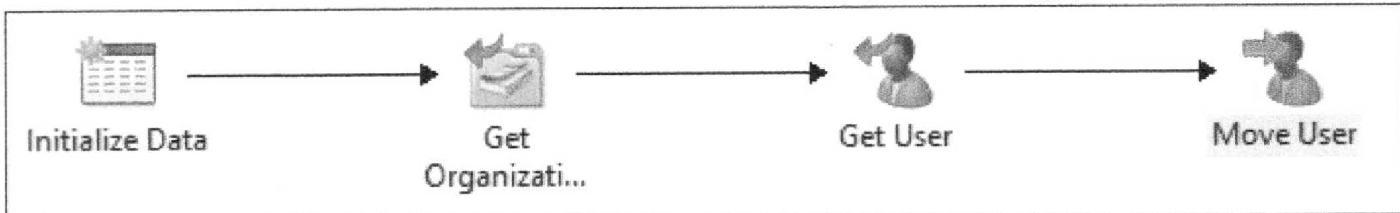

How it works...

When the Runbook is invoked in the Runbook designer or Orchestration Console website you will be prompted for a user name and an OU name (**Initialize Data** activity).

The OUname will be used as input for the **Get Organizational Unit** activity to get the Distinguished Name (DN) of the OU object.

The username will be used as input for the **Get User** activity to get the Distinguished Name (DN) of the user object.

The user object will be moved to the specified OU object. Both objects are defined by the Distinguished Name in the **Move User** activity.

There's more...

Moving computers or groups to a new OU

You can also move computer accounts or groups to a new OU to meet the organizational structure of your enterprise in Active Directory. You can automate this with the **Move Computer** or **Move Group** activities in the Active Directory integration pack.

The required information is the same as what you supply for moving a user object but targeted at computer or group objects.

An example of a move computer to OU Runbook is shown in the following diagram:

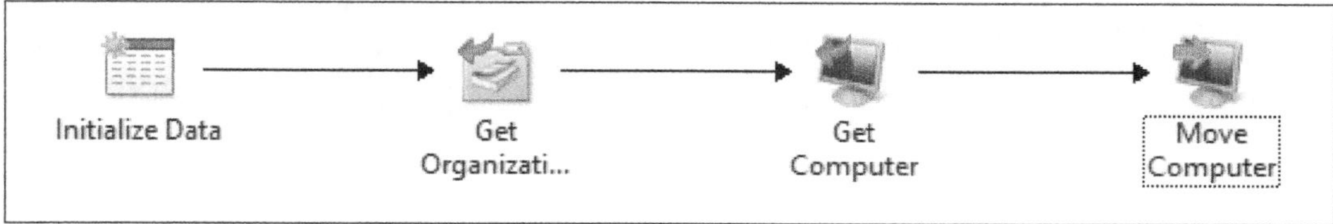

An example of a move group to OU Runbook is as follows:

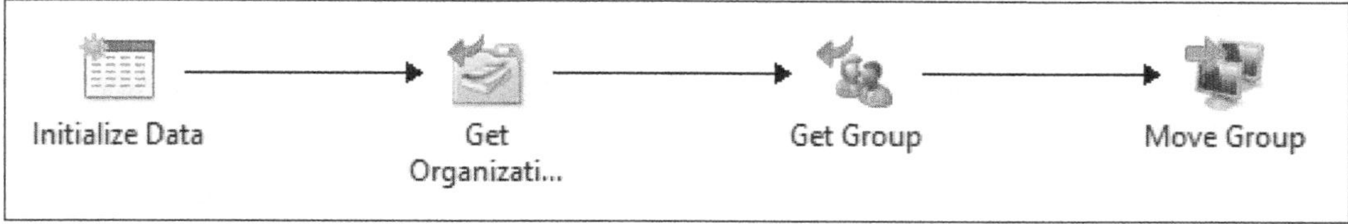

See also

Detailed information for the activities used in this Runbook can be found here:

- **Microsoft Technet – Get Organizational Unit activity**: `http://technet.microsoft.com/en-us/library/hh553468.aspx`
- **Microsoft Technet – Get User activity**: `http://technet.microsoft.com/en-us/library/hh553476.aspx`
- **Microsoft Technet – Move User activity**: `http://technet.microsoft.com/en-us/library/hh564143.aspx`

Disabling user accounts in Active Directory

It is a common security policy of an organization to disable inactive user accounts. This might happen for a number of reasons, for example an employee on a long break.

Instead of using an **Initialize Data** activity at the start of the Runbook we will use a different approach to automate the process. The business process to disable user accounts in Active Directory is described in the following diagram:

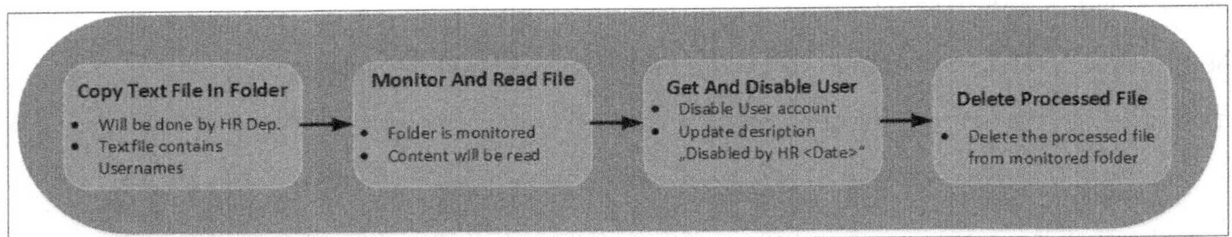

Getting ready

We need a shared folder (on the SCORCH 2012 server or access to shared on another server) as this Runbook would be triggered by monitoring a folder. Create and share the folder if required.

In addition to the preparation in the introduction of this chapter we need to create a new Runbook in the Runbook Designer.

1. In the Runbook Designer expand the connection to the SCORCH 2012 server.
2. Right-click on **Runbooks** and click on **New** (you can also right-click on a folder in **Runbooks**).
3. Right-click on the newly created Runbook and rename it to `Disable Inactive Users`.

How to do it...

1. In the newly created Runbook navigate to **File Management** under **Activities** click and drag a **Monitor File** activity into the middle pane of Runbook.

> A **Monitor Folder** activity doesn't work here because we need the exact filename dropped into the folder by HR department.

2. Add the following parameter into this activity on the **Details** section by double-clicking on **Monitor File Activity**:

Name of parameter	Value	Contents
In Folder:	`C:\PACKT8505EN-Chapter04\DisableUsers` Or your choice of folder or share: `\\server\<NameOfShare>`	Contains the folder monitored for new files by SCORCH 2012.

3. Click on the **Triggers** tab and mark **Created** under **Trigger if one of these files was** section. Click on **Finish**.

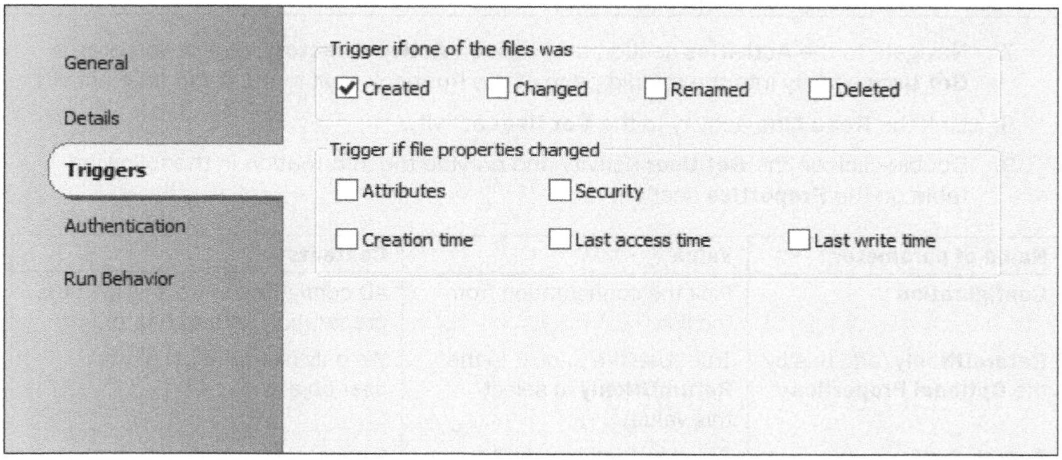

4. Navigate to the **Activities** section in the Runbook Designer, click on **Text File Management** | select and drag a **Read Line** activity into the middle pane of Runbook next to the **Monitor File** activity.
5. Link the **Monitor File** activity to the **Read Line** activity.

6. Double-click on the **Read Line** activity and provide the information in the following table in the **Properties** section:

Name of parameter	Value	Contains information
File Name	Right-click in the field and select **Subscribe** and click on **Published data**. Choose **Monitor File** and select **Name and path of the file** from the list of available properties.	File name and path of the file dropped in the folder.
File encoding	ASCII (Use the **...** next to the **File encoding:** to select this value).	Encoding of the text in the file.

7. Navigate to the **Activities** section and click on **Active Directory**. Select and drag a **Get User** activity into the middle pane of the Runbook next to the **Read Line** activity.
8. Link the **Read Line** activity to the **Get User** activity.
9. Double-click on the **Get User** activity and provide the information in the following table on the **Properties** section:

Name of parameter	Value	Contents
Configuration	Pick the configuration from the list.	AD configuration we set up in the preparation of this chapter.
ReturnDNonly (add this by the **Optional Properties**)	True (Use the **...** next to the **ReturnDNonly** to select this value).	We only need the DN of the user object.
Search Root	Type the Distinguished Name of the domain (you may also subscribe to a variable if this has been defined for this value).	For instance, `DC=TrustLab, DC=local`.
Search Scope	**Sub Tree** (Use the **...** next to **Search Scope** to select this value).	All OUs under **Search Root** will be enumerated.

10. In the **Filters** section of the **Get User** activity add the following filter using the **Add** button:

Name of parameter	Value	Contents
Name	`SAM Account Name`	Property of the filter.
Relation	`Equals`	We need the specific user object in this case.
Value	Right-click in the field and select **Subscribe** and click on **Published data**. Choose **Read Line** and select **Line text**.	Username in the text file.

11. Navigate to the **Activities** section click on **Active Directory**. Select and drag a **Disable User** activity into the middle pane of the Runbook next to the **Get User** activity.
12. Link the **Get User** activity to the **Disable User** activity.
13. Double-click on the **Disable User** activity and provide the following information in the **Properties** section:

Name of parameter	Value	Contents
Configuration	Pick the configuration from the list.	AD configuration we set up in the preparation of this chapter.
Distinguished Name	Right-click in the field and select **Subscribe**. Click on **Published Data**. Choose **Get User** and select **Distinguished Name** from the list of available properties.	The Distinguished Name of the user object.

14. Navigate to the **Activities** section and click on **Active Directory.** Select and drag an **Update User** activity into the middle pane of the Runbook next to the **Disable User** activity.
15. Link the **Disable User** activity to the **Update User** activity.
16. Double-click on the **Update User** activity and provide the following information on the **Properties** section:

Name of parameter	Value	Contents
Configuration	Pick the configuration from the list.	AD configuration we set up in the preparation of this chapter.
Distinguished Name	Right-click in the field and select **Subscribe**. Click on **Published Data**. Choose **Get User** and select **Distinguished Name** from the list of available properties.	The Distinguished Name of the created user object.

Name of parameter	Value	Contents
Description (add this by the **Optional Properties**)	Type in the text related to the requirement of the business process: **- User Account disable by HR runbook** Add the required date information by using the **Subscribe** and **Published Data** option. Select **Disable User** and uncheck the **Show common Published Data** option. Select the required Activity date properties.	Text put in the description of the user object.

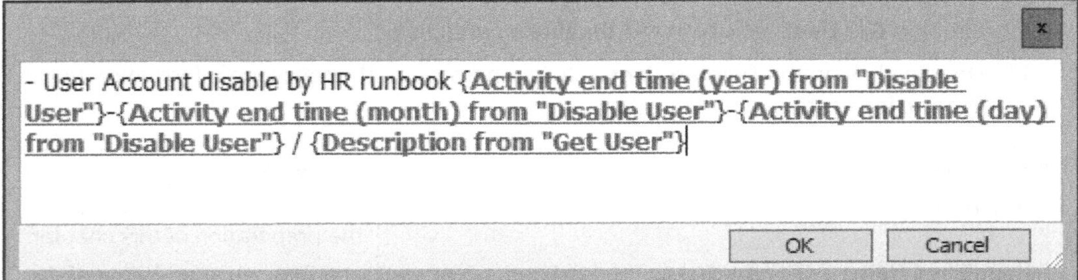
- User Account disable by HR runbook {Activity end time (year) from "Disable User"}-{Activity end time (month) from "Disable User"}-{Activity end time (day) from "Disable User"} / {Description from "Get User"}
OK
Cancel

This will ensure the description of the user object in AD is filled in! In this case the new text will be appended to an existing description.

17. Navigate to and click on **Runbook Control** under **Activities**. Select and drag a **Junction** activity into the Runbook.
18. Link the **Update User** activity to the **Junction** activity.
19. Link the **Monitor File** activity to the **Junction** activity.
20. Double-click on the **Junction** activity and provide the following information on the **Details** section. Click on **...** next to the **Return data from:** field and select **Monitor File** | **Finish**.

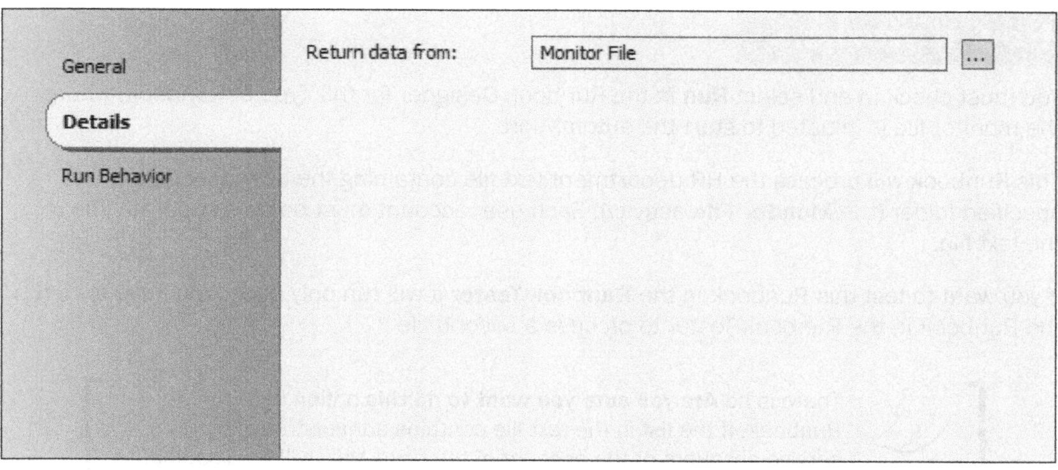

21. Navigate to **File Management** under **Activities.** Select and drag a **Delete File** activity into the middle pane of the Runbook.
22. Link the **Junction** activity to the **Delete File** activity.
23. Double-click on the **Delete File** activity and provide the following information on the **Details** section:

Name of parameter	Value	Contents
Path	Right-click in the field and select **Subscribe** | **Published Data.** Choose **Monitor File** and select **Name and path of the file.**	File name and path of the file dropped in the folder.

The Runbook should look like this now:

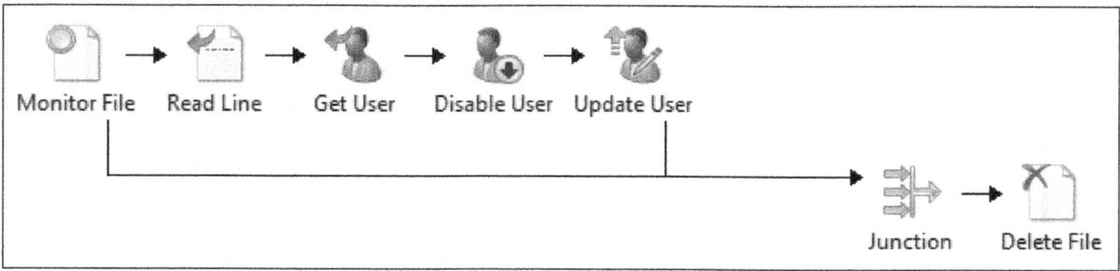

How it works...

You must check in and select **Run** in the Runbook Designer for this type of Runbook; where the monitor file is initiated to start the automation.

This Runbook will process the HR department text file containing the user accounts in the specified folder (the **Monitor File** activity). Each user account must be on a separate line in the text file.

If you want to test this Runbook in the **Runbook Tester** it will run only once. You have to re-run the Runbook in the Runbook Tester to process a second file.

[There is no **Are you sure you want to do this** option in the Runbook. If the list in the text file contains administrative or service accounts or the account of the boss, they will be disabled.]

The **Read Line** activity will process each line in the text file. Each line of will be pushed to the **Get User** activity.

In the Runbook Tester you will see a new **Get User** activity for each username in the file. The username of the **Read Line** activity will be used as input for the **Get User** activity to get the Distinguished Name of the user object.

The DN of the user object will be passed to the **Disable User** activity. Similar to the **Get User** activity, the **Disable User** activity will process each user in the text file. The same DN information of the **Get User** activity will be used in the **Update user** activity. The description of each user will be modified.

As the activities are run for each user in the list we have to use a junction to prevent the Runbook from deleting the file before all users in the list are processed. This is why a **Junction** activity is added and linked to the **Monitor File** activity and the **Update User** activity.

[A junction in SCORCH is essentially a demarcation (check) point that causes two things. 1: All branches have to complete executing to the point of the junction before continuing with the next activity and 2: Merge processing down to one branch. In our scenario the junction reduces the action of looping and disabling *n* amount of users into one virtual activity. The result is our Runbook monitors a file, processes *n* users as one action and then we can delete the file. A very important fact to note is that the junction will wait for all branches to complete before proceeding; this may slow down the overall processing of the Runbook based on the slowest branch.]

The **Monitor File** and **Delete File** activity are only run once in for each instance of the Runbook. When the **Delete File** activity runs, the corresponding text file is deleted.

There's more...

Specify additional filters in the Monitor File activity

You can add additional file property checks to the Runbook. You must add additional filters to the **Monitor File** activity.

1. Double-click the **Monitor File** activity.
2. Click on **Add** under **Filters** on the **Details** tab.
3. Pick the criteria from the field **Name**.
4. The **Name** field has a list of filter options. The filter option you select dictates what relation and value you can use. For example selecting **Accessed** allows an **After** or **Before Relation** with date time as your value option.
5. Specify the filter criteria.

Prevent to overwrite the description of user accounts

To prevent overwriting the existing description of a user object in the **Update User** activity you can add the existing description of the user by following these steps:

1. In the **Disable Inactive Users** Runbook, double-click on the **Update User** activity.
2. Right-click on the text in the **Description** field. Select **Expand**.
3. Type / at the end of the last character. Right click on the space after / and select **Subscribe | Published Data**.
4. Choose **Get User** activity.
5. Choose **Description**. Click on **OK** and then on **Finish**.

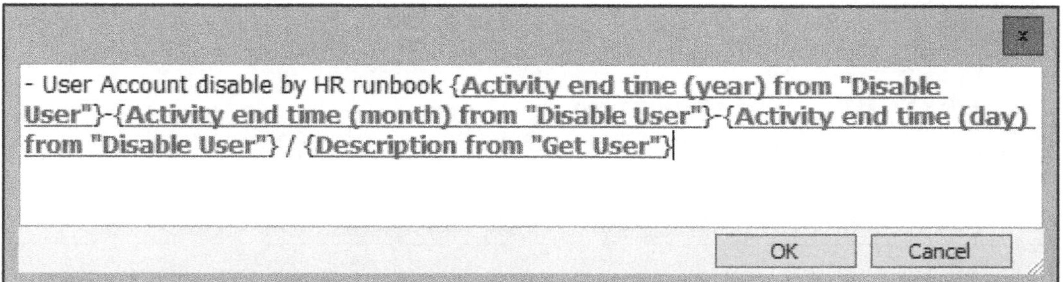
- User Account disable by HR runbook {Activity end time (year) from "Disable User"}-{Activity end time (month) from "Disable User"}-{Activity end time (day) from "Disable User"} / {Description from "Get User"}
OK
Cancel

Disabling computer accounts instead of user accounts

To disable computer accounts there is also an activity in the Active Directory integration pack called **Disable Computer**. The information that is required is the same as the **Disable User** activity (Distinguished Name of the computer account).

See also

Detailed information for the activities used in this Runbook can be found here:

- Microsoft Technet – the **Monitor File** activity: `http://technet.microsoft.com/en-us/library/hh206083.aspx`
- Microsoft Technet – the **Read Line** activity :`http://technet.microsoft.com/en-us/library/hh206041.aspx`
- Microsoft Technet – the **Get User** activity: `http://technet.microsoft.com/en-us/library/hh553476.aspx`
- Microsoft Technet – the **Disable User** activity: `http://technet.microsoft.com/en-us/library/hh553459.aspx`
- Microsoft Technet – the **Update User** activity: `http://technet.microsoft.com/en-us/library/hh565918.aspx`
- Microsoft Technet – the **Junction** activity: `http://technet.microsoft.com/en-us/library/hh206089.aspx`
- Microsoft Technet – the **Delete File** activity:`http://technet.microsoft.com/en-us/library/hh225024.aspx`

Using SCORCH to remove obsolete user accounts

You can schedule a Runbook in System Center 2012 Orchestrator to automatically remove disabled and obsolete user accounts from Active Directory.

The business process of this workflow is defined in the following diagram:

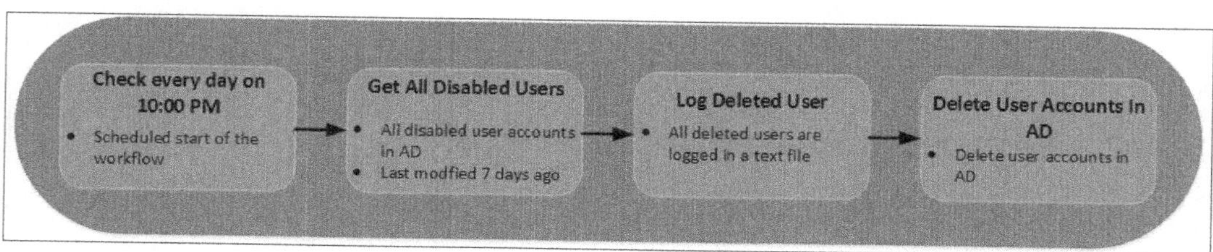

Getting ready

In addition to the preparation in the introduction of this chapter we need to create a new Runbook in the **Runbook Designer**.

1. In the **Runbook Designer** expand the connection to the SCORCH 2012 server
2. Right-click on **Runbooks** and then click on **New** (you can also right-click on a folder in **Runbooks**)
3. Right-click the newly created Runbook and rename it to **Delete Obsolete Users**.

How to do it...

This Runbook requires a schedule, which is the first activity we need in our Runbook.

1. In the newly created Runbook navigate to and click on **Scheduling** under **Activities** | select and drag a **Monitor Date/Time** activity into the middle pane of the Runbook.
2. Double-click on the **Monitor Date/Time activity**. Configure the **Interval** on the **Details** section using the information in the following table:

Name of parameter	Value	Contents
Interval At	`22:00` or `10:00 PM`	This contains the time the Runbook will be triggered every day.

3. Navigate to the **Activities** section and click on **Active Directory** select and drag a **Get User** activity into the middle pane of the Runbook next to the **Monitor Date/Time** activity.
4. Link the **Monitor Date/Time** activity to the **Get User** activity.
5. Double-click on the **Get User** activity and provide the information in the following table on the **Properties** section:

Name of parameter	Value	Contains information
Configuration	Pick the configuration from the list.	AD configuration we set up in the preparation of this chapter.
`ReturnDNonly` (add this by the **Optional Properties** value)	**False**	We need all information of the user object.
Search Root	Distinguished Name of the domain or OU	For instance: `DC=TrustLab, DC=local`.
Search Scope	Subtree	All OUs under Search Root will be enumerated.

6. On the **Filters** section of the **Get User** activity add the following filter:

Name of parameter	Value	Contents
Name	**Disabled**	Property of the filter.
Relation	**Equals**	We need the specific user object in this case.
Value	**TRUE**	We need all disabled user accounts.

7. Navigate to the **Activities** section click on **Utilities**. Select and drag a **Format Date/Time Modification Date** activity into the Runbook next to the **Get User** activity.
8. Link the **Get User** activity to the **Format Date/Time Modification Date** activity
9. Double-click on the **Format Date/Time Modification Date** activity and provide the information shown. Right-click on in the space next to **Date/Time** and select **Subscribe | Published Data | Get User | Modification Date**. Type `dd/MM/yyyy hh:mm:ss` in the **Format:** field under the **Output** section. Click on **Finish**.

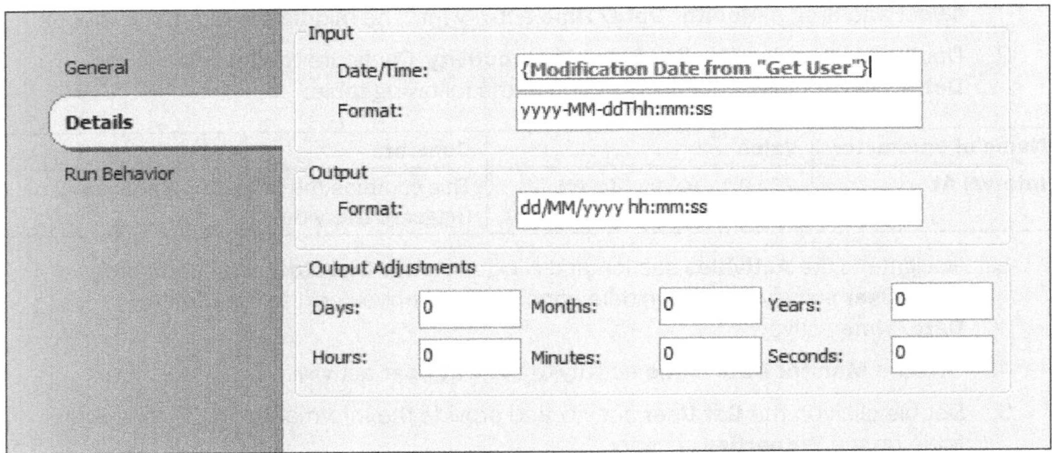

10. Navigate to the **Activities** section, click on **System** and drag a **Run .Net Script** activity into the middle pane of the Runbook next to the **Format Date/Time Modification Date** activity.
11. Link the **Format Date/Time Modification Date** activity to the **Run .Net Script** activity.
12. Rename the **Run .Net Script** activity to **PowerShell Script Compare Modfication Date**.
13. Double-click on the **PowerShell Script Compare Modification Date** activity and select PowerShell in the **Language | Type** field on the **Details** section (use the **...** button to select).

14. Right-click in the **Script** field and select **Expand** to open up the **Script** field. Add the code shown in the following screenshot into the **Script** field:

The following information needs to be added by right-clicking and selecting **Subscribe | Published Data** in the script:

```
$UserDN = "{Distinguished Name from "GetUser"}"
$LastmodifiedDate = "{Format Result without
adjustments from "Format Date/Time Modification
Date"}"
```

```
$UserDN = "{Distinguished Name from "Get User"}"

$LastmodifiedDate = "{Format Result without adjustments from "Format Date/Time Modification Date"}"

$BeforeDate = (Get-Date).AddDays(-7).ToString("dd/MM/yyyy HH:mm:ss")

IF ($LastmodifiedDate -lt $BeforeDate)
{
$DeleteUser = "TRUE"
}
ELSE
{
$DeleteUser = "FALSE"
}
```

OK Cancel

15. In the **PowerShell Script Compare Modification date** activity, select the **Published Data** tab and add the two properties with their respective values, using the table below (Click on **Finish** on completion):

Name	Type	Variable Name
`DeleteUser`	String	`DeleteUser`
`UserDN`	String	`UserDN`

16. Navigate to the **Activities** section in the Runbook Designer. Click on **Text File Management** select and drag an **Append Line** activity into the Runbook next to the **PowerShell Script Compare Modification Date**.

17. Link the **PowerShell Script Compare Modification Date** activity to the **Append Line** activity.

18. Double-click on the link (link is the arrowed line between the two activities) and modify the **Include Filter**. Double-click on the existing information in the **Include Filter** and select **DeleteUser**, click on **OK** and then on **value**. Type `TRUE`. Click on **OK** and then on **Finish**.

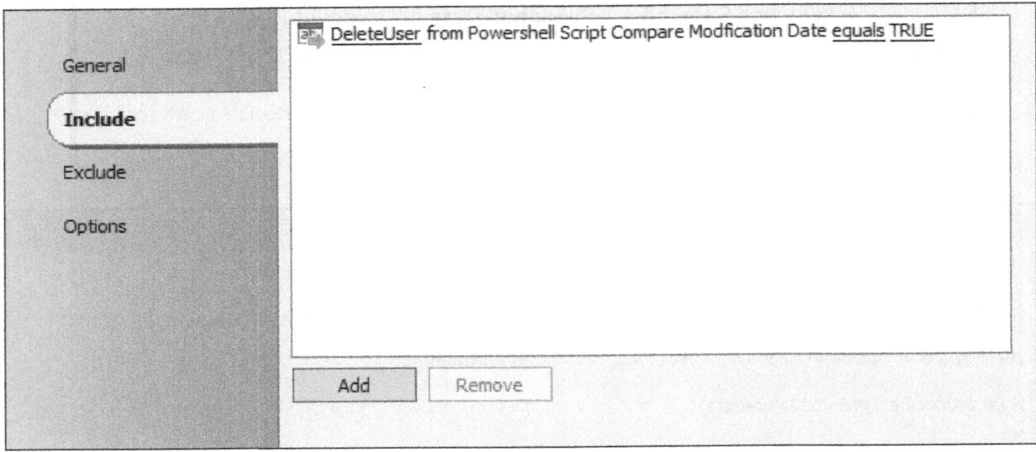

19. Double-click on the **Append Line** activity and configure the activity with the information from the following table:

Name of the parameter	Value	Contents
File	Right-click in the field and select **Expand**. Type the path of the file. For example, `C:\PACKT8505EN-Chapter04\DeletedUsers.txt`.	The name of the logfile you plan to use for the Runbook.
File encoding	ASCII (Use the **...** button to select)	Encoding of the file.
Text	Right-click in the field and click on **Expand**. Type the text you want to proceed the logfile entry of users deleted by the Runbook add additional specific Runbook data by subscribing to **Published Data** (check **Show common Published Data** to get a list of additional properties indicated from the **PowerShell Script Compare Modification Data** activity **Published Data**).	The text of the log entry.

The result might look like this:

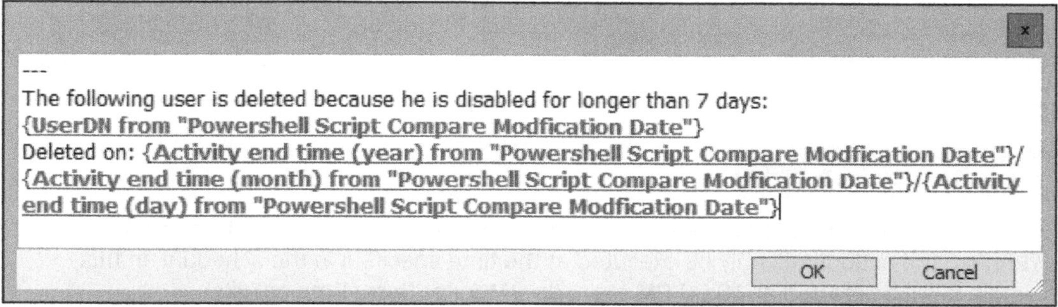

The following user is deleted because he is disabled for longer than 7 days:
{UserDN from "Powershell Script Compare Modfication Date"}
Deleted on: {Activity end time (year) from "Powershell Script Compare Modfication Date"}/
{Activity end time (month) from "Powershell Script Compare Modfication Date"}/{Activity
end time (day) from "Powershell Script Compare Modfication Date"}
OK
Cancel

20. Navigate to the Activities section in the **Runbook Designer** click "**Active Directory**" select and drag a **Delete User** activity into the middle pane of the runbook next to the **Append Line** activity.
21. Link the **Append Line** activity to the **Delete User** activity
22. Double-click on the **Delete User** activity and provide the following information on the "**Properties**" section:

Name of parameter	Value	Contains information
Configuration	Pick the configuration from the list	AD configuration we setup in the preparation of this chapter
Distinguished Name	Right-click in the field | Subscribe | Published Data Choose **Powershell Script Compare Modification Date** and select **UserDN**	The Distinguished Name (DN) of the user object

Using the **Runbook Tester** to test this runbook: As a recommended best practise, you should plan to test this in a lab/development environment. The user accounts found by the **Get User** activity and filtered into the PowerShell script will be deleted even if the runbook is run in the Runbook Tester! For testing in a production environment it is a good idea to disable the **link** between the **Append Line** activity and the **Delete User** activity" (right-click on the **link** and deselect **Enabled**). This way the filtered users are logged in the text file but not deleted during the test.

The runbook should look like this now:

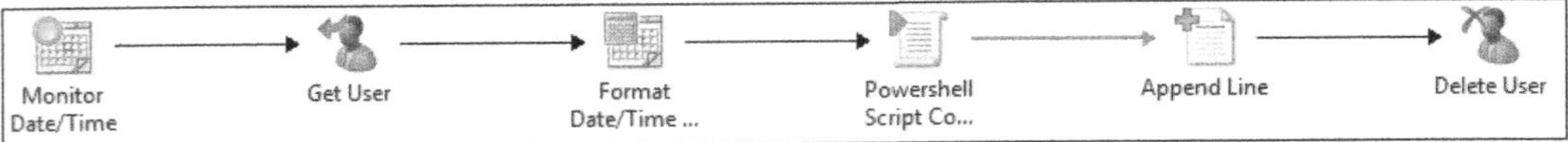

How it works...

This runbook needs to be **Checked In** and started (Run) to execute. Though the runbook is running, the actions will only be executed at the time specified in the schedule. In this example it will be started at 10:00 PM every day (Monitor Date/Time activity).

In the **Get User** activity the disabled users will be queried from Active Directory. The **Modification Date** is formatted in the **Format Date/Time Modification Date** activity for the next step.

For each disabled user discovered by the Active Directory query, the PowerShell Script will compare the formatted **Modification Date** against the current date -7 days before. See the comment lines in the script for details:

```
#Set UserDN variable to Distinguished Name from "Get User" activity
$UserDN = "{Distinguished Name from "GetUser"}"
#Set LastmodifiedDate variable
$LastmodifiedDate = "{Format Result without adjustments from "Format
Date/Time Modification Date"}"
#Get the current date -7 days and format the date
$BeforeDate = (Get-Date).AddDays(-7).ToString("dd/MM/yyyyHH:mm:ss")
#If LastModifiedDate is less the Before date set DeleteUser variable
TRUE
IF ($LastmodifiedDate -lt $BeforeDate)
{
$DeleteUser = "TRUE"
}
#If LastModifiedDate is greater thanBefore date set DeleteUser
variable FALSE
ELSE
{
$DeleteUser = "FALSE"
}
```

If the **DeleteUser** variable is equal to **TRUE** the Distinguished Name of the user and the current date are logged in a text file (**Append Line** activity). If the **DeleteUser** variable is **FALSE** nothing will happen.

In the last activity the disabled user accounts which were last modified 7 days ago are deleted in Active Directory (**Delete User** activity).

There's more...

Deleting obsolete computer accounts in Active Directory:

To delete obsolete computer accounts you can use the activities **Get Computer** and **Delete Computer** of the Active Directory integration pack.

See also

Detailed information for the activities used in this runbook you can find here:

Microsoft Technet - Monitor Date/Time activity: `http://technet.microsoft.com/en-us/library/hh225031.aspx`

Microsoft Technet - Get User activity: `http://technet.microsoft.com/en-us/library/hh553476.aspx`

Microsoft Technet - Format Date/Time activity: `http://technet.microsoft.com/en-us/library/hh206037.aspx`

Microsoft Technet - Run .Net Script activity: `http://technet.microsoft.com/en-us/library/hh206103.aspx`

Microsoft Technet - Append Line activity: `http://technet.microsoft.com/en-us/library/hh206072.aspx`

Microsoft Technet - Delete User activity: `http://technet.microsoft.com/en-us/library/hh553462.aspx`

5

Creating Runbooks for System Center 2012 Configuration Manager Tasks

In this chapter, we will cover the following topics:

- Deploying software updates
- Deploying software applications
- Deploying client agents to workgroup devices
- Gathering the client deployment status

Introduction

System Center 2012 Orchestrator is not only designed to help automate a single system but is also able to automate across "silos" of systems in a typical IT environment.

This chapter focuses on automating some of the common tasks which requires System Center 2012 Configuration Manager to interact with other configuration management processes and systems. This level of cross silo automation helps to alleviate some of the more repetitive manual tasks. The aim is to free up some of the IT admins' time for better valued proactive work.

The common tasks for Configuration Management described in this chapter will cover the following scenarios:

- Deploying software updates to servers
    - Deploying software updates to a specific device on demand.
- Deploying software applications

  Users requesting approval-required applications using the Configuration Manager self-service Software Catalog
- Deploying clients to workgroup devices
    - Pushing the agent from the ConfigMgr console to a domain joined device is simple, but now we can simplify and automate the process to workgroup devices
- Gathering client deployment status
    - Gather information related to the deployments of the ConfigMgr agent to a client machine for review

We will define a process for all of these configuration management tasks with the required steps in each recipe.

The requirements for all recipes in this chapter are:

- Installed and deployed System Center 2012 Configuration Manager integration pack. For how to install integration packs in SCO, please see the *How to load Integration Packs (IP)* recipe in *Chapter 2, Initial Configuration and Making SCORCH Highly Available*.
- The Configuration Manager console installed on the Runbook server.
- A user account with appropriate permissions in System Center 2012 Configuration Manager is needed to fulfill the tasks (create, modify, and deploy the following: Software Update Groups, Collections, Task Sequences, Software, Alerts, Status Notifications).

You must perform the following for all recipes in this chapter:

Create a connection in SCORCH 2012 Runbook Designer to your System Center 2012 Configuration Manager site server. To do this, follow these steps:

1. Start the SCORCH 2012 Runbook Designer.
2. Choose **Options** in the Menu and click on **SC 2012 Configuration Manager**.
3. Click on **Add**.

4. Provide the information using the following table:

Name for the Connection Entry	Descriptive name for this ConfigMgr connection
Configuration Manager Server Name (FQDN)	Full Qualified Domain Name of your Configuration Manager server.
Username	User with appropriate permissions in ConfigMgr.
Password	Password of the user.

5. Click on **Test Connection** to ensure the connection to your Configuration Manager server can be made successfully.

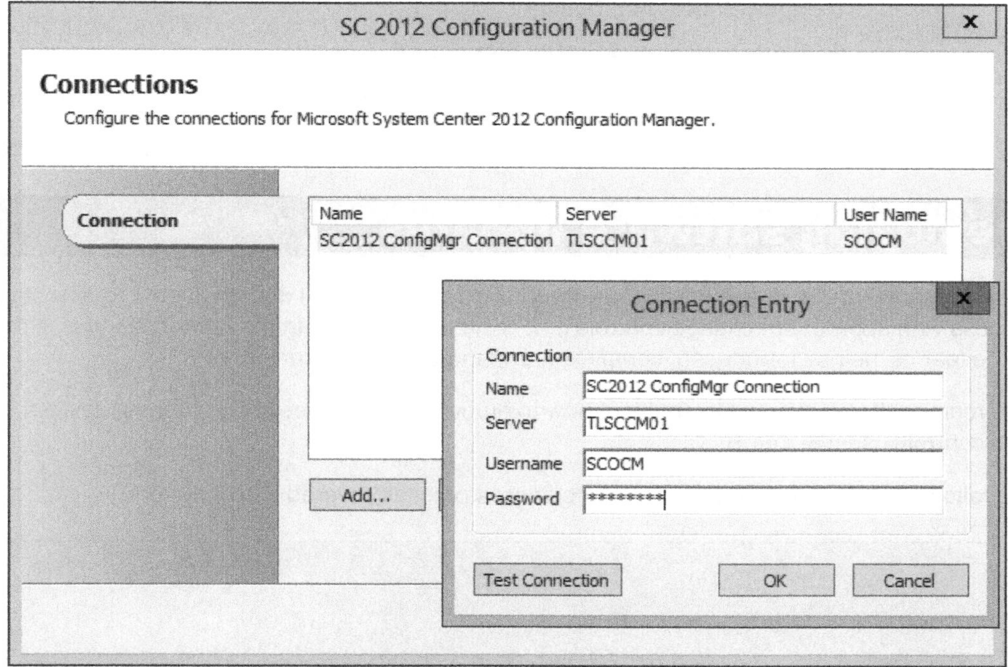

6. Click on **OK**.
7. Click on **Finish**.

Before you begin, you will also need to create some new Runbooks to use with the recipes.

The following steps show how to create a new Runbook:

1. Right-click on **Runbooks** to the left of the Runbook Designer and choose **New | Runbook**.
2. Right-click on the **New Runbook** tab that appears above the workspace, click on **Yes** in the **Confirm Check out** message box. Name the Runbook **1.Deploy Software Update**.
3. Repeat the steps above to create four additional Runbooks with the following names:
   - **2a.Check for Requests**
   - **2b.Deploy App**
   - **3.Deploy Workgroup Device**
   - **4.Client Deployment Status Monitoring**

Deploying software updates

Deploying software updates for organizations is usually a very well documented and executed process with appropriate change controls or it is simply not done. In the latter case, this is due to the fear of the risk introduced, complexity, and the time it can consume.

This recipe will show you an example of how to automate your process for patching devices with controls using SCORCH.

The following diagram shows the defined business process covered in this recipe:

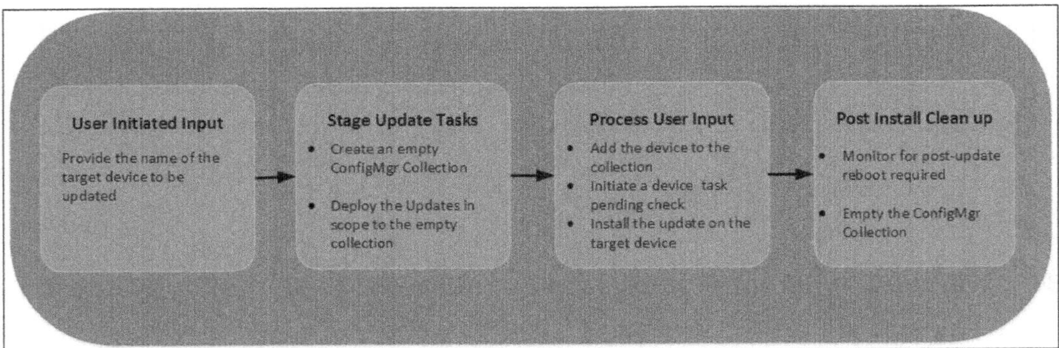

Getting ready

This recipe will leverage System Center 2012 Configuration Manager (ConfigMgr) to deploy a set of updates to a device.

Before creating this recipe you will need to create an Update Group in ConfigMgr. In this recipe it is assumed that you will be using an Update Group in ConfigMgr called **Monthly Security Updates**. You will also need to create a deployment template for this recipe.

How to do it...

The following steps will show you how to configure the activities in the Runbook (**1.Deploy Software Update**) for this recipe:

1. Navigate to the **Activities** section in the Runbook Designer, select **Runbook Control** and drag an **Initialize Data** activity into the middle pane of the Runbook (the workspace).
2. Right-click on the activity and select **Properties**. Click on **Add** in the **Details** section and specify the information shown in the following table. Click on **Finish**.

Name of parameter	Data type	Contains information
NetBIOSName	String	This will be used for the name of the device to patch.

3. Navigate to the **Activities** section, select **SC 2012 Configuration Manager** and drag a **Create Collection** activity to the Runbook next to the **Initialize Data** object.
4. Link the **Initialize Data** activity to the **Create Collection** activity.

5. Double-click on the **Create Collection** activity and provide the following information in the **Details** section, shown in the following image:

Name of parameter	Value
Connection	Pick the ConfigMgr configuration we set up in the preparation of this chapter from the list.
Collection Name	Type `Automated Patching-` and then right-click in the field **Subscribe** | **Published Data**. Choose **Initialize Data** in the **Activity** field and select **NetBIOSName**.
Collection Type	Device
Limiting Collection	All Systems
Limiting Collection Value Type	Name (click on **...** to select)
Comment	Collection for Automated Patching.
Use incremental updates	Click on **False** (click on **...** to select)

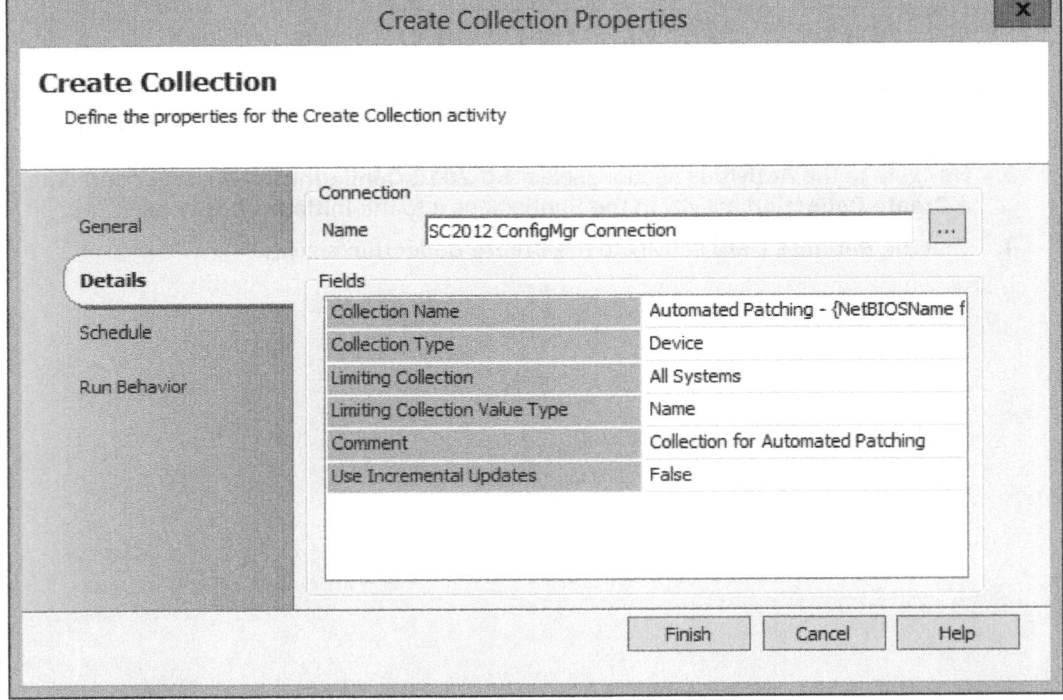

6. Navigate to the **Activities** section, select **SC 2012 Configuration Manager** and drag a **Deploy Software Update** activity to the Runbook next to the **Create Collection** object.

7. Link the **Create Collection** activity to the **Deploy Software Update** activity.
8. Double-click on the **Deploy Software Update** activity and provide the following information in the **Details** section:

Name of parameter	Value
Connection	Pick the ConfigMgr configuration we set up in the preparation of this chapter from the list.
Deployment Name	Automated Patching.
Deployment Description	Automated Patching using Orchestrator.
Deployment Template	Select your deployment template from the list (click on **...** to select).
Deployment Template Value Type	**Name** (click on **...** to select)
Update/Update Group	Select the Update Group you created earlier as outlined in the preparation of this chapter from the list.
Update Value Type	Update Group Name (click on **...** to select).
Purpose	Required (click on **...** to select)
User Notification	Hide all notifications (click on **...** to select).
Collection	Right-click in the field and select **Subscribe** | **Published Data**. Choose **Create Collection** from the **Activity** field and select **Collection ID**.
Collection Value Type	**ID** (click **...** to select)

9. Navigate to the **Activities** section, select **SC 2012 Configuration Manager** and drag an **Add Collection Rule** activity to the Runbook next to the **Deploy Software Update** object.
10. Right-click on the **Add Collection Rule** activity and choose rename. Rename it to `Add Device to Collection`.
11. Link the **Deploy Software Update** activity to the **Add Device to Collection** activity.
12. Double-click on the **Add Device to Collection** activity and provide the following information in the **Details** section:

Name of parameter	Value
Connection	Pick the ConfigMgr configuration we set up in the preparation of this chapter from the list.
Collection	Right-click in the field and select **Subscribe** | **Published Data** Choose **Create Collection** in the Activity field and select **Collection ID**.
Collection Value Type	**ID** (click **...** to select)
Rule Name	Automated Patching.

Name of parameter	Value
Rule Type	**Direct Rule** (click **...** to select)
Rule Definition	Right-click in the field and select **Subscribe** | **Published Data**. Choose **Initialize Data** in the **Activity** field and select **NetBIOSName**.
Rule Definition Value Type	**Resource Names** (click **...** to select)

13. Navigate to the **Activities** section, select **SC 2012 Configuration Manager** and drag an **Update Collection Membership** activity to the Runbook next to the **Add Device to Collection** object.
14. Link the **Add Device to Collection** activity to the **Update Collection Membership** activity.
15. Double-click on the **Update Collection Membership** activity and provide the following information in the **Details** section:

Name of parameter	Value
Connection	Pick the ConfigMgr configuration we set up in the preparation of this chapter from the list.
Collection	Right-click in the field and select **Subscribe** | **Published Data**. Choose **Create Collection** in the **Activity** field and select **Collection ID**.
Collection Value Type	`ID`
Wait for Refresh Completion	`True`
Polling Interval (seconds)	`5`

16. Navigate to the **Activities** section, select **SC 2012 Configuration Manager** and drag a **Perform Client Action** activity to the Runbook next to the **Update Collection Membership** object.
17. Right-click on the **Perform Client Action** activity and choose rename. Rename it to `Refresh Machine Policy`.
18. Link the **Update Collection Membership** activity to the **Refresh Machine Policy** activity.
19. Double-click on the **Refresh Machine Policy** activity and provide the following information in the **Details** section:

Name of parameter	Value
Computer	Right-click in the field and select **Subscribe** | **Published Data**. Choose **Initialize Data** in the Activity field and select **NetBIOSName**.
Action	Click on the ellipsis button and choose Software **Machine Policy Retrieval & Evaluation Cycle** from the list.

20. Navigate to the **Activities** section, select **SC 2012 Configuration Manager** and drag a **Perform Client Action** activity to the Runbook next to the **Refresh Machine Policy** object.
21. Right-click on the **Perform Client Action** activity and choose rename. Rename it to **Software Updates Scan**.
22. Link the **Refresh Machine Policy** activity to the **Software Updates Scan** activity.
23. Double-click on the link between **Refresh Machine Policy** and **Software Updates Scan**, click on the **Options** tab to the left of the **Link Properties** screen, shown below.
24. Change the **Trigger delay** value to **30**, and click on **Finish**.

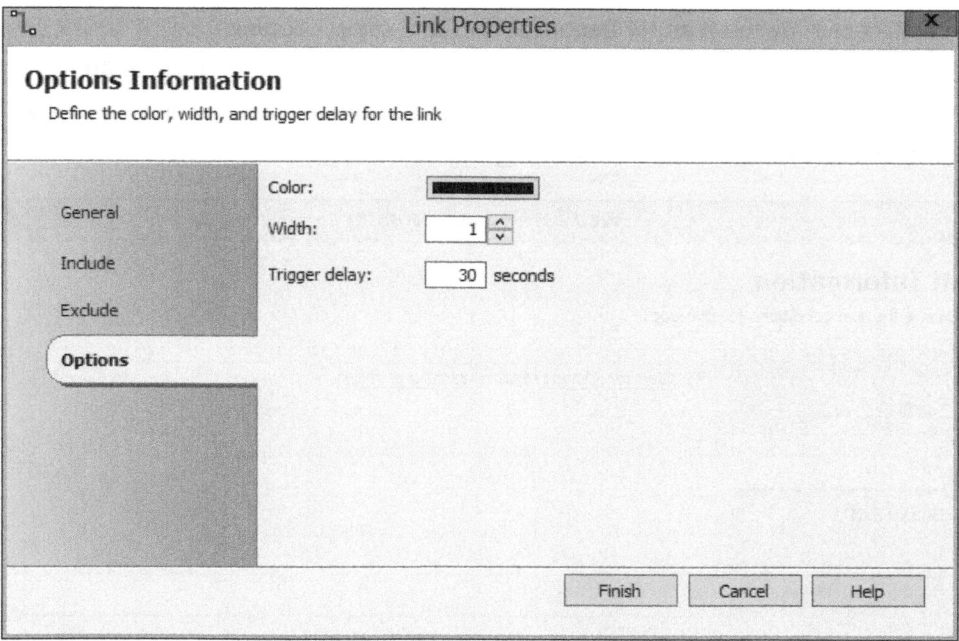

25. Double-click on the **Software Updates Scan** activity and provide the following information in the **Details** section:

Name of parameter	Value
Computer	Right-click in the field and select **Subscribe | Published Data**. Choose **Initialize Data** in the **Activity** field and select **NetBIOSName**.
Action	Click on the ellipsis button and choose **Software Updates Scan and Deployment Re-evaluation** from the list.

26. Navigate to the **Activities** section, select **Monitoring** and drag a **Get Computer/IP Status** activity to the Runbook next to the **Software Updates Scan** object.

27. Right-click on the **Get Computer/IP Status** activity and choose rename. Rename it to `Wait for Reboot`.
28. Link the **Software Updates Scan** activity to the **Wait for Reboot** activity.
29. Double-click on the **Wait for Reboot** activity and provide the following information in the **Details** section:

Name of parameter	Value
Computer	Right-click in the field and select **Subscribe | Published Data**. Choose **Initialize Data** in the **Activity** field and select **NetBIOSName**.

30. Right-click on the **Wait for Reboot** activity and select **Looping**.
31. Check the box to enable looping and set the delay between attempts to **30**.
32. Click on the **Exit** tab on the left of the screen and click on the underlined **success** word.
33. Uncheck **success** and check **warning** and **failed**.

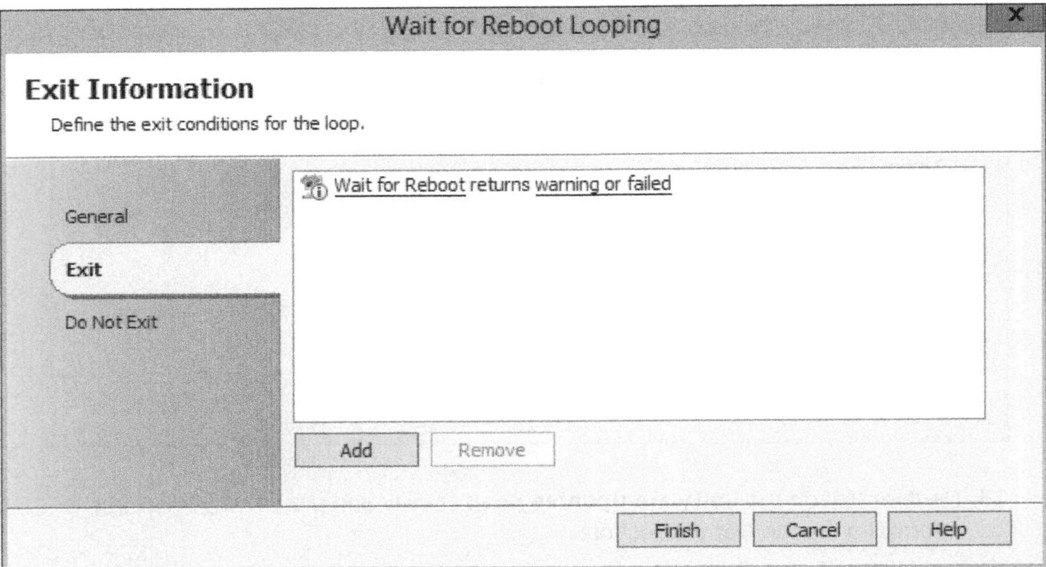

34. Click on the **Do Not Exit** tab to the left of the screen and click on **Add** to get an entry that says **Wait for Reboot returns success**.
35. Click on **Finish**.
36. Navigate to the **Activities** section, select **Monitoring** and drag a **Get Computer/IP Status** activity to the Runbook next to the **Wait for Reboot** object.
37. Right-click on the **Get Computer/IP Status** activity and choose rename. Rename it to `Wait for OS boot`.

38. Link the **Wait for Reboot** activity to the **Wait for OS boot** activity.
39. Double-click the link between **Wait for Reboot** and **Wait for OS boot** click on the **Options** tab to the left of the **Link Properties** screen.
40. Click the **Include** tab on the left of the screen and click on the underlined **success**.
41. Uncheck **success** and check **warning** and **failed** instead.
42. Click on **Finish**.
43. Double-click on the **Wait for OS boot** activity and provide the following information in the **Details** section:

Name of parameter	Value
Computer	Right-click in the field and select **Subscribe | Published Data**. Choose **Initialize Data** in the **Activity** field and select **NetBIOSName**.

44. Right-click on the **Wait for OS boot** activity and choose **Looping**.
45. Check the box to enable looping and set the delay between attempts to **30**.
46. Click on the **Do Not Exit** tab on the left of the screen and click on **Add**.
47. Click on the underlined **success** word and uncheck **success** and check **warning** and **failed** instead.
48. Click on **Finish**.
49. Navigate to the **Activities** section, select **SC 2012 Configuration Manager** and drag a **Delete Collection** activity to the Runbook next to the **Wait for OS boot** object.
50. Link the **Wait for OS boot** activity to the **Delete Collection** activity.
51. Double-click on the **Delete Collection** activity and provide the following information in the **Details** section:

Name of parameter	Value
Connection	Pick the ConfigMgr configuration we set up in the preparation of this chapter from the list.
Collection	Right-click in the field and select **Subscribe | Published Data**. Choose **Create Collection** in the Activity field and select **Collection ID**.
Collection Value Type	`ID`
Delete members from database	`False`

52. Click the **Advanced** tab on the left of the screen and provide the following information:

Name of parameter	Value
Has assigned deployments (including auto-deployments)	False
Is used in any deployment templates	False
Has custom client settings assignments	False
Has antimalware policy assignments	False
Is used in any queries	False

The final Runbook should look like this:

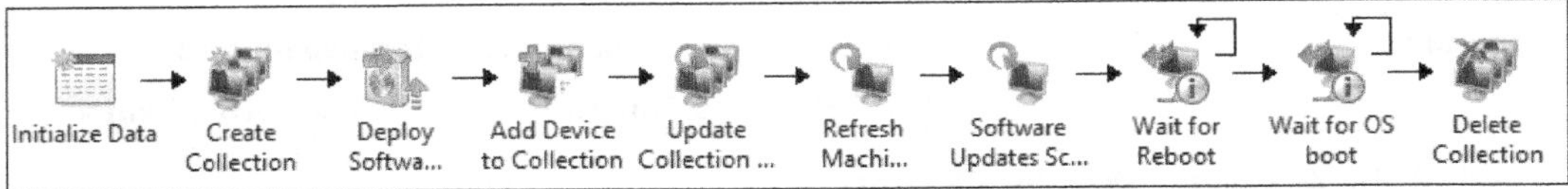

How it works...

This Runbook takes a prompt for the name of the device to be patched. The Runbook passes the device name entered in to the databus in Orchestrator to automate the patching process.

A temporary collection is created in ConfigMgr. The Software Update Group you created in ConfigMgr for the Runbook is deployed to this temporary collection.

The device is made a member of the collection and ConfigMgr is instructed to update the collection membership information. Following the update of the collection membership, Orchestrator instructs the device to update its client policies. The client is instructed to perform a software update scan and deployment evaluation which starts the installation of the updates.

The Runbook goes into a loop until the device reboots. The Runbook loops again until the client is confirmed as rebooted (when the operating system is available).

The final task the Runbook performs is cleaning up the temporary collection created by the Runbook specifically for this update deployment.

There's more...

This is a basic Runbook to deploy a set of already staged updates to a device, but it lays the foundation for expanding out your process for patching.

Software updates and Automatic Deployment rules

An alternative to creating and maintaining the software updates group manually each month is to use the Automatic Deployment rules in ConfigMgr to automate the selection and download of the updates each month. You can then use a Runbook to extract a list of the new updates, send a notification for review and an approval before initiating the actual update process.

Suppressing alerts and health checking after updating

Take a look at the recipes in *Chapter 6, Creating Runbooks for System Center 2012 Operations Manager Tasks*, to see how suppressing monitoring alerts can fit into your software update automation process. The objective is to suppress alerts during the patching and rebooting of devices. You can also expand on the post update checks to include a full health state analysis, rather than relying on a simple IP ping routine.

Create a safety net

The recipe uses automation to execute a high risk task, patching devices. You can reduce this risk using example virtualization best practices discussed in the recipes in *Chapter 7, Creating Runbooks for System Center 2012 Virtual Machine Manager Tasks*.

Moving to a change control process for software update deployment

The Runbook discussed is simple in principle and also applies to one device at a time. This approach is not typical or practical in production environments. You can expand the automation by integrating the Runbook into your change and service management processes. An example will be to extract the software updates as a list of **Configuration Items** (**CIs**). A change request can be initiated to apply the extracted CIs to a list of servers, for example. On approval by a change board, the updates can be applied to all servers in scope of the change.

Chapter 8, Creating Runbooks for System Center 2012 Service Manager Tasks, provides recipes on integrating change management into the tasks you automate with SCORCH.

System Center 2012 Configuration Manager Integration Pack

The Integration Pack for System Center 2012 SP1 components can be found at:

`http://www.microsoft.com/en-gb/download/details.aspx?id=34611`

The full set of System Center 2012 Configuration Manager activities can be found at:

`http://technet.microsoft.com/en-us/library/hh967525.aspx`

See also

Detailed information for the activities used in this Runbook can be found at:

- Microsoft TechNet - Create Collection activity: `http://technet.microsoft.com/en-us/library/hh967526.aspx`
- Microsoft TechNet - Deploy Software Update activity: `http://technet.microsoft.com/en-us/library/hh967530.aspx`
- Microsoft TechNet - Add Collection Rule activity: `http://technet.microsoft.com/en-us/library/hh967533.aspx`
- Microsoft TechNet - Update Collection Membership activity: `http://technet.microsoft.com/en-us/library/hh967527.aspx`
- Microsoft TechNet - Perform Client Activity activity: `http://technet.microsoft.com/en-us/library/hh967538.aspx`
- Microsoft TechNet - Delete Collection activity: `http://technet.microsoft.com/en-us/library/hh967528.aspx`

Deploying software applications

System Center 2012 Configuration Manager has a new Application Catalog website where users can view and request software for self-installation. This catalog can be configured to require approval for all or specific software before a user can install it. The resulting user request is only presented in the ConfigMgr console. This process requires an administrator to manually launch the console in order to view pending requests.

This recipe will show you how to automate the manual administrative process for handling requests for software. The recipe also integrates the request process with the ITSM team responsible for standard service requests in an organization.

The following diagram shows the defined business process covered in this recipe:

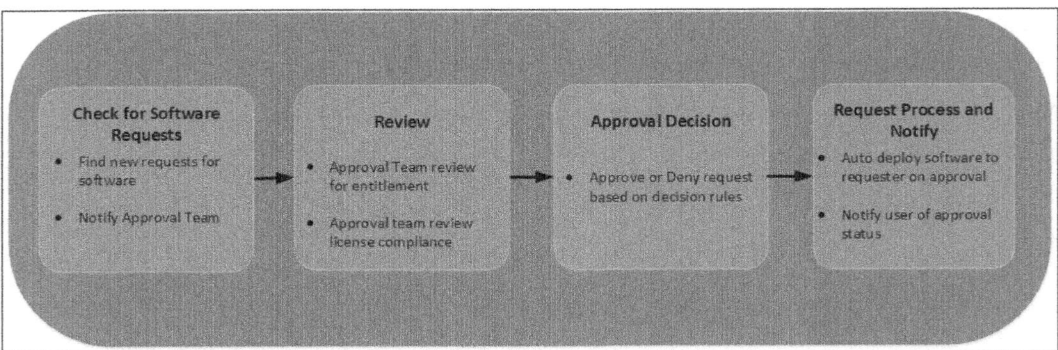

Getting ready

This recipe will leverage System Center 2012 Configuration Manager Service Pack 1. The need for SP1 is due to the support for PowerShell in this release of ConfigMgr.

The ConfigMgr console must be installed on your Runbook server and the `SMS_ADMIN_UI_PATH` system environment variable on your Orchestrator server must point to the folder path of your ConfigMgr console.

How to do it...

This recipe is split into two Runbooks.

The first Runbook will periodically check for new software application requests and notify the Service Desk by e-mail.

The second Runbook takes the resultant approval status input from an analyst (approves or denies the request) for the application and notifies the requesting user. Approving the request will allow the installation to occur at the next ConfigMgr client policy check.

Here are the steps for the Check for Requests Runbook (**2a.Check for Requests**)

1. Navigate to the **Activities** section in the Runbook Designer, select **Scheduling**, and drag a **Monitor Date/Time** activity into the middle pane of the Runbook (the workspace).
2. Right-click on the **Monitor Date/Time** activity and choose rename. Rename it to `Check every 5 minutes`.

3. Right-click on the activity and select **Properties**. Change the interval to every 5 minutes:

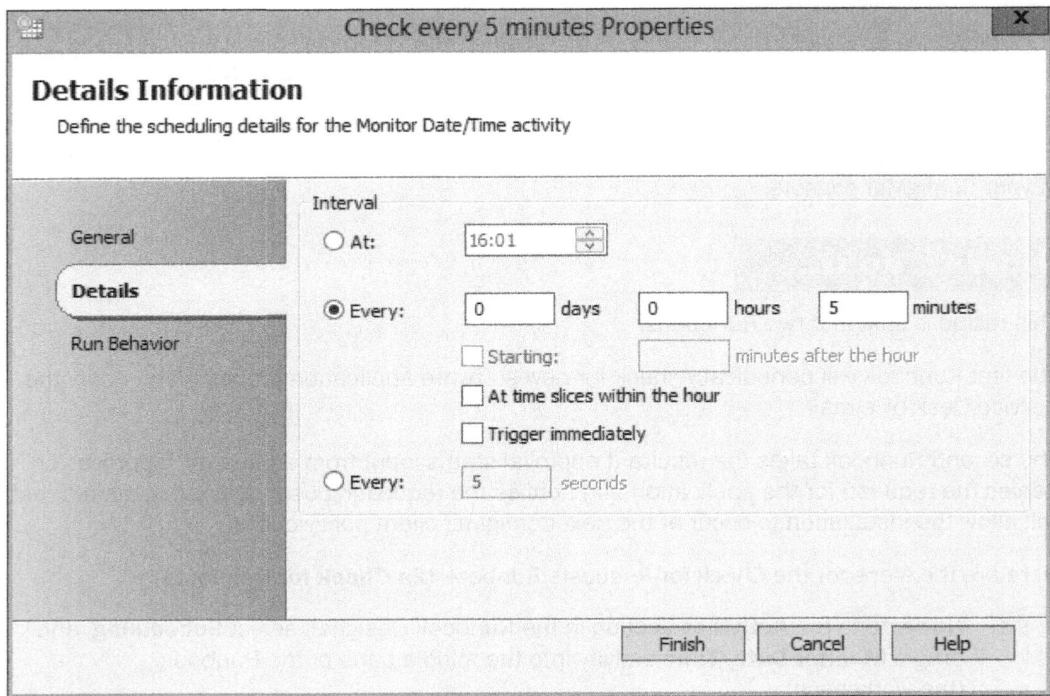

4. Click on **Finish**.
5. Navigate to the **Activities** section, select **System**, and drag a **Run .Net Script** activity to the Runbook next to the **Check every 5 minutes** object.
6. Right-click on the **Run .Net Script** activity and choose rename. Rename it to `Check for requests`.
7. Link the **Check every 5 minutes** activity to the **Check for requests** activity.
8. Double-click on the **Check for requests** activity and change the language type to **PowerShell**.
9. Enter the following PowerShell script into the **Script** box:

```
$ErrorActionPreference = "Stop"
try
{
$RequestedID= @()
$RequestedApp= @()
$RequestedComment= @()
$RequestedUser= @()
```

```
    $Results = C:\Windows\syswow64\WindowsPowerShell\v1.0\
powershell.exe {
import-module ($Env:SMS_ADMIN_UI_PATH.Substring(0,$Env:SMS_ADMIN_
UI_PATH.Length-5) + '\ConfigurationManager.psd1') -force
if ((get-psdrive CAS -erroraction SilentlyContinue | measure).
Count -ne 1) {
new-psdrive -Name "CAS" -PSProvider "AdminUI.PS.Provider\CMSite"
-Root "<ServerFQDN>"
            }
        Set-Location "CAS:"
new-object pscustomobject -property @{
            RequestID = Get-CMApprovalRequest | Where-Object {$_.
CurrentState -eq 1} | Select RequestGuid
            RequestApp = Get-CMApprovalRequest | Where-Object {$_.
CurrentState -eq 1} | Select Application
            RequestComments = Get-CMApprovalRequest | Where-Object
{$_.CurrentState -eq 1} | Select Comments
            RequestUser = Get-CMApprovalRequest | Where-Object
{$_.CurrentState -eq 1} | Select User
            }
        }
$RequestedID+=$Results.RequestID
$RequestedApp+=$Results.RequestApp
$RequestedComment+=$Results.RequestComments
$RequestedUser+=$Results.RequestUser
}
catch
{
    Throw $_.Exception
}
```

Customizing the PowerShell script for your environment

The following section of the script should be customized for your environment, where CAS equals the site code for your site and replace `<ServerFQDN>` with the Fully Qualified Domain Name of your server:

```
if ((get-psdrive CAS -erroraction SilentlyContinue |
measure).Count -ne 1) {
new-psdrive -Name "CAS" -PSProvider "AdminUI.
PS.Provider\CMSite" -Root "<ServerFQDN>"
            }
        Set-Location "CAS:"
```

10. Click on the **Published Data** tab on the left of the screen.
11. Click on **Add** and enter the following details, also shown in the following screenshot:

Name	Type	Variable name
`SCO_RequestedID`	`String`	`RequestedID`
`SCO_RequestedApp`	`String`	`RequestedApp`
`SCO_RequestedComment`	`String`	`RequestedComment`
`SCO_RequestedUser`	`String`	`RequestedUser`

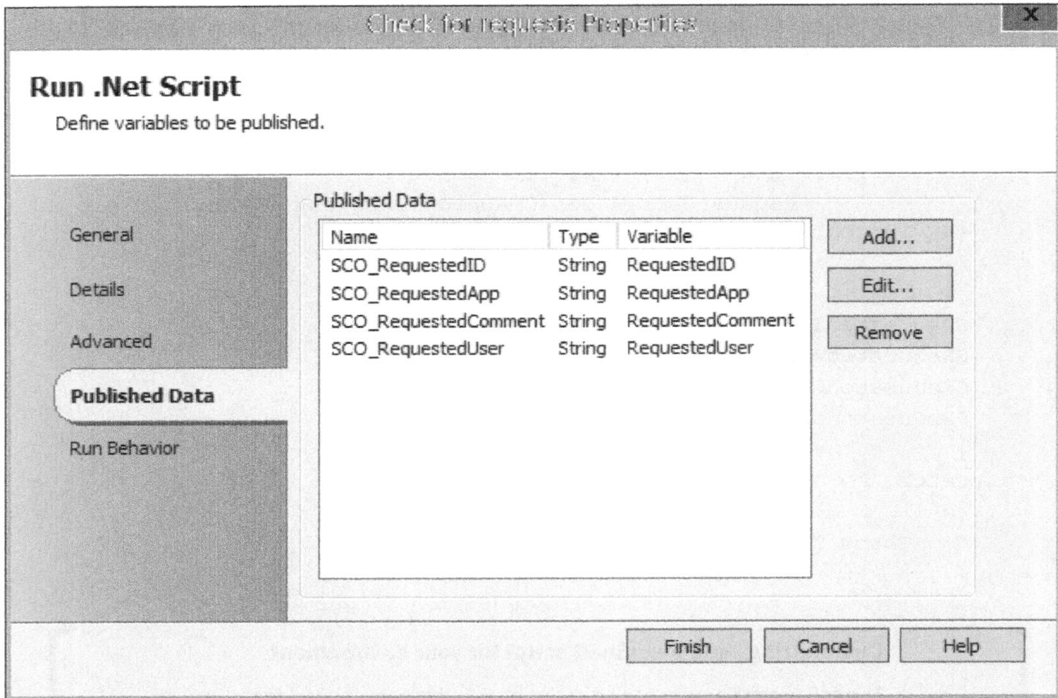

12. Click on **Finish**.
13. Navigate to the **Activities** section in the Runbook Designer, select **Email** and drag a **Send Email** activity to the Runbook next to the **Check for requests** object.
14. Right-click on the **Send Email** activity and choose rename. Rename it to `Send Request Notification`.
15. Link the **Check for requests** activity to the **Send Request Notification** activity.
16. Double-click on the link between **Check for requests** and **Send Request Notification**. Click on the underlined **Check for Requests** word.
17. Select the **SCO_RequestID** from the **Check for requests** activity and click on **OK**.

18. Click on the underlined **equals** word and change it to **does not match pattern**. Click on **OK**.
19. Click on the underlined **value** word and type `^$`.

> This creates a condition that only sends an e-mail when the `SCO_RequestID` published data is not blank, otherwise an e-mail will be sent every 5 minutes.
>
> The `^$` value is interpreted as "blank".

20. Double-click on the **Send Request Notification** activity and provide the following information in the **Details** section:

Name of parameter	Data
`Subject`	New Request for Application
`Recipients`	E-mail address of the Service Desk or relevant member of staff that will deal with these requests.
`Message`	Please review this request for an application. Request ID: Right-click in the field and select **Subscribe** | **Published Data**. Choose **Check for Requests** in the **Activity** field and select **SCO_RequestedID**. Application Name: Right-click in the field and select **Subscribe** | **Published Data**. Choose **Check for Requests** in the **Activity** field and select **SCO_RequestedApp**. User: Right-click in the field and select **Subscribe** | **Published Data**. Choose **Check for Requests** in the **Activity** field and select **SCO_RequestedUser**. Requesters Comment: Right-click in the field and select **Subscribe** | **Published Data**. Choose **Check for Requests** in the **Activity** field and select **SCO_RequestedComment**.
`Attachments`	Uncheck **Task fails if an attachment is missing**.

21. Click on the **Connect** tab on the left of the screen and specify the server that will handle the SMTP connection and the notification sender's e-mail address.

The final Runbook should look like this:

These steps have set up a very simple Runbook that will check for submitted requests from users using the ConfigMgr Software self-service Catalog website.

The next set of steps will create the second Runbook that manages an approval or a denial of a request.

Here are the steps for the Deploy Application Runbook (**2b.Deploy App**):

1. Navigate to the **Activities** section in the Runbook Designer, select **Runbook Control**, and drag an **Initialize Data** activity into the middle pane of the Runbook (the workspace).
2. Right-click on the **Initialize Data** activity and select **Properties**. Add the following parameters in this activity in the **Details** section:

Name of parameter	Data type	Contains information
`RequestID`	`String`	Contains the name of the ConfigMgr app requested.
`ApproveOrDeny`	`String`	Either the word `Approve` or the word `Deny` should be passed to this variable.
`Comment`	`String`	Any comment about the application request and its approval or rejection should be passed to this variable.

3. Navigate to the **Activities** section, select **System**, and drag a **Run .Net Script** activity to the Runbook to the right and above the **Initialize Data** object.
4. Right-click on the **Run .Net Script** activity and choose rename. Rename it to `Approve Request`.
5. Link the **Initialize Data** activity to the **Approve Request** activity.

6. Double-click on the link between **Initialize Data** and **Approve Request**, and click on the underlined **Initialize Data** and choose the **ApproveOrDeny** published data from the **Initialize Data** activity. Click on **OK**.
7. Click on the underlined **value** at the end of the line and type `Approved`.

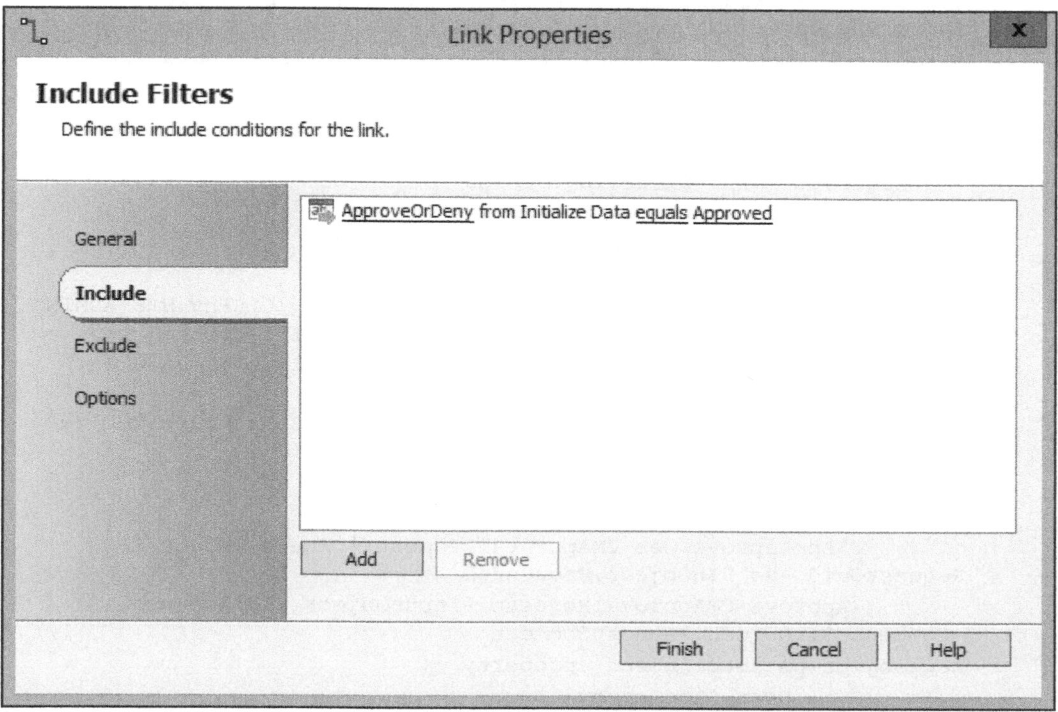

8. Click on the **Options** tab on the left.
9. Change the color to green and the width to 3.
10. Click on **Finish**.
11. Double-click on the **Approve Request** activity and change the language type to **PowerShell**.

12. Enter the following PowerShell script into the **Script** box:

```
$ErrorActionPreference = "Stop"
try
{
$IncomingID= '<Subscribe to RequestID published Data from
Initalize Data>'
$IncomingComment = '<Subscribe to Comment published Data from
Initalize Data>'
$InObj=new-object pscustomobject -property @{
    RequestID=$IncomingID
    RequestComment=$IncomingComment
    }
    $Results = $InObj | powershell {
        $InObject=$input | Select -first 1
import-module ($Env:SMS_ADMIN_UI_PATH.Substring(0,$Env:SMS_ADMIN_
UI_PATH.Length-5) + '\ConfigurationManager.psd1') -force
if ((get-psdrive CAS -erroraction SilentlyContinue | measure).
Count -ne 1) {
new-psdrive -Name "CAS" -PSProvider "AdminUI.PS.Provider\CMSite"
-Root "<ServerFQDN>"
            }
        Set-Location "CAS:"
        $AppApprove=Get-CMApprovalRequest | Where-Object {$_.
RequestGuid -eq $InObject.RequestID}
        Approve-CMApprovalRequest -InputObject $AppApprove
-Comment $InObject.RequestComment
new-object pscustomobject -property @{
            User=$AppApprove.User
            App=$AppApprove.Application
            }


        }
$WhoIsUser=$Results.User.Substring(9)
$App=$Results.App
}
catch
{
    Throw $_.Exception
}
```

Within the PowerShell script, the variables `$IncomingID` and `$IncomingComment` at the top of the script need modifying to capture the values of `RequestID` and `Comment` published data.

Delete the existing text within the ''. Right-click within the '' and choose **Subscribe | Published Data**. Choose the correct published data from the **Initialize Data** activity.

The final script should look like this:

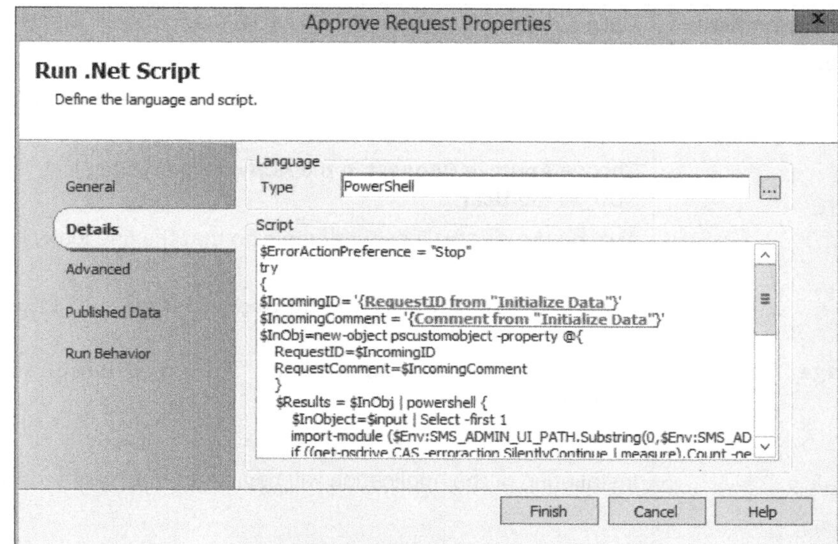

The following section of the script should also be customized for your environment, where `CAS` equals the site code for your site and replace `<ServerFQDN>` with the name of your server:

```
if ((get-psdrive CAS -erroraction SilentlyContinue |
measure).Count -ne 1) {
new-psdrive -Name "CAS" -PSProvider "AdminUI.
PS.Provider\CMSite" -Root "<ServerFQDN>"
            }
        Set-Location "CAS:"
```

13. Click on the **Published Data** tab on the left of the screen.
14. Click on **Add** and enter the following details:

Name	Type	Variable name
`SCO_WhoIsUser`	`String`	`WhoIsUser`
`SCO_App`	`String`	`App`

15. Navigate to the **Activities** section in the Runbook Designer, select **Email**, and drag a **Send Email** activity to the Runbook next to the **Approve Request** object.
16. Right-click on the **Send Email** activity and choose rename. Rename it to `Send Approved Notification`.
17. Link the **Approve Request** activity to the **Send Approved Notification** activity.
18. Double-click on the **Send Approved Notification** activity and provide the following information in the **Details** section:

Name of parameter	Data
Subject	Application Request Approved
Recipients	Click on **Add**. Right-click in the field and select **Subscribe** | **Published Data**. Choose **Approve Request** in the **Activity** field and select **SCO_WhoIsUser**. Append the `@FQDN` for your domain so that the line looks like this example: `{SCO_WhoIsUser from "Approve Request"}@Trustlab.local`
Message	Your request for `{SCO_App from "Approve Request"}` has been approved. Installation of the application will begin automatically shortly. Regards, Your friendly neighborhood Service Desk team. Note: Replace `{SCO_App from "Approve Request"}` by right-clicking in the field and selecting **Subscribe** | **Published Data**. Choose **Approve Request** in the **Activity** field and select **SCO_App**.
Attachments	Ensure that the option for **Task fails if an attachment is missing** is unchecked.

19. Click on the **Connect** tab on the left of the screen and specify the server that will handle the SMTP connection and the e-mail address that the notification e-mail will appear to have come from.

20. Navigate to the **Activities** section, select **System**, and drag a **Run .Net Script** activity to the Runbook next to the right and below the **Initialize Data** object, as shown in the following screenshot:

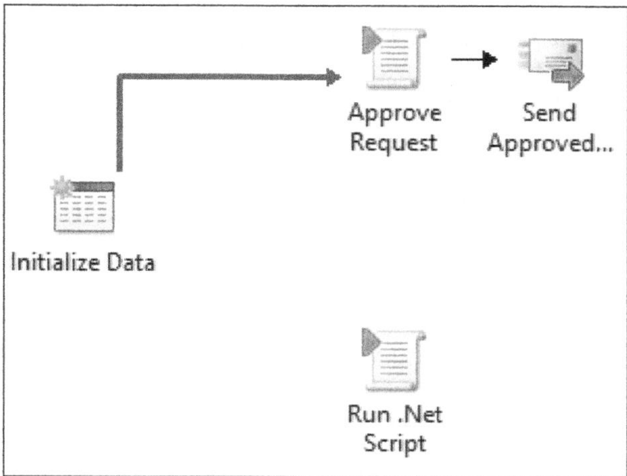

21. Right-click on the **Run .Net Script** activity and choose rename. Rename it to `Deny request`.
22. Link the **Initialize Data** activity to the **Deny Request** activity.
23. Double-click the link between **Initialize Data** and **Deny Request**, and click on the underlined **Initialize Data** and choose the **ApproveOrDeny** published data from the **Initialize Data** activity and click on **OK**.
24. Click on the underlined **value** at the end of the line and type `Denied`.
25. Click on the **Options** tab on the left.
26. Change the color to red and the width to 3.
27. Click on **Finish**.
28. Double-click on the **Deny Request** activity and change the language type to **PowerShell**.

29. Enter the following PowerShell script into the **Script** box:

```
$ErrorActionPreference = "Stop"
try
{
$IncomingID= '<Subscribe to RequestID published Data from
Initalize Data>'
$IncomingComment = '<Subscribe to Comment published Data from
Initalize Data>'
$InObj=new-object pscustomobject -property @{
    RequestID=$IncomingID
    RequestComment=$IncomingComment
    }
    $Results = $InObj | powershell {
        $InObject=$input | Select -first 1
import-module ($Env:SMS_ADMIN_UI_PATH.Substring(0,$Env:SMS_ADMIN_
UI_PATH.Length-5) + '\ConfigurationManager.psd1') -force
if ((get-psdrive CAS -erroraction SilentlyContinue | measure).
Count -ne 1) {
new-psdrive -Name "CAS" -PSProvider "AdminUI.PS.Provider\CMSite"
-Root "<ServerFQDN>"
            }
        Set-Location "CAS:"
        $AppDeny=Get-CMApprovalRequest | Where-Object {$_.
RequestGuid -eq $InObject.RequestID}
Deny-CMApprovalRequest -InputObject $AppDeny -Comment $InObject.
RequestComment
new-object pscustomobject -property @{
            User=$AppDeny.User
            App=$AppDeny.Application
            }

        }
$WhoIsUser=$Results.User.Substring(9)
$App=$Results.App
}
catch
{
    Throw $_.Exception
}
```

Within the PowerShell script, the variables `$IncomingID` and `$IncomingComment` at the top of the script need modifying to capture the values of `RequestID` and `Comment` published data.

Delete the existing text within the ''. Right-click within the '' and choose **Subscribe | Published Data**. Choose the correct published data from the **Initialize Data** activity.

The final script should look like this:

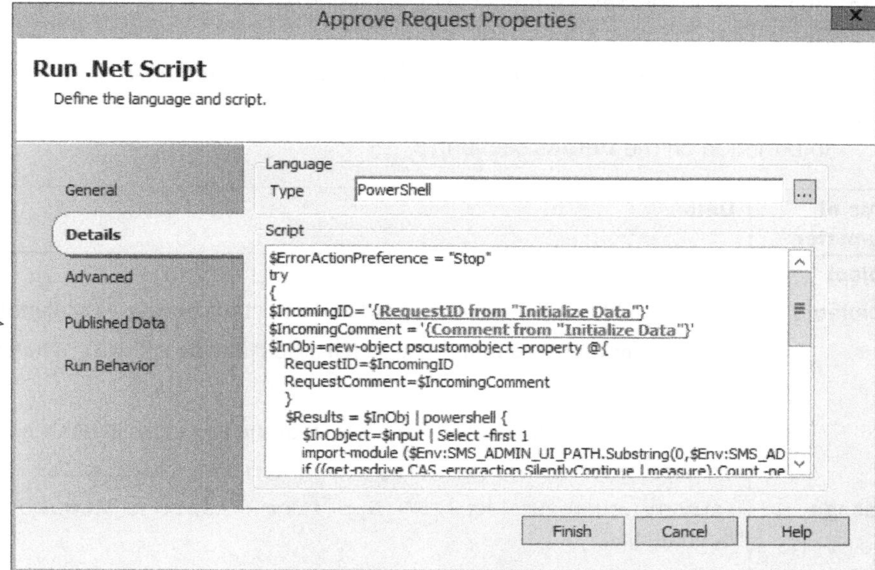

This section of the script should also be customized for your environment, where `CAS` equals the site code for your site and replace `<ServerFQDN>`with the name of your server.

```
if ((get-psdrive CAS -erroraction SilentlyContinue |
measure).Count -ne 1) {
new-psdrive -Name "CAS" -PSProvider "AdminUI.
PS.Provider\CMSite" -Root "<ServerFQDN>"
            }
        Set-Location "CAS:"
```

30. Click on the **Published Data** tab on the left of the screen.

31. Click on **Add** and enter the following details:

Name	Type	Variable name
`SCO_WhoIsUser`	`String`	`WhoIsUser`
`SCO_App`	`String`	`App`

32. Navigate to the **Activities** section in the Runbook Designer, select **Email** and drag a **Send Email** activity to the Runbook next to the **Deny Request** object.
33. Right-click on the **Send Email** activity and choose rename. Rename it to `Send Denied Notification`.
34. Link the **Deny Request** activity to the **Send Denied Notification** activity.
35. Double-click on the **Send Denied Notification** activity and provide the following information on the **Details** section:

Name of parameter	Data
Subject	Application Request Denied
Recipients	Click on **Add**. Right-click in the field and select **Subscribe** | **Published Data**. Choose **Approve Request** in the **Activity** field and select **SCO_WhoIsUser**. Append the `@FQDN` for your domain so that the line looks like this example: `{SCO_WhoIsUser from "Approve Request"}@Trustlab.local`
Message	I'm sorry, your request for `{SCO_App from "Approve Request"}` has been denied. Reason for denial: `{Comment from "Initialize Data"}` Regards, Your friendly neighborhood Service Desk team. Note: Replace `{SCO_App from "Approve Request"}` by right-clicking in the field and selecting **Subscribe** | **Published Data**. Choose **Approve Request** in the **Activity** field and select **SCO_App**. Replace `{Comment from "Initialize Data"}` by right-clicking in the field and selecting **Subscribe** | **Published Data**. Choose **Initialize Data** in the **Activity** field and select **Comment**.
Attachments	Ensure that the option for **Task fails if an attachment is missing** is unchecked.

36. Click on the **Connect** tab on the left of the screen and specify the server that will handle the SMTP connection and the notification sender's e-mail address.

The final Runbook should look like this:

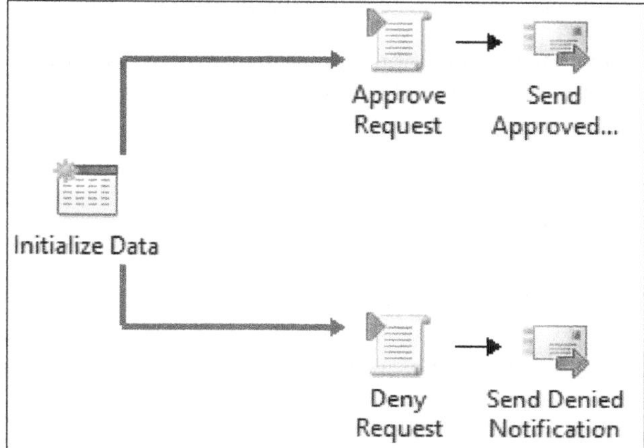

How it works...

This recipe uses two Runbooks to achieve the goal of deploying an application which requires approval.

The first Runbook (**2a.Check for Requests**) runs every 5 minutes. The Runbook executes a PowerShell script to check for pending requests logged by a user using the Software Catalog.

A PowerShell script is used because there is no native activity in the SC 2012 Configuration Manager Integration Pack.

The PowerShell script consists of the following segments:

- Declare the variables:

```
$RequestedID= @()
$RequestedApp= @()
$RequestedComment= @()
$RequestedUser= @()
```

- Spawn a PowerShell v3 32-bit instance and pass a script block to the child PowerShell. Orchestrator currently natively uses PowerShell v2 and the ConfigMgr cmdlets require a 32-bit PowerShell v3 environment.

```
$Results = C:\Windows\syswow64\WindowsPowerShell\v1.0\powershell.
exe {
```

- Import the PowerShell modules using a dynamic path to the Configuration Manager console. This relies on having the `SMS_ADMIN_UI_PATH` system environment variable on your Orchestrator server pointing to the folder path of your console:

```
import-module ($Env:SMS_ADMIN_UI_PATH.Substring(0,$Env:SMS_ADMIN_
UI_PATH.Length-5) + '\ConfigurationManager.psd1') -force
```

- Check for a PowerShell Drive mapping (PSDrive) called **CAS** (the example script uses the site code of the target ConfigMgr site. You must update the script to reflect the site code of your environment).

```
if ((get-psdrive CAS -erroraction SilentlyContinue | measure).
Count -ne 1) {
new-psdrive -Name "CAS" -PSProvider "AdminUI.PS.Provider\CMSite"
-Root "TLSCCMCAS01.Trustlab.local"
            }
        Set-Location "CAS:"
```

- Create a new object and put the output of the Application Requests into it for consumption by the Orchestrator databus.

```
new-object pscustomobject -property @{
            RequestID = Get-CMApprovalRequest | Where-Object {$_.
CurrentState -eq 1} | Select RequestGuid
            RequestApp = Get-CMApprovalRequest | Where-Object {$_.
CurrentState -eq 1} | Select Application
            RequestComments = Get-CMApprovalRequest | Where-Object
{$_.CurrentState -eq 1} | Select Comments
            RequestUser = Get-CMApprovalRequest | Where-Object
{$_.CurrentState -eq 1} | Select User
            }
```

- Output the ConfigMgr data into distinct variables for consumption by the Orchestrator databus.

```
$RequestedID+=$Results.RequestID
$RequestedApp+=$Results.RequestApp
$RequestedComment+=$Results.RequestComments
$RequestedUser+=$Results.RequestUser
```

- The code is wrapped in an error trapping code snippet, so that the errors from the child PowerShell environment can be passed back to Orchestrator for troubleshooting.

```
$ErrorActionPreference = "Stop"
try
{
}
catch
{
    Throw $_.Exception
}
```

The Service Desk, or relevant IT personnel (review team), is sent the information in an e-mail for approving or denying the request.

The second Runbook (**2b.Deploy App**) is used by the Service Desk once they have reviewed the request e-mail to approve or deny the request.

The review team uses the Orchestrator web console to execute the second Runbook which will prompt for the values of `RequestID` (the one sent in the e-mail from the previous Runbook), a comment about the request and either the word `Approved` or `Denied`.

The review team output will be passed as the inputs into a PowerShell script that will either approve or deny the request.

The script is similar to the script in the first Runbook except for the following areas.

Input variables passed to the Runbook pass to the child PowerShell session:

```
$IncomingID= '{RequestID from "Initialize Data"}'
$IncomingComment = '{Comment from "Initialize Data"}'
$InObj=new-object pscustomobject -property @{
    RequestID=$IncomingID
    RequestComment=$IncomingComment
    }
```

We get the request details based on `RequestID` passed into the Runbook. Approve the request and add the comment to the request, as follows:

```
$AppApprove=Get-CMApprovalRequest | Where-Object {$_.RequestGuid -eq
$InObject.RequestID}
Approve-CMApprovalRequest -InputObject $AppApprove -Comment $InObject.
RequestComment
```

A similar thing happens for the deny request using the `Deny-CMApprovalRequest` command instead.

We take the username and remove the domain part of the name to get the `SamAccountName`:

```
$WhoIsUser=$Results.User.Substring(9)
```

In this example, we used a value `(9)` along with the PowerShell command `Substring` to remove the domain part of the returned username. You will need to modify this for your environment.

Substring allows us to output just a part of a string. If only one argument is provided, it is used as the starting position, and the remainder of the string is output. In this example, `Trustlab\` is the starting position of the string which is 9 characters in length. `Substring(9)` returns only the characters after the ninth character in the string back to the `$WhoIsUser` variable.

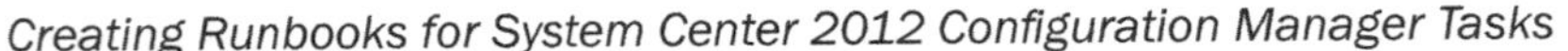

An e-mail is generated to the user explaining that the request has either been approved and will install shortly, or that it is denied with an explanation using the comments provided. This is the returned user from the request.

There's more...

This is a basic Runbook to deploy applications which require approval requested using the Software Catalog in Configuration Manager.

Microsoft Application Approval Workflow Solution Accelerator

If you are also using System Center 2012 Service Manager in your environment, a recommendation would be to look at the Application Approval Workflow Solution Accelerator from Microsoft:

`http://www.microsoft.com/en-us/download/details.aspx?id=29687`

This Solution Accelerator is a collection of Runbooks for Orchestrator, and management packs for Service Manager, that automates the retrieval of application requests from ConfigMgr and creates service requests automatically in Service Manager.

This has the distinct advantage of allowing you to create templates for the applications, define the process workflow for the checking license-compliance, and routing to the relevant people for approval.

Multiple request notification e-mails

The Runbook **2a.Check for Requests** is currently set to gather all pending requests and email the list every 5 minutes. With the Runbook in its basic form you will get an e-mail every 5 minutes for the same requests until they are approved or denied.

A highly-recommend method would be to log the results to an external database and assign a value to indicate that it's been notified and then put an extra step to validate the status of this value before sending an e-mail.

Testing tip

While you're testing this Runbook, do your testing with the denied branch since once a request has been approved you cannot request the same application.

Denying the request will generate the e-mail for testing purposes but, will also allow you to resubmit the test request.

See also

Detailed information for the activities used in this Runbook can be found at:

- Microsoft TechNet – Run .Net Script activity: `http://technet.microsoft.com/en-us/library/hh206103.aspx`
- Microsoft TechNet – Send Email activity: `http://technet.microsoft.com/en-gb/library/hh206081.aspx`
- Microsoft TechNet – Monitor Date/Time activity: `http://technet.microsoft.com/en-us/library/hh225031.aspx`
- Microsoft TechNet – Delete Collection activity: `http://technet.microsoft.com/en-us/library/hh967528.aspx`

Deploying client agents to workgroup devices

System Center 2012 Configuration Manager can easily deploy its client agent to Active Directory joined devices. During and post deployment, these devices can gather client settings from the AD Published Information provided by ConfigMgr.

Installing client agents on non-Domain joined or Workgroup devices is a manual process. You need to be a user with local administrative rights on the device. Additionally, you must specify credentials for the ConfigMgr site share used by the client. You must also specify command line options for the client installation string.

This Runbook will automate the process of connecting to multiple workgroup devices to perform the install with the required switches.

The following diagram shows the defined business process covered in this recipe:

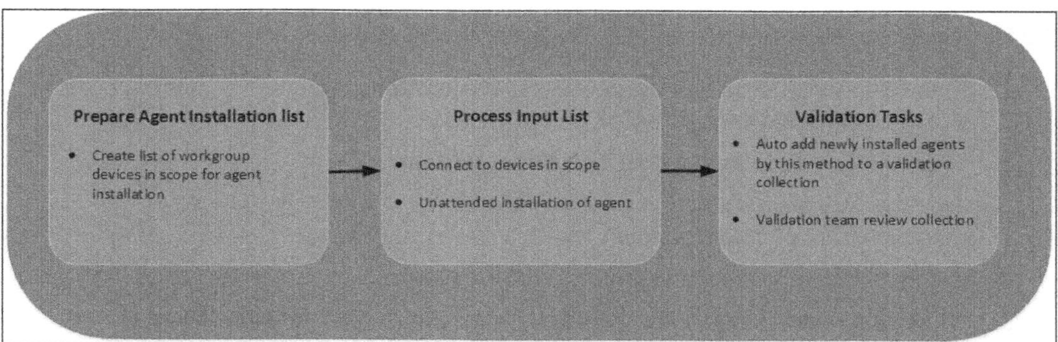

Getting ready

This recipe will leverage System Center 2012 Configuration Manager Service Pack 1.

The need for SP1 is due to the support for PowerShell in this release of ConfigMgr.

The ConfigMgr console must be installed on your Runbook server, and the `SMS_ADMIN_UI_PATH` system environment variable on your Orchestrator server must point to the folder path of your ConfigMgr console.

This recipe assumes that the workgroup devices you are deploying will have the File and Printer Sharing (SMB-In) inbound rule enabled for any firewalls, and the local accounts on the workgroup computer are allowed to have authenticated access to the C$ share.

Since the release of Windows Vista, local account access to administrative shares are restricted. To remove this restriction see the following Microsoft Knowledgebase article: `http://support.microsoft.com/kb/947232`.

Microsoft Sysinternal PSExec is used in this Runbook and must be downloaded from `http://technet.microsoft.com/en-us/sysinternals/bb795533` and copied to the `C:\Windows\System32` directory on the Runbook server.

In preparation for the Runbook, you must create a CSV file containing the workgroup devices in scope of the deployment. The CSV file must also contain their local admin account and password. The file should be in the following format:

```
Device,User,Password
```

You must also create a blank text file for the Runbook to output basic logging information.

The two files should be located in a network share and ensure that the Orchestrator service account has read and write access rights to the share.

For this Runbook we will also be subscribing to Orchestrator custom variables.

The following steps show how to create the required variables:

1. In the Runbook Designer, navigate to the **Connections** explorer tree interface and expand **Global Settings** and click on **Variables**.
2. Right-click on **Variables** and choose **New** | **Variable**.
3. Type the variable `SMSMP` with a value of the FQDN of your ConfigMgr management point. For example, `TLSCCMPRI01.Trustlab.local`.
4. Optionally, provide a description and click on **Finish**.
5. Create another variable called `SMSSITECODE` with a value of your ConfigMgr site code. For example, `PRI`.

How to do it...

The Runbook takes an input from a CSV file which contains a list of devices in scope of the client installation. The Runbook will connect to each device in the list and execute a client agent installation. The client will be approved for the ConfigMgr site post installation.

Here are the steps for the Deploy Workgroup Device Runbook (**3.Deploy Workgroup Device**):

1. Navigate to the **Activities** section in the Runbook Designer, select **Text File Management**, and drag a **Read Line** activity into the middle pane of the Runbook (the workspace).
2. Right-click on the **Read Line** activity and choose rename. Rename it to `Get list of devices`.
3. Double-click on the **Get list of devices** activity and provide the following information in the **Details** section:

Name of parameter	Data
File	Network share and file name location of the input CSV file created ready for this recipe.
File encoding	Click on the ellipsis and choose **Auto** from the list.
Line numbers	Type the following text: `1-END`.

4. Navigate to the **Activities** section in the Runbook Designer, select **System**, and drag a **Run .NET Script** activity next to the **Get list of devices** activity.
5. Right-click on the **Run .NET Script** activity and choose rename. Rename it to **Split Data**.
6. Link the **Get list of devices** activity to the **Split Data** activity.
7. Double-click on the **Split Data** activity and provide the following information in the **Details** section:

Name of parameter	Data
Language Type	PowerShell

Script	`$Device='[Field('{Line text from "Get list of devices"}',',',1)]'`
	`$User='[Field('{Line text from "Get list of devices"}',',',2)]'`
	`$Password='[Field('{Line text from "Get list of devices"}',',',3)]'`
	Replace `{Line text from "Get list of devices"}` with an actual subscription by right-clicking and choosing **Subscribe | Published Data**, and selecting **Line text** from the **Get list of devices** activity on the databus.

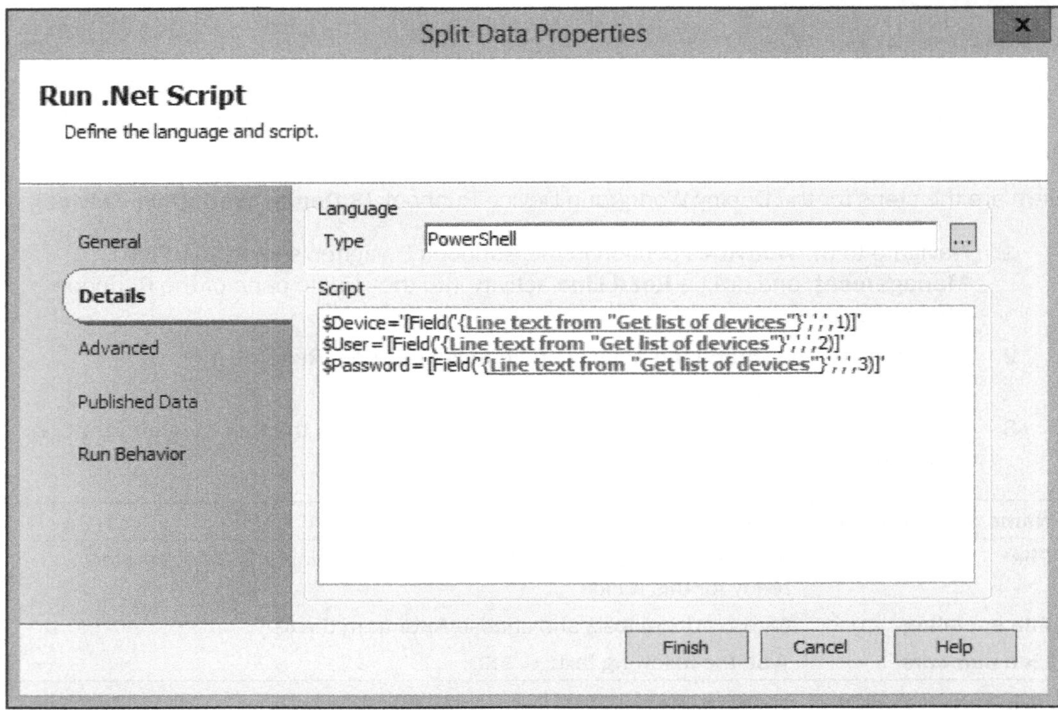

8. Click on the **Published Data** tab on the left of the screen.
9. Click on **Add** and enter the following details:

Name	Type	Variable name
SCO_Device	String	Device
SCO_User	String	User
SCO_Password	String	Password

10. Navigate to the **Activities** section in the Runbook Designer, select **System**, and drag a **Run .NET Script** activity next to the **Split Data** activity.
11. Right-click on the **Run .NET Script** activity and choose rename. Rename it to `Install Client Agent`.
12. Link the **Split Data** activity to the **Install Client Agent** activity.

13. Double-click on the **Install Client Agent** activity and provide the following information in the **Details** section:

Name of parameter	Data
Language Type	PowerShell

Script	`$PSE=PowerShell{`
	`$DeviceName='{SCO_Device from "Split Data"}'`
	`$UserName = "$DeviceName\{SCO_User from "Split Data"}"`
	`$Password = '{SCO_Password from "Split Data"}'`
	`$SMSMP='{SMSMP}'`
	`$SMSSITECODE='{SMSSITECODE}'`
	
	`$SecurePassword = ConvertTo-SecureString -String $Password -AsPlainText -Force`
	`$Cred = New-Object -TypeName System.Management.Automation.PSCredential -ArgumentList $UserName, $SecurePassword`
	
	`New-PSDrive -Name Workgroup -PSProvider FileSystem -Root \\$DeviceName\C$ -Credential $Cred`
	`Copy-Item -Path "\\$SMSMP\SMS_$SMSSITECODE\Client" -Destination Workgroup: -Recurse`
	`$cmdResult = Start-Process -FilePath C:\SysInternals\psexec -ArgumentList "\\$DeviceName -u $UserName -p $Password -s C:\Client\ccmsetup.exe /noservice /source:C:\Client SMSSITECODE=$SMSSITECODE SMSMP=$SMSMP event=fullexport" -NoNewWindow -Wait -PassThru`
	`Remove-Item -Path Workgroup:\Client -Recurse -Force`
	`Remove-PSDrive -Name Workgroup`
	`}`
	Replace the `{SCO_Device from "Split Data"}` with an actual subscription by right-clicking and choosing **Subscribe** | **Published Data** and selecting **SCO_Device** from the **Split Data** activity on the data bus. Repeat this for the `UserName` and `Password` variable with their relevant published data.
	Replace the `{SMSMP}` and `{SMSSITECODE}` text with a subscription to the variables you created earlier by right-clicking and choosing **Subscribe** | **Variable** and selecting the appropriate variable.

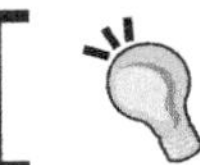

You can right-click in the script area and choose **Expand...** to open a bigger window to enter the PowerShell script into.

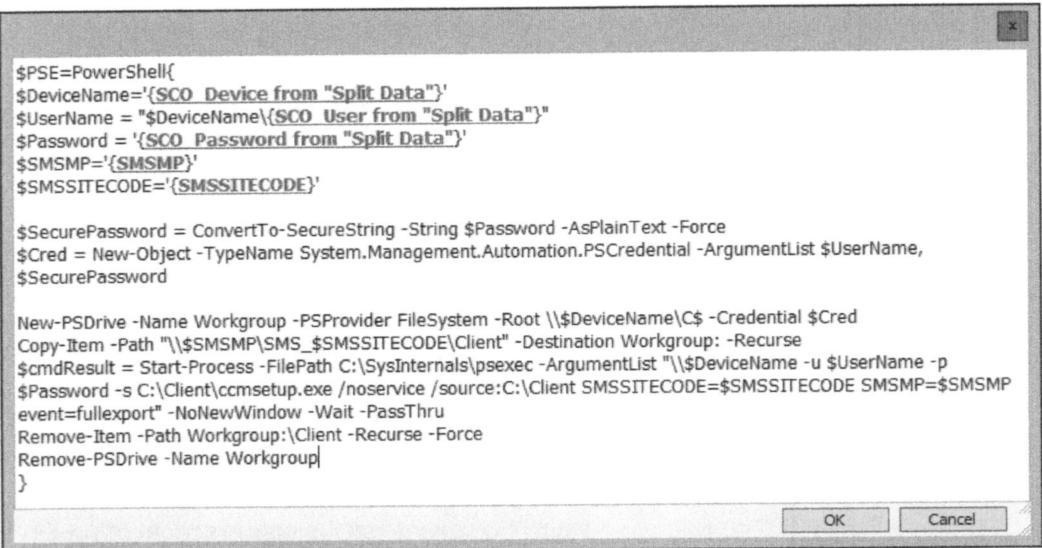

```
$PSE=PowerShell{
$DeviceName='{SCO_Device from "Split Data"}'
$UserName = "$DeviceName\{SCO_User from "Split Data"}"
$Password = '{SCO_Password from "Split Data"}'
$SMSMP='{SMSMP}'
$SMSSITECODE='{SMSSITECODE}'

$SecurePassword = ConvertTo-SecureString -String $Password -AsPlainText -Force
$Cred = New-Object -TypeName System.Management.Automation.PSCredential -ArgumentList $UserName,
$SecurePassword

New-PSDrive -Name Workgroup -PSProvider FileSystem -Root \\$DeviceName\C$ -Credential $Cred
Copy-Item -Path "\\$SMSMP\SMS_$SMSSITECODE\Client" -Destination Workgroup: -Recurse
$cmdResult = Start-Process -FilePath C:\SysInternals\psexec -ArgumentList "\\$DeviceName -u $UserName -p
$Password -s C:\Client\ccmsetup.exe /noservice /source:C:\Client SMSSITECODE=$SMSSITECODE SMSMP=$SMSMP
event=fullexport" -NoNewWindow -Wait -PassThru
Remove-Item -Path Workgroup:\Client -Recurse -Force
Remove-PSDrive -Name Workgroup
}
```

14. Click on **Finish**.
15. Navigate to the **Activities** section, select **SC 2012 Configuration Manager** and drag an **Update Collection Membership** activity to the Runbook next to the **Install Client Agent** object.
16. Link the **Install Client Agent** activity to the **Update Collection Membership** activity.
17. Double-click on the **Update Collection Membership** activity and provide the following information in the **Details** section:

Name of parameter	Value
Connection	Pick the ConfigMgr configuration we set up in the preparation of this chapter from the list.
Collection	Click on the ellipsis button and choose **All Systems**.
Collection Value Type	**Name**
Wait for Refresh Completion	**True**
Polling Interval (seconds)	**5**

18. Navigate to the **Activities** section in the Runbook Designer, select **System**, and drag a **Run .NET Script** activity next to the **Update Collection Membership** activity.
19. Right-click on the **Run .NET Script** activity and choose rename. Rename it to `Approve Devices`.

20. Link the **Update Collection Membership** activity to the **Approve Devices** activity.
21. Double-click on the **Approve Devices** activity and provide the following information in the **Details** section:

<table>
<tr><th>Name of parameter</th><th>Data</th></tr>
<tr><td>Language Type</td><td>PowerShell</td></tr>
<tr><td>Script</td><td><pre><code>$ErrorActionPreference = "Stop"
try
{
$Device= '{SCO_Device from "Split Data"}'
$SMSMP='{SMSMP}'
$SMSSITECODE='{SMSSITECODE}'

$InObj=new-object pscustomobject -property @{
    Device=$Device
    SMSSITECODE=$SMSSITECODE
    SMSMP=$SMSMP
    }
    $Results = $InObj | C:\Windows\syswow64\
WindowsPowerShell\v1.0\powershell.exe {
        $InObject=$input | Select -first 1
        import-module ($Env:SMS_ADMIN_UI_PATH.
Substring(0,$Env:SMS_ADMIN_UI_PATH.Length-5) + '\
ConfigurationManager.psd1') -force
        if ((get-psdrive $InObject.SMSSITECODE
-erroraction SilentlyContinue | measure).Count -ne
1) {
            new-psdrive -Name $InObject.SMSSITECODE
-PSProvider "AdminUI.PS.Provider\CMSite" -Root
$InObject.SMSMP
            }
        $drive=$InObject.SMSSITECODE+":"
        Set-Location $Drive
        Approve-CMDevice -DeviceName $InObject.
Device
        }
}
catch
{
    Throw $_.Exception
}</code></pre>
Replace <code>{SCO_Device from "Split Data"}</code> with an actual subscription by right-clicking and choosing Subscribe | Published Data, and selecting SCO_Device from the Split Data activity on the data bus.
Replace the <code>{SMSMP}</code> and <code>{SMSSITECODE}</code> text with a subscription to the variables you created earlier by right-clicking and choosing Subscribe | Variable and selecting the appropriate variable. </td></tr>
</table>

22. Navigate to the **Activities** section in the Runbook Designer, select **Text File Management**, and drag an **Append Line** activity next to the **Approve Devices** activity.
23. Right-click on the **Append Line** activity and choose rename. Rename it to `Log Success`.
24. Link the **Approve Devices** activity to the **Log Success** activity.
25. Double-click on the **Log Success** activity and provide the following information in the **Details** section:

Name of parameter	Data
File	Network share and filename location of the output logfile created in preparation for this recipe.
File encoding	Click on the ellipsis (**...**) and choose **Auto** from the list.
Text	-- PC {`SCO_Device from "Split Data"`} Installed ConfigMgr Client and is Approved. Replace {`SCO_Device from "Split Data"`} with an actual subscription by right-clicking and choosing **Subscribe** | **Published Data**, and selecting **SCO_Device** from the **Split Data** activity on the data bus.

26. Navigate to the **Activities** section in the Runbook Designer, select **Text File Management**, and drag an **Append Line** activity below the **Install Client Agent** activity,
27. Right-click on the **Append Line** activity and choose rename. Rename it to `Log Failed`.
28. Link the **Install Client Agent** activity to the **Log Failed** activity.
29. Double-click the link between **Install Client Agent** and **Log Failed**, and click on the underlined word **success** at the end of the line.
30. Uncheck **success** and check **warning** and **failed**. Click on **OK**.
31. Click on the **Options** tab on the left.
32. Change the color to red and increase the width to 3.
33. Click on **Finish**.

34. Double-click on the **Log Failed** activity and provide the following information in the **Details** section:

Name of parameter	Data
File	Network share and filename location of the output logfile created ready for this recipe.
File encoding	Click on the ellipsis (**...**) button and choose **Auto** from the list.
Text	-- PC `{SCO_Device from "Split Data"}` Failed to install Client. Replace `{SCO_Device from "Split Data"}` with an actual subscription by right-clicking and choosing **Subscribe | Published Data**, and selecting **SCO_Device** from the **Split Data** activity on the databus.

The final Runbook, **3.Deploy Workgroup Device**, should look like this:

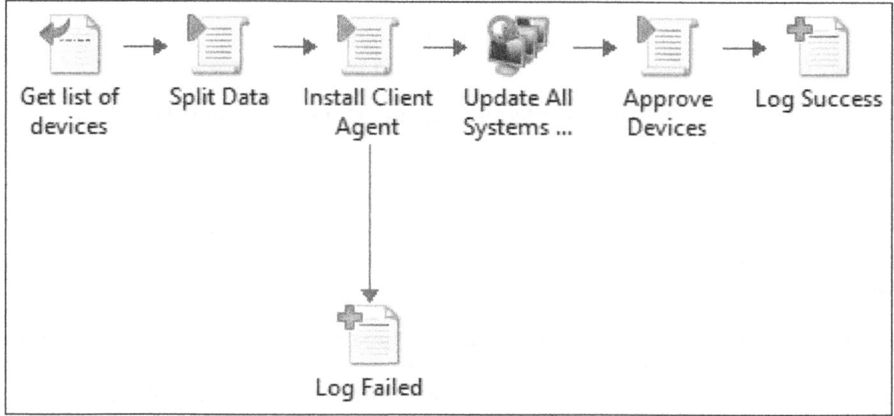

How it works...

This recipe starts by reading in the list of workgroup devices with their associated administrative usernames and password input from the CSV file.

The Split Data PowerShell script splits each line into three separate variables based on the comma separator.

The Install Client Agent script uses the three CSV input variables and the pre-created Orchestrator variables for the Site Code and FQDN of the Management Server in this section:

```
$DeviceName='{SCO_Device from "Split Data"}'
$UserName = "$DeviceName\{SCO_User from "Split Data"}"
$Password = '{SCO_Password from "Split Data"}'
$SMSMP='{SMSMP}'
$SMSSITECODE='{SMSSITECODE}'
```

The script converts the credentials into PowerShell credential objects and passes these into the New-PSDrive command, which mounts the workgroup C$ share as a PowerShell drive called workgroup:

```
$SecurePassword = ConvertTo-SecureString -String $Password
-AsPlainText -Force
$Cred = New-Object -TypeName System.Management.Automation.PSCredential
-ArgumentList $UserName, $SecurePassword
New-PSDrive -Name Workgroup -PSProvider FileSystem -Root
\\$DeviceName\C$ -Credential $Cred
```

The `Copy-Item` command is used to copy the ConfigMgr client install files to the workgroup device:

```
Copy-Item -Path "\\$SMSMP\SMS_$SMSSITECODE\Client" -Destination
Workgroup: -Recurse
```

The PSExec command starts the installation on the remote host. The process does not run as a service so we can wait for it to complete. The process uses the source files on the workgroup device that we copied and uses the Management Point and Site Code for the installation configuration.

```
$cmdResult = Start-Process -FilePath C:\SysInternals\psexec -ArgumentList
"\\$DeviceName -u $UserName -p $Password -s C:\Client\ccmsetup.exe /
noservice /source:C:\Client SMSSITECODE=$SMSSITECODE SMSMP=$SMSMP
event=fullexport" -NoNewWindow -Wait -PassThru
```

The next part of the script is a tidy operation to remove the client installation files from the workgroup device:

```
Remove-Item -Path Workgroup:\Client -Recurse -Force
Remove-PSDrive -Name Workgroup
```

The Runbook proceeds to refresh the **All Systems** collection and runs another PowerShell script to approve the clients. The default setting in ConfigMgr does not auto-approve workgroup clients, hence this step.

The following command in the script handles the approval, using the input variable as the device name:

```
Approve-CMDevice -DeviceName $InObject.Device
```

There's more...

This is a basic Runbook to help deploy ConfigMgr agents to workgroup-based devices.

It works on the assumption that the workgroup devices can resolve the FQDN of the ConfigMgr management point server and that the Runbook can resolve the names of the devices supplied in the input CSV file using DNS.

Resolving the FQDN name of the ConfigMgr Management Point

If the Workgroup devices cannot resolve the Fully Qualified Domain Name of the ConfigMgr Management Point server, you must configure an additional step.

The easiest method is to update the hosts file on the workgroup device with the IP and name of the Management Point.

The Install Client Agent PowerShell script could be modified to append a line to the hosts file using the PSDrive mounted using a command such as:

```
Add-Content workgroup:\windows\system32\drivers\etc\hosts "n172.16.1.28
TLSCCMPRI01.Trustlab.local"
```

Why PSExec and not Run Program activity?

Orchestrator has its own version of PSExec which creates a service on a remote device and runs a specified command or program.

During creation and testing of this example Runbook, the Run Program activity was launching the `ccmsetup.exe` under the credentials supplied to access the remote device. Though the credentials have administrative privileges, **User Account Control** (**UAC**) was blocking the `ccmsetup.exe` from executing.

PSExec can be run under the system context which overcomes the UAC blocking (which is what we do in the script).

Split data script

Another option for the splitting of data into variables is a community Integration Pack is available on CodePlex called the *Orchestrator IP for Data Manipulation* by *Charles Joy*.

This IP includes an activity called **Split Fields** that could be used instead of scripting.

`http://orchestrator.codeplex.com/releases/view/83934`

Configuration Manager Client Agent Installation commands

The Configuration Manager agent cannot be installed directly from the MSI file and must be launched from the `ccmsetup.exe` file.

The following URL shows all of the possible command-line properties to help with installations in your environment:

`http://technet.microsoft.com/en-us/library/gg699356.aspx`

See also

Detailed information for the activities used in this Runbook can be found at:

- Microsoft TechNet – Run .Net Script activity: `http://technet.microsoft.com/en-us/library/hh206103.aspx`
- Microsoft TechNet – Update Collection Membership activity: `http://technet.microsoft.com/en-us/library/hh967527.aspx`
- Microsoft TechNet – Read Line activity: `http://technet.microsoft.com/en-us/library/hh206041.aspx`
- Microsoft TechNet – Append Line activity: `http://technet.microsoft.com/en-us/library/hh206072.aspx`

Gathering the client deployment status

This Runbook helps to gather deployment-related information for clients.

The following diagram will show the defined business process covered in this recipe:

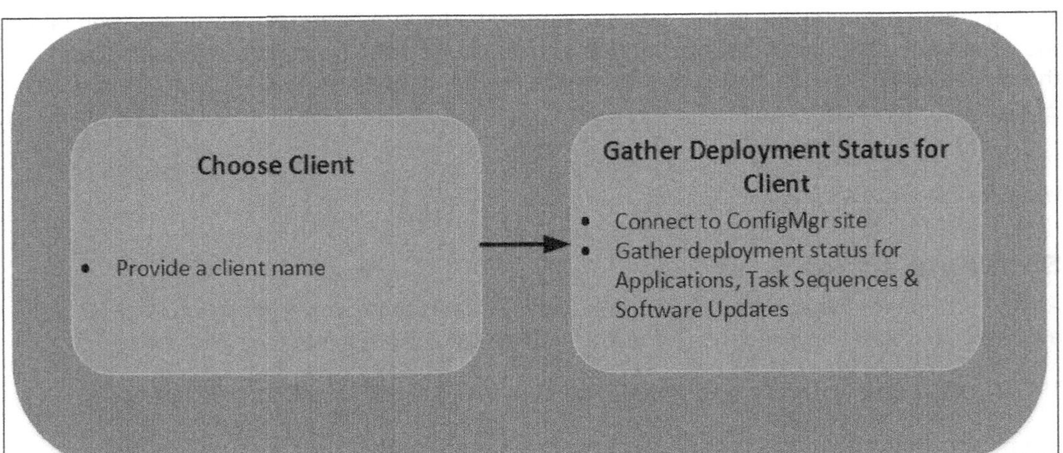

Getting ready

This recipe will leverage System Center 2012 Configuration Manager Service Pack 1.

The need for SP1 is due to the support for PowerShell in this release of ConfigMgr.

The ConfigMgr console must be installed on your Runbook server and the `SMS_ADMIN_UI_PATH` system environment variable on your Orchestrator server must point to the folder path of your ConfigMgr console. The Runbook will also be subscribing to Orchestrator custom variables.

This recipe requires the custom variables to be created in advance. If you haven't already created these variables from the previous recipe, follow the steps in the *Getting ready* section of the *Deploying client agents to workgroup devices* recipe.

How to do it...

The Runbook takes an input of a device name which the Runbook will use to gather the deployment status information and send as a logfile to an administrator.

The following steps will show you how to configure the activities in the Runbook (**4.Client Deployment Status Monitor**) for this recipe:

1. Navigate to the **Activities** section in the Runbook Designer, select **Runbook Control**, and drag an **Initialize Data** activity into the middle pane of the Runbook (the workspace).
2. Right-click the activity and select **Properties**. Add one parameter in this activity in the **Details** section:

Name of parameter	Data type	Contains information
`MachineName`	`String`	Contains the name of the device to gather information for.

3. Navigate to the **Activities** section, select **SC 2012 Configuration Manager**, and drag a **Get Deployment Status** activity to the Runbook next to the **Initialize Data** object to the right and above it.
4. Rename the activity to `Application Deployment Status`.
5. Link the **Initialize Data** activity to the **Application Deployment Status** activity.
6. Double-click on the **Application Deployment Status** activity and provide the following information in the **Details** section:

Name of parameter	Value
Connection	Pick the ConfigMgr configuration we set up in the preparation of this chapter from the list.
Deployment Type	Click on the ellipsis and choose **Application**.

7. Click on **Add** under **Filters** section and choose the following settings:

Name	Relation	Value
MachineName	**Equals**	Right-click and select **Subscribe** | **Published Data**. Select **MachineName** from the **Initialize Data** activity.

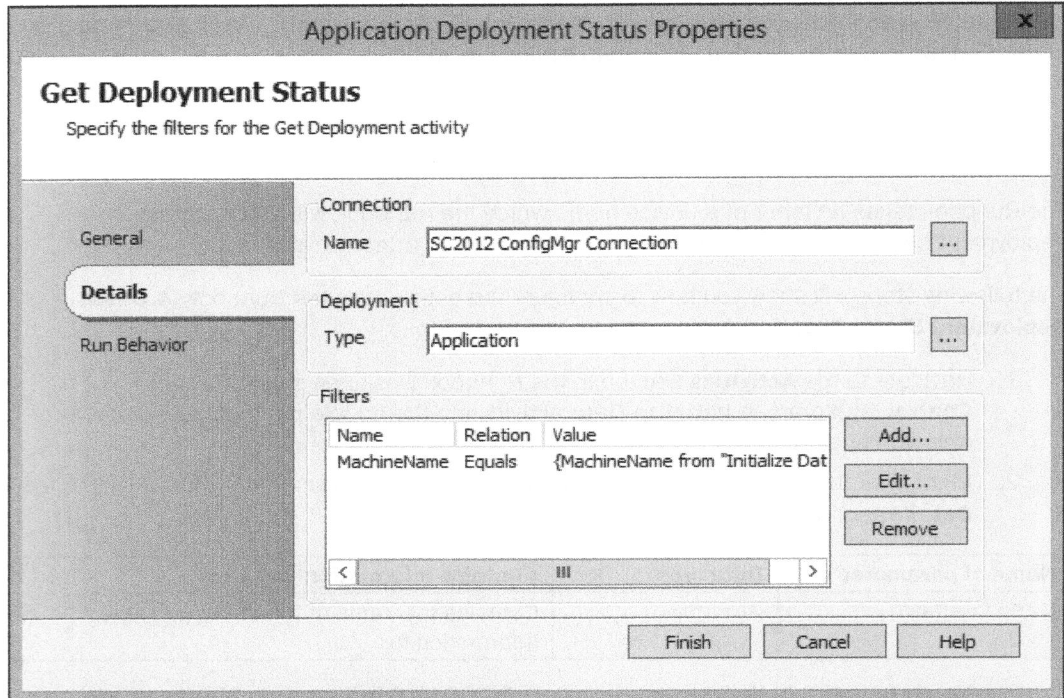

8. Click on **Finish**.
9. Navigate to the **Activities** section in the Runbook Designer, select **System**, and drag a **Run .NET Script** activity next to the **Initialize Data** activity.
10. Right-click on the **Run .NET Script** activity and choose rename. Rename it to `Get ResourceID`.
11. Link the **Initialize Data** activity to the **Get ResourceID** activity.

12. Double-click on the **Get ResourceID** activity and provide the following information in the **Details** section:

<table>
<tr><th>Name of parameter</th><th>Data</th></tr>
<tr><td>Language Type</td><td><code>PowerShell</code></td></tr>
<tr><td>Script</td><td><pre>
$ErrorActionPreference = "Stop"
try
{
$Device= '{MachineName from "Initialize Data"}'
$SMSSITECODE='{SMSSITECODE}'
$SMSMP='{SMSMP}'

$InObj=new-object pscustomobject -property @{
    Device=$Device
    SMSSITECODE=$SMSSITECODE
    SMSMP=$SMSMP
    }
    $Results = $InObj | C:\Windows\syswow64\
WindowsPowerShell\v1.0\powershell.exe {
        $InObject=$input | Select -first 1
        import-module ($Env:SMS_ADMIN_UI_PATH.
Substring(0,$Env:SMS_ADMIN_UI_PATH.Length-5) + '\
ConfigurationManager.psd1') -force
        if ((get-psdrive $InObject.SMSSITECODE
-erroraction SilentlyContinue | measure).Count -ne
1) {
            new-psdrive -Name $InObject.
SMSSITECODE -PSProvider "AdminUI.PS.Provider\
CMSite" -Root $InObject.SMSMP
            }
        $drive=$InObject.SMSSITECODE+":"
        Set-Location $Drive
        get-cmdevice -Name $InObject.Device
        }
$ResourceID=$Results.ResourceID
$ResourceID
}
catch
{
    Throw $_.Exception
}
</pre>
Replace the <code>{MachineName from "Initialize Data"}</code> with an actual subscription by right-clicking and choosing Subscribe | Published Data, and selecting MachineName from the Initialize Data activity on the databus.

Replace the <code>{SMSSITECODE}</code> and <code>{SMSMP}</code> text by right-clicking, choosing Subscribe | Variable, and selecting the relevant variables.</td></tr>
</table>

13. Click on the **Published Data** tab on the left of the screen.
14. Click on **Add** and enter the following details:

Name	Type	Variable name
`SCO_ResourceID`	`String`	`ResourceID`

15. Click on **Finish**.

At this point in the Runbook we are creating multiple parallel tracks. The next step will add another activity which will give you three activities that will be linked to the **Initialize Data** activity, and all three activities will be executed in parallel when the Runbook is executed.

16. Navigate to the **Activities** section, select **SC 2012 Configuration Manager**, and drag a **Get Deployment Status** activity to the Runbook next to the **Initialize Data** object to the right and below it.
17. Rename the activity to `Software Update Deployment Status`.
18. Link the **Initialize Data** activity to the **Software Update Deployment Status** activity.
19. Double-click on the **Software Update Deployment Status** activity and provide the following information in the **Details** section:

Name of parameter	Value
Connection	Pick the ConfigMgr configuration we set up in the preparation of this chapter from the list.
Deployment Type	Click on the ellipsis and choose **Software Update**.

20. Click on **Add** next to the **Filters** section and choose the following settings:

Name	Relation	Value
DeviceName	**Equals**	Right-click and choose **Subscribe** | **Published Data**. Select **MachineName** from the **Initialize Data** activity.

21. Click on **Finish**. The Runbook should look like this:

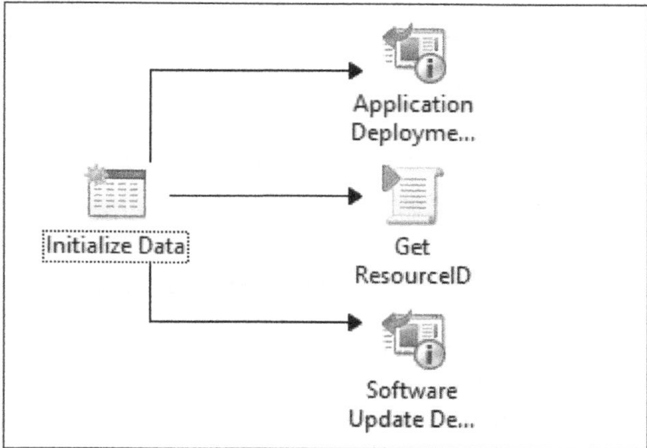

22. Navigate to the **Activities** section, select **SC 2012 Configuration Manager**, and drag a **Get Deployment Status** activity to the Runbook next to the **Get ResourceID** object.
23. Rename the activity to `Task Sequence Deployment Status`.
24. Link the **Get ResourceID** activity to the **Task Sequence Deployment Status** activity.
25. Double-click on the **Task Sequence Deployment Status** activity and provide the following information in the **Details** section:

Name of parameter	Value
Connection	Pick the ConfigMgr configuration we set up in the preparation of this chapter from the list.
Deployment Type	Click on the ellipsis and choose **Task Sequence**.

26. Click on **Add** under the **Filters** section and choose the following settings:

Name	Relation	Value
ResourceID	**Equals**	Right-click and choose **Subscribe** | **Published Data**. Select **SCO_ResourceID** from the **Get ResourceID** activity.

27. Click on **Finish**.
28. Navigate to the **Activities** section in the Runbook Designer, select **System**, and drag a **Run .NET Script** activity next to the **Task Sequence Deployment Status** activity.
29. Right-click on the **Run .NET Script** activity and choose rename. Rename it to `Get TS Name`.
30. Link the **Task Sequence Deployment Status** activity to the **Get TS Name** activity.

31. Double-click on the **Get TS Name** activity and provide the following information in the **Details** section:

Name of parameter	Data
Language Type	**PowerShell**
Script	(see below)

```
$ErrorActionPreference = "Stop"
try
{
$PackID= '{AdvertisementID from "Task Sequence Deployment
Status"}'
$SMSSITECODE='{SMSSITECODE}'
$SMSMP='{SMSMP}'
$InObj=new-object pscustomobject -property @{
    PackageID=$PackID
    SMSSITECODE=$SMSSITECODE
    SMSMP=$SMSMP
    }
    $Results = $InObj | C:\Windows\syswow64\
WindowsPowerShell\v1.0\powershell.exe {
        $InObject=$input | Select -first 1
        import-module ($Env:SMS_ADMIN_UI_PATH.
Substring(0,$Env:SMS_ADMIN_UI_PATH.Length-5) + '\
ConfigurationManager.psd1') -force
        if ((get-psdrive $InObject.SMSSITECODE
-erroraction SilentlyContinue | measure).Count -ne 1) {
            new-psdrive -Name $InObject.SMSSITECODE
-PSProvider "AdminUI.PS.Provider\CMSite" -Root $InObject.
SMSMP
            }
        $drive=$InObject.SMSSITECODE+":"
        Set-Location $Drive
        Get-CMTaskSequence -PackageId $InObject.PackageID
        }
$TSName=$Results.Name
$TSName
}
catch
{
    Throw $_.Exception
}
```

Replace `{MachineName from "Initialize Data"}` with an actual subscription by right-clicking and choosing **Subscribe** | **Published Data**, and selecting **MachineName** from the **Initialize Data** activity on the databus.

Replace the `{SMSSITECODE}` and `{SMSMP}` text by right-clicking, choosing **Subscribe** | **Variable**, and selecting the relevant variables.

32. Click on the **Published Data** tab on the left of the screen.
33. Click on **Add** and enter the following details:

Name	**Type**	**Variable name**
SCO_TSName	String	TSName

34. Click on **Finish**.
35. Navigate to the **Activities** section in the Runbook Designer, select **Text File Management**, and drag an **Append Line** activity next to the **Application Deployment Status** activity.
36. Right-click on the **Append Line** activity and choose rename. Rename it to `App Log`.
37. Link the **Application Deployment Status** activity to the **App Log** activity.
38. Double-click on the **App Log** activity and provide the following information in the **Details** section:

Name of parameter	**Data**
File	Network share and filename location of the output logfile created ready for this recipe.
File encoding	Click on the ellipsis (**...**) and choose **Auto** from the list.
Text	------------------------ Application Deployment Details Application: {`AppName from "Application Deployment Status`} App Status: {`StatusType from "Application Deployment Status`} Compliance State: {`ComplianceState from "Application Deployment Status`} Enforcement State: {`Enforcement State from "Application Deployment Status`} ------------------------ Replace the references above with an actual subscription by right-clicking and choosing **Subscribe** | **Published Data**, and selecting relevant data from the **Application Deployment Status** activity.

39. Click on **Finish**.
40. Navigate to the **Activities** section in the Runbook Designer, select **Text File Management**, and drag an **Append Line** activity next to the **Get TS Name** activity.

41. Right-click on the **Append Line** activity and choose rename. Rename it to `Task Log`.
42. Link the **Get TS Name** activity to the **Task Log** activity.
43. Double-click on the new link, choose the **Options** tab, change the **Trigger delay** value to 10, and click on **Finish**.
44. Double-click on the **Task Log** activity and provide the following information in the **Details** section:

Name of parameter	Data
File	Network share and filename location of the output logfile created ready for this recipe.
File encoding	Click on the ellipsis and choose **Auto** from the list.

Text	------------------------------------
	Task Sequence Detail
	
	Advertisment ID:
	`{AdvertisementID from "Task Sequence Deployment Status"}`
	
	Task Sequence Name:
	`{SCO_TSName from "Get TS Name"}`
	
	Last Status Time:
	`{LastStateTime from "Task Sequence Deployment Status"}`
	
	Last State:
	`{LastStateName from "Task Sequence Deployment Status"}`
	
	Last Acceptance Message Name:
	`{LastAcceptanceMessageIDName from "Task Sequence Deployment Status"}`
	------------------------------------ 	
	
	Replace the references above with an actual subscription by right-clicking, choosing **Subscribe** | **Published Data**, and selecting relevant data from the **Task Sequence Deployment Status** activity.

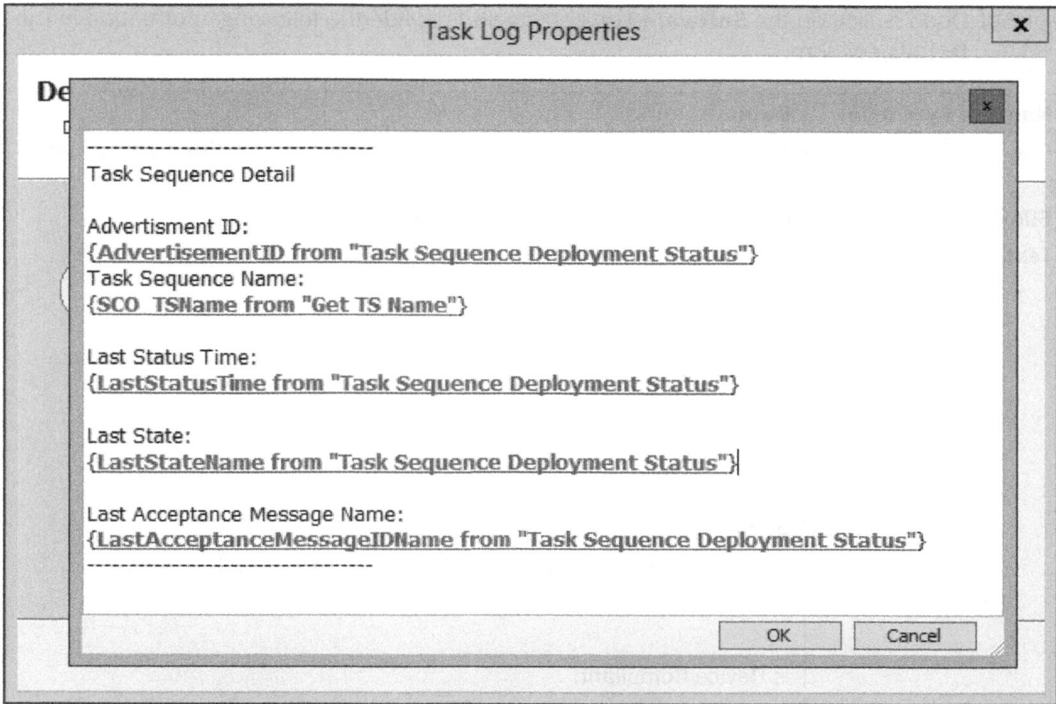
Task Log Properties

Task Sequence Detail
Advertisment ID:
{AdvertisementID from "Task Sequence Deployment Status"}
Task Sequence Name:
{SCO_TSName from "Get TS Name"}
Last Status Time:
{LastStatusTime from "Task Sequence Deployment Status"}
Last State:
{LastStateName from "Task Sequence Deployment Status"}
Last Acceptance Message Name:
{LastAcceptanceMessageIDName from "Task Sequence Deployment Status"}

OK
Cancel

45. Click on **Finish**.
46. Navigate to the **Activities** section in the Runbook Designer, select **Text File Management**, and drag an **Append Line** activity next to the **Software Update Deployment Status** activity.
47. Right-click on the **Append Line** activity and choose rename. Rename it to `Software Log`.
48. Link the **Software Update Deployment Status** activity to the **Software Log** activity.
49. Double-click the new link, choose the **Options** tab, change the **Trigger delay** value to 15, and click on **Finish**.

50. Double-click on the **Software Log** activity and provide the following information in the **Details** section:

Name of parameter	Data
File	Network share and filename location of the output logfile created ready for this recipe.
File encoding	Click on the ellipsis and choose **Auto** from the list.

Text	------------------------------
	Software Update Details:
	
	Assignment Name:
	`{AssignmentName from "Software Update Deployment Status"}`
	
	Status Type:
	`{StatusType from "Software Update Deployment Status"}`
	
	Is Device Compliant:
	`{IsCompliant from "Software Update Deployment Status"}`
	
	------------------------------ 	
	
	Replace the references above with an actual subscription by right-clicking, choosing **Subscribe** | **Published Data**, and selecting relevant data from the **Software Update Deployment Status** activity.

51. Click on **Finish**.
52. Navigate to the **Activities** section in the Runbook Designer, select **Runbook Control**, and drag a **Junction** activity in front of the logfile activities.
53. Link the three logfile activities to the **Junction** activity.
54. Double-click on the **Junction** activity, click on the ellipsis, and choose the **Software Log** activity. Click on **OK** and then click on **Finish**.
55. Navigate to the **Activities** section in the Runbook Designer, select **Email**, and drag a **Send Email** activity to the Runbook next to the **Junction** object.
56. Link the **Junction** activity to the **Send Email** activity.

57. Double-click on the **Send Email** activity and provide the following information in the **Details** section:

Name of parameter	Data
Subject	Client Status Monitoring
Recipients	Click on **Add** and choose an e-mail address for whom to send the e-mail to
Message	Attached logfile with device client status.
Attachments	Click on the **Add** button and provide the path to the logfile used to log the deployment status to.

58. Click on the **Connect** tab on the left of the screen and specify the server that will handle the SMTP connection and the notification sender's e-mail address.

The final Runbook, **4.Client Deployment Monitoring**, should look like this:

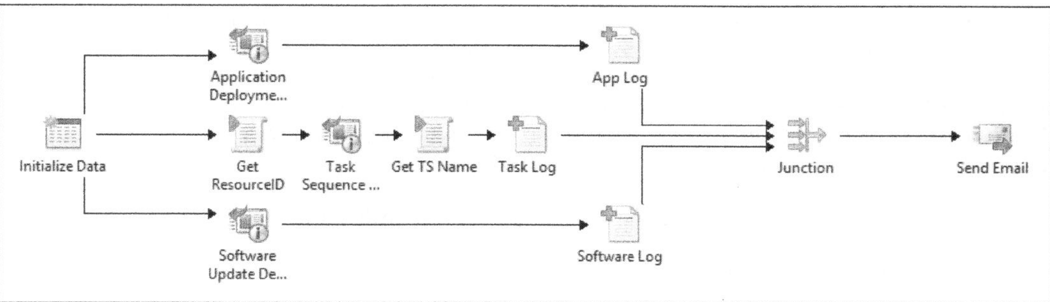

How it works...

The Runbook uses **Get Deployment Status** to query Configuration Manager for the status of specific deployments for the machine name you specify when the Runbook is initiated.

The Runbook gathers the deployment status of:

- Application Deployments
- Task Sequence Deployments
- Software Update Deployments

However, the **Get Deployment Status** activity requires extra steps to get additional relevant information to make it easier to understand.

The PowerShell script executed before the Get Deployment Status activity gets the ResourceID of the machine specified from ConfigMgr. This is due to the fact that the Task Sequence deployment status cannot be queried based on machine name, and must be queried using the ResourceID.

The PowerShell script executed after the **Get Deployment Status** activity gets the Task Sequence name as this is not returned by the activity.

All of this information is then logged to a file and is then e-mailed as an attachment for review. The delay is introduced to prevent a file in use error during the email file attachment action.

There's more...

This is a basic Runbook to help gather the status of Application, Software Updates, and Task Sequence Deployments to devices.

The example data logged can be changed to log whichever data is most relevant for your purposes by subscribing to the relevant published data.

"App/Compliance Status equals 2" means what exactly?

The status value returned by the Runbook is a numeric value. The numeric value requires ConfigMgr knowledge to understand its meaning. A recommended approach is to convert this value into its actual status value (for example, Pending).

You can use the Map Published Data standard activity to achieve this as it allows you to define a source value and its corresponding friendly alias for consumption by the databus. More information can be found here:

`http://technet.microsoft.com/en-us/library/hh225025.aspx`

See also

Detailed information for the activities used in this Runbook can be found at:

- Microsoft TechNet - Run .Net Script activity: `http://technet.microsoft.com/en-us/library/hh206103.aspx`
- Microsoft TechNet - Get Deployment Status activity: `http://technet.microsoft.com/en-us/library/hh967532.aspx`
- Microsoft TechNet - Junction activity: `http://technet.microsoft.com/en-us/library/hh206089.aspx`
- Microsoft TechNet - Append Line activity: `http://technet.microsoft.com/en-us/library/hh206072.aspx`

6

Creating Runbooks for System Center 2012 Operations Manager Tasks

In this chapter, we will provide recipes on how to manage a number of System Center 2012 Operations Manager tasks with Microsoft System Center 2012 Orchestrator Runbooks:

- Checking the health status of a managed device
- Remediating an alert
- Bulk-enabling the maintenance mode

Introduction

This chapter focuses on how to automate examples of the common tasks addressed with **System Center 2012 Operations Manager** (**SCOM**), in the areas of alert management and remediation.

For all recipes in this chapter the requirements are:

- Installed and deployed SCOM integration pack
    - *The installation of integration packs in SCO* is described in the *How to load Integration Packs (IP)* recipe in *Chapter 2, Initial Configuration and Making SCORCH Highly Available*
- A user account with appropriate permissions in SCOM
- Installed the SCOM console on the Runbook Designer computer

The following preparation needs to be performed for all the recipes in this chapter:

1. You must create a connection in SCORCH 2012 Runbook Designer to your SCOM management group.
2. Start SCORCH 2012 Runbook Designer.
3. Choose **Options** in the Menu and click on **SC 2012 Operations Manager**.
4. Click on **Add**.
5. Provide the information specified in the following table:

Name for the Connection Entry	**Descriptive name for this SCOM connection**
Server	Name of your SCOM server
Domain	Domain Name of your environment
User Name	User with appropriate permissions in SCOM
Password	Password of the user
Monitoring Interval - Polling	10 Seconds
Monitoring Interval - Reconnect	10 Seconds

6. Click on **Test Connection** to ensure a successful connection to your SCOM server.
7. Click on **OK**.
8. Click on **Finish**.

As an additional preparation step, you must create three new Runbooks to use with the recipes.

The following steps show you how to create a new Runbook:

1. Right-click on the **Runbooks** heading in the explorer view on the left of the Runbook Designer and navigate to **New | Runbook**.
2. Right-click on the **New Runbook** tab that appears above the main workspace. Navigate to **Rename**, click **Yes** on the **Confirm Check out message box**, and then name the Runbook `Check Health State`.

3. Repeat the preceding steps to create two additional Runbooks and name them: `Remediating an Alert` and `Bulk Maintenance Mode`, as shown in the following screenshot:

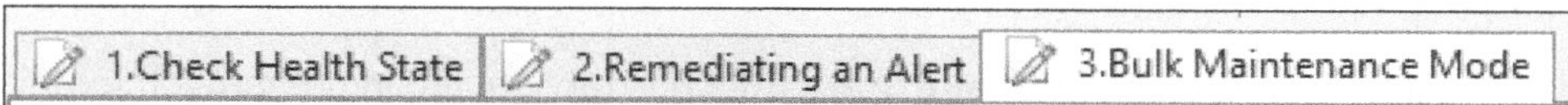

Checking the health status of a managed device

When designing Runbooks to automate processes, it is highly recommended to check the health status of the managed device first. This ensures a health state baseline is established prior to any automation-triggered activities. You can leverage this baseline by ensuring that the automated activities are only triggered on healthy devices. An additional benefit of this approach is that the baseline can assist with troubleshooting, as the state of the device is known before the automation activity is executed.

The following diagram shows the defined business process covered in this recipe:

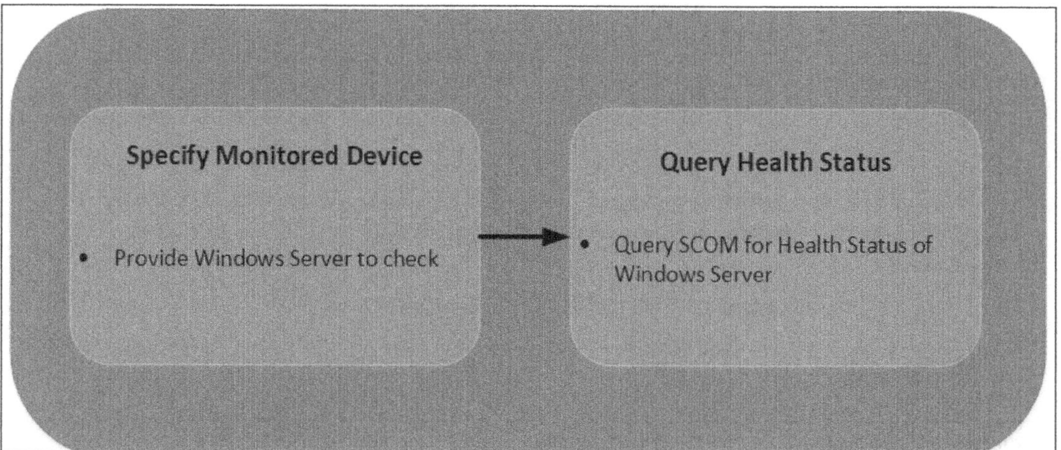

Getting ready

This recipe will leverage SCOM to query the health status of a Windows Server. This requires the SCOM IP to be registered with Orchestrator and deployed to the Runbook Designer as specified in the introduction to this chapter.

You must create the Runbook (**Check Health State**) as part of the chapter preparation.

How to do it...

The following steps will show you how to configure the activities to create the Runbook for this recipe:

1. Right-click on the **Check Health State** Runbook tab created in preparation for this chapter and then click on **Properties**.
2. Click on the **Returned Data** tab and then click on the **Add** button.
3. Provide the following details:

Name	Type	Description
Health State	`String`	Contains health state of the Windows server

4. Click on **OK** and then click on **Finish**.
5. Navigate to the **Activities** section in the Runbook Designer, then click on **Runbook Control**, and drag an **Initialize Data** activity into the middle pane of the Runbook (the workspace).
6. Right-click on **Activity**, navigate to **Properties** | **Add** one parameter (click on **Parameter 1** to make the change) in this activity in the **Details** section using the details below.

Name of parameter	Data Type	Contains information
`ServerName`	`String`	Contains the server name of the Windows Server to query the health status

7. Navigate to the **Activities** section in the Runbook Designer, click on **SC 2012 Operations Manager**, and drag a **Get Monitor** activity next to the **Initialize Data** activity.
8. Link the **Initialize Data** activity to the **Get Monitor** activity.
9. Double-click on the **Get Monitor** activity and provide the following information on the **Details** section:

Property	Value	Description
Connection	SCOM Connection	The connection setup in the preparation for this chapter

10. Click on **Add** under the **Filters** section to add two filters.

Name	Relation	Value
HealthState	**Does not equal**	**Uninitialized**
FullName	**Contains**	**Microsoft.Windows.Computer:**`{ServerFQDN from "Initialize Data"}` Replace `{ServerFQDN from "Initialize Data"}` with a subscription to the ServerName Published Data from the **Initialize Data** activity by right-clicking in the field **Subscribe | Published Data**. Choose **Initialize Data** in the Activity field and select **ServerName**.

11. Navigate to the **Activities** section in the Runbook Designer, click on **Runbook Control**, and drag a **Return Data** activity next to the **Get Monitor** activity.
12. Right-click on the **Return Data** activity, select **Rename**, and rename the activity to **Health State**.
13. Link the **Get Monitor** activity to the **Health State** activity.
14. Double-click on the **Health State** activity and provide the following information on the **Details** section:

Property	Value
HealthState	Right-click in the field **Subscribe | Published Data**. Choose **Get Monitor** in the Activity field and select **HealthState**.

15. Click on **Finish**.

The final Runbook should look like this:

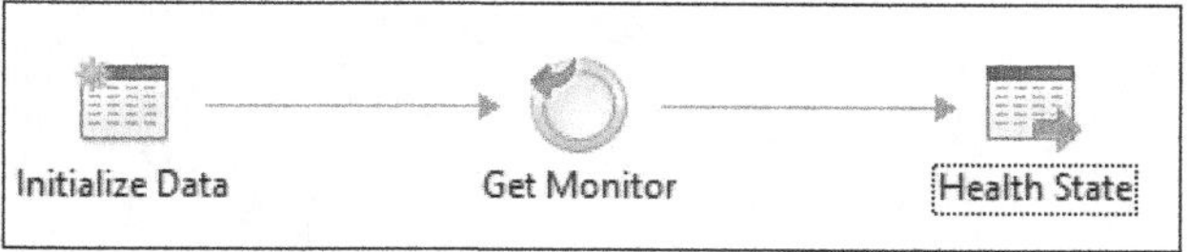

How it works...

This Runbook takes an input of a server name supplied using the Orchestration Web Console and queries the health state for the Windows computer object. Following the query, the health state of the server is passed to the **Health State** activity.

The objective of this Runbook is to provide a useful standalone health check Runbook. This stand-alone Runbook can serve as a prerequisite check activity for Runbooks designed to perform actions on managed server devices.

- Microsoft TechNet – Get Monitor activity from `http://technet.microsoft.com/en-us/library/hh830695.aspx`

Remediating an alert

When an alert is raised in Operations Manager you have two options available to you: either investigate the alert and manually resolve the issue, or preconfigure an auto-recovery rule to attempt a remediation.

This recipe will show you how to expand on the second choice by performing multiple defined remediation steps to resolve the issue using SCORCH. This is automating the initial steps a typical administrator will perform. The advantage over the default SCOM auto-recovery is introducing consistency in the execution by using a SCORCH Runbook.

The following diagram shows the defined business process covered in this recipe:

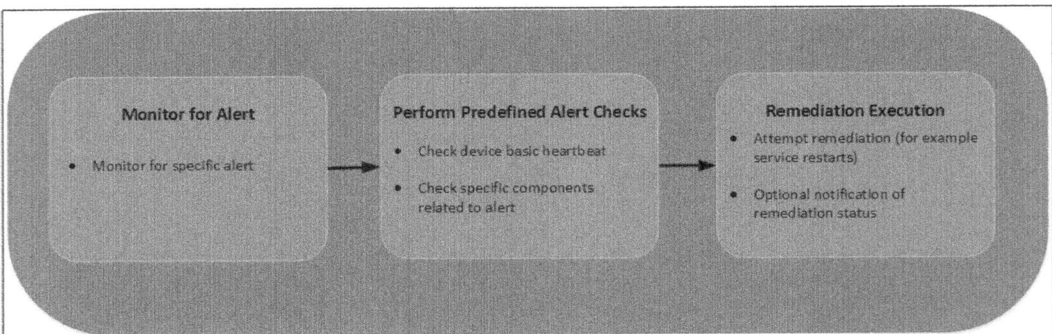

Getting ready

This recipe will leverage SCOM to monitor for a specific alert and then attempt to remediate it using a SCORCH Runbook. This requires the SCOM IP to be registered with Orchestrator and deployed to the Runbook Designer, as specified in the *Introduction* section to this chapter.

You must create the Runbook (**Remediating an Alert**) as part of the chapter preparation.

How to do it...

The following steps will show you how to configure the activities to create the Runbook for this recipe:

1. Navigate to the **Activities** section in the Runbook Designer, click on **SC 2012 Operations Manager**, and drag a **Monitor Alert** activity into the middle pane of the Runbook (the workspace).
2. Double-click on the **Monitor Alert** activity and provide the following information on the **Details** section:

Property	Value	Data
Connection	SCOM Connection	The connection setup in the preparation for this chapter
Trigger	New Alerts	Ensure only **New Alerts** is checked under the **Trigger** section
Filters	Name (click on **Add** under the **Filters** section)	Navigate to **Relation** | **Contains.** Type `IIS 8 Web Site is unavailable` in the **Value** field

3. Navigate to the **Activities** section, click on **Monitoring**, and drag a **Get Computer/IP Status** activity to the Runbook next to the **Monitor Alert** object.
4. Link the **Monitor Alert** activity to the **Get Computer/IP Status** activity.
5. Double-click on the **Get Computer/IP Status** activity and provide the following information on the **Details** section:

Property	Data
Computer	Right-click in the field. Navigate to **Subscribe** | **Published Data.** Choose **Monitor Alert** in the Activity field and select **NetBIOSComputerName**.

6. Click on **Finish**.

7. Navigate to the **Activities** section, click on **Monitoring**, and drag a **Get Computer/IP Status** activity to the Runbook below the **Get Computer/IP Status** object.
8. Link the **Monitor Alert** activity to the **Get Computer/IP Status(2)** activity.
9. Double-click on the link between **Monitor Alert** and **Get Computer/IP Status(2)**, modify the **Get Computer/IP Status returns success**, check **warning** and **failed** by clicking on the word **success**, and uncheck **success**.
10. Right-click on the **Get Computer/IP Status (2)** activity and click on **rename**. Rename the activity to `Ping Loop`.
11. Double-click on the **Ping Loop** activity and provide the following information on the **Details** section:

Property	Data
Computer	Right-click in the field. Navigate to **Subscribe | Published Data**. Choose **Monitor Alert** in the Activity field and select **NetBIOSComputerName**.

12. Right-click on the **Ping Loop** activity and click on **Looping**.
13. Check the **Enable** box under **Looping** and set the **delay between attempts** value to **10**.
14. Click on the **Exit** tab on the left of the screen.
15. Click on the word **Ping Loop** and check the **Show common Published Data** box.
16. Select **Loop: Total Number of attempts** and click on **OK**.
17. Click on the word **Value** and enter the value `36`.
18. Click on **Add** to add another **Ping Loop returns success**.
19. Click on the **Do Not Exit** tab on the left of the screen and click on **Add**.
20. Click on the word **Success,** uncheck the box for **success**, and check **warning** and **failed**.
21. Click on **Finish**.
22. Navigate to the **Activities** section, click on **Runbook Control**, and drag a **Junction** activity to the Runbook to the right of the **Get Computer/IP Status** objects.

23. Link the **Get Computer/IP Status** and **Ping Loop** activities to the **Junction** activity, as shown below:

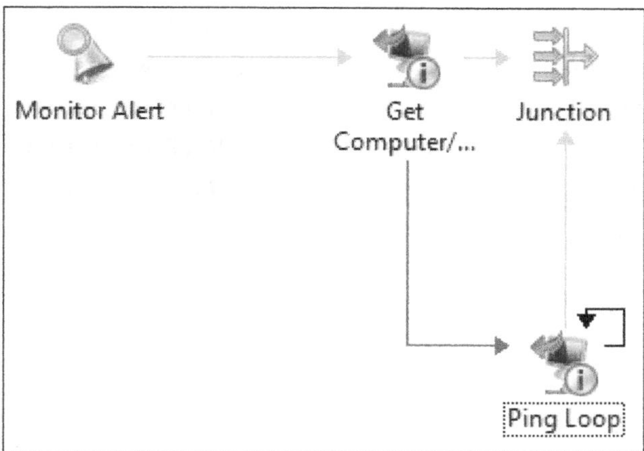

24. Navigate to the **Activities** section, click on **Monitoring**, and drag a **Get Service Status** activity into the Runbook to the right of the **Junction** object.
25. Link the **Junction** activity to the **Get Service Status** activity.
26. Right-click on the **Get Service Status** activity and click on **rename**. Rename the activity to `Get W3SVC Service Status`.
27. Double-click on the **Get W3SVC Service Status** activity and provide the following information on the **Details** section:

Property	**Value**
Computer	Right-click in the field. Navigate to **Subscribe** | **Published Data**. Choose **Monitor Alert** in the Activity field and select **NetBIOSComputerName**.
Service	**World Wide Web Publishing Service**

28. Repeat the preceding steps for the **Get Service Status** activity for four additional activities.

29. Rename the activities and change the service value to the information in the following table:

Activity Name	Service Value
`Get WAS Service Status`	**Windows Process Activation Service**
`Get NetMsmqActivator Service Status`	**Net.Msmq Listener Adapter**
`Get NetPipeActivator Service Status`	**Net.Pipe Listener Adapter**
`Get NetTcpActivator Service Status`	**Net.Tcp Listener Adapter**

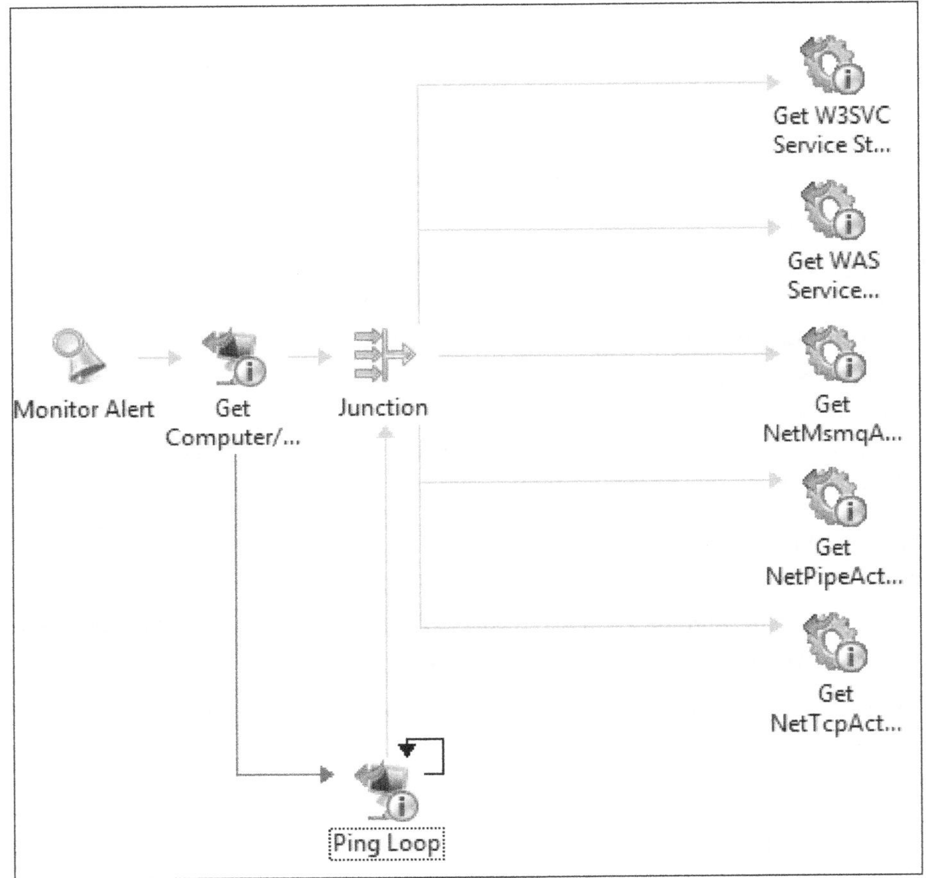

30. Navigate to the **Activities** section, click on **System**, and drag a **Start/Stop Service** activity to the Runbook to the right of the **Get W3SVC Service Status** object.

31. Link the **Get W3SVC Service Status** activity to the **Start/Stop Service** activity.
32. Right-click on the **Start/Stop Service** activity and click on **rename**. Rename the activity to `Start W3SVC Service`.
33. Double-click on the **Start W3SVC Service** activity and provide the following information on the **Details** section:

Property	Value
Action	**Start Service**
Computer	Right-click in the field. Navigate to **Subscribe | Published Data**. Choose **Monitor Alert** in the Activity field and select **NetBIOSComputerName**.
Service	Right-click in the field. Navigate to **Subscribe | Published Data**. Choose **Get W3SVC Service Status** in the Activity field and select **Service display name**.

34. Repeat the preceding steps you used for the **Start W3SVC Service** activity for the other services.
35. Rename the activities and change the service value to the information in the following table:

Activity Name	Service Value
`Start WAS Service`	Right-click in the field. Navigate to **Subscribe | Published Data**. Choose **Get WAS Service Status** in the Activity field and select **Service display name**.
`StartNetMsmqActivator Service`	Right-click in the field. Navigate to **Subscribe | Published Data**. Choose **Get NetMsmqActivator Service Status** in the Activity field and select **Service display name**.
`StartNetPipeActivator Service`	Right-click in the field. Navigate to **Subscribe | Published Data**. Choose **Get NetPipeActivatorService Status** in the Activity field and select **Service display name**.
`StartNetTcpActivator Service`	Right-click in the field. Navigate to **Subscribe | Published Data**. Choose **Get NetTcpActivator Service Status** in the Activity field and select **Service display name**.

36. Double-click on each of the links between the **Get Service Status** activity and the **Start Service** activity.

37. Click on the **Get Service Status** text, click on **Service Status**, and then click on OK.
38. Click on the text **Value**, type `Stopped` as the value and then click on **OK**.
39. Click on **Finish**.

The final Runbook should look like this:

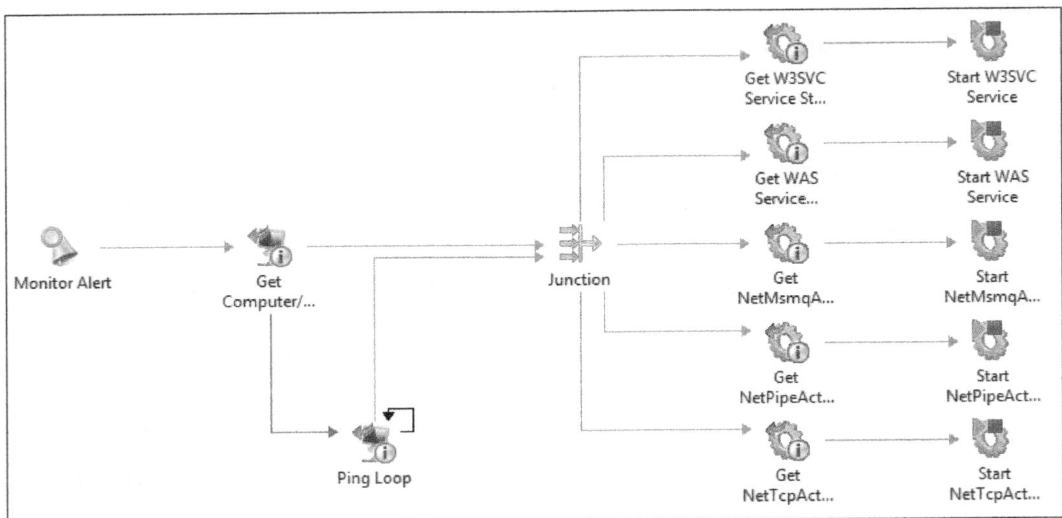

How it works...

This Runbook monitors for alerts with a name of IIS 8 Web Site is unavailable. The Runbook sends a ping to monitored server to check the current status. If the ping is unsuccessful the Runbook enters a ping loop (the server might be unavailable due to a reboot). If the server is available the Runbook checks the specified services related to IIS. If any of the services are in a stopped state the Runbook attempts to start the affected service.

There's more...

This is a basic example that shows how a Runbook can monitor for an alert and then attempt to remediate it.

Failure handling and notifications

This example can be expanded to include error/failure handling and notification. For example, notification activities can be added after the **Ping Loop** activity in case the server is unavailable for a period of time. Further activities could be added after the attempts to restart the services to recheck the status, and either restart again or restart the entire server. An additional option in a virtualized environment is to use a virtualization specific activity to restart the virtual machine.

See also

- Microsoft TechNet - Monitor Alert activity from `http://technet.microsoft.com/en-us/library/hh830707.aspx`

Bulk-enabling the maintenance mode

The ability to suppress alerts in Microsoft System 2012 Operations Manager during planned maintenance activities in a production IT environment is known as **maintenance mode**. Typically maintenance mode is initiated by using the Operation Manager console.

You may want to delegate this task to a user without access to the console, but with authority and approval to perform the maintenance activity. For example, applying application updates to a list of servers.

This recipe will show you how to create a simple Runbook to put a list of Windows Servers supplied in the Orchestration console with a comma separator into a predefined duration of maintenance mode.

The following diagram shows the defined business process covered in this recipe:

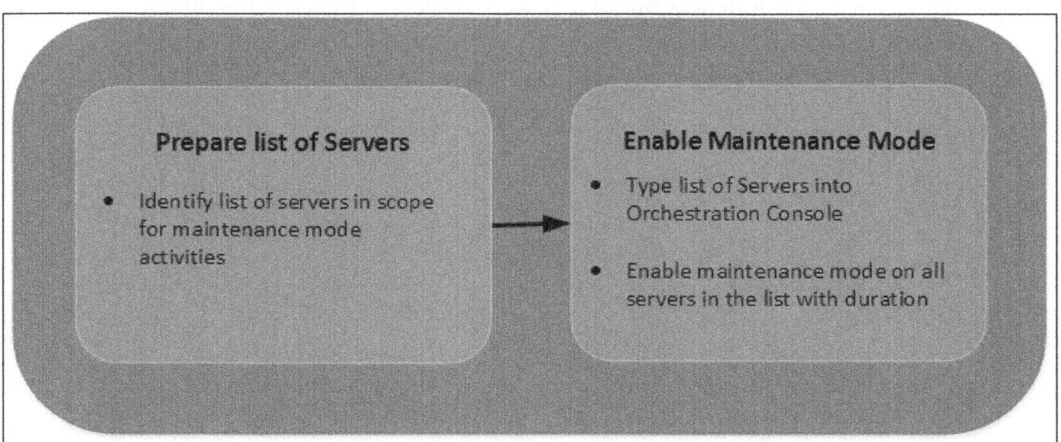

Getting ready

This recipe will leverage SCOM to enable maintenance mode to suppress alerts for a list of Windows Servers. The recipe requires the SCOM IP to be registered with Orchestrator and deployed to the Runbook Designer, as specified in the introduction to this chapter.

You must create the Runbook (**Bulk Maintenance Mode**) as part of the recipe preparation.

How to do it...

The following steps will show you how to configure the activities to create the Runbook for this recipe:

1. Navigate to the **Activities** section in the Runbook Designer, click on **Runbook Control**, and drag an **Initialize Data** activity into the middle pane of the Runbook (the workspace).
2. Right-Click on the **Activity**, navigate to **Properties** | **Add**. Add three parameters in this activity in the **Details** section:

Name of parameter	Data Type	Contains information
`ServerFQDN`	string	Contains the Fully Qualified Domain name of the Windows Server to enable maintenance mode on
`Duration`	integer	Length of time in minutes to enable maintenance mode
`Reason`	string	Comment or reason for enabling maintenance mode

3. Navigate to the **Activities** section, click on **System**, and drag a **Run .Net Script** activity to the Runbook next to the **Initialize Data** object.
4. Right-click on the **Run .Net Script** activity and click on **rename**. Rename it to `Split Array`.
5. Link the **Initialize Data** activity to the **Split Array** activity.

6. Double-click on the **Split Array** activity and provide the following information on the **Details** section:

<table>
<tr><th>Name of parameter</th><th>Data</th></tr>
<tr><td>Language Type</td><td>PowerShell</td></tr>
<tr><td>Script</td><td><pre><code>$ErrorActionPreference = "Stop"
try
{
$Servers=@()
$List"{ServerFQDN from Initalize Data}"
$Lists=$List.Split(',')
foreach($l in $lists){$Servers+=$l}
}
catch
{
    Throw $_.Exception
}</code></pre>
Replace the <code>{ServerFQDN from "Initialize Data"}</code> with an actual subscription by navigating to Subscribe | Published Data and selecting ServerFQDN from the Initialize Data activity on the databus.</td></tr>
</table>

7. Click on the **Published Data** tab on the left of the screen.
8. Click on **Add** and enter the following details:

Name	Type	Variable name
`SCO_Servers`	`string`	`Servers`

9. Click on **Finish**.
10. Navigate to the **Activities** section, click on **SC 2012 Operations Manager**, and drag a **Start Maintenance Mode** activity to the Runbook next to the **Split Array** object.
11. Link the **Split Array** activity to the **Start Maintenance Mode** activity.

12. Double-click on the **Start Maintenance Mode** activity and provide the following information on the **Details** section:

Name of parameter	Value
Connection	Pick the SCOM configuration we set up in the preparation of this chapter from the list.
Monitor	`{SCO_Servers from "Split Array"}` **:** Microsoft.Windows. Computer**:**`{SCO_Servers from "Split Array"}` Replace `{SCO_Servers from "Split Array"}`with a subscription by navigating to **Subscribe** | **Published Data** and selecting **SCO_Servers** from the **Split Array** activity on the databus. There is a space between the subscribed data and **:** but there is no space between and after Microsoft.Windows.Computer and "**:**".
Reason	Click the ellipsis button and choose **PlannedOther** from the list.
Duration	Delete the exiting value, right-click in the field, and navigate to **Subscribe** | **Published Data.** Choose **Initialize Data** in the Activity field and select **Duration**.
Comment	Right-click in the field, navigate to **Subscribe** | **Published Data**. Choose **Initialize Data** in the Activity field and select **Reason**.

The final Runbook should look like this:

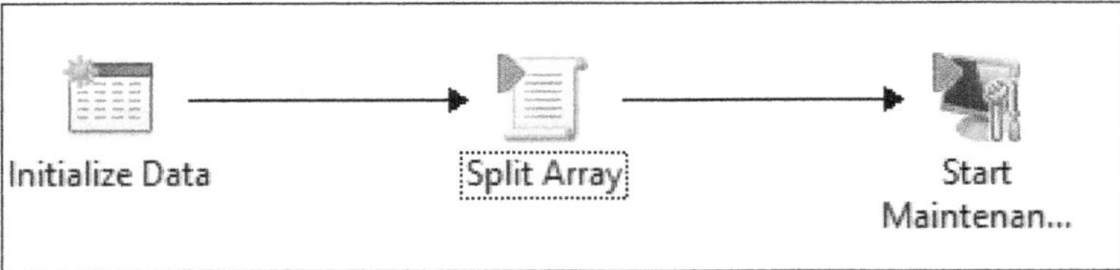

How it works...

You must type the FQDN of the servers separated by a comma to initiate this Runbook. The Runbook takes the list of Windows Servers with the required duration value and the reason for initiating the maintenance mode.

The **PowerShell** script splits this comma separated list into an array and then runs the **Start Maintenance Mode** activity for each member of the array. The maintenance is set to the duration specified and the reason supplied is logged as a comment.

The Runbook for putting devices into maintenance mode can be triggered from the Orchestration web console. Using the Orchestration web console for this activity removes the requirement to deploy the Operations Manager console to non-essential users.

There's more...

This is a basic Runbook to enable maintenance mode for a list of servers, but it forms the foundation for expanding out your process.

Service Request driven maintenance mode

A real world progression of this basic Runbook would be to leverage the Service Request process and Self Service Portal of Microsoft System Center 2012 Service Manager. You could create a Request Offering that allows the application owner or server administrator to select a list of servers using the portal. Once the selection process is complete, the process would launch the Runbook to put the selected servers into maintenance mode.

Reading from a CSV

Instead of entering a comma separated list of servers in the Orchestration web console, you could add a step to the process to read a CSV file. The content of the CSV file would be processed using the Read Line activity from the Text File Management IP.

Using SCOM groups

SCOM allows you to create groups of servers. You can utilize the groups you create in SCOM as an alternative source of input for this recipe.

You can use an SQL query to obtain SCOM group membership and use the results as the input to the Runbook for the maintenance mode targets.

A sample of such an SQL query may look like the following code:

```
select TargetObjectDisplayName as 'Group Members'
from RelationshipGenericView
where isDeleted=0
AND SourceObjectDisplayName = 'GROUP NAME'
ORDER BY TargetObjectDisplayName
```

System Center 2012 Operations Manager integration pack

- The integration pack for System Center 2012 SP1 components can be found at `http://www.microsoft.com/en-gb/download/details.aspx?id=34611`
- The full set of System Center 2012 Configuration Manager activities can be found at `http://technet.microsoft.com/en-us/library/hh830720.aspx`

See also

- Microsoft TechNet – Start Maintenance Mode activity from `http://technet.microsoft.com/en-us/library/hh830730.aspx`

7

Creating Runbooks for System Center 2012 Virtual Machine Manager Tasks

In this chapter, we will provide recipes on how to manage common System Center 2012 Virtual Machine Manager Scenarios with Microsoft System Center 2012 Orchestrator Runbooks:

- Removing attached ISOs from Virtual Machines (VMs)
- Remediating host compliance
- Working with Virtual Machine snapshots (Create, Delete, and Revert)

Introduction

This chapter focuses on how to automate examples of the common tasks addressed with **System Center 2012 Virtual Machine Manager** (**SCVMM**). The tasks in this chapter focus on the virtualization management team in a typical IT environment. Similar to other expert domains in IT, virtualization management requires a number of general manual repetitive tasks. The automation provided by SCORCH reduces and simplifies these manual tasks. The additional benefit of the automation is that IT admins gain additional time to work on often neglected proactive tasks due to time constraints.

The common tasks for Virtual Infrastructure Management described in the recipes of this chapter will cover the following scenarios:

- Remove attached ISOs from VMs

  Hyper-V is unable to successfully live migrate Virtual Machines (VM) in the case where an ISO image is still linked to the VM. As a result, high availability is impacted during host maintenance and servicing.

- Host Compliance Remediation

  SCVMM has the ability to monitor and remediate Hyper-V host compliance. This recipe will help automate that task and adhere to maintenance windows.

- Working with Virtual Machine checkpoints (Create, Delete, Revert)

  One heavily used feature of virtualization is the ability to take checkpoints of virtual machines. Taking snapshots provides a level of protection/rollback before a task is performed on the VM operating system. This recipe will help show how to utilize some of the activities in Orchestrator to automate working with checkpoints.

For all of these Virtual Infrastructure management tasks, we will define a process with the required steps in each recipe.

For all recipes in this chapter the requirements are:

- Installed and deployed System Center 2012 Virtual Machine Manager integration pack

  The installation of integration packs in SCORCH is described in *Chapter 2, Initial Configuration and Making SCORCH Highly Available*, as to how to load **Integration Packs** (**IP**)

- A user account with appropriate permissions in System Center 2012 Virtual Machine Manager to fulfill the tasks (Create, Modify, and Deploy VM's; Manage Hyper-V Hosts)

The following preparation needs to be performed for all recipes in this chapter:

Create a connection in SCORCH 2012 Runbook Designer to your System Center 2012 Virtual Machine Manager server:

1. Start the SCORCH Runbook Designer.
2. Choose the **Options** menu and click on **SC 2012 Virtual Machine Manager**.
3. Click on **Add**.

4. Provide the information specified in the following table:

Name	**Descriptive name for this SCVMM connection**
Type	Click the ellipsis (**...**) button and select **System Center Virtual Machine Manager**
VMM Server	Full qualified domain name of your Virtual Machine Manager server
User	User with appropriate permissions in SCVMM
Password	Password of the user
Domain	Domain containing the user account
Authentication Type (Remote Only)	Default
Port (Remote Only)	5985
Use SSL (Remote Only)	False
Cache Session Timeout (Min.)	10
VM Administrator Console	Full qualified domain name of your Virtual Machine Manager server

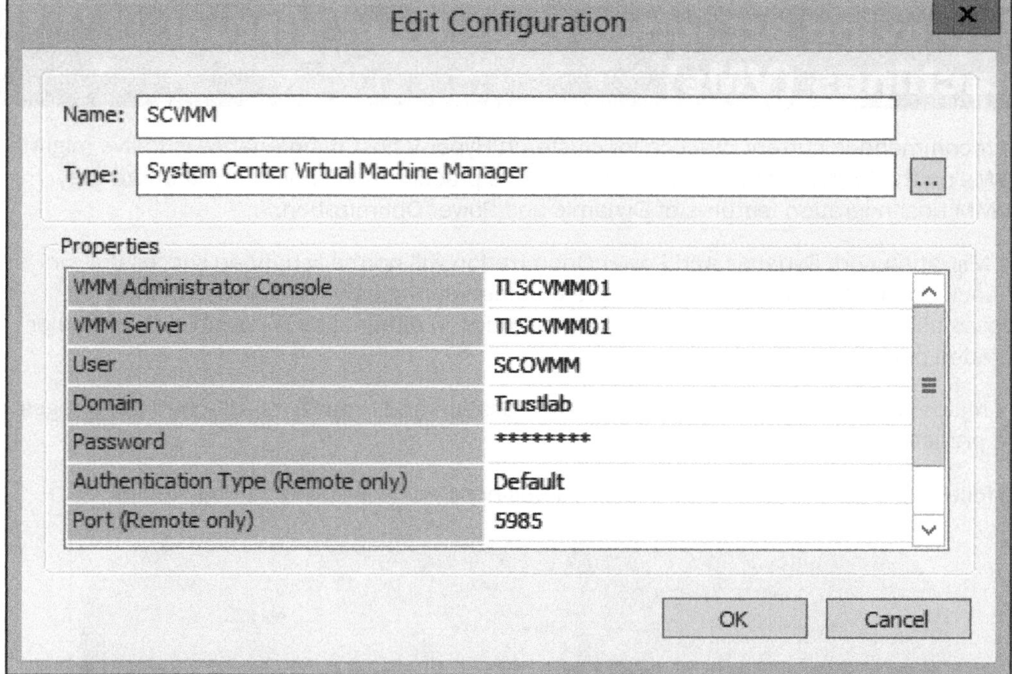

5. Click on **OK**.

6. Click on **Finish**.

   As an additional preparation step for the recipes, you must create three new Runbooks.

   The following steps show how to create a new Runbook:

7. Right-click on the Runbooks heading in the explorer view on the left of the Runbook Designer and choose **New | Runbook**.
8. Right-click on the **New Runbook** tab that appears above the main workspace, click on **Rename** and then click on **Yes** on the **Confirm Check out** message box then name the Runbook as **1.Remove Attached ISO**.
9. Repeat the preceding steps to create two additional Runbooks with the following names, also seen in the following screenshot:
   - **2.Host Compliance**
   - **3.VM Snapshots**

Removing attached ISOs from Virtual Machines (VMs)

The recommended current practice for clustered Hyper-V host maintenance is to live migrate all VMs on the target host to a different host. This practice also applies if you utilize the SCVMM host migration features of Dynamic and Power Optimization.

Live Migration and, Dynamic and Power Optimization will normally happen successfully in the background. Any VMs with ISO images attached during either of these tasks will not successfully migrate. The result of a failed migration in either case is possible downtime or degraded performance.

This recipe will show you how to automate the location and removal of attached ISO images on a predefined schedule.

The following diagram will show the defined business process covered in this recipe:

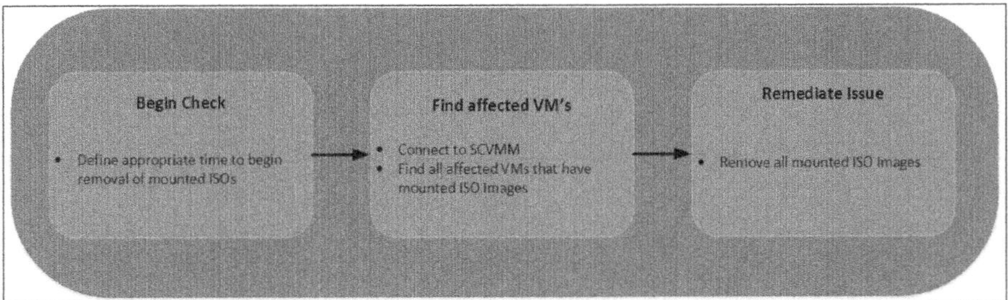

Getting ready

This recipe will leverage System Center 2012 Virtual Machine Manager to find and remediate all VM's with mounted ISO Images.

You will need to mount an ISO image to at least one VM for testing.

You must create the Runbook (**1.Remove Attached ISO**) as part of the chapter preparation for this recipe.

How to do it...

The following steps will show you how to configure the activities to create the Runbook for this recipe:

1. Navigate to the **Activities** section in the Runbook Designer, select **Scheduling** and drag a **Monitor Date/Time** activity into the middle pane of the Runbook (the workspace).
2. Right-click on the activity and choose **Rename**. Rename the activity to **Start at 21:30**.
3. Right-click on the activity and choose **Properties**.
4. Change the **Interval** to **At: 21:30** and click on **Finish**.
5. Navigate to the **Activities** section, select **SC 2012 Virtual Machine Manager** and drag a **Get VM** activity into the Runbook next to the **Start at 21:30** activity.
6. Link the **Start at 21:30** activity to the **Get VM** activity.
7. Double-click on the **Get VM** activity and provide the following information on the **Filters** section:

Name of parameter	Value
Configuration Name	Pick the SCVMM configuration you set up in the preparation of this chapter from the list

8. Click on **Finish**.
9. Navigate to the **Activities** section, select **SC 2012 Virtual Machine Manager** and drag a **Run VMM PowerShell Script** activity to the Runbook next to the **Get VM** object.
10. Link the **Get VM** activity to the **Run VMM PowerShell Script** activity.
11. Right-click on the **Run VMM PowerShell Script** and choose **Rename**.
12. Rename the activity to **Find VMs with ISO Attached**.

13. Double-click on the **Find VMs with ISO Attached** activity and provide the following information:

Name of parameter	Value
Configuration name	Pick the SCVMM configuration you setup in the preparation of this chapter from the list.

PowerShell script	`$VM = '{VM Name from "Get VM"}'`
	`$ISO = get-scvirtualdvddrive -VM $VM`
	`$HasISO = $ISO.ISOLinked`
	Replace the `{VM Name from "Get VM"}` by right-clicking on the PowerShell Script field and navigate to **Subscribe** | **Published Data**. Choose Get VM in the Activity field and select VM Name.

Output variable 1	`$HasISO`

14. Click on **Finish**.
15. Navigate to the **Activities** section, select **SC 2012 Virtual Machine Manager** and drag a **Run VMM PowerShell Script** activity to the Runbook next to the **Find VMs with ISO Attached** object.
16. Link the **Find VMs with ISO Attached** activity to the **Run VMM PowerShell Script** activity.
17. Right-click on the **Run VMM PowerShell Script** and select **Rename**.
18. Rename the activity to **Remove ISO**.
19. Double-click the link between **Find VMs with ISO Attached** and **Remove ISO** activities.
20. Click on the **Find VMs with ISO Attached** text.
21. Select **Output Variable 01** from the list and click **OK**.
22. Click the underlined text value.
23. Type `True` and click on **OK**.
24. Click on **Finish**.
25. Double-click on the **Remove ISO** activity and provide the following information:

Name of parameter	Value
Configuration name	Pick the SCVMM configuration we set up in the preparation of this chapter from the list.

PowerShell script	`$VM = '{VM Name from "Get VM"}'`
	`$ISO = Get-SCVirtualDVDDrive -VM $VM`
	`$UnMount = Set-SCVirtualDVDDrive -VirtualDVDDrive`
	`$ISO -NoMedia`
	`$IsISOLinked = $UnMount.ISOLinked`
	Replace the `{VM Name from "Get VM"}` by right-clicking on the PowerShell Script field and navigate to **Subscribe** | **Published Data**. Choose **Get VM** in the **Activity** field and select **VM Name**.

Output variable 1	`$IsISOLinked`

26. Click on **Finish**.
27. Navigate to the **Activities** section, select **Notification** and drag a **Send Platform Event** activity to the Runbook next to the **Remove ISO activity**.
28. Right-click on the **Send Platform Event** and select **Rename**.
29. Rename the activity to **Log Removal**.
30. Link the **Remove ISO** activity to the **Log Remova**l activity.
31. Double-click on the link between **Remove ISO** and **Log Removal** activities.
32. Click on the **Remove ISO** text.
33. Select **Output Variable 01** from the list and click on **OK**.
34. Click the underlined word value.
35. Type `False` and click on **OK**.
36. Click on the **Options** tab and change the **Color** to **Green**.
37. Click on **Finish**.

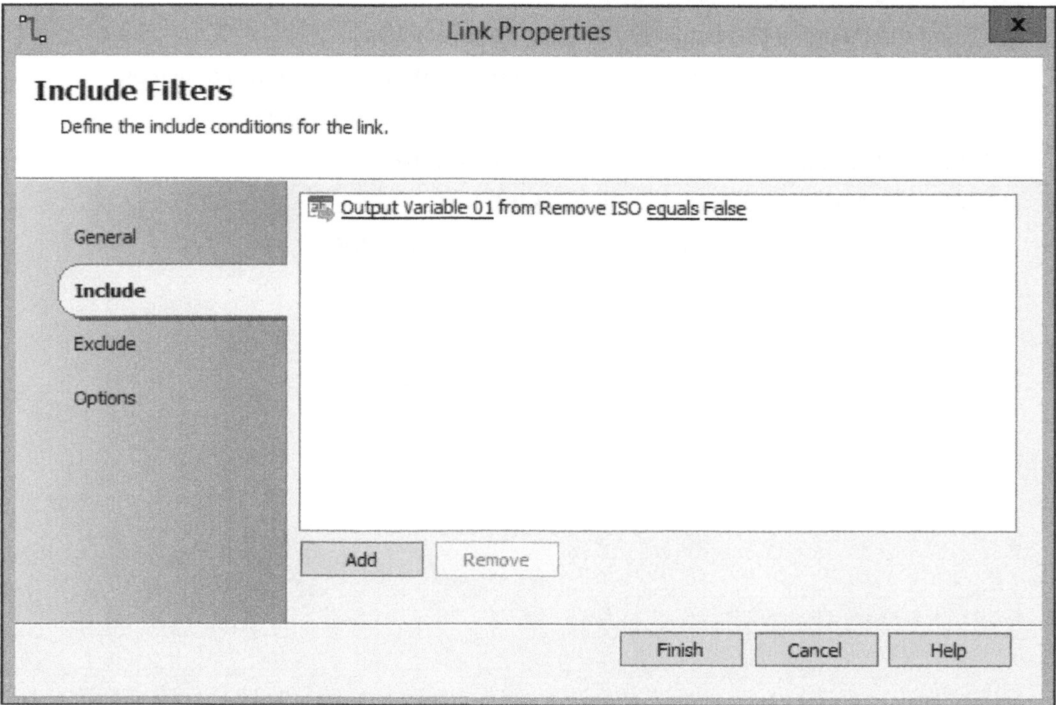

38. Double-click on the **Log Removal** activity and provide the following information on the **Details** section:

Name of parameter	Value
Type	Information
Summary	Type the following text: `Removed ISO Image`
Details	Type the following text: `Removed ISO Image from` Then, right-click on the space after the word "from" and navigate to **Subscribe** | **Published Data**. Choose **Get VM** in the **Activity** field and select **VM Name**.

39. Click on **Finish**.
40. Navigate to the **Activities** section, select **Notification** and drag a **Send Platform Event** activity to the Runbook below the **Remove ISO** activity.
41. Right-click on the **Send Platform Event** activity and select **Rename**.
42. Rename the activity to **Log Failure**.
43. Link the **Remove ISO** activity to the **Log Failure** activity.
44. Double-click on the link between the **Remove ISO** and **Log Failure** activities.
45. Click on the word **success** next to the **Remove ISO** returns text.
46. Uncheck **success** and check failed then click on **OK**.
47. Click on **Add** then click on the **Remove ISO** text.
48. Choose **Output Variable 01** from the list and click on **OK**.
49. Click the underlined word value.

50. Type `True` and click on **OK**.

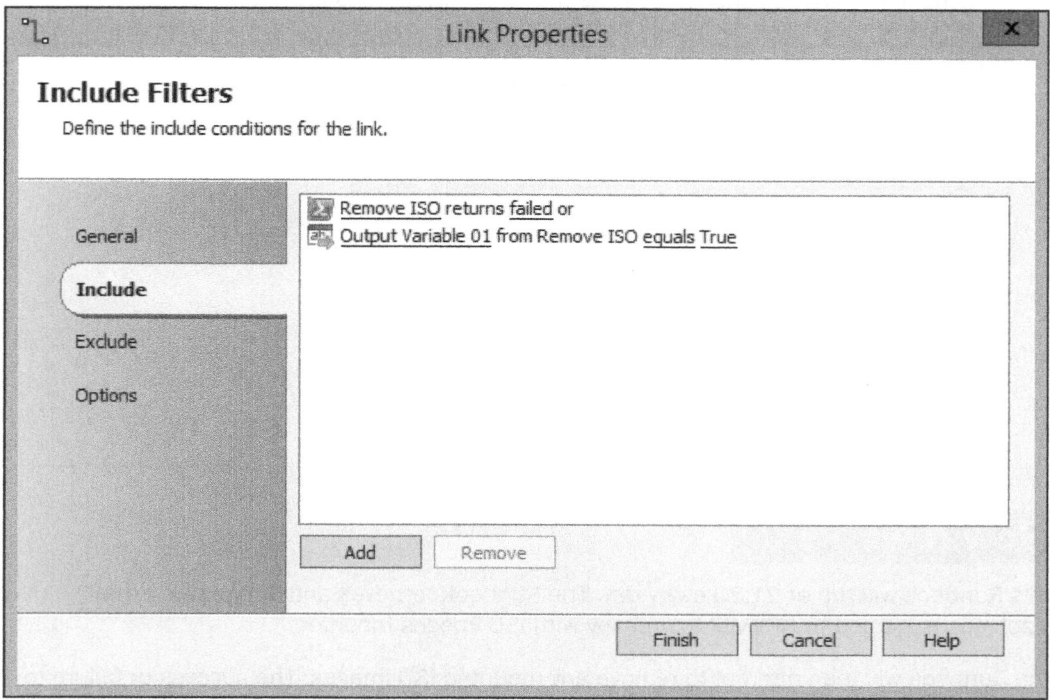

51. Click on the **Options** tab and change the **Color** to **Red**.
52. Click on **Finish**.
53. Double-click on the **Log Failure** activity and provide the following information on the **Details** section:

Name of parameter	Value
Type	Error
Summary	Type the following text: `Failed to Remove ISO`
Details	Type the following text: `Failed to Remove ISO from` Then, right-click on the space after the word **from** and navigate to **Subscribe | Published Data**. Select **Get VM** in the **Activity** field and select **VM Name**.

54. Click on **Finish**.

    The final Runbook should look like the following screenshot:

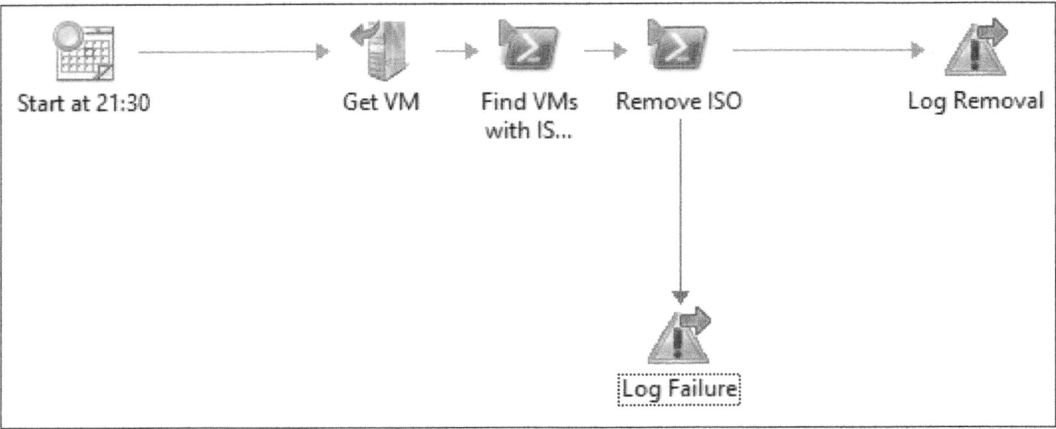

How it works...

This Runbook will run at 21:30 every day. The Runbook retrieves and queries all virtual machines managed by SCVMM to find any with ISO images mounted.

The Runbook will then attempt to remove any mounted ISO images. The success or failure to remove the ISO is logged, as seen in the following screenshot:

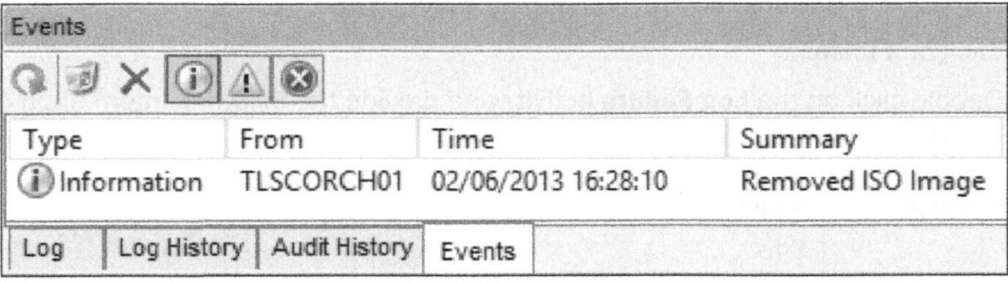

There's more...

You have the option to change this Runbook to your specific environment, for example, the start time. You can either adjust the start time, or replace it with an **Initialize Data** activity, and alternatively invoke this Runbook from another part of an automated process.

Logging events to Orchestrator

This recipe uses the **Send Platform Event** activity to log either the success or failure of the action to remove an ISO Image from a VM.

These events can be viewed in the Runbook Designer by navigating to the Runbook and selecting the **Events** tab.

However, you need access to the Runbook Designer. The Runbook can be modified to send e-mail notifications to users without access to the Runbook designer. An additional extension is to automatically log an incident within your Service Desk system.

System Center 2012 Virtual Machine Manager Integration Pack

The integration pack for System Center 2012 SP1 components can be found at `http://www.microsoft.com/en-gb/download/details.aspx?id=34611`.

The full set of System Center 2012 Virtual Machine Manager activities can be found at `http://technet.microsoft.com/en-us/library/hh830704.aspx`.

See also

Detailed information for the activities used in this Runbook can be found at the following locations:

- Microsoft TechNet – Get VM activity: `http://technet.microsoft.com/en-us/library/hh830744.aspx`
- Microsoft TechNet – Run VMM PowerShell Script activity: `http://technet.microsoft.com/en-us/library/hh830716.aspx`

Remediating host compliance

SCVMM has a feature that allows for you to manage patching of the Hyper-V hosts. This feature, which is based on the integration with **Windows Server Updates Services** (**WSUS**), and is managed using the SCVMM console.

SCVMM also has the ability to set servicing windows (used for maintenance activities) for the Hyper-V hosts using the same console.

However, these two related operational features from SCVMM do not automatically work together. The SCVVM administrator must manually initiate both tasks in the right order during a patch maintenance cycle.

This recipe will show you how to automate patching of Hyper-V hosts in your environment using the serving windows you have defined in SCVMM.

The following diagram will show the defined business process covered in this recipe:

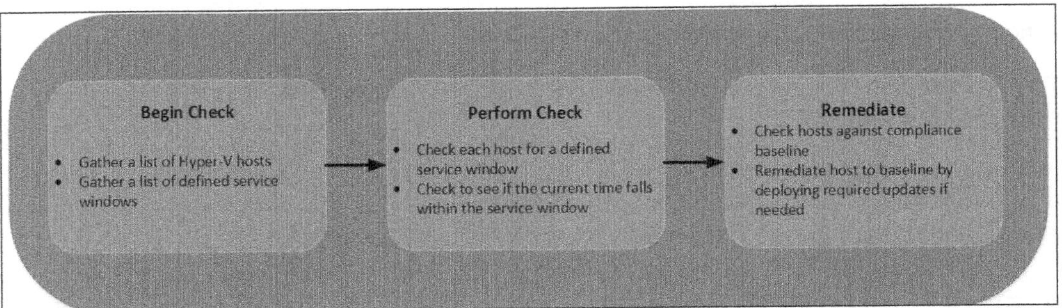

Getting ready

This recipe will use System Center 2012 Virtual Machine Manager to deploy patches to Hyper-V hosts according to defined Service Windows.

Before creating this recipe, you will need to have completed the steps in SCVMM to add a WSUS server. You must also approve the relevant updates in a baseline and create appropriate Service Windows.

For more information on these steps, refer to the following TechNet Library documents:

- Managing Fabric Updates in VMM:`http://technet.microsoft.com/en-us/library/gg675084.aspx`
- How to Create and Assign a Service Window in VMM:`http://technet.microsoft.com/en-us/library/hh416221.aspx`

You must create the Runbook (**2.Host Compliance**) as part of the preparation for this recipe.

How to do it...

The following steps will show you how to configure the activities to create the Runbook for this recipe:

1. Navigate to the **Activities** section in the Runbook Designer, select **Scheduling** and drag a **Monitor Date/Time** activity into the middle pane of the Runbook (the workspace).
2. Right-click on the activity and select **Rename.** Rename the activity to **Run Every 15 Mins.**
3. Right-click on the **Run Every 15 Mins** activity and select **Properties.**
4. Change the **Interval to Every: 15 Minutes** and click on **Finish.**
5. Navigate to the **Activities** section, select **SC 2012 Virtual Machine Manager** and drag a **Get VM Host** activity to the Runbook next to the **Run Every 15 Mins** activity.
6. Link the **Run Every 15 Mins** activity to the **Get VM Host** activity.
7. Double-click on the **Get VM Host** activity and provide the following information on the **Filters** section:

Name of parameter	Value
Configuration name	Pick the SCVMM configuration you set up in the preparation of this chapter from the list.

8. Click on **Finish.**
9. Navigate to the **Activities** section, select **SC 2012 Virtual Machine Manager** and drag a **Run VMM PowerShell Script** activity to the Runbook next to the **Get VM** object.
10. Link the **Get VM** activity to the **Run VMM PowerShell Script** activity.
11. Right-click on the **Run VMM PowerShell Script** and select **Rename.**
12. Rename the activity to **Check Servicing Window.**
13. Double-click on the **Check Servicing Window** activity and provide the following information in the **Properties** section:

Name of parameter	Value
Configuration name	Pick the SCVMM configuration you set up in the preparation of this chapter from the list.

Name of parameter	Value

PowerShell script	$StartMaintDate = $false
	$StartMaintDay = $false
	$StartMaintTime = $false
	$StartMaintDuration = $false
	$CurrDate = get-date
	$CurrTime = ([string](get-date).hour + ":" +
	[string](get-date).minute)
	
	$SvcWindow = Get-SCServicingWindow -VMHost '{VM
	Host Name from "Get VM Host"}'
	If ($SvcWindow) {
	
	#Check if the Date is after the start date for the
	Servicing Window
	[DateTime]$StartDate = $SvcWindow.StartDate
	if ($CurrDate -gt $StartDate) {$StartMaintDate =
	$true} else {$StartMaintDate = $false}
	
	#Check if today is a day allowed for servicing
	$Day = $CurrDate.DayOfWeek
	If ($SvcWindow.WeeklyScheduleDayOfWeek –match $Day)
	{$StartMaintDay = $true} else {$StartMaintDay =
	$false}
	
	#Check if it's after the Service Windows start time
	$StartHour = $SvcWindow.StartTimeOfDay.Hours
	$StartMin = $SvcWindow.StartTimeOfDay.Minutes
	$WindowStartTime = ("$StartHour" + ':' +
	"$StartMin")
	if ($CurrTime -eq $WindowStartTime)
	{$StartMaintTime = $true}
	elseif ($CurrTime -gt $WindowStartTime)
	{$StartMaintTime = $true}
	else {$StartMaintTime = $false}
	
	#Calculate end time of the servicing window and
	give it 1 Hour for completion
	$Duration = $SvcWindow.MinutesDuration
	$Duration = $Duration-60
	$WindowStartTime = [DateTime]([string]$SvcWindow.
	StartTimeOfDay.Hours + ":" + [string]$SvcWindow.
	StartTimeOfDay.Minutes)
	$WindowEndTime = $WindowStartTime.
	AddMinutes($Duration)
	#Compare this to current time to determine if still
	within servicing window
	if ($CurrDate -lt $WindowEndTime)
	{$StartMaintDuration = $true} else
	{$StartMaintDuration = $false}
	}

Name of parameter	Value
PowerShell script	Replace the `{VM Host Name from "Get VM Host"}` by right-clicking on the position of script where the value is highlighted and navigate to **Subscribe** | **Published Data** select **Get VM Host** in the **Activity** field and select **VM Host Name**.
Output Variable 1	Click on **Optional Properties ...** and then type `$StartMaintDate`.
Output Variable 2	Click on **Optional Properties ...** and then type `$StartMaintDay`.
Output Variable 3	Click on **Optional Properties ...** and then type `$StartMaintTime`.
Output Variable 4	Click on **Optional Properties ...** and then type `$StartMaintDuration`.

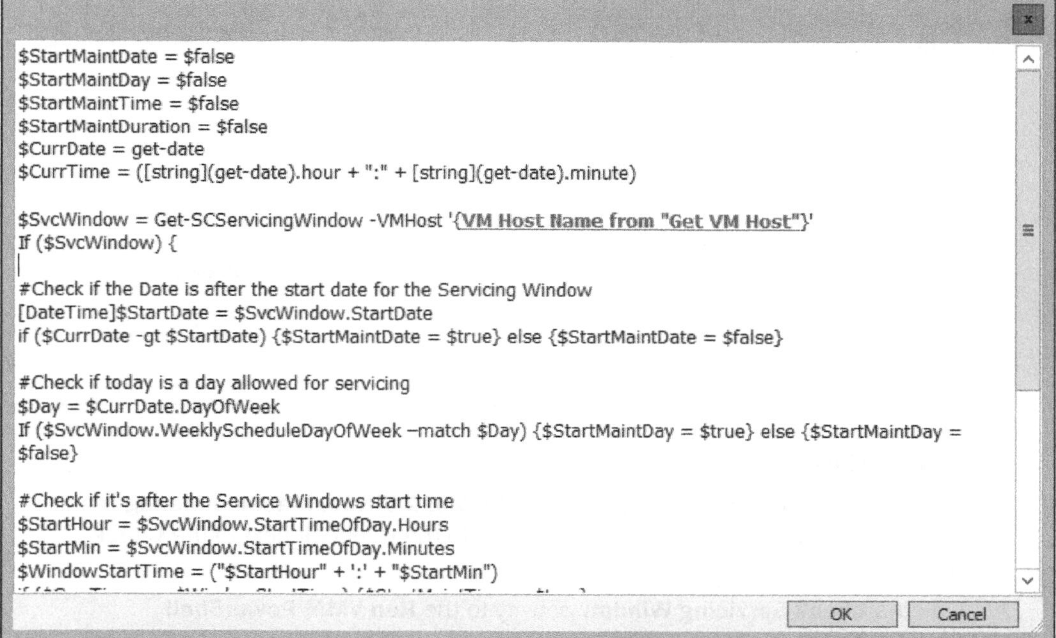
$StartMaintDate = $false
$StartMaintDay = $false
$StartMaintTime = $false
$StartMaintDuration = $false
$CurrDate = get-date
$CurrTime = ([string](get-date).hour + ":" + [string](get-date).minute)
$SvcWindow = Get-SCServicingWindow -VMHost '{VM Host Name from "Get VM Host"}'
If ($SvcWindow) {
#Check if the Date is after the start date for the Servicing Window
[DateTime]$StartDate = $SvcWindow.StartDate
if ($CurrDate -gt $StartDate) {$StartMaintDate = $true} else {$StartMaintDate = $false}
#Check if today is a day allowed for servicing
$Day = $CurrDate.DayOfWeek
If ($SvcWindow.WeeklyScheduleDayOfWeek –match $Day) {$StartMaintDay = $true} else {$StartMaintDay = $false}
#Check if it's after the Service Windows start time
$StartHour = $SvcWindow.StartTimeOfDay.Hours
$StartMin = $SvcWindow.StartTimeOfDay.Minutes
$WindowStartTime = ("$StartHour" + ':' + "$StartMin")
OK
Cancel

14. Click on the **Optional Properties...** button to add more Output Variables to the list, as shown in the following screenshot:

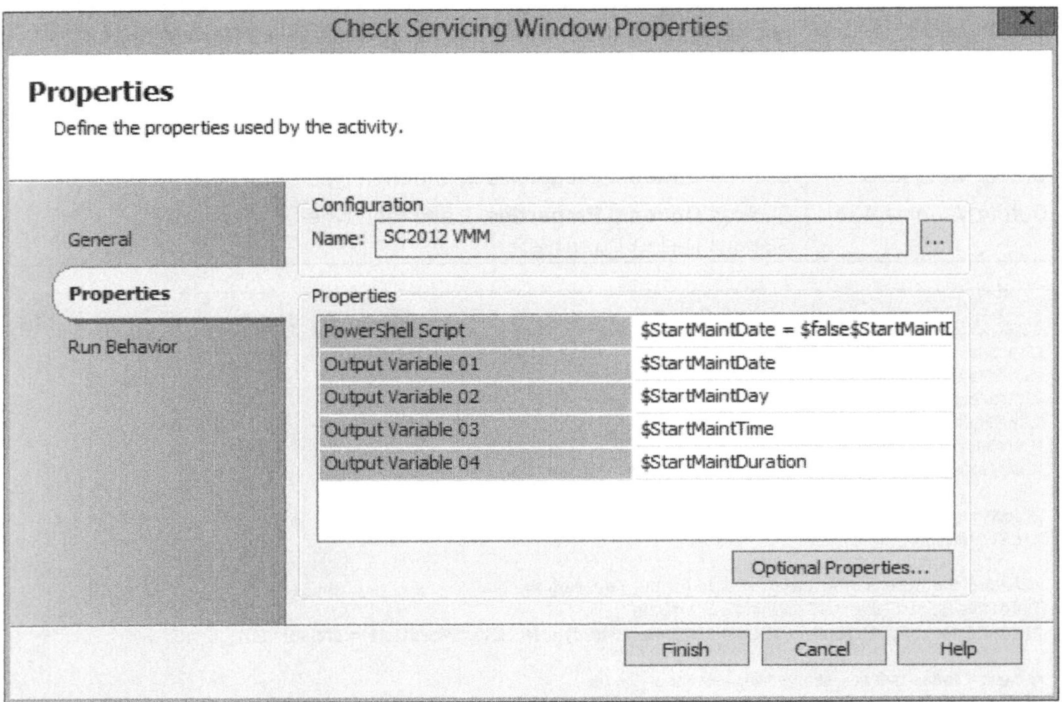

15. Click on **Finish**.
16. Navigate to the **Activities** section, select **SC 2012 Virtual Machine Manager** and drag a **Run VMM PowerShell Script** activity to the Runbook next to the **Check Servicing Window** object.
17. Link the **Check Servicing Window** activity to the **Run VMM PowerShell Script** activity.
18. Right-click on the **Run VMM PowerShell Script** and select **Rename**.
19. Rename the activity to **Perform Compliance Scan**.
20. Double-click on the link between the **Check Servicing Window** and **Perform Compliance Scan** activities, select the **Exclude** tab on the left of the window.
21. Click on **Add** and click on the underlined word **Check Servicing Window** and select **Output Variable 01** from the list and click on **OK**.
22. Click on the underlined word value and type `False` into the data window and click on **OK**.

23. Repeat the Add and Data value process for **Output Variable 02-04** then click on **Finish**.

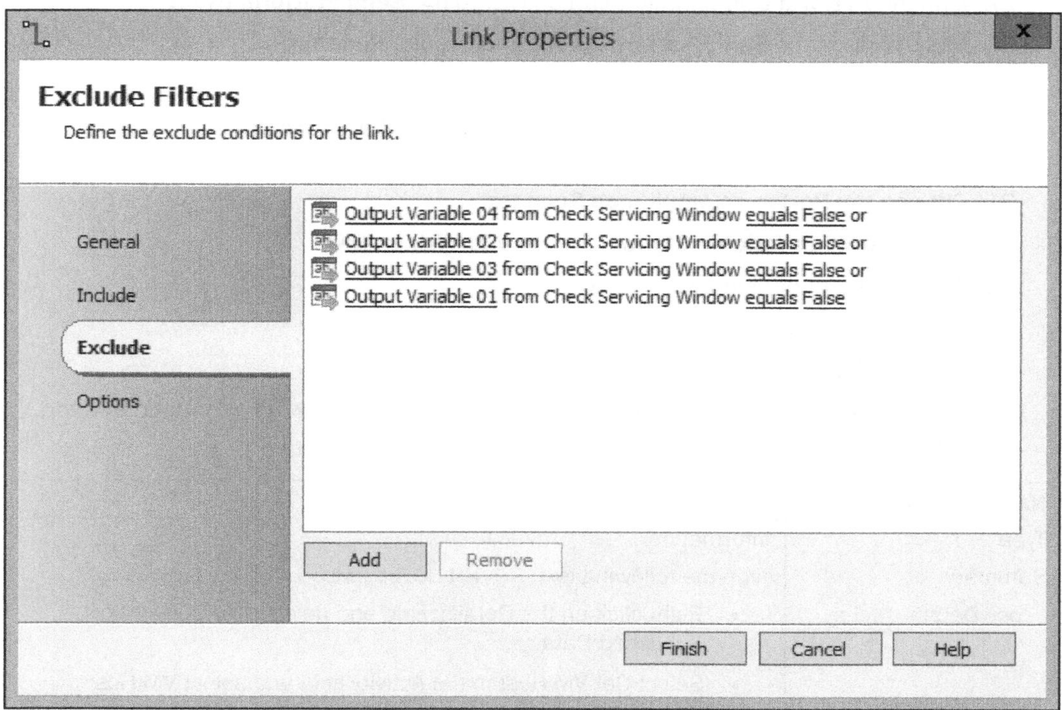

24. Double-click on the **Perform Compliance Scan** activity and provide the following information on the **Properties** section:

Name of parameter	Value
Configuration name	Pick the SCVMM configuration you set up in the preparation of this chapter from the list.

PowerShell script	`$VMHost = Get-SCVMMManagedComputer \| Where-Object {$_.Name -eq '{VM Host Name from "Get VM Host"}'}`
	`$Scan = Start-SCComplianceScan -VMMManagedComputer $VMHost`
	`$Result=$Scan.OverallComplianceState`
	Replace the `{VM Host Name from "Get VM Host"}` by right-clicking on the highlighted script section and then navigate to **Subscribe | Published Data** select **Get VM Host** in the **Activity** field and select **VM Host Name**.

Output Variable 1	Type `$Result`.

25. Click on **Finish**.

26. Navigate to the **Activities** section, select **Notification** and drag a **Send Platform Event** activity to the Runbook underneath the **Perform Compliance Scan** activity.
27. Link the **Perform Compliance Scan** activity to the **Send Platform Event** activity.
28. Right-click on the **Send Platform Event** and choose **Rename**.
29. Rename the activity to **Compliant**.
30. Double-click on the link between the **Perform Compliance Scan** and **Compliant** activities.
31. Click on the **Perform Compliance Scan** text.
32. Choose **Output Variable 01** from the list and click on **OK**.
33. Click on the underlined word value.
34. Type `Compliant` and click on **OK**.
35. Click on **Finish**.
36. Double-click on the **Compliant** activity and provide the following information on the **Details** section:

Name of parameter	Value
Type	Information
Summary	Type the following text: `SCVMM Automated Patching`
▶ Details	▶ Right-click on the Details: field and navigate to Subscribe | Published Data. ▶ Select Get VM Host in the Activity field and select VM Host Name. ▶ Add the additional text after the subscription: is compliant, no patching performed.

37. Click on **Finish**.
38. Navigate to the **Activities** section, select **SC 2012 Virtual Machine Manager** and drag a **Run VMM PowerShell Script** activity to the Runbook next to the **Perform Compliance Scan** object.
39. Link the **Perform Compliance Scan** activity to the **Run VMM PowerShell Script** activity.
40. Right-click on the **Run VMM PowerShell Script** and select **Rename**.
41. Rename the activity to **Remediate**.
42. Double-click on the link between the **Perform Compliance Scan** and **Remediate** activities.

43. Click on the **Perform Compliance Scan** text.
44. Select **Output Variable 01** from the list and click on **OK**.
45. Click on the underlined word value.
46. Type `NonCompliant` and click on **OK**.
47. Click on **Finish**.
48. Double-click on the **Remediate** activity and provide the following information on the **Properties** section:

Name of parameter	Value
Configuration name	Pick the SCVMM configuration you setup in the preparation of this chapter from the list.
PowerShell script	`$VMHost = Get-SCVMMManagedComputer \| Where-Object {$_.Name -eq '{VM Host Name from "Get VM Host"}'}` `$Remediate = Start-SCUpdateRemediation -VMMManagedComputer $VMHost` **`$Result=$Remediate.OverallComplianceState`** Replace the `{VM Host Name from "Get VM Host"}` by right-clicking in the highlighted section of the script and navigate to **Subscribe | Published Data** and select **Get VM Host** in the **Activity** field and select **VM Host Name**.
Output Variable 1	Type `$Result`.

49. Click on **Finish**.
50. Navigate to the **Activities** section, select **Notification** and drag a **Send Platform Event** activity above and to the right of the **Remediate** activity.
51. Link the **Remediate** activity to the **Send Platform Event** activity.
52. Right-click on the **Send Platform Event** and choose **Rename**.
53. Rename the activity to **Finished Remediating**.
54. Double-click on the link between the **Remediate** and **Finished Remediating** activities.
55. Click on the **Remediate text**.
56. Select **Output Variable 01** from the list and click on **OK**.
57. Click the underlined word value.
58. Type `Compliant` and click on **OK**.
59. Click on **Finish**.

60. Double-click on the **Finished Remediating** activity and provide the following information on the **Details** section:

Name of parameter	Value
Type	Information
Summary	Type the following text: `SCVMM Automated Patching`
Details	Right-click on the **Details:** field and navigate to **Subscribe** | **Published Data**. Select **Get VM Host** in the Activity field and select **VM Host Name**. Add the following additional text after the subscription: `Has successfully deployed updates.`

61. Click on **Finish**.
62. Navigate to the **Activities** section, select **Notification** and drag a **Send Platform Event** activity to the Runbook below and to the right of the **Remediate** activity.
63. Link the **Remediate** activity to the **Send Platform Event** activity.
64. Right-click on the **Send Platform Event** and select **Rename**.
65. Rename the activity to **Failed Remediating**.
66. Double-click on the link between the **Remediate** and the **Failed Remediating** activities.
67. Click on the **Remediate text**.
68. Select **Output Variable 01** from the list and click on **OK**.
69. Click on the underlined word value.
70. Type NonCompliant and click on **OK**.
71. Click on **Finish**.
72. Double-click on the **Failed Remediating** activity and provide the following information on the **Details** section:

Name of parameter	Value
Type	Error
Summary	Type the following text: `SCVMM Automated Patching`
Details	Right-click on the **Details:** field and navigate to **Subscribe** | **Published Data**. Select **Get VM Host** in the **Activity** field and select **VM Host Name**. Add the following additional text after the subscription: `is not fully compliant.`

73. Click on **Finish**.

    The final Runbook should look like the following screenshot:

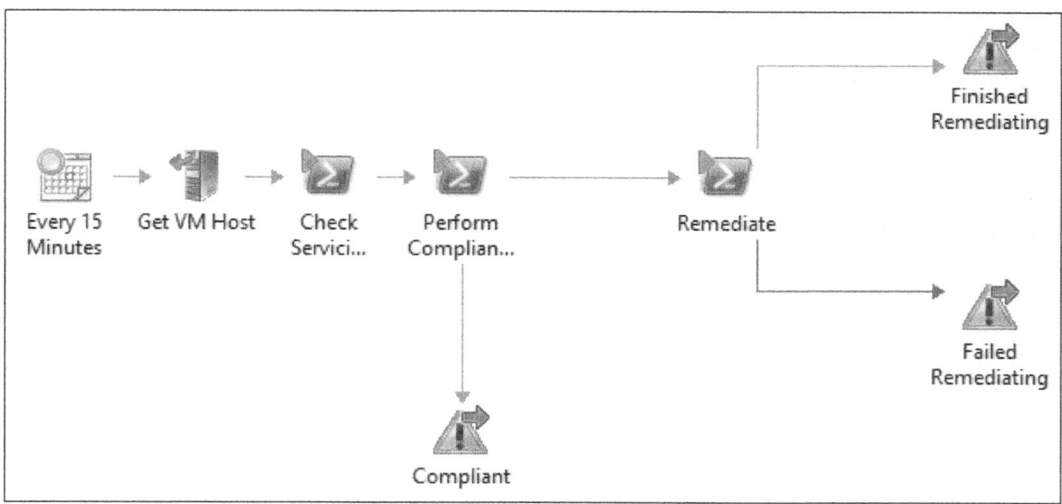

How it works...

Every 15 minutes this Runbook checks the Hyper-V hosts managed by SCVMM for their applied Service Windows.

If a Service Window is present, the Runbook checks if the current time falls within the defined Service Window. A host compliance scan is initiated if the time check against the service window returns true. The host compliance scan uses baselines assigned to the specific hosts in scope.

If the Hyper-V host returns a non-compliant state after a scan, a remediation job will be initiated. The remediation job will attempt to apply all applicable updates to the Hyper-V host.

There's more...

The Runbook will run every 15 minutes in this recipe. The 15 minute interval is not appropriate for production environments. In a production environment, you must align the time to the Service Windows defined for your hosts (this is typically out of hours).

VM's with ISO images attached?

A mounted ISO image on a VM will prevent the Host from live migration activities in the case where the remediation requires a restart.

You could enhance this Runbook book to include automatically unmounting ISO images from VMs running on the host in scope.

The previous recipe in this chapter shows how to automate the process of checking for mounted and unmounting ISO images.

Maintenance mode

You must plan to place the hosts in maintenance mode before triggering patching activities in your environment using this type of Runbook. The maintenance mode would either live migrate the VMs, or place the VMs in a save state depending on your SCVMM environment configuration.

While there is no Orchestrator activity for this within the SCVMM Integration Pack, you could utilize the `Disable-SCVMHost` and `Enable-SCVMHost PowerShell` commands to achieve this.

See also

Detailed information for the activities used in this Runbook can be found at the following locations:

- Microsoft TechNet – Get VM Host activity: `http://technet.microsoft.com/en-us/library/jj656637.aspx`
- Microsoft TechNet – Run VMM PowerShell Script activity: `http://technet.microsoft.com/en-us/library/hh830716.aspx`

Working with Virtual Machine snapshots (Create, Delete, and Revert)

It is a common recommended practice to perform a checkpoint (also referred to as a snapshot) of the virtual machine before performing tasks on the operating system or applications running on the virtual machine.

Performing checkpoints before a maintenance task (install/update/configuration change) provides you with the option to revert the VMs to the specific point in time before the task was initiated.

However, checkpoints do have associated risks. Checks may be accidentally applied causing the VMs to revert to an undesired state! Another risk is disk usage due to multiple checkpoints (each check point requires disk space).

This recipe will show you how to use the SCVMM activities to manage and eliminate the check points risks typically found in production environments.

Getting ready

This recipe will leverage System Center 2012 Virtual Machine Manager to create, restore, and remove checkpoints.

Before creating this recipe, you will need a test virtual machine on which to perform these checkpoint tasks.

You must create the Runbook (**3.VM Snapshots**) as part of the preparation for this recipe.

How to do it...

The following steps will show you how to configure the activities to create the Runbook for this recipe:

1. Navigate to the **Activities** section in the Runbook Designer, select **Runbook Control** and drag an **Initialize Data** activity into the middle pane of the Runbook (the workspace).
2. Right-click on the **Activity** and navigate to **Properties**, then click on **Add** and provide the following parameters to this activity in the **Details** section:

Name of parameter	Data Type	Contains information
`ServerName`	`String`	Contains the name of the virtual machine to work with
`Reason`	`String`	Reason for performing the checkpoint operation
`CheckPointType`	`String`	Use this parameter to determine whether to perform a `Create`, `Restore`, or `Remove` checkpoint operation by providing one of the following values: `Create`, `Restore`, and `Remove`

3. Navigate to the **Activities** section, select **SC 2012 Virtual Machine Manager** and drag a **Get VM** activity next to the **Initialize Data** activity.
4. Link the **Initialize Data** activity to the **Get VM** activity.
5. Double-click on the **Get VM** activity and provide the following information on the **Filters** section:

Name of parameter	Value
Configuration name	Pick the SCVMM configuration we set up in the preparation of this chapter from the list

6. Under the **Filters** area in the **Filters** tab, click on **Add** and provide the following details for the filter:

Name	Relation	Value
Computer Name	Contains	Right-click on the **Value:** field and navigate to **Subscribe** | **Published Data**. Choose **Initialize Data** in the **Activity** field and select **ServerName**.

7. Click on **OK**, and then click on **Finish**. Rename the **Get VM** activity to Get **VM for Remove**.
8. Repeat the preceding steps for two additional activities, called **Get VM for Restore** and **Get VM for Create**.
9. Arrange the three activities in the following order next to the **Initialize data** activity: **Get VM for Remove** (above and to the right of **Initialize Data**), **Get VM for Restore** (next to **Initialize Data**), and Get VM for Create (below and to the right of Initialize Data).
10. Double-click on the link between **Initialize Data** and **Get VM for Remove**.
11. Click on the **Initialize Data** text.
12. Choose **CheckPointType** from the list and click on **OK**.
13. Click on the underlined word value.
14. Type `Remove` and click on **OK**.
15. Click on **Finish**.

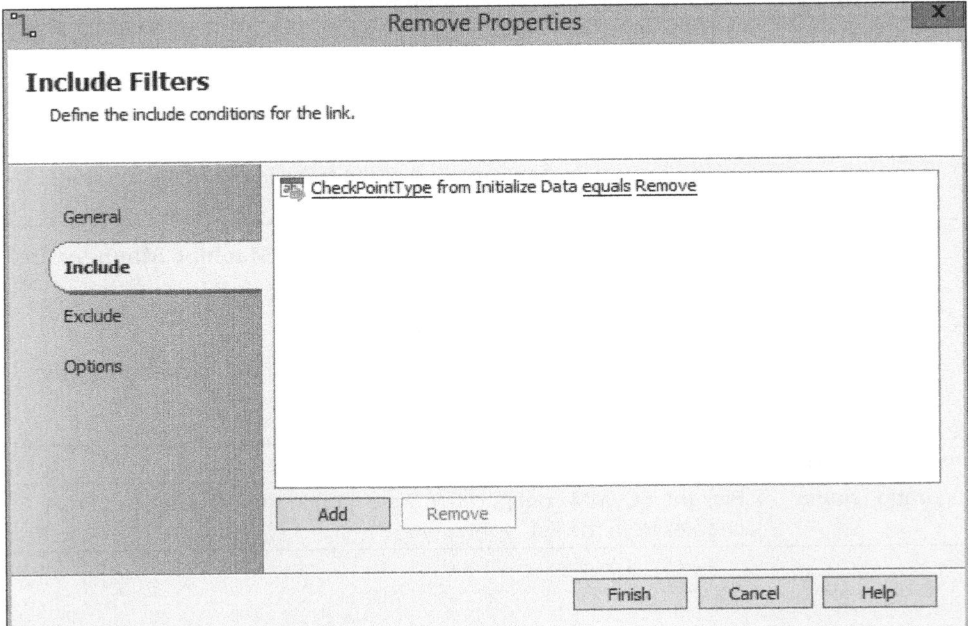

16. Repeat the preceding steps on the link between **Initialize Data** and **Get VM for Restore** but use **Restore** as the value you type.
17. Repeat the preceding steps on the link between **Initialize Data** and **Get VM** for **Create** but use **Create** as the value you type.
18. Navigate to the **Activities** section, select **SC 2012 Virtual Machine Manager** and drag a **Get Checkpoint** activity to the runbook next to the **Get VM for Restore** object.
19. Link the **Get VM** for **Restore** activity to the **Get Checkpoint** activity.
20. Right-click on the **Get Checkpoint** and select **Rename**.
21. Rename the activity to **Get Checkpoint** for **Restore**.
22. Double-click on the **Get Checkpoint for Restore** activity and provide the following information on the **Filters** tab:

Name of parameter	Value
Configuration name	Pick the SCVMM configuration you set up in the preparation of this chapter from the list

23. Under the **Filters** area in the **Filters** tab, click on **Add** and add the following details for the filter:

Name	Relation	Value
VM ID	Equals	Right-click on the **Value:** field and navigate to **Subscribe | Published Data**. Choose **Get VM for Restore** in the Activity field and select **VM ID**.
Most Recent	Equals	True (click on **...**).

24. Click on **Finish**.
25. Repeat the preceding steps for the **Get Checkpoint** activity **Get VM for Remove**. Rename the **Get Checkpoint** activity to **Get Checkpoint for Remove**.
26. Navigate to the **Activities** section, select **SC 2012 Virtual Machine Manager** and drag a **Manage Checkpoint** activity to the Runbook next to the **Get Checkpoint** for **Restore** activity.
27. Link the **Get Checkpoint for Restore** activity to the **Manage Checkpoint** activity.
28. Right-click on the **Manage Checkpoint** and choose **Rename**.
29. Rename the activity to **Restore Checkpoint**.

30. Double-click on the **Restore Checkpoint** activity and provide the following information on the **Filters** section:

Name of parameter	Value
Configuration name	Pick the SCVMM configuration you set up in the preparation of this chapter from the list

31. Provide the following details for the properties:

Name	Value
Action	Use the ellipsis (**...**) button and select the **Restore** action.
ID	Right-click on the **ID** field and navigate to **Subscribe** | **Published Data**. Choose **Get Checkpoint for Restore** in the **Activity** field and select **ID**.

32. Click on **Finish**.
33. Repeat the preceding steps for the **Manage Checkpoint** for the **Get Checkpoint for Remove** activity. Rename it to **Remove Checkpoint** and set the action to **Remove**.
34. Navigate to the **Activities** section, select **SC 2012 Virtual Machine Manager** and drag a **Create Checkpoint** activity to the Runbook next to the **Get VM for Create** object.
35. Link the **Get VM for Create** activity to the **Create Checkpoint** activity.
36. Double-click on the **Create Checkpoint** activity and provide the following information on the **Details** section:

Name of parameter	Value
Configuration name	Pick the SCVMM configuration we set up in the preparation of this chapter from the list

37. Click on **Optional Properties** and select **Description** and **Name** then click on **OK**.
38. Provide the following details for the properties:

Name	Value
VM ID	Right-click on the VM ID field and navigate to **Subscribe** | **Published Data**. Select **Get VM for Create** in the **Activity** field and select **VM ID**.
Description	Right-click on the **Description** field and navigate to **Subscribe** | **Published Data**. Choose **Initialize Data** in the **Activity** field and select **Reason**.
Name	Type the following text: `Orchestrator Created Checkpoint`

39. Click on **Finish**.

    The final Runbook should look like the following screenshot:

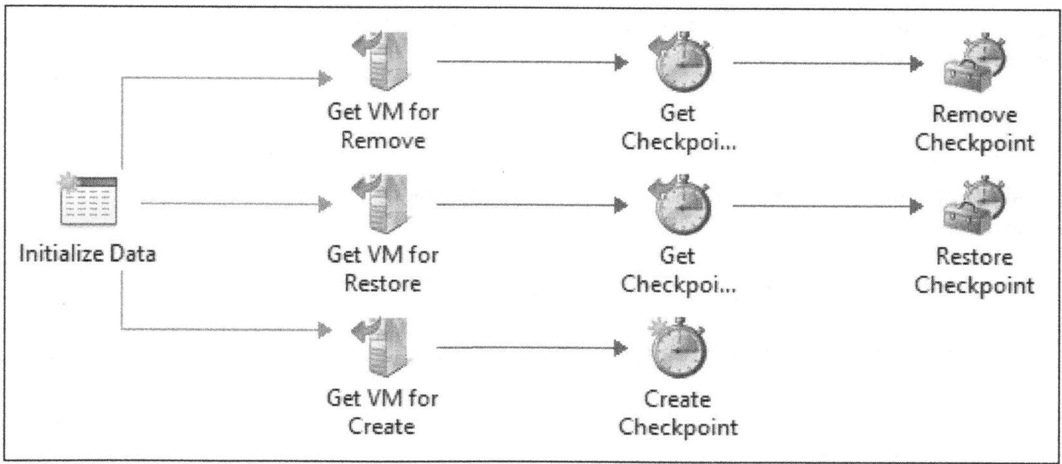

How it works...

When you run this Runbook using the tester, or from the Orchestrator Web Console, the Runbook will prompt you for a virtual server name, a reason for the checkpoint and the action to perform (Create, Restore, or Remove).

The Runbook will then query SCVMM for details about the VM (VM ID). The ID is passed to the other activities.

The Remove and Restore activities get the most recent checkpoint of the VM using the **Get Checkpoint** activity. The **Manage Checkpoint** activity uses the Checkpoint ID to either perform a restore or remove action.

To create a checkpoint, the VM ID from SCVMM is passed to a **Create Checkpoint** activity. The **Create Checkpoint** activity uses the VM ID to trigger the checkpoint creation on the VM using the reason value as the description.

There's more...

This Runbook can be used to enhance maintenance Runbooks. The maintenance Runbooks can invoke this Runbook and perform the checkpoint action before executing the specific maintenance action.

See also

Detailed information for the activities used in this Runbook can be found at the following locations:

- Microsoft TechNet - Create Checkpoint activity: `http://technet.microsoft.com/en-us/library/hh830696.aspx`
- Microsoft TechNet - Get Checkpoint activity: `http://technet.microsoft.com/en-us/library/hh830709.aspx`
- Microsoft TechNet - Manage Checkpoint activity: `http://technet.microsoft.com/en-us/library/hh830711.aspx`
- Microsoft TechNet - Get VM activity: `http://technet.microsoft.com/en-us/library/hh830744.aspx`

8
Creating Runbooks for System Center 2012 Service Manager Tasks

In this chapter we will cover the following topics:

- Changing incident priority for affected services
- Automating manual user creation service request fulfilment
- Automating manual activities for change request tasks on infrastructure servers

Introduction

IT Service Management processes are good candidates for automation. Most of the processes are usually well-documented and can consistently be repeated.

In this chapter we will provide recipes for the following topics:

- Changing incident priority for affected services:
    - Incidents may initially be recorded with the wrong priority by service desk analysts because of insufficient information or human selection errors
    - Setting a wrong priority for an incident might result in a longer outage of important business services
    - This Runbook will set the right priority based on the affected service(s)

- Automating manual user creation service request fulfillment:
  - Using the self-service portal and service requests in Microsoft System Center 2012 Service Manager for the new employee user creation process
  - Following approval of a service request, a **Runbook Activity** will be used to trigger the user account creation in Active Directory
- Automating manual activities (tasks) for infrastructure servers change requests:
  - A "Runbook Activity" in the change request will automatically add the related computers to a collection in System Center 2012 Configuration Manager (ConfigMgr)
  - ConfigMgr will install the required service pack on the computers based on the membership of this collection

For all recipes in this chapter, the requirements and preparations tasks are:

- Installed and deployed Service Manager 2012 integration pack
- To install integration packs in SCO refer to the *How to load Integration Packs* and *Configuring Integration Pack Connections* recipes in *Chapter 2, Initial Configuration and Making SCORCH Highly Available*
- A user account with appropriate permissions in Service Manager 2012 to create work items and modify existing work items

Changing incident priority for affected services

A very important and vital aspect of the incident management process is **prioritization**. One of the core aims of incident management is to ensure that all incidents related to a specified business service get the same priority. The priority allocation is based on the urgency and impact to the related service. The use of an Orchestrator Runbook can eliminate errors in priorities when allocated manually.

The following business process diagram shows the defined process covered in this recipe:

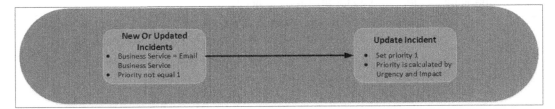

Getting ready

Perform the following steps before creating this Runbook:

1. The SC 2012 Service Manager integration pack needs to be installed and deployed to all SCORCH Runbook Designers.
2. The connection needs to be configured with the appropriate account. Navigate to **SCO 2012 Runbook Designer** | **Options** | **SC 2012 Service Manager** | **Connections** | **Add a connection**, and provide the required information.
3. In Service Manager create a Business Service. The example used in this recipe is an Email Business Service. Navigate to SCSM 2012 console | **Configuration Items** | **Business Services** | **All Business Services** | **Create Service**.

[For more information on Business Services in SCSM 2012, refer to the *Creating a business service* recipe in *Chapter 4, Building the Configuration Management Database (CMDB)* of *Microsoft System Center 2012 Service Manager Cookbook, Samuel Erskine (MCT), Steven Beaumont, Anders Asp (MVP), Dieter Gasser, Andreas Baumgarten (MVP).*]

4. In SCSM 2012 configure the priority calculation table to reflect your organization rules. SCSM 2012 console | **Administration** | **Settings** | **Incident Setting** | **Priority Calculation**. This recipe is based on the following priority calculation table:

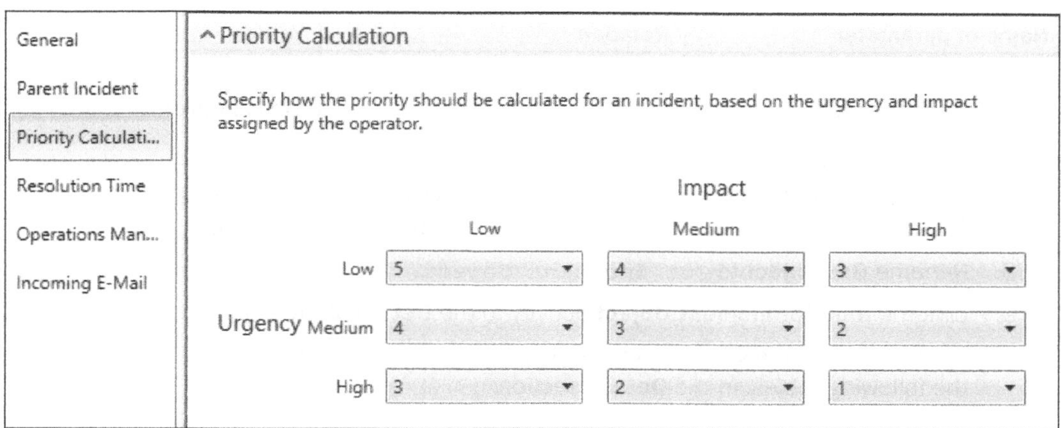

[For more information regarding the Incident Settings and the configuration of Priority Calculation matrix, refer to the *Configuring Priority and Urgency for your SLA targets* recipe in *Chapter 2, Personalizing SCSM 2012 Administration* of *Microsoft System Center 2012 Service Manager Cookbook*.]

Now, create a new Runbook in SCO 2012 Runbook Designer:

1. In the Runbook Designer expand the connection to the SCO 2012 server.
2. Right-click on **Runbooks** and click on **New** (you can also right-click on a folder in **Runbooks**).
3. Right-click on the newly created Runbook and rename it to `SetPriorityBasedOnAffectedService` (Click on **Yes** on the **Confirm Check out** dialog when prompted).

How to do it...

The following steps describe the configuration of the Runbook:

1. Navigate to the **Activities** section **SC 2012 Service Manager** and drag a **Monitor Object** activity into the newly created Runbook (middle pane).
2. Rename the activity to `Monitor Incident Object`.
3. Double-click on the activity in the **Details** tab under **Properties** | **Connection** and select the connection you configured to SCSM 2012.
4. Select **Incident** in the **Class** field.
5. Check **Updated** as **Trigger**.
6. Add three filters under the **Filters** section using the details in the following table (Click on **Finish** on completion of the filters):

Name of parameter	Relation	Value
Status	Equals	Active
Classification category	Equals	Email Problem
Priority	Does not equal	1

7. Navigate to the **Activities** section **SC 2012 Service Manager** and drag a **Get Object** activity into the Runbook next to the **Monitor Incident Object** activity.
8. Rename **Get Object** to `Get Incident Object`.
9. Link the **Monitor Incident Object** activity to the **Get Incident Object** activity.
10. Double-click on the **Get Incident Object** activity and provide the information given in the following tables, in the **Details** section:

Name of parameter	Value	Description
Connection	Choose connection to SCSM 2012.	The SCSM 2012 connection.
Class	Incident	The class we want to monitor.

Filter (Name)	Relation	Value
SC Object Guid	Equal	Right-click in the **Value** field and select **Subscribe** | **Published Data**. Choose the **Monitor Incident Object** activity and select **SC Object Guid**.

11. Navigate to the **Activities** section, go to **SC 2012 Service Manager** and drag a **Get Relationship** activity into the Runbook next to the **Get Incident Object** activity.
12. Rename the **Get Relationship** to **Get Relationship Incident About CI**.
13. Link the **Get Incident Object** activity to the **Get Relationship Incident About CI** activity.
14. Double-click on the **Get Relationship Incident About CI** activity and provide the information given in the following table, in the **Details** section:

Name of the parameter	Value	Description
Connection	Choose connection to SCSM 2012.	The SCSM 2012 connection.
Object Class	Incident	The class we want to get the information from.
Object Guid	Right-click in the Object Guid field and select **Subscribe** | **Published Data.** Choose **Get Incident Object** activity and **select SC Object Guid**.	Object Guid from Incident.
Related Class	**Business Service**	Related Business Service class.

15. Navigate to the **Activities** section **SC 2012 Service Manager** and drag a **Get Object** activity into the Runbook next to the **Get Relationship Incident About CI** activity.
16. Rename the **Get Object** activity to `Get Related Business Service Object`.
17. Link the **Get Relationship Incident About CI** activity to the **Get Related Business Service Object** activity.

18. Double-click on the link between the **Get Relationship Incident About CI** and the **Get Related Business Service Object** activities and modify **Include Filters** | **Include** to `Number of objects from Get Relationship Incident About CI does not equal 0`, as shown in the following screenshot:

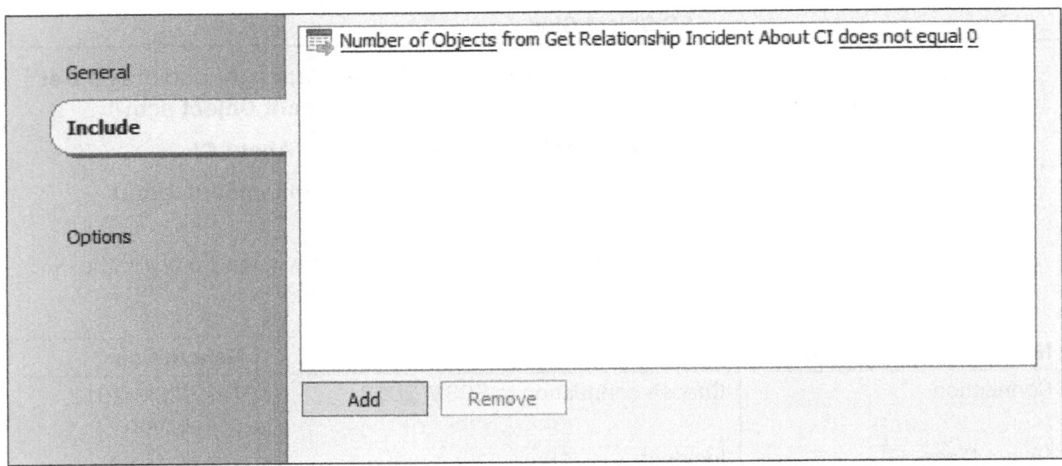

19. Double-click on the **Get Related Business Service Object** activity and provide the information given in the following tables, in the **Details** section:

Name of the parameter	Value	Description
Connection	Choose connection to SCSM 2012	The SCSM 2012 connection.
Class	Business Service	The class we want the information from.

Filter (Name)	Relation	Value
SC Object Guid	Equal	Right-click in the **Value** field and select **Subscribe** | **Published Data**. Choose the **Get Relationship Incident About CI** activity and **Related Object Guid**.

20. Navigate to the **Activities** section **SC 2012 Service Manager** and drag an **Update Object** activity in the Runbook next to the **Get Related Business Service Object** activity.
21. Rename the **Update Object** activity to **Update Incident Object**.
22. Link the **Get Related Business Service Object** activity to the **Update Incident Object** activity.

23. Double-click on the link between the **Get Related Business Service Object** and **Update Incident Object** activities and modify the **Include Filters** to `Display Name from get Related Business Service Object equals to Email Business Service` (you must type the value):

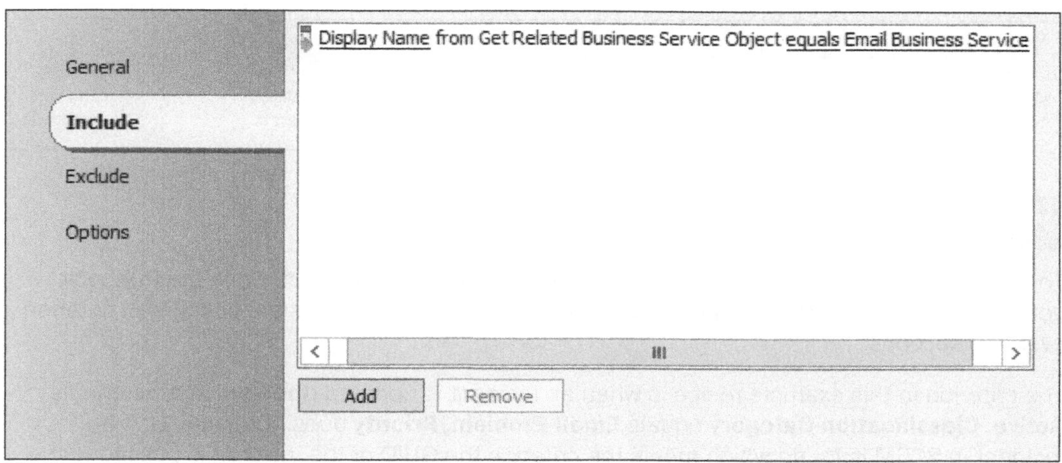

24. Double-click on the **Update Incident Object** activity and provide the information given in the following tables, in the **Details** section:

Name of the parameter	Value	Description
Connection	Choose connection to SCSM 2012	The SCSM 2012 connection.
Class	Incident	The class we want to update.
Object Guid	Right-click in the **Object Guid field** and select **Subscribe** | **Published Data**. Choose the **Get Incident Object** activity and select **SC Object Guid**.	The GUID of the incident we want to update.

Field (Name) (Click Select optional fields...)	Value	Description
Urgency	**High** (Click **...** on the right of the field to select)	Priority 1 needs Urgency value = High.
Impact	**High** (Click **...** on the right of the field to select)	Priority 1 needs Impact value = High.

25. Check in the Runbook.
26. Click on **Run** in the SCO 2012 Runbook Designer.

The Runbook should look like this:

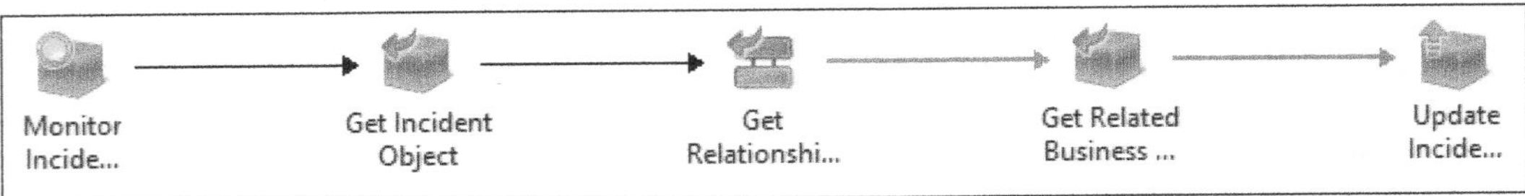

How it works...

The Runbook becomes active when it is checked in and you select run. Once the Runbook gets into a running state, the **Monitor Incident Object** activity checks the configured criterion every 10 seconds.

The criterion in this example recipe is when an incident is updated (**Incident Status** equals **Active**, **Classification Category** equals **Email Problem**, **Priority** does not equal **1**). If an incident in SCSM is found which meets the criterion the GUID of the incident is passed to the **Get Incident Object** activity. The Runbook uses the **Updated** trigger because in SCSM when you create an incident, the Business Service selection is an update action. This is in the case of either a new or existing incident.

The **Get Incident Object** activity gets all of the information related to the incident detected by **Monitor Incident Object**.

In the next step of the Runbook the related Business Service is discovered by the **Get Relationship Incident About Configuration Item** activity.

If there is a related Configuration Item/Business Service and Number of objects does not equal 0, the details of the related business service is discovered by the **Get Related Business Service Object** activity.

If **Display Name** of the related Business Service is equal to **Email Business Service** the **Update Incident Object** activity will set the **Impact** and **Urgency** of the incident to **High**. An SCSM internal workflow uses the configured settings in the Priority Calculation to set a value in the incident. In this example, the value is 1 based on the settings specified.

There's more...

Extending Runbook for different business services

To extend this Runbook to update the incident priority for different business services, you need an additional **Update Incident Object** activity to set the appropriate **Urgency** and **Impact**. This **Update Incident Object** activity must be linked to the **Get Related Business Service Object** activity. Configure each of the links with an **Include Filter**. For instance:

- **Display Name** from **Get Related Business Service Object** equals **to ERP Business Service**
- **Display Name** from **Get Related Business Service Object** equals to **Webshop Business Service**

Caution

This scenario is based on a one-to-one relationship between a business service and an incident. This is the cookbook organizations defined business process. You must modify the Runbook to manage the scenario of more than one business service to an incident. Using this Runbook with multiple business services attached to the same incident will result in a flip-flop state where the priority allocation will get into a loop.

See also

The detailed information for the activities used in this Runbook can be found at:

- Microsoft Technet – Monitor Object activity: `http://technet.microsoft.com/en-us/library/hh832009.aspx`
- Microsoft Technet – Get Object activity: `http://technet.microsoft.com/en-us/library/hh832002.aspx`
- Microsoft Technet – Get Relationship activity: `http://technet.microsoft.com/en-us/library/hh832006.aspx`
- Microsoft Technet – Update Object activity: `http://technet.microsoft.com/en-us/library/hh832004.aspx`

Automating manual user creation service request fulfilment

This recipe is based on the recipe in the Creating new users in Active Directory recipe in *Chapter 4, Creating Runbooks for Active Directory Tasks*. In this recipe we will combine the automated process to create a user in AD with the service request fulfillment in System Center 2012 Service Manager (SCSM 2012). The input for the request will be initiated from the self-service portal of SCSM 2012. When the service request is approved, a Runbook will create the user in AD.

The following diagram shows the defined business process covered in this recipe:

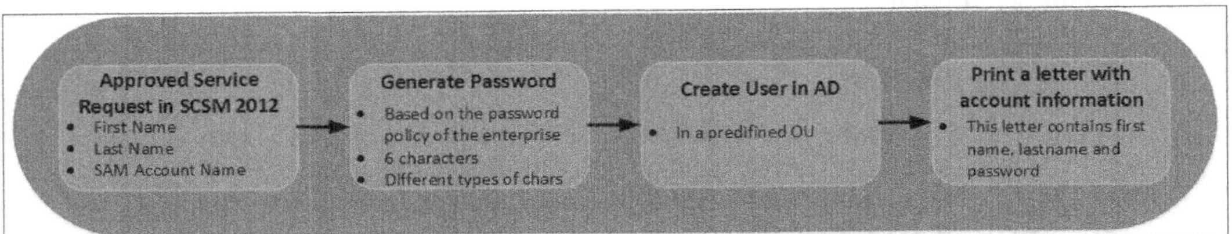

Getting ready

For this recipe we need the Active Directory integration pack installed and deployed to all SCORCH 2012 Runbook Designers (refer to the *How to load Integration Packs* and *Configuring Integration Pack Connections* recipes in *Chapter 2, Initial Configuration and Making SCORCH Highly Available*). You need a user account with appropriate permissions in Active Directory to fulfill the following tasks, create a user account and enable a user account.

The Orchestrator connector in SCSM 2012 needs to be configured and running.

For more information regarding the Orchestrator Connector in SCSM 2012 refer to the *Importing Orchestrator Runbooks* recipe in *Chapter 4* of *Microsoft System Center 2012 Service Manager Cookbook.*

Before we begin configuring the activities of the process we need to create a new Runbook in the Runbook Designer.

1. In the Runbook Designer expand the connection to the SCORCH 2012 server.
2. Right-click on **Runbooks** and click on **New** (you can also right-click on a folder under **Runbooks**).
3. Right-click on the newly created Runbook and rename it to **SRCreateNewUserInAD**.
4. Check in the Runbook.

5. Switch to the SCSM 2012 console | **Administration** | **Connectors** and sync the Orchestrator connector. Wait until the sync is completed.
6. In the SCSM 2012 console navigate to **Library** | **Runbooks** and check if the Runbook **SRCreateNewUserInAD** is synced.

How to do it...

The configuration of this solution is split in two parts. The first part is to configure the Runbook in the SCORCH 2012 Runbook Designer. The second part is to configure the Runbook Automation and a Request Offering in SCSM 2012.

This recipe is mainly focused on SCO 2012. You are provided with a summary of steps required for the SCSM configuration in part 2. For detailed information on Service Requests and Request Offerings in SCSM 2012, refer to the *Microsoft System Center 2012 Service Manager Cookbook* and Microsoft online resources.

Part 1 – configuring the Runbook in System Center 2012 Orchestrator Runbook Designer

1. In the SCO 2012 Runbook Designer console, navigate to the Runbook **SRCreateNewUserInAD**.
2. Navigate to the **Activities** section in the Runbook Designer. Select **Runbook Control** and drag an **Initialize Data** activity into the middle pane of the Runbook.
3. Right-click on the **Activity** and select **Properties**. Add one parameter in this activity in the **Details** section named **WorkItemID** as **String**.
4. Navigate to the **Activities** section and select **SC 2012 Service Manager** and drag a **Get Object** activity into the Runbook below the **Initialize Data** object.
5. Right-click on the **Get Object** and rename to **Get Runbook Activity Object**.
6. Link the **Initialize Data** and **Get Runbook Activity Object** activity.
7. Double-click on the **Get Runbook Activity Object** activity and provide the information from the following tables in the **Details** section:

Name of the parameter	Value	Description
Connection	Choose connection to SCSM 2012	The SCSM 2012 connection
Class	Runbook Automation Activity	The class we want to get the details

Filter (Name)	Relation	Value
ID	equal	Right-click in the **Value** field and select **Subscribe** | **Published Data**. Choose **Initialize Data** and **WorkItemID**.

8. Navigate to the **Activities** section **SC 2012 Service Manager** and drag a **Get Relationship** activity in the Runbook next to the **Get Runbook Activity Object** activity.
9. Rename the **Get Relationship** to `Get Service Request Relationship`.
10. Link the **Get Runbook Activity Object** activity to the **Get Service Request Relationship** activity.
11. Double-click on the **Get Service Request Relationship** activity and provide the information given in the following table on the **Details** section:

Name of the parameter	Value	Description
Connection	Choose connection to SCSM 2012	The SCSM 2012 connection.
Object Class	Runbook Automation Activity	The class we want to get the information from.
Object Guid	Right-click in the **Value** field and select **Subscribe** | **Published Data**. Choose the **Get Runbook Activity Object** activity and select **SC Object Guid**.	Object Guid from Runbook Activity Object.
Related Class	**Service Request**	Related Service Request

12. Click on **Finish**.
13. Navigate to the **Activities** section **SC 2012 Service Manager** and drag a **Get Object** activity in the Runbook above and to the right of the **Get Service Request Relationship** activity.
14. Rename the **Get Object** activity to `Get Service Request Object`.
15. Link the **Get Service Request Relationship** activity to the **Get Service Request Object** activity.
16. Double-click on the **Get Service Request Object** activity and provide the information on the **Details** section:

Name of the parameter	Value	Description
Connection	Choose connection to SCSM 2012	The SCSM 2012 connection.
Object Class	Service Request	The class we want to get the information from.

Filter (Name)	Relation	Value
SC Object Guid	Equals	Right-click in the **Value** field and select **Subscribe** | **Published Data**. Choose the **Get Service Request Relationship** activity and select **Related Object Guid**.

17. Click on **Finish**.
18. Navigate to the **Activities** section **SC 2012 Service Manager** and drag a **Get Relationship** activity into the Runbook next to the **Get Service Request Object** activity.
19. Rename the **Get Relationship** activity to `Get Review Activity Relationship`.
20. Link the **Get Service Request Object** activity to the **Get Review Activity Relationship** activity.
21. Double-click on the **Get Review Activity Relationship** activity and provide the information given in the following table on the **Details** section:

Name of the parameter	Value	Description
Connection	Choose connection to SCSM 2012	The SCSM 2012 connection.
Object Class	Service Request	The class we want to get the information from.
Object Guid	Right-click in the **Object Guid** field and select **Subscribe** | **Published Data.** Choose the **Get Service Request Object** activity and select **SC Object Guid.**	Object Guid from Service Request Object.
Related Class	Review Activity	Related Review Activity

22. Click on **Finish**.
23. Navigate to the **Activities** section **SC 2012 Service Manager** and drag a **Get Object** activity into the Runbook next to the **Get Review Activity Relationship** activity.
24. Rename the **Get Object** activity to `Get Review Activity Object`.
25. Link the **Get Review Activity Relationship** activity to the **Get Review Activity Object** activity.
26. Double-click on the **Get Review Activity Object** activity and provide the information given in the following tables on the **Details** section:

Name of the parameter	Value	Description
Connection	Choose connection to SCSM 2012	The SCSM 2012 connection.
Object Class	Review Activity	The class we want to get the information from.

Filter (Name)	Relation	Value
SC Object Guid	Equals	Right-click in the **SC Object Guid** field and select **Subscribe** | **Published Data**. Choose the **Get Review Activity Relationship** activity and select **Related Object Guid**.

27. Navigate to the **Activities** section **Utilities** and drag a **Generate Random Text** activity in the Runbook below and to the right of the **Get Review Activity Object** object.
28. Rename the **Generate Random Text** to **Generate Random Password**.
29. Link the **Get Review Activity Object** and **Generate Random Password** activity.
30. Double-click on the **Generate Random Password** activity and provide the information from the following table in the **Details** section:

Name of parameter	Value	Contains information
Text length (Type the value)	6	Password policy. Length of passwords.
Lower-Case Characters (check box and value)	1	At least 1 lower-case character. Complexity of passwords.
Upper-Case Characters (check box and value)	1	At least 1 upper-case character. Complexity of passwords.
Numbers (check box and value)	1	At least 1 number character. Complexity of passwords.
Symbols	Leave this option unchecked	Not required to meet the password policy in our example

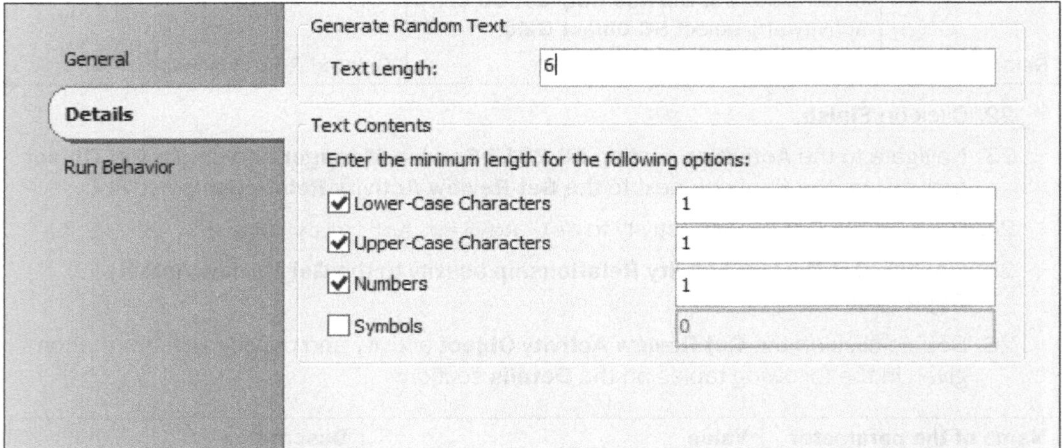

31. Navigate to the **Activities** section **Active Directory** and drag a **Create User** activity into the Runbook above and to the right of the **Generate Random Password** Activity.
32. Link the **Generate Random Password** activity to the **Create User** activity.

33. Double-click on the **Create User** activity and provide the information given in the following table on the **Properties** section:

Name of the parameter	Value	Contains information
Configuration	Pick the configuration from the list.	AD configuration we setup in the preparation of this chapter.
Common Name	Right-click in the **Common Name** field and select **Subscribe** | **Published Data**. Choose the **Get Review Activity Object** in the **Activity** field and select **Description**.	The username as part of the new distinguished name of the user object.
First Name (add this by using **Optional Properties**)	Click on **Optional Properties....** Select the field name from the **Available** section and click on **OK**. Right-click in the **First Name** field and select **Subscribe** | **Published Data**. Choose the **Get Service Request Object** activity and select **Description**.	The first name of the new user.
Last Name (add this by using **Optional Properties**)	Right-click in the **Last Name** field and select **Subscribe** | **Published Data**. Choose the **Get Service Request** activity and select **Alternate Contact Method**.	The last name of the new user.
Container Distinguished Name (add this by using **Optional Properties**)	Provide the Distinguished Name (DN) of the OU in AD. We will use this DN in our Runbook: `OU=PACKT8505EN-04,DC=TrustLab,DC=local`	The Organizational Unit in which, the user object will be created in AD.
SAM Account Name (add this by using **Optional Properties**)	Right-click in the **SAM Account Name** field and select **Subscribe** | **Published Data**. Choose the **Get Review Activity Object** in the **Activity:** field and select **Description**.	The login name of the new user.

Name of the parameter	Value	Contains information
Password	Right-click in the **Password** field and select **Subscribe** | **Published Data**. Choose the **Generate Random Password** activity and select **Random Text**.	The random password.
Description	Right-click in the **Description** field and select **Subscribe** | **Published Data**. Choose the **Get Service Request Object** in the **Activity:** field and select **ID**.	Use the Service request ID.

34. Navigate to the **Activities** section **Active Directory** and drag an **Enable User** activity into the Runbook below and to the right of the **Create User** activity.
35. Link the **Create User** activity to the **Enable User** activity.
36. Double-click on the **Enable User** activity and provide the following information in the **Properties** section:

Name of parameter	Value	Contains information
Configuration	Pick the configuration from the list	AD configuration we setup in the preparation section of this chapter
Distinguished Name	Right-click in the **Distinguished Name** field | **Subscribe** | **Published Data** Choose the "**Create User**" activity and select "**Distinguished Name**"	The Distinguished Name (DN) of the created user object

37. Navigate to the **Activities** section **Text File Management** and drag an **Append Line** activity into the Runbook above and to the right of the **Enable User** activity.
38. Right-click on the **Append Line** activity and rename the activity to **Generate Password Letter**.
39. Link the **Enable User** activity to the **Generate Password Letter** activity.

40. Double-click on the **Generate Password Letter** and provide the following information in the **Details** section:

Name of parameter	Value	Contains information
File	Right-click in the **File** field and select **Expand....** Type the path of the file for example `\\Server1\PACKT8505EN-Chapter08\` (using a shared folder is recommended). Right-click in the field after the last character in the file path \ and select **Subscribe** | **Published Data**. Choose the **Get Review Activity Object** and select **Description**. Type `.txt` (suffix of the file).	The filename of the password letter. Generated using the description from the review activity.
File encoding	Unicode	Encoding of the file.
Text	Right-click in the **Text** field and select **Expand....** Type the text as you would like it to appear in the letter. Add dynamic additional data by subscribing to **Published Data** in the relevant part of the text.	The text of the password letter. Note that the mapped fields from the subscription is based on how the Request Offering is configured in SCSM. In our example, the first name is mapped to the description entered in the Service Request. The description field is presented in the portal as a request for first name.

The result might look like the following:

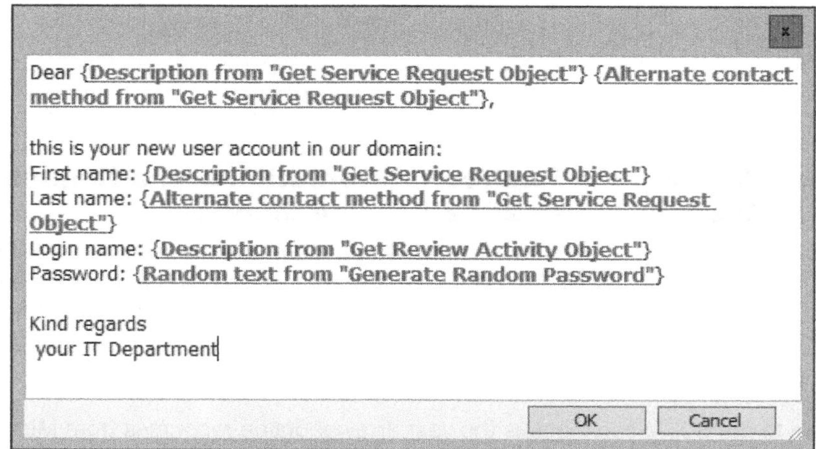

41. Navigate to the **Activities** section **File Management** and drag a **Print File** activity into the Runbook to the right and above of the **Generate Password Letter** activity.
42. Link the **Generate Password Letter** activity to the **Print File** activity.
43. Double-click on the **Print File** activity and provide the following information in the **Details** section:

Name of parameter	Value	Contains information
File	Right-click in the **File** field and select **Subscribe** | **Published Data**. Choose the Generate Password Letter activity and select **File path**.	The file name of the password letter.
Printer	Search and choose a printer.	The printer the password letter is send to.
Filter	(no age filter)	Keep the default setting.

44. Check in the Runbook in the SCO 2012 Runbook Designer. Right-click on the Runbook and select **Check In**.

The created Runbook should look like below:

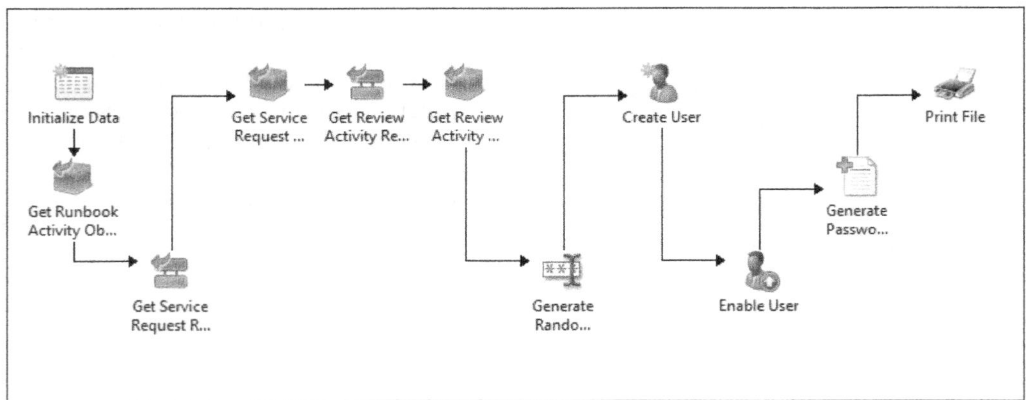

Part 2 – configuring the Runbook Automation and a Request Offering in System Center 2012 Service Manager

The first part of this recipe provides you with the steps required to create the SCORCH Runbook for the business process. The complete solution requires you to perform additional steps in System Center 2012 Service Manager. This cookbook is scoped to SCORCH and requires you to refer to the System Center 2012 Service Manager cookbook on how to perform the detailed steps in part 2.

An alternative to the SCSM cookbook is the vast array of online resources from Microsoft and the user community.

Here are the steps you must perform in SCSM:

1. In the SCSM 2012 console, ensure you have a connector to the SCORCH management server.
2. Perform a synchronization of Runbooks after you have perform the Runbook Check-In step in part 1.
3. Create a Review Activity Template for the Create User Process. Configure the reviewers to match the organization rules for this type of request.
4. Create a Runbook Activity Template based on the **SRCreateNewUserInAD** Runbook you created in part 1. You must ensure the SCSM SCORCH connector synchronization is complete and successful.
5. Create a Request Offering. Map the fields used in part 1 to the prompt questions.
6. Assign the Request Offering to a Service Offering. The Offerings must be assigned to a catalog group which is assigned to end users with rights to request new users.
7. Publish the Request and Service Offerings.

How it works...

The Runbook is invoked when you create a new service request with this specific Runbook Activity in the SCSM 2012 Self-Service portal.

You must fill the required fields in the service request and submit the service request in the SCSM 2012 Self-Service portal.

The input of the Self-Service portal form will be automatically mapped to the following fields if configured appropriately in the prompts section of the Request Offering:

Name of the parameter	Field	Contains information
Firstname	Description of the Service Request	First name of the new user.
Lastname	Alternate Contact Method of the Service Request	Last name of the new user.
Loginname	Description of the Review Activity	Login name of the new user.

For detailed information on Service Requests and the Self-Service portal in SCSM 2012, refer to *the Microsoft System Center 2012 Service Manager Cookbook*.

Upon successful submission of the request, the next step is to approve the request. The approval step is the Review Activity of the Service Request.

You might need to wait for the internal workflow to populate the review activity. This process can take a few minutes before the activity is listed in the SCSM console.

Following the approval of the Review Activity, an internal SCSM workflow changes the status of the Service Request to **In-Progress**. This status automatically triggers the Runbook in SCORCH.

The following happens once the Runbook is initiated:

1. The Initialize Data activity receives the ID from SCSM.
2. SCSM 2012 sets the ID in the **Initialize Data** activity of the **Runbook Automation Activity**.
3. The **Get Runbook Automation Activity Object** activity uses this ID to get the details of the Runbook Automation Activity.
4. The **Get Service Request Relationship** activity discovers the relationship between the Runbook Automation Activity and Service Request.
5. Using the details of the previous activities, the Get Service Request Object discovers additional detailed information of the related Service Request.
6. The next activity gets the relationship between the Service Request object and the related Review Activity (**Get Review Activity Relationship** activity).
7. The details of the Review Activity is read by the **Get Review Activity Object** activity.
8. Following the previous activities, SCORCH can access all of the required information to create the user in AD which is now available on the SCORCH Data Bus.
9. A random password is generated (**Generate Password** activity).
10. The Create User activity creates a new user object in the OU specified in Active Directory. The **Create User Runbook** activity gets the required information from the **Get Service Request Object** activity and the **Get Review Activity Object** activity.
11. The new user will be enabled by the **Enable User** activity (by default new user objects are disabled.)
12. A password letter will be created and stored in the specified folder using the **Generate Password Letter** activity. The **Print File** activity sends the file to the configured printer.

There's more...

There are more options available to you to automate processes in Microsoft System Center Service Manager. One option could be the automated update of the Implementation Result in a Service Request.

Updating the implementation results in the Service Request

To automatically update the result of the implementation in the Service Request you need to add one more activity into the Runbook:

1. Select the **SRCreateNewUserInAD** Runbook and navigate to the **Activities** section **SC 2012 Service Manager**. Drag an **Update Object** activity into the Runbook to the right and below the **Generate Password Letter** activity. Click on **Yes** to check out the Runbook.
2. Rename the **Update Object** activity to **Update Service Request Object**.
3. Link the **Generate Password Letter** activity to the **Update Service Request Object** activity.
4. Double-click on the **Update Service Request** activity and provide the following information in the **Properties** section, as seen in the following screenshot:

Name of the parameter	Value	Description
Connection	Choose connection to SCSM 2012.	The SCSM 2012 connection.
Object Class	Service Request	The class we want to get the information from.
Object Guid	Right-click in the **Object Guid** field and select **Subscribe** | **Published Data**. Choose the **Get Service Request Object** activity and select **SC Object Guid**.	Object Guid from Service Request Object.
Field (Name) (Click on Select optional fields...)	**Value**	**Description**
Implementation Results	Click on **...** and select **Successfully Implemented**.	List item from SCSM.
Notes	Type `Done by a SCO 2012 runbook`.	Free text

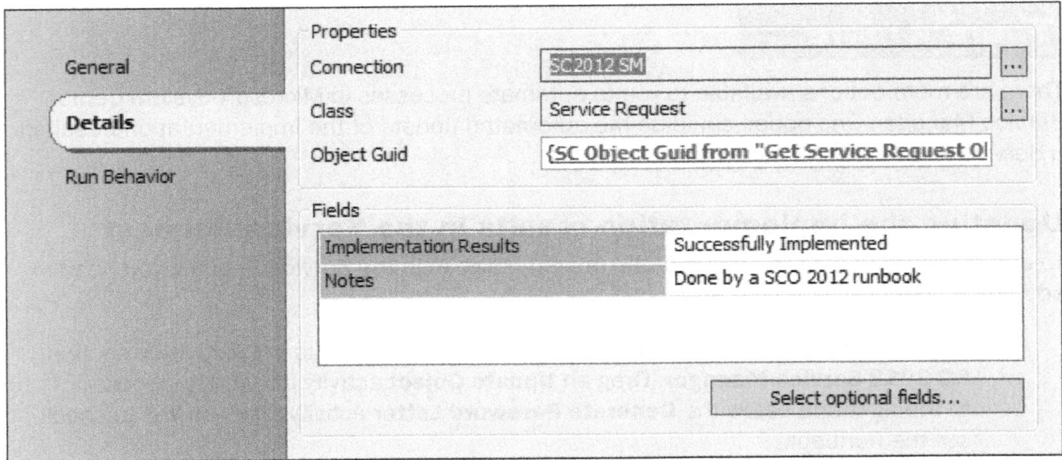

The Runbook should now look like the following:

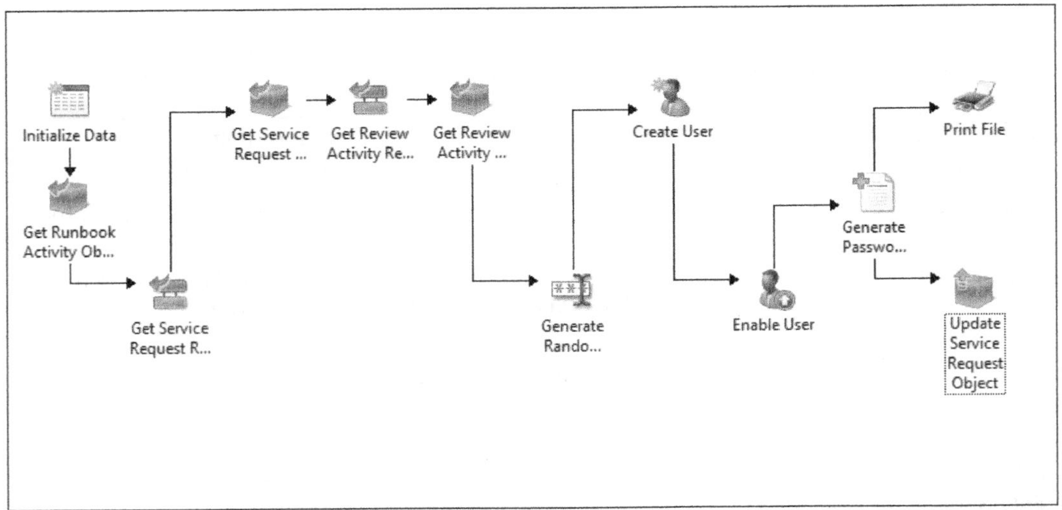

See also

Detailed information for the activities used in this Runbook you can be found at the following links:

- Microsoft Technet – Get Object activity: `http://technet.microsoft.com/en-us/library/hh832002.aspx`
- Microsoft Technet – Get Relationship activity: `http://technet.microsoft.com/en-us/library/hh832006.aspx`

- Microsoft Technet – Update Object activity: `http://technet.microsoft.com/en-us/library/hh832004.aspx`
- Microsoft Technet – Create User activity: `http://technet.microsoft.com/en-us/library/hh553464.aspx`
- Microsoft Technet – Enable User activity: `http://technet.microsoft.com/en-us/library/hh553486.aspx`
- Microsoft Technet – Generate Random Text activity: `http://technet.microsoft.com/en-us/library/hh206114.aspx`
- Microsoft Technet – Append Line activity: `http://technet.microsoft.com/en-us/library/hh206072.aspx`
- Microsoft Technet – Print File activity: `http://technet.microsoft.com/en-us/library/hh206045.aspx`

Automating manual activities for change request tasks on infrastructure servers

In this recipe, we will provide a Runbook to automate a manual task in the change management process.

Applying security updates and installing service packs on servers is a common and repetitive requirement for data center administrators. The change management process supports the task rated to these requirements.

System Center 2012 Service Manager (SCSM 2012) provides the means to raise and manage change requests in line with the organization's policies. System Center 2012 Configuration Manager (ConfigMgr 2012) provides the ability to deploy software and updates to computers.

Typically, the two components need to be bridged with manual processes. For example, you must add the applicable servers to a ConfigMgr deployment collection once a SCSM change has been approved to deploy updates.

This process can be automated with a SCORCH 2012 Runbook. You can use a Runbook to add a computer, defined in a SCSM 2012 change request as **Config Item To Change**, to a ConfigMgr 2012 Collection.

The following diagram illustrates the defined business process covered in this recipe:

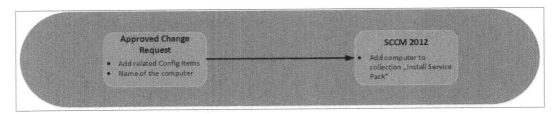

Getting ready

For this recipe you need the SC 2012 Configuration Manager integration pack installed and deployed to all SCORCH 2012 Runbook Designers (refer to the *How to load Integration Packs* and *Configuring Integration Pack Connections* recipes in *Chapter 2, Initial Configuration and Making SCORCH Highly Available*). We will also need a user account with appropriate permissions in ConfigMgr 2012 to fulfill the tasks automated in this Runbook.

In ConfigMgr 2012, you need a pre-defined collection (for example, **Install Service Pack**). ConfigMgr 2012 also needs to be configured to deploy the appropriate updates/service packs to this collection.

The computer you want to add to this collection must be managed by ConfigMgr 2012.

The Orchestrator connector in SCSM 2012 needs to be configured and running.

For more information regarding the Orchestrator Connector in SCSM 2012, refer to the *Importing Orchestrator runbooks* recipe in *Chapter 4, Building the Configuration Management Database (CMDB)* of *Microsoft System Center 2012 Service Manager Cookbook, Samuel Erskine (MCT), Steven Beaumont, Anders Asp (MVP), Dieter Gasser, Andreas Baumgarten (MVP)*.

How to do it...

Before we begin configuring the activities of the process, you need to create a new Runbook in the Runbook Designer.

1. In the Runbook Designer console expand the connection to the SCO 2012 server.
2. Right-click on **Runbooks** and click on **New**.
3. Right-click on the newly created Runbook and rename it to **CRAddComputerToSCCMCollection**.

4. Navigate to the **Activities** section in the Runbook Designer. Select **Runbook Control** and drag an **Initialize Data** activity into the middle pane of the Runbook.
5. Right-click the activity and select **Properties**. Add one parameter in this activity in the **Details** section named **WorkItemID** as **String**.
6. Check in the Runbook.
7. Switch to the SCSM 2012 console, select **Administration** | **Connectors**, and sync the Orchestrator connector. Wait until the sync is completed.
8. In the SCSM 2012 console, navigate to **Library** | **Runbooks** and check that the Runbook **CRAddComputerToSCCMCollection** is synced.

The rest of the configuration of this solution is split in two parts. The first part is to configure the Runbook Automation Activity in SCSM 2012.

This recipe is mainly focused on SCORCH 2012. For detailed information on Service Requests in SCSM 2012, refer to *Microsoft System Center 2012 Service Manager Cookbook*.

The second part is to configure the Runbook in the SCO 2012 Runbook Designer.

Part 1 – configuring the Runbook Automation Activity in System Center 2012 Service Manager

1. In the SCSM 2012 console navigate to **Library** | **Runbooks**.
2. Click on the synced Runbook named **CRAddComputerToSCCMCollection** and click on **Tasks** | **Create Runbook Automation Activity Template**.
3. Provide the following information:

Name of the parameter	Value	Contains information
Name	For example, `Runbook Activity Template CR - Add Computer To SCCM Collection`.	Name of the Runbook Automation Activity Template.
Description	For example, `Packt SCO 2012 Cookbook Chapter 8`.	Optional description of this template.
Class	Runbook Automation Activity	Class the template is related to.
Management Pack	Use an existing management pack or create a new management pack.	Management packs is storing the configuration of the template in SCSM 2012.

4. Click on **OK**.

5. Provide the following information on the **General** tab of the Runbook Automation Activity template (**Title**, **Description**, and **Is Ready For Automation** checkbox):

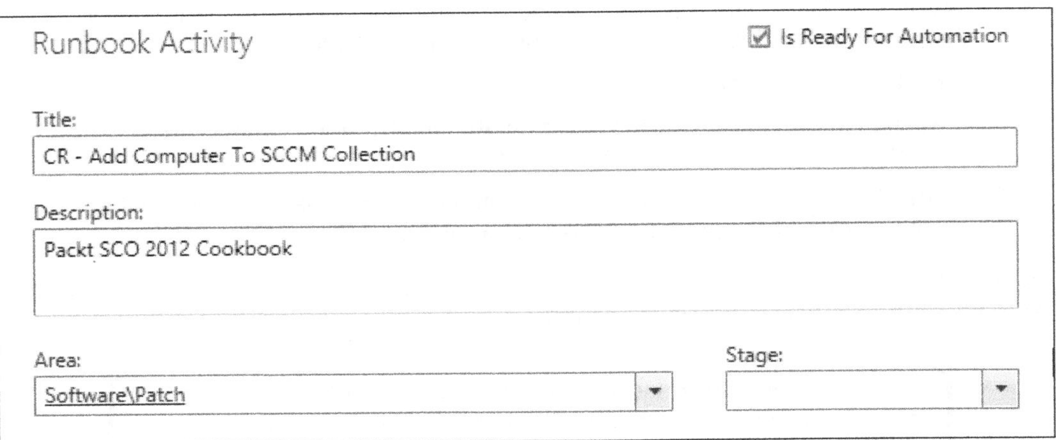

6. Navigate to the **Runbook** tab of the Runbook Automation Activity template.
7. Click on **Edit mapping** next to **WorkItemID** and select **Runbook Automation Activity | Work Item | Id**, as shown below:

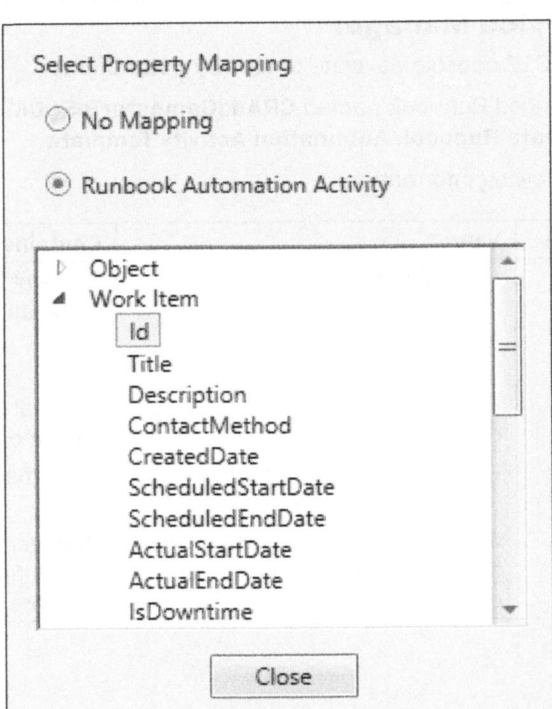

Part 2 – configuring the Runbook in System Center 2012 Orchestrator Runbook Designer

1. In the SCORCH 2012 Runbook Designer console navigate to the Runbook **CRAddComputerToSCCMCollection**. Right-click on the Runbook and select **Check Out**.
2. Navigate to the **Activities** section **SC 2012 Service Manager** and drag a **Get Object** activity into the Runbook below the **Initialize Data** object.
3. Rename the **Get Object** to `Get Runbook Activity Object`.
4. Link the **Initialize Data** and **Get Runbook Activity Object** activity.
5. Double-click on the **Get Runbook Activity Object** activity and provide the information given in the following table in the **Details** section:

Name of the parameter	Value	Description
Connection	Choose connection to SCSM 2012.	The SCSM 2012 connection.
Class	Runbook Automation Activity.	The class we want to get the details.
Filter (Name) (click Add under the Filters section)	**Relation**	**Value**
ID	Equal	Right-click in the **Value** field and select **Subscribe | Published Data**. Choose the **Initialize Data** activity and select **WorkItemID**.

6. Navigate to the **Activities** section **SC 2012 Service Manager** and drag a **Get Relationship** activity in the Runbook next to the **Get Runbook Activity Object** activity.
7. Rename the **Get Relationship** to `Get Change Request Relationship`.
8. Link the **Get Runbook Activity Object** activity to the **Get Change Request Relationship** activity.

9. Double-click on the **Get Change Request Relationship** activity and provide the following information in the **Details** section:

Name of the parameter	Value	Description
Connection	Choose connection to SCSM 2012.	The SCSM 2012 connection.
Object Class	Runbook Automation Activity.	The class we want to get the information from.
Object Guid	Right-click in the **Object Guid** field and select **Subscribe** | **Published Data**. Choose the **Get Runbook Activity Object** activity and select **SC Object Guid**.	Object Guid from Runbook Activity Object.
Related Class	Change Request	Related Change Request

10. Navigate to the **Activities** section **SC 2012 Service Manager** and drag a **Get Object** activity into the Runbook to the right and above the **Get Change Request Relationship** activity.
11. Rename the **Get Object** activity to `Get Change Request Object`.
12. Link the **Get Service Request Relationship** activity to the **Get Change Request Object** activity.
13. Double-click on the **Get Change Request Object** activity and provide the following information in the **Details** section:

Name of the parameter	Value	Description
Connection	Choose connection to SCSM 2012	The SCSM 2012 connection.
Object Class	Change Request	The class we want to get the information from.
Filter (Name)	**Relation**	**Value**
SC Object Guid	Equals	Right-click in the **SC Object Guid** field and select **Subscribe** | **Published Data**. Choose the **Get Change Request Relationship** activity and select **Related Object Guid**.

14. Navigate to the **Activities** section **SC 2012 Service Manager** and drag a **Get Relationship** activity in the Runbook next to the **Get Change Request Object** activity.
15. Rename the **Get Relationship** to `Get Computer Relationship`.
16. Link the **Get Change Request Object** activity to the **Get Computer Relationship** activity.

17. Double-click on the **Get Computer Relationship** activity and provide the following information in the **Details** section:

Name of parameter	Value	Description
Connection	Choose connection to SCSM 2012.	The SCSM 2012 connection.
Object Class	Change Request	The class we want to get the information from.
Object Guid	Right-click in the **Object Guid** field and select **Subscribe | Published Data**. Choose the **Get Change Request Object** activity and select **SC Object Guid**.	Object Guid from Change Request Object.
Related Class	Windows Computer	Related Change Request

18. Navigate to the **Activities** section **SC 2012 Service Manager** and drag a **Get Object** activity in the Runbook next to the "**Get Computer Relationship**" activity.
19. Rename the **Get Object** activity to `Get Windows Computer Object.`
20. Link the **Get ComputerRelationship** activity to the **Get Windows Computer Object** activity.
21. Double-click on the **Get Windows Computer Object** activity and provide the following information in the **Details** section:

Name of parameter	Value	Description
Connection	Choose connection to SCSM 2012.	The SCSM 2012 connection.
Object Class	Windows Computer	The class we want to get the information from.
Filter (Name)	**Relation**	**Value**
SC Object Guid	Equals	Right-click in the **SC Object Guid** field and select **Subscribe | Published Data**. Choose **Get Computer Relationship** and select **Related Object Guid**.

22. Navigate to the **Activities** section **SC 2012 Configuration Manager** and drag a **Add Collection Rule** activity into the Runbook below the **Get Computer Object** activity.
23. Link the **Get Computer Object** activity to the **Add collection rule** activity.

24. Double-click on the **Add collection rule** activity and provide the following information in the **Details** section:

Name of the parameter	Value	Description
Connection	Choose connection to SCCM 2012.	The SCCM 2012 connection
Fields (Name)	**Value**	**Value**
Collection	For instance, `Install Service Pack`.	Name of the SCCM 2012 collection the computer will be added to
Collection Value Type	Name	The collection is defined by name and not by ID
Rule Name	<keep it empty>	Not required
Rule Type	Direct Rule	The computer is added by name instead of a query.
Rule Definition	Right-click in the **Rule Definition** field and select **Subscribe | Published Data**. Choose the **Get Computer Object** activity and select **NetBIOS Computer Name**.	Name of the computer.
Rule Definition Value Type	Resource Name	The computer is specified by the computer name.

25. Navigate to the **Activities** section **SC 2012 Configuration Manager** and drag an **Update Collection Membership** activity into the Runbook next to the **Add collection rule** activity.
26. Link the **Add collection rule** activity to the **Update Collection Membership** activity.
27. Double-click on the **Update Collection Membership** activity and provide the following information in the **Details** section:

Name of the parameter	Value	Description
Connection	Choose connection to SCCM 2012.	The SCCM 2012 connection.
Fields (Name)	**Value**	**Value**
Collection	For instance `Install Service Pack`.	Name of the SCCM 2012 collection the computer will be added to.
Collection Value Type	Name	The collection is defined by name and not by ID.

Name of the parameter	Value	Description
Wait for Refresh Completion	`False`	The Runbook should not wait until the membership of the collection is refreshed.
Polling Interval (in seconds)	`5`	This interval is used if `Wait for Refresh Completion` is set to `True`.

28. Check in the Runbook in the SCO 2012 Runbook Designer.

The Runbook should look like the following:

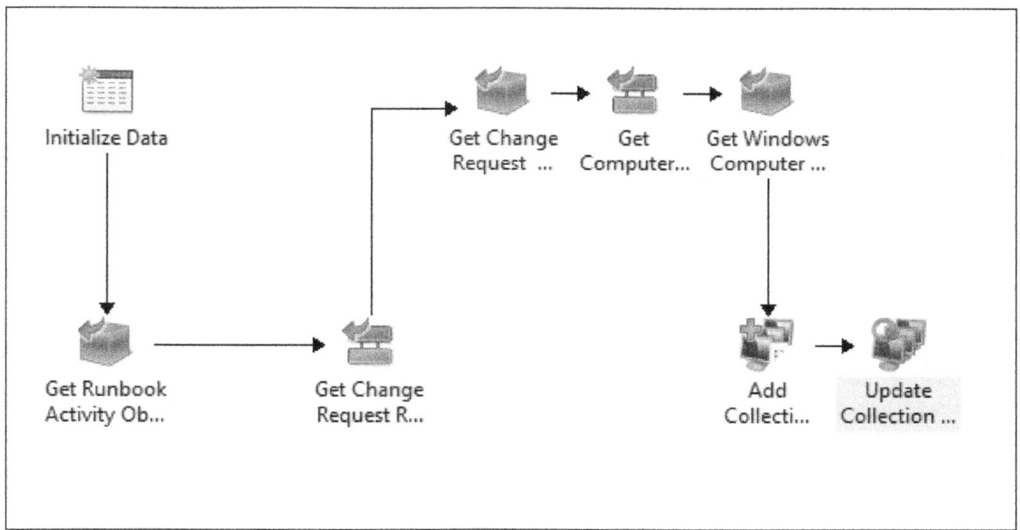

How it works...

The automation process is triggered by creating a new change request in the SCSM 2012 console. You must choose an appropriate Change Request template which has the Runbook Automation Activity configured. In our example, we are using the Major Change Request Template.

Provide the required information to the change request:

Change Request Information

Title:
Major Change Request / Install Service Pack

Description:
Packt SCO 2012 Cookbook Chapter 8

Reason:
Service Pack needs to be installed

Created By:

Alternate contact method:

Area:
Software\Patch

Assigned To:

Priority: Medium
Impact: Minor
Risk: Medium

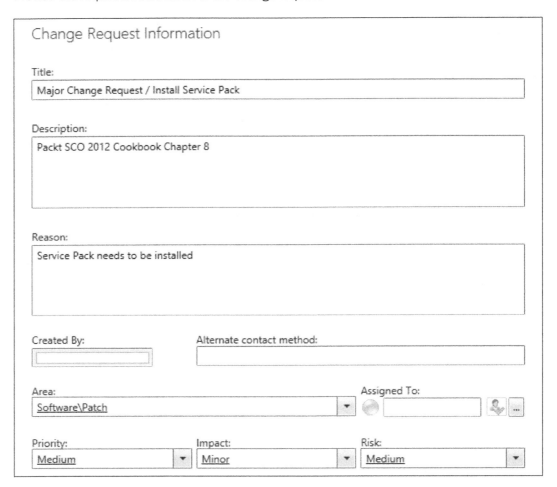

Add at least one computer in the **Config ItemsTo Change** section by clicking on **Add** and selecting a computer:

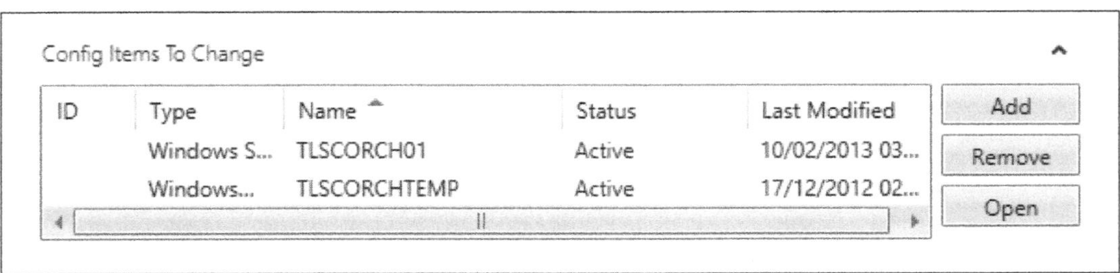

Ensure the selected computer(s) is/are already managed by ConfigMgr 2012 and are active.

Navigate to the **Activities** tab of the change request.

Delete all existing activities except the first **Approval** activity.

Add the Runbook Automation Activity you created in this recipe called **CR - Add Computer To SCCM Collection** by clicking on the **+ Activities**.

On the **Runbook Automation Activity** click on **OK** to close.

The change request should look like the following:

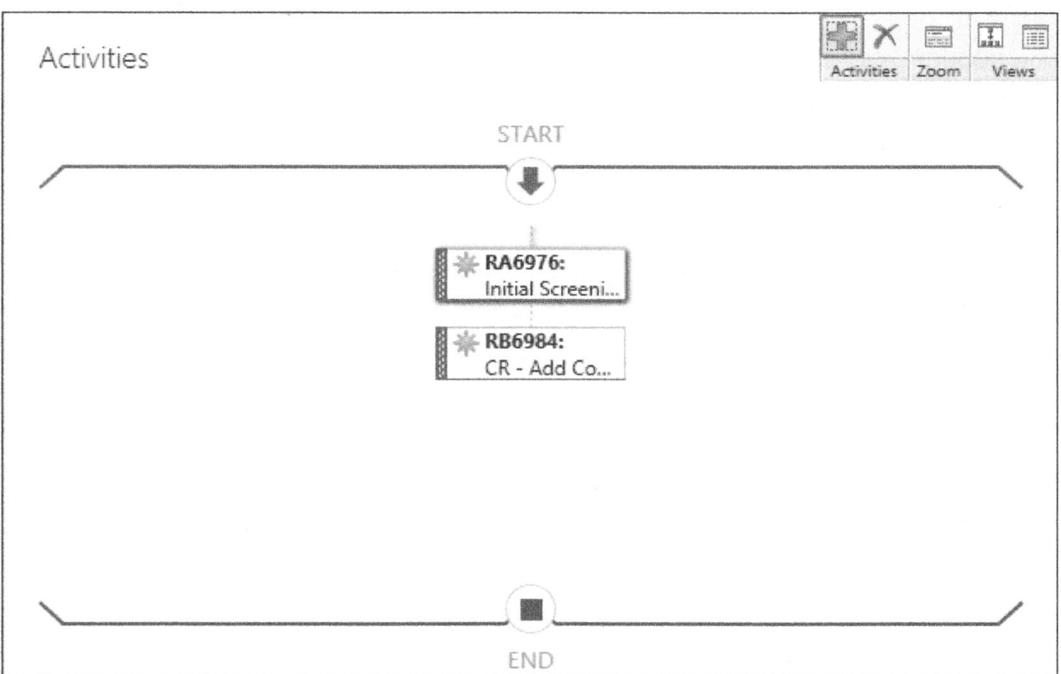

On the Change Request click on **OK** to close.

Wait until the new Change Request gets the status of **In Progress**.

Approve the Review Activity of the new Change Request in the SCSM 2012 console.

When the approval is complete SCSM 2012 will set the **Runbook Automation Activity** to a status of **In Progress**. This will trigger the execution of the Runbook in SCO 2012.

The ID of the Runbook Automation Activity is transferred to the **Initialize Data** activity in the Runbook.

This ID is used by **Get Runbook Automation Activity Object** to get the details of the **Runbook Automation Activity**.

The **Get Change Request Relationship** activity discovers the relationship between **Runbook Automation Activity** and **Change Request**.

Using these details, **Get Change Request Object** retrieves the detailed information of the related Change Request.

The next activity will get the relationship between the **Change Request** object and **Config Items To Change** using the Windows Computer class (**Get Computer Relationship** activity).

The details of the related computers will be provided by the **Get Computer Object** activity.

Now SCORCH 2012 can access all of the required information to add the computer(s) to the specified ConfigMgr collection from the SCO 2012 Data Bus.

The **Add Collection Rule** activity will get the NetBIOS Computer Names to add to the specified the collection (for example, a collection called `Install Service Pack`).

The last activity updates the membership of this collection in ConfigMgr 2012.

The result after the Runbook executes should look like the following in the ConfigMgr 2012 console (in our example, the computers are `TLSCORCH01` and `TLSCORCHTEMP`):

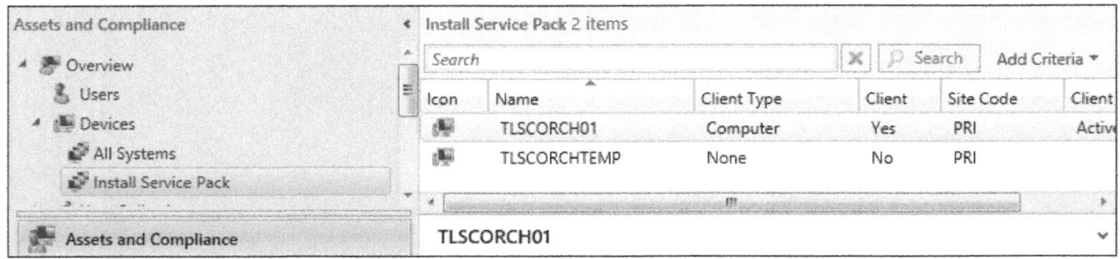

There's more...

Updating the implementation results in the Change Request

To automatically update the result of the implementation in the Change Request one more activity is required:

1. Select **CRAddComputerToSCCMCollection**, navigate to the **Activities** section **SC 2012 Service Manager**, and drag a **Update Object** activity in the Runbook next to the **Update Collection Membership** activity. Click on **Yes** to check out the Runbook.

2. Rename the **Update Object** activity to `Update Change Request Object`.
3. Link the **Update Collection Membership** activity to the **Update Change Request Object** activity.
4. Double-click on the **Update Change Request** activity and provide the following information in the **Properties** section, also shown in the following screenshot:

Name of the parameter	Value	Description
Connection	Choose connection to SCSM 2012.	The SCSM 2012 connection.
Object Class	Change Request	The class we want to get the information from.
Object Guid	Right-click in the **Object Guid** field and select **Subscribe** | **Published Data**. Choose the **Get Change Request Object** activity and select **SC Object Guid**.	Object Guid from Service Request Object.
Field (Name) (Click on Select optional fields...)	**Value**	**Description**
Implementation Results	Click on **...** and | select **Successfully Implemented**.	List item from SCSM
Notes	Type `Computer Items to Change added to the collection.`	Free text

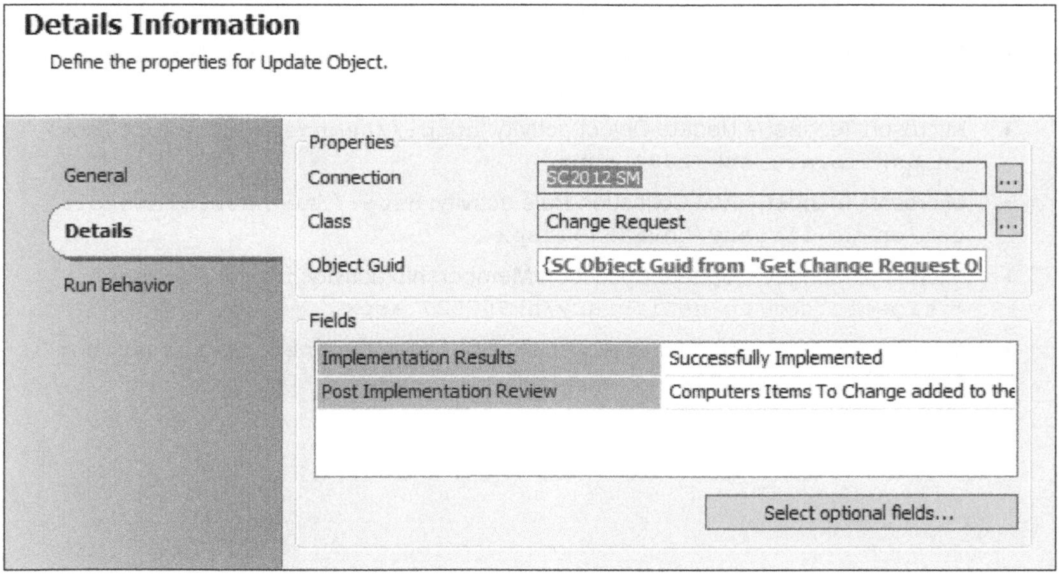

Details Information
Define the properties for Update Object.
General
Details
Run Behavior
Properties
Connection SC2012 SM
Class Change Request
Object Guid {SC Object Guid from "Get Change Request O
Fields
Implementation Results Successfully Implemented
Post Implementation Review Computers Items To Change added to the
Select optional fields...

The Runbook should now look like the following:

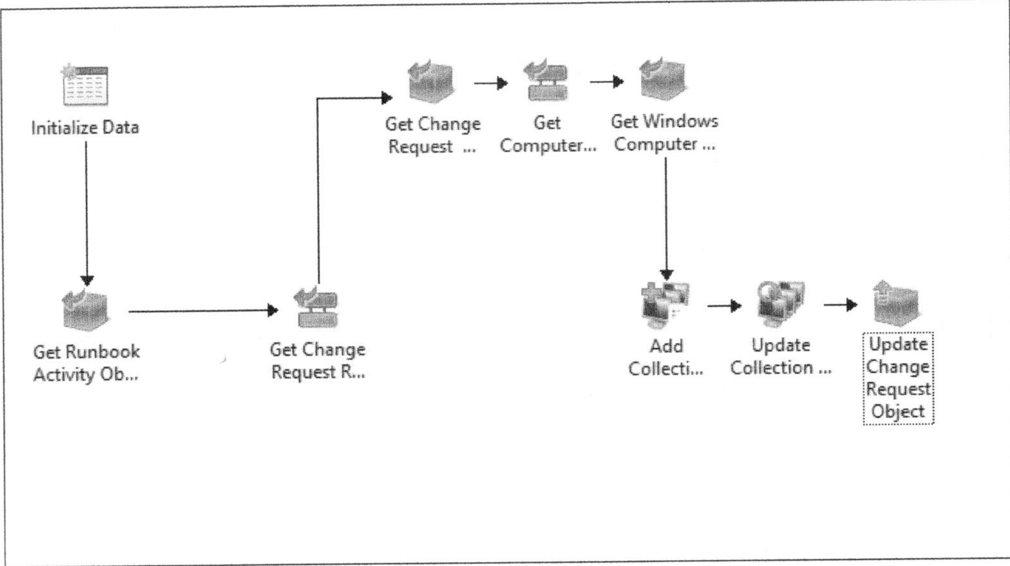

See also

Detailed information for the activities used in this Runbook you can be found here:

- Microsoft Technet – Get Object activity: `http://technet.microsoft.com/en-us/library/hh832002.aspx`
- Microsoft Technet – Get Relationship activity: `http://technet.microsoft.com/en-us/library/hh832006.aspx`
- Microsoft Technet – Update Object activity: `http://technet.microsoft.com/en-us/library/hh832004.aspx`
- Microsoft Technet – Add Collection Rule activity: `http://technet.microsoft.com/en-us/library/hh967533.aspx`
- Microsoft Technet – Update Collection Membership activity:`http://technet.microsoft.com/en-us/library/hh967527.aspx`
- Microsoft Technet – Update Object activity: `http://technet.microsoft.com/en-us/library/hh832004.aspx`

9
Using Advanced Techniques in Runbooks

In this chapter, we will be providing recipes on how to enhance and create advance System Center 2012 Orchestrator Runbooks:

- Creating child Runbooks
- Implementing error handling in your Runbooks
- Implementing logging in your Runbooks
- Creating looping Runbooks

Introduction

There are a variety of methods and options available to you to enhance **System Center 2012 Orchestrator (SCORCH)** Runbooks. The recipes in this chapter provide steps on how to utilize some of the common options available to enhance your Runbooks.

The recipes in this chapter will cover the following scenarios:

- Creating child Runbooks

  Use existing Runbooks for tasks instead of creating multiple Runbooks with duplicate, overlapping activities.

- Implementing error handling in your Runbooks

  This recipe will show how to proactively handle activity and Runbook errors.

- Implementing logging in your Runbook

  Different options on how to log the result of activities in Runbooks.

- Creating looping Runbooks

  Runbooks designed and created to wait for scenarios which require a specific condition to be met before executing.

The requirements for all recipes in this chapter are:

- Installed and deployed Active Directory integration pack

  Installing integration packs in SCORCH is described in *Chapter 2, Initial Configuration and Making SCORCH Highly Available*, how to load Integration Packs and Configuring Integration Pack Connections.

- A user account with appropriate permissions in **Active Directory** (**AD**) to fulfill the following tasks: create a user account, modify group membership, and move AD objects between OUs.

Creating child Runbooks

This recipe will describe how to call a child Runbook. This method allows you to be modular in your approach to Runbook activity designs. You can create common shared (functional) activity Runbooks. These common functional Runbooks can be used in new or existing Runbooks that require this functionality without duplicating the effort.

In this recipe you will use two of the Runbooks you created in *Chapter 4, Creating Runbooks for Active Directory Tasks*.

The specific scenario for the Runbook in this recipe is to create and add a new user to an Active Directory group.

Getting ready

The preparation for this recipe requires you to create the following two Runbooks described in *Chapter 4, Creating Runbooks for Active Directory Tasks*:

- Creating new users in Active Directory
- Adding users to groups in Active Directory

The two Runbooks you created in *Chapter 4, Creating Runbooks for Active Directory Tasks* should look and be called as shown:

"Create New User In AD"

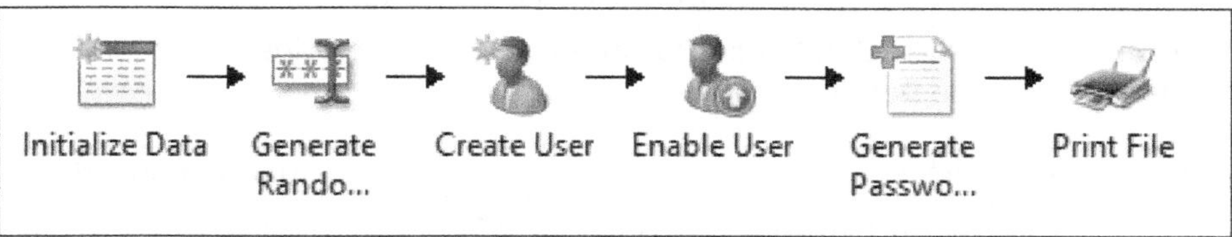

"Add User To Group In AD"

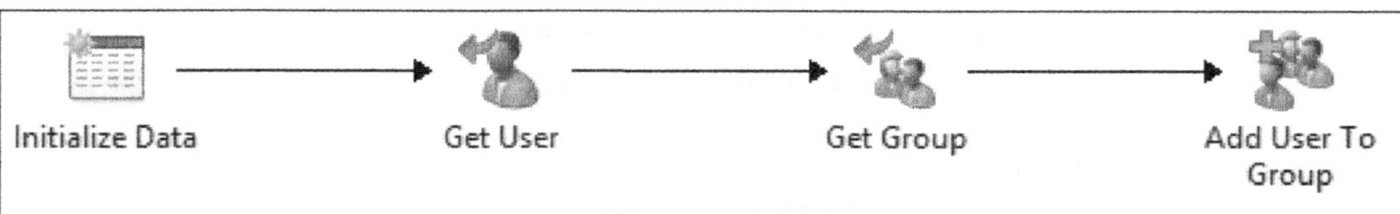

How to do it...

Follow these steps to call an existing child Runbook:

1. Navigate to the Runbook you created in *Chapter 4, Creating Runbooks for Active Directory Tasks* called "Create New User In AD", right-click on the Runbook and select **Check Out** | **Yes** to the prompt.
2. Double-click on the activity **Initialize Data**.
3. Add a new property called `GroupName` as `String` and close the property with **OK**, then click on **Finish** to close the activity.

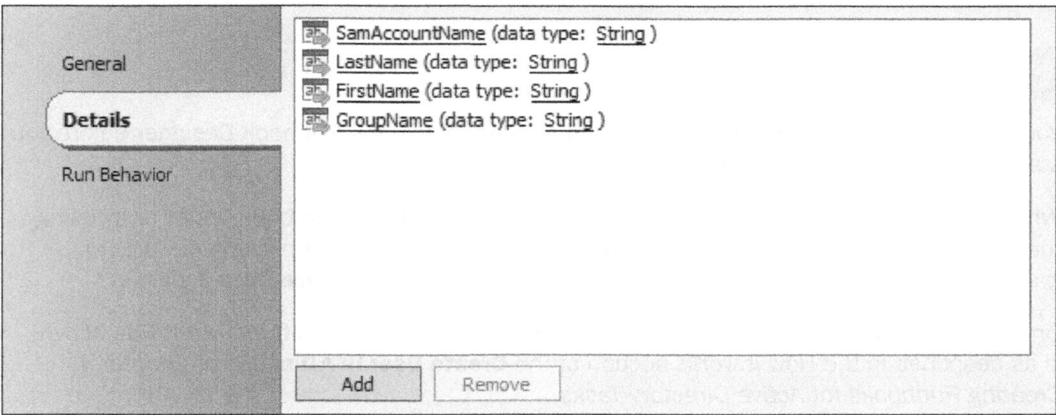

4. Navigate to the **Activities** | **Runbook Control** and drag an **Invoke Runbook** activity in the Runbook next to the **Print File** activity.
5. Right-click on the **Invoke Runbook** and rename it to **RB- Add User To Group**.
6. Link the **Print File** activity to the **RB- Add User To Group** activity.
7. Double-click on the **RB- Add User To Group** activity and provide the following information in the **Details** section:

Name of parameter	Value	Contains information
`Runbook`	Choose the **Add User To Group In AD** Runbook by clicking **...** and navigating to the Runbook.	The child Runbook that we are invoking with this activity.
`GroupName`	Right-click on the **GroupName** field and navigate to **Subscribe** | **Published Data**. Choose the **Initialize Data** activity and select **GroupName**.	The name of the new user's assigned group.
`Username`	Right-click on the **Username** field and navigate to **Subscribe** | **Published Data**. Choose the **Create User** activity and select **SAM Account Name**.	Name of the user that should be added to the group.

The result of the modified **Create User In AD** Runbook should look similar to the following screenshot:

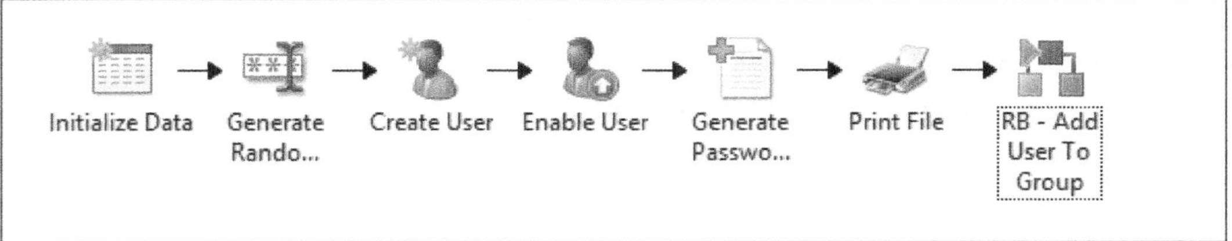

How it works...

You must check in the **Add User To Group In AD** Runbook in the Runbook Designer before you start the modified **Create User In AD** Runbook.

When you start this modified Runbook either in the Orchestrator Runbook Tester or by using the Orchestration Console website, you will be prompted for the four parameters: `First Name`, `Last Name`, `SAM Account Name`, and `GroupName` (**Initialize Data** activity).

Once the required information is provided the Runbook execution up to the **Print File** activity is as described in the *How it works* section of the **Create User In AD** recipe of *Chapter 4, Creating Runbooks for Active Directory Tasks*.

The modified part of this Runbook, **Invoke Runbook** activity (**RB-Add User To Group**), will call the specified **Add User To Group in AD** Runbook. The **Add User To Group** is known as the child Runbook. The child Runbook consumes the required information from the initiating parent Runbook which is, `GroupName` and `Username`.

The information from the parent Runbook (**Create User In AD**) is passed to the **Initialize Data** activity of the child Runbook (**Add User To Group**).

The username will be used as input for the **Get User** activity (**Distinguished Name** (**DN**) of the user object).

The `GroupName` parameter will be used as input for the **Get Group** activity (Distinguished Name of the group object).

The user object will be as assigned as a member of the group object. The two objects are defined by the Distinguished Name in the **Add User To Group** activity.

See also

Detailed information for the activities used in this Runbook are available at the following locations:

- Microsoft Technet – Create User activity: `http://technet.microsoft.com/en-us/library/hh553464.aspx`
- Microsoft Technet – Enable User activity: `http://technet.microsoft.com/en-us/library/hh553486.aspx`
- Microsoft Technet – Generate Random Text activity: `http://technet.microsoft.com/en-us/library/hh206114.aspx`
- Microsoft Technet – Append Line activity: `http://technet.microsoft.com/en-us/library/hh206072.aspx`
- Microsoft Technet – Print File activity: `http://technet.microsoft.com/en-us/library/hh206045.aspx`
- Microsoft Technet – Invoke Runbook activity: `http://technet.microsoft.com/en-us/library/hh206078.aspx`
- Microsoft Technet – Get User activity:`http://technet.microsoft.com/en-us/library/hh553476.aspx`
- Microsoft Technet – Get Group activity: `http://technet.microsoft.com/en-us/library/hh553470.aspx`
- Microsoft Technet – Add User To Group activity: `http://technet.microsoft.com/en-us/library/hh564142.aspx`

Implementing error handling in your Runbooks

This recipe will describe different methods of error handling in a Runbook. The current recommended practice is to ensure you implement error handling in all your Runbooks. Typical reasons why errors occur are incorrectly typed inputs and missing expected inputs.

In this recipe, you will enhance the recipe *Add User To Group In AD* you created in *Chapter 4, Creating Runbooks for Active Directory Tasks*, to include error handling.

Getting ready

The preparation for this recipe requires you to create the Adding users to groups in Active Directory Runbook described in *Chapter 4, Creating Runbooks for Active Directory tasks*.

The Runbook should look like and be called:

"Add User To Group In AD"

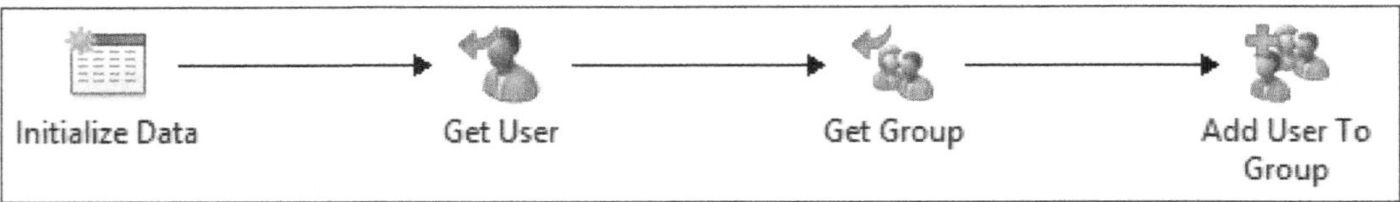

You must also define the error handling criterion for the Runbook and the corresponding action to perform when an error occurs.

In this scenario you can assume the process of error handling is defined as follows:

- If the `GroupName` is empty, create a log entry in the Windows event log
- If the `GroupName` is not empty but the group does not exist in the AD, then create a new group with the name provided

How to do it...

Follow these steps to add error handling to the existing Runbook:

1. Navigate to the Runbook **Add User To Group In AD**. Right-click on the Runbook and select **Check Out** | **Yes** to the prompt.
2. Navigate to the **Activities** section and select **Notification** and drag a **Send Event Log Message** activity into the Runbook above the **Initialize Data** activity.
3. Link the **Initialize Data** activity to the **Send Event Log Message** activity (you must start the link action from the **Initialize Data** activity).

4. Double-click on the link between the **Initialize Data** and **Send Event Log Message** activities.
5. Modify the **Include** filter of the link as follows:

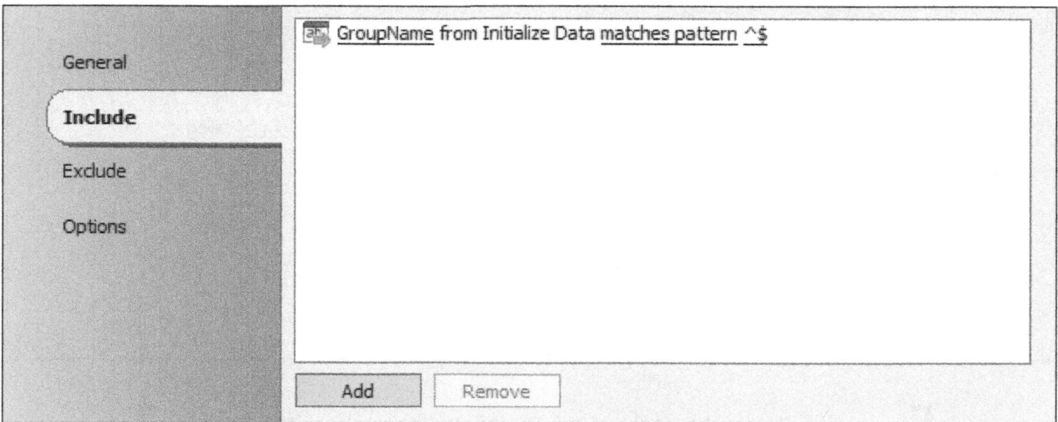

The regular expression **^$** is interpreted as a blank or NULL value.

6. Double-click on the created link between **Initialize Data** activity and **Get User** activities.
7. Modify the **Include** filter of the link as follows:

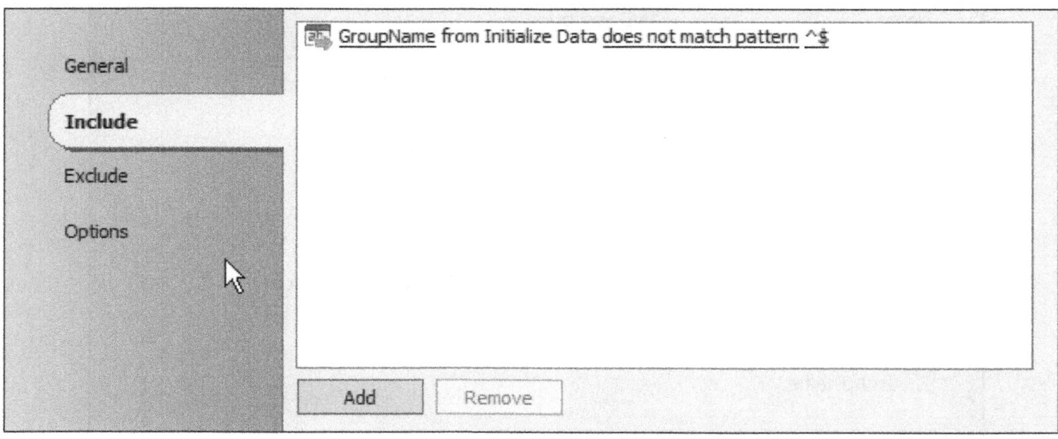

8. Double-click on the **Send Event Log Message** activity. In the **Computer:** field type the name of the Runbook Server.

9. In the **Message** section type the message as indicated in the following screenshot and select **Error** as the **Severity** option (you must subscribe to the published data from the data bus to get the Runbook name from the **Initialize Data** activity).

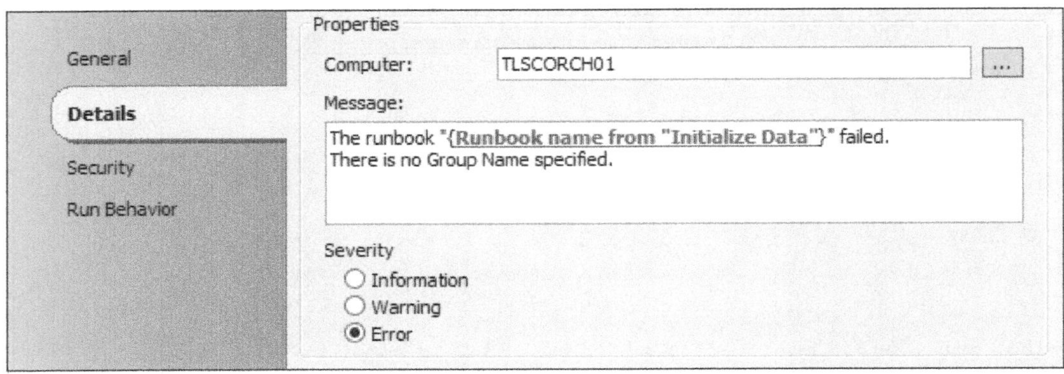

To get the name of the Runbook please check the **Show common Published Data** option in the **Published Data** window and scroll down.

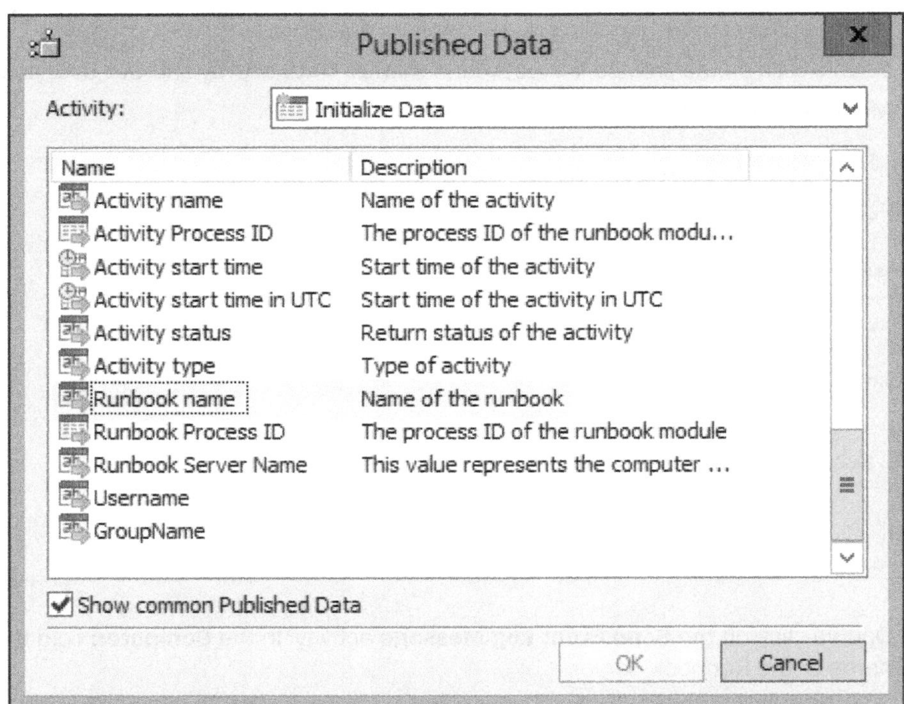

10. Navigate to the **Activities** section and select **Active Directory** and drag a **Create Group** activity into the Runbook above the **Get Group** activity.
11. Link the **Get Group** activity to the **Create Group** activity (you must start the link from the **Get Group** activity).
12. Double-click in between the **Get Group** and **Create Group** activities.
13. Modify the **Include** filter of the link as follows:

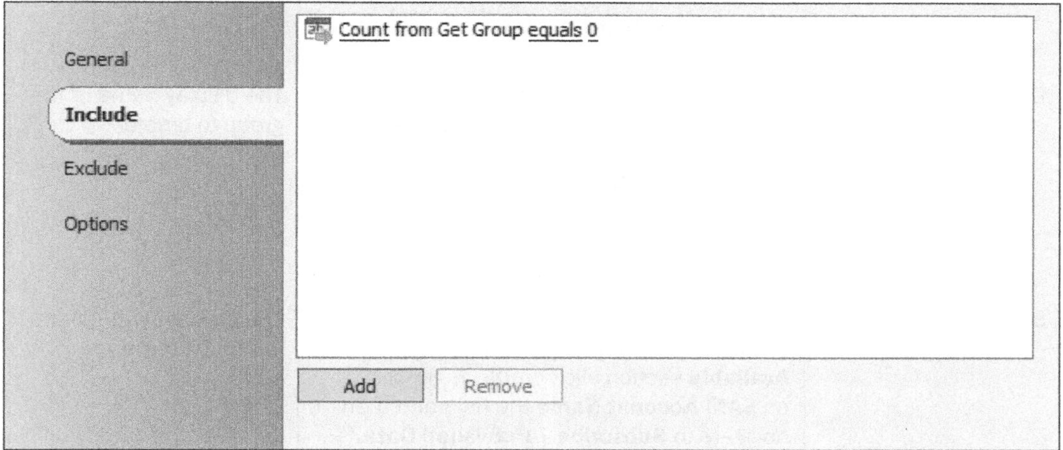

14. Double-click on the link between **Get Group** activity and **Add User To Group** activities.
15. Modify the **Include** filter of the link as follows:

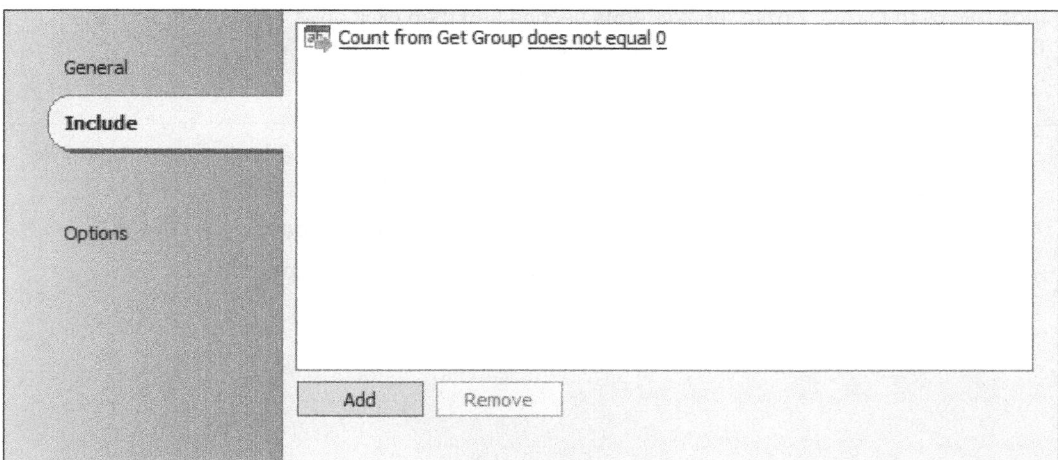

16. Double-click on the **Create Group** activity and provide the following information:

Name of parameter	Value	Contains information
Configuration	Pick the configuration from the list.	AD configuration we set up in preparation for this chapter.
Common Name	Right-click on the **Common Name** field | **Subscribe** | **Published Data**. Select the **Initialize Data** activity and select **GroupName**.	The common name of the group to create.
Display Name	Click on **Optional Properties....** Select the **Display Name** from the **Available** section and then click on **OK**. Right-click on the **Display Name** field and navigate to **Subscribe** | **Published Data**. Select the **Initialize Data** activity and select **GroupName**.	The display name of the group to create.
SAM Account Name	Click **Optional Properties....** Select the **SAM Account Name** field name from the **Available** section click on **OK**. Right-click on **SAM Account Name** the field and then navigate to **Subscribe** | **Published Data**. Select the **Initialize Data** in the **Activity:** field and select **GroupName**.	The display name of the group to create.
Container Distinguished Name (add this by the **Optional Properties**)	Click on **Optional Properties....** Select the **Container Distinguished Name** field name from the **Available** section and then click on OK. Provide the **Distinguished** name of the OU in AD. For instance: OU=PACKT8505EN,DC=TrustLab,DC=local.	The Organizational Unit in AD where the group object will be created.

17. Navigate to the **Activities** section. Click on **Active Directory** and drag a **Add User To Group** activity into the Runbook next to the **Create Group** activity.
18. Rename the **Add User To Group (2)** to **Add User To New Group**.
19. Link the **Create Group** activity to the **Add User To New Group** activity.

20. Double-click on the **Add User To New Group** activity and provide the following information:

Name of parameter	Value	Contains information
Configuration	Pick the configuration from the list.	AD configuration we set up in the preparation of this chapter.
Group Distinguished Name	Right-click on the **Group Distinguished Name** field and navigate to **Subscribe** | **Published Data**. Choose the **Create Group** activity and select **Distinguished Name**.	The Distinguished Name of the group.
User Distinguished Name	Right-click on the **User Distinguished Name** field and navigate to **Subscribe** | **Published Data**. Choose the **Get User** activity and select **Distinguished Name**.	The Distinguished Name of the user.

The difference between the original **Add User To Group** activity and the **Add User To New Group** activity is the different **Group Distinguished Name** value.

The result of the modified **Add User To Group In AD** Runbook should look like the following screenshot:

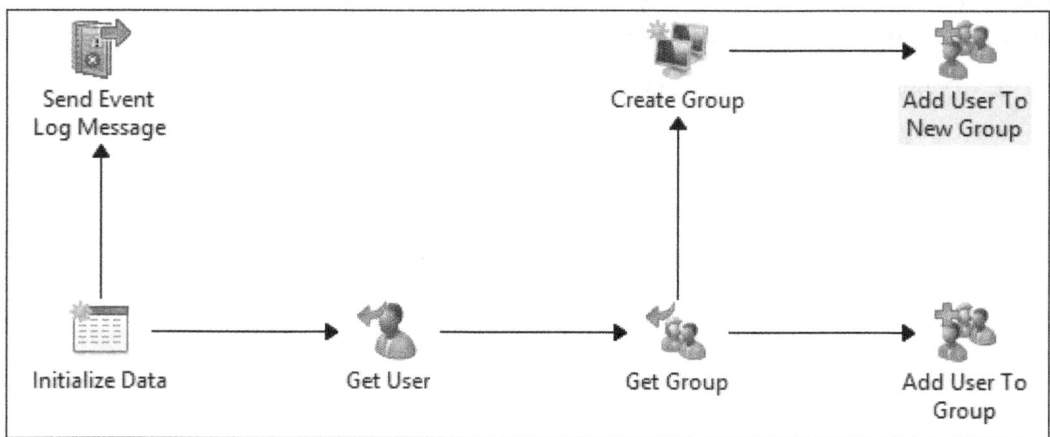

How it works...

When the Runbook is invoked in the Runbook designer or Orchestration Console website you will be prompted for a username and a group name.

Depending on the input of the Runbook:

- If `GroupName` property is empty/blank, a new entry is logged in the Event Log. (Send Event Log Message)
- If `GroupName` property is not empty/blank, the username is used as input for the **Get User** activity (Distinguished Name (DN) of the user object).

The `Groupname` will be used as input for the **Get Group** activity (Distinguished Name (DN) of the group object).

Depending on the result of the **Get Group** activity:

- If the group does not exists in AD, the group specified in the **Initialize Data** will be created and the user object will be added as a member of the new group.
- If group exists in AD, the user object will be added as a member of the group object. Both objects are defined by the Distinguished Name in the **Add User To Group** activity.

There's more...

Use different colors on links between activities:

To visualize different conditions on links you can choose different colors for the link:

1. Double-click on a related link.
2. Navigate to the **Options** tab.
3. Choose a different **Color** for instance red and choose a different **Width**.

This would show the different paths in the Runbook Designer for the error handling as indicated in the next screenshot (the links to the Send Event Log Message and **Create Group** activities have been modified):

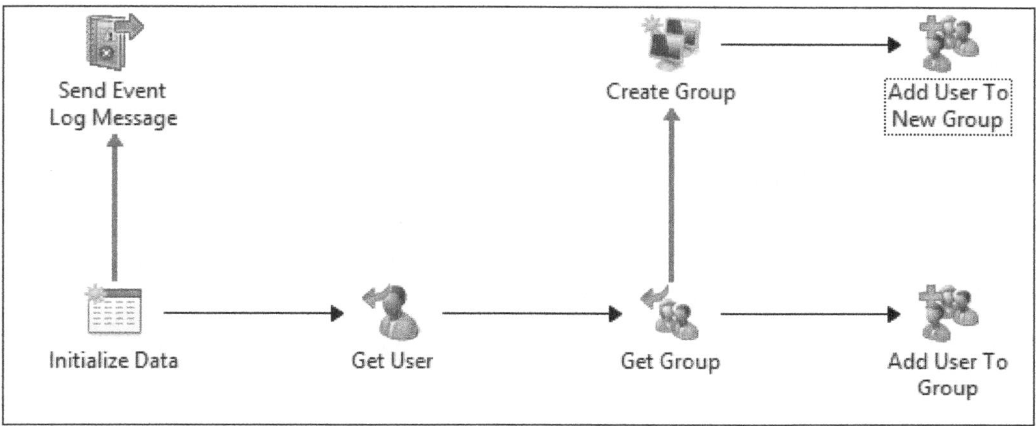

See also

Detailed information for the activities used in this Runbook are available at the following locations:

- Microsoft Technet – Send Event Log Message activity: `http://technet.microsoft.com/en-us/library/hh206038.aspx`
- Microsoft Technet – Get User activity: `http://technet.microsoft.com/en-us/library/hh553476.aspx`
- Microsoft Technet – Get Group activity: `http://technet.microsoft.com/en-us/library/hh553470.aspx`
- Microsoft Technet – Create Group activity: `http://technet.microsoft.com/en-us/library/hh553473.aspx`
- Microsoft Technet – Add User To Group activity: `http://technet.microsoft.com/en-us/library/hh564142.aspx`

Implementing logging in your Runbooks

Automating IT management processes often requires logging of results and changes to the environment. These requirements ensure there is an audit trail of changes as well as providing a troubleshooting aid. This recipe will describe how to log the output of a Runbook to comply with the auditing policies of an organization when automating.

There are a number of options available to you for logging in SCO 2012:

- Write output data of a Runbook to a text file
- Write output data of a Runbook to the Event Log of the Windows Server Operating System
- Write output data of a Runbook to a SQL Server database

Writing data of a Runbook to a text file is described in *Chapter 4, Creating Runbooks for Active Directory Tasks*, in the recipe *Using SCO to remove obsolete user accounts*. This is done by using the **Append Line** activity.

Writing data of a Runbook to the Event Log of the Windows Server Operating System is described in this chapter in the recipe *Implementing error handling in your Runbooks*. This is done by using the **Send Event Log Message** activity.

This recipe is focusing on how to use SCO to write output data to a SQL Server database for logging.

Getting ready

The preparation for this recipe requires you to create the using SCO to remove obsolete user accounts Runbook described in *Chapter 4, Creating Runbooks for Active Directory Tasks*.

The **DeleteObsoleteUsers** Runbook should look like the following screenshot:

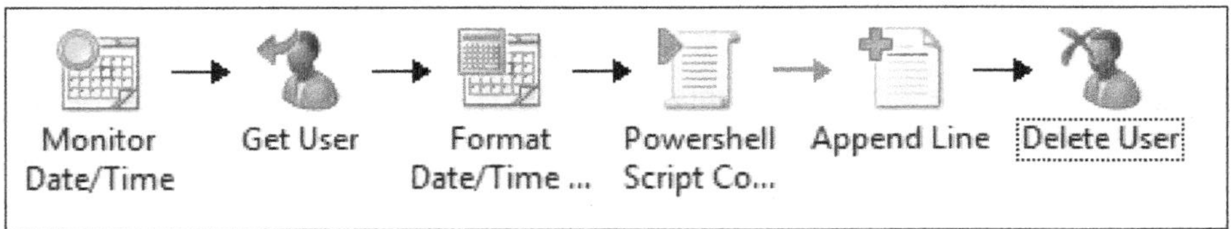

To log the output of the Runbook to a database you need a database called `SCO-Logging` on a SQL Server. You must create this database in your target Microsoft SQL Server before running the SQL script in this recipe.

For this recipe you need one table named `tblSCOlog` with the following columns:

Column name	Data type	Allow NULLS
ID	`int`	`False / Primary Key / Is Identity = yes / Identity Increment = 1`
RunbookName	`nvarchar(50)`	`True`
Description	`nvarchar(250)`	`True`
DateTime	`datetime`	`True`

The following SQL script will generate this table:

```
USE [SCO-Logging]
GO
CREATE TABLE [dbo].[tblSCOlog](
  [ID] [int] IDENTITY(1,1) NOT NULL,
  [Runbook] [nvarchar](50) NULL,
  [Description] [nvarchar](200) NULL,
  [DateTime] [datetime] NULL
) ON [PRIMARY]
GO
```

How to do it...

Follow these steps to add SQL database logging to the existing Runbook:

1. Navigate to the **Delete Obsolete Users** Runbook you created in *Chapter 4, Creating Runbooks for Active Directory Tasks*, using the Runbook Designer. You must check out the Runbook.
2. Navigate to the **Activities** section and then select **Utilities** and drag a **Query Database** activity into the runbook next to the **Delete User** activity.
3. Link the **Delete User** activity to the **Query Database** activity.
4. Double-click on the **Query Database** activity and provide the following connection information (**Database type** and **Authentication**):

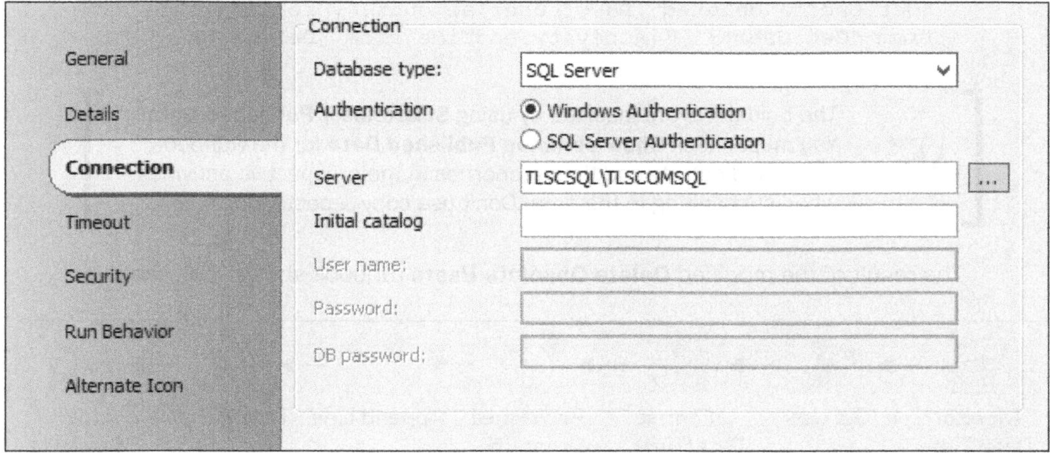

Enter your SQL Server in the **Server** field that is hosting the `SCO-Logging` database.

5. On the **Details** tab enter the following SQL query:

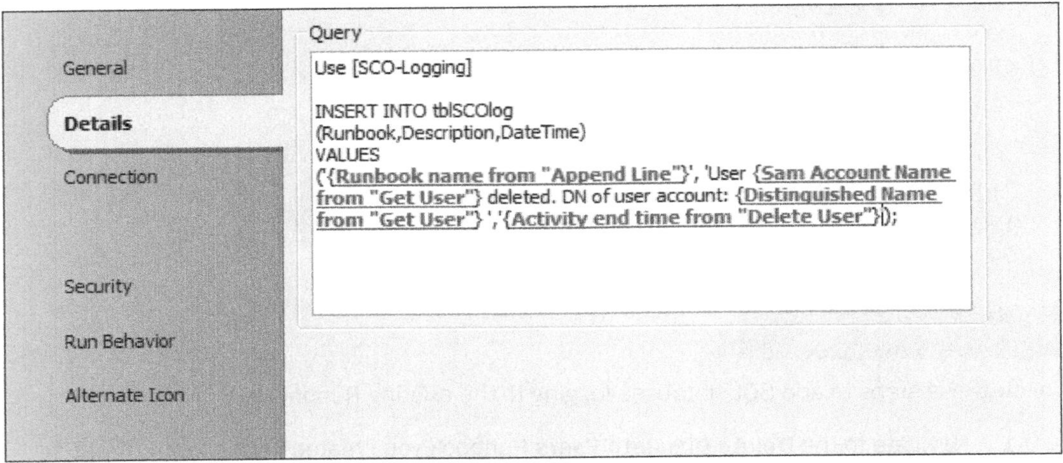

Here is the SQL query:

```
Use [SCO-Logging]

INSERT INTO tblSCOlog
(Runbook,Description,DateTime)
VALUES
('{Runbookname from "Append Line"}', 'User {SAM Account Name from
  "Get User"} deleted. DN of user account: {Distinguished Name
  from "Get User"}','{Activity endTime from "Delete User"}');
```

> The bold parts are inserted by using **Subscribe | Published Data**. You must check **Show common Published Data** for the Runbook name and activity end time properties in their respective activities when subscribing to the data. Don't use copy & paste in this case.

The result of the modified **Delete Obsolete Users** runbook should look like this:

How it works...

This Runbook must be checked in after completion in other for it to execute on the schedule specified in the **Monitor Date/Time** activity. In this example, it will be started at 10:00 PM every day (**Monitor Date/Time** activity).

In the **Get User** activity all disabled users will be queried from **Active Directory**.

The **Modification Date** is formatted in the **Format Date/Time Modification Date** activity.

For each disabled user the PowerShell Script will compare the formatted **Modification Date** against the current date -7 days. See the comment lines in the script for details:

```
#Set UserDN variable to Distinguished Name from "Get User" activity
$UserDN = "{Distinguished Name from "GetUser"}"
#Set LastmodifiedDate variable
$LastmodifiedDate = "{Format Result without adjustments from "Format
Date/Time Modification Date"}"
#Get the current date -7 days and format the date
$BeforeDate = (Get-Date).AddDays(-7).ToString("dd/MM/yyyy HH:mm:ss")
#If LastModifiedDate is less the Before date set DeleteUser variable
TRUE
IF ($LastmodifiedDate -lt $BeforeDate)
{
$DeleteUser = "TRUE"
}
#If LastModifiedDate is greater than Before date set DeleteUser
variable FALSE
ELSE
{
$DeleteUser = "FALSE"
}
```

If the `DeleteUser` variable is equal to `TRUE`, the Distinguished Name of the user and the current date are logged in a text file (the **Append Line** activity). If the `DeleteUser` variable is `FALSE` nothing will happen.

The **Delete User** activity in this Runbook will delete all user accounts in a disabled state which were last modified seven days ago (offset against the current time the Runbook is executed).

The **Query Database** activity will insert the specified information into the specified database (SCO-Logging) using the table `tblSCOlog`. To see the result after executing the Runbook, run the following query in the SQL Server Management Studio:

```
Use [SCO-Logging]
Select*From tblSCOlog
```

The result set should look like the following screenshot:

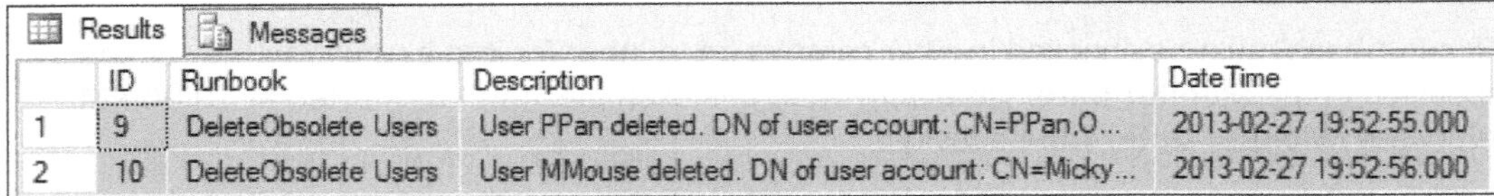

	ID	Runbook	Description	DateTime
1	9	DeleteObsolete Users	User PPan deleted. DN of user account: CN=PPan,O...	2013-02-27 19:52:55.000
2	10	DeleteObsolete Users	User MMouse deleted. DN of user account: CN=Micky...	2013-02-27 19:52:56.000

There's more...

Using a result set of a database query in a Runbook

If you need to use the result set of database entries in a later activity you can do this with the following example.

This example is based on the database and table we are using in this recipe.

1. Create a new Runbook called **SQLQuery**.
2. Navigate to the **Activities** section and then select **Utilities** and drag a **Query Database** activity into the Runbook.
3. Double-click on the **Query Database** activity and provide the following information:

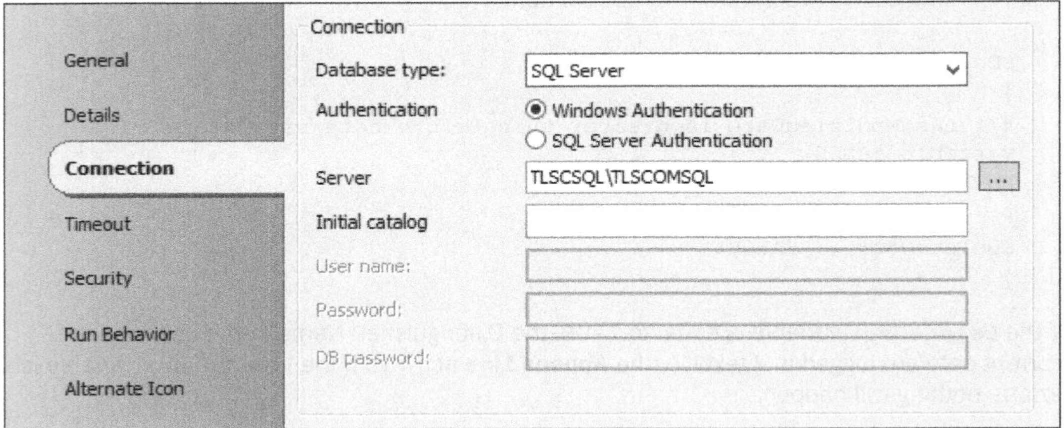

Enter your SQL Server in the **Server** field that is hosting the `SCO-Logging` database.

4. On the Details tab enter the following SQL query:

```
Use [SCO-Logging]

SELECT * from tblSCOlog
```

5. Navigate to the **Activities** section and then select **Text File Management** and drag an **Append Line** activity into the Runbook next to the **Query Database** activity.
6. Link the **Query Database** activity to the **Append Line** activity.
7. Double-click on the **Append Line** activity and configure the activity:

File	Right-click on the field **Expand**. Add the path of the file, for example `C:\PACKT8505EN-Chapter04\SQLTest.txt`.	The name of the text file for this Runbook.
File encoding	ASCII	Encoding of the file.

Add the following text in the **Text** field of the **Append Line** activity:

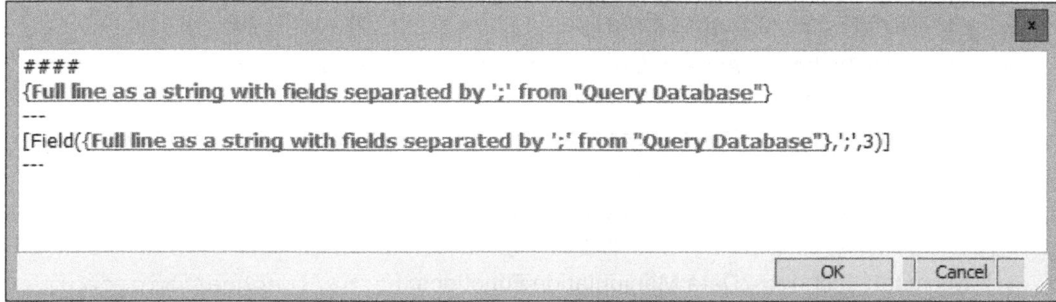

The first line retrieves all of the data as a single string.

The second line splits the result (separator/delimiter is ";") and only takes the third field information.

The result in the text file should look like the following screenshot:

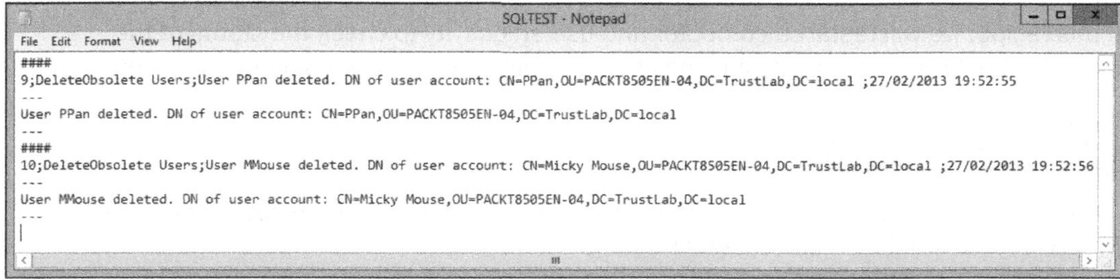

See also

Detailed information for the activities used in this Runbook can be found at the following locations:

- Microsoft Technet – Monitor Date/Time activity: `http://technet.microsoft.com/en-us/library/hh225031.aspx`
- Microsoft Technet – Get User activity: `http://technet.microsoft.com/en-us/library/hh553476.aspx`
- Microsoft Technet – Format Date/Time activity: `http://technet.microsoft.com/en-us/library/hh206037.aspx`
- Microsoft Technet – Run .Net Script activity: `http://technet.microsoft.com/en-us/library/hh206103.aspx`
- Microsoft Technet – Append Line activity: `http://technet.microsoft.com/en-us/library/hh206072.aspx`
- Microsoft Technet – Delete User activity: `http://technet.microsoft.com/en-us/library/hh553462.aspx`
- Microsoft Technet – Query Database activity: `http://technet.microsoft.com/en-us/library/hh206073.aspx`
- Microsoft Technet – Data Manipulation Functions: `http://technet.microsoft.com/en-us/library/hh440537.aspx`

Creating looping Runbooks

Looping in a Runbook is an option to wait for a specified condition and repeat an activity until the criteria is met.

In this recipe, we will restart a computer and use an activity to check the status of the computer until it is available again. The final step will be to log the result into the event log.

Getting ready

For this recipe you need a computer that can be restarted. On the nominated computer the Print Spooler should be available and running.

You must create a new Runbook in the Runbook Designer before configuring the activities of the process:

1. In the Runbook Designer expand the connection to the SCO 2012 server.
2. Right-click on **Runbooks** and click on **New** (you can also right-click on a folder under **Runbooks**).
3. Right-click on the newly created Runbook and rename it to **RestartComputer**.

How to do it...

Follow the next steps to add and configure different activities in the Runbook to restart a computer:

1. Navigate to the **Activities** section in the Runbook Designer and select **Runbook Control** and drag an **Initialize Data** activity into the middle pane of the Runbook.
2. Right-click on the **Initialize Data** Activity and then navigate to **Properties**. **Add** one parameter in this activity on the **Details** section:

Name of parameter	Data type	Contains information
ComputerName	String	Contains theNetBIOS name of the computer

3. Navigate to the **Activities** section and select **System** and drag a **Restart System** activity into the Runbook next to the **Initialize Data** activity.
4. Link the **Initialize Data** to the **Restart System** activity.
5. Double-click on the **Restart System** activity and provide the information of the following table on the **Details** section:

Name of parameter	Value	Contains information
Computer	Right-click on the **Computer** field and navigate to **Subscribe** | **Published Data**. Choose the **Initialize Data** in the **Activity:** field and select **ComputerName**.	NetBIOS name of the computer.
Message (Max. 120 characters)	Restarting triggered by Runbook.	Text displayed on the computer before restarted.
Wait before rebooting (seconds)	30 (30 seconds are the minimum value)	At least 1 uppercase character Complexity of passwords.
Force applications to close	Checked	Force running application to close before restarting the computer.

6. Navigate to the **Activities** section and select **Monitoring** and drag a **Get Service Status** activity into the Runbook next to the **Restart System** activity.
7. Link the **Restart System** activity to the **Get Service Status** activity.
8. Double-click on the link between the **Restart System** and **Get Service Status** activity.
9. Select the **Options** tab, change the **Trigger Delay** value to `40`, and click on **Finish**.

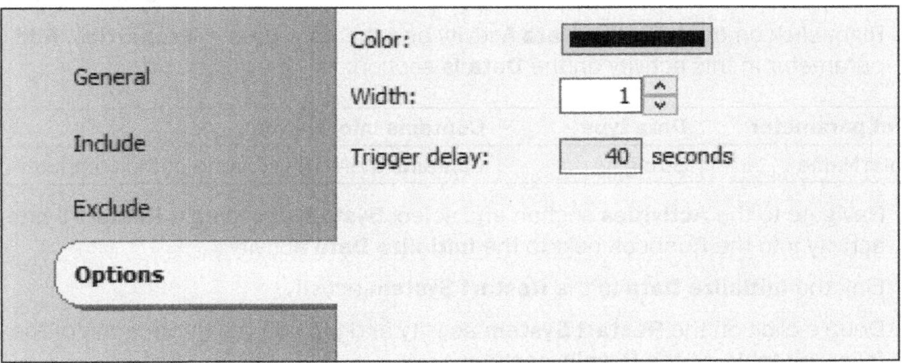

10. Double-click on the **Get Service Status** and provide the information using the following table on the **Details** section:

Name of parameter	Value	Contains information
Computer	Right-click on the Computer field and navigate to **Subscribe** | **Published Data**. Select **Initialize Data** in the **Activity:** field and select **ComputerName**.	NetBIOS name of the computer
Service	Pick the **Print Spooler** from the list (click on **...** to get a list of the available services).	The name of the service

11. Click on **Finish**.
12. Right-click on the **Get Service Status** activity and select **Looping ...**.

13. On the **General** tab in the **Get Service Status Looping** window check **Enable** under the **Looping** section and add a **Delay** between attempts of `20`.
14. On the **Exit** tab in the **Get Service Status Looping** window add three conditions (click on the **Get Service Status** value to start the process, and add the remaining conditions using the **Add** button):

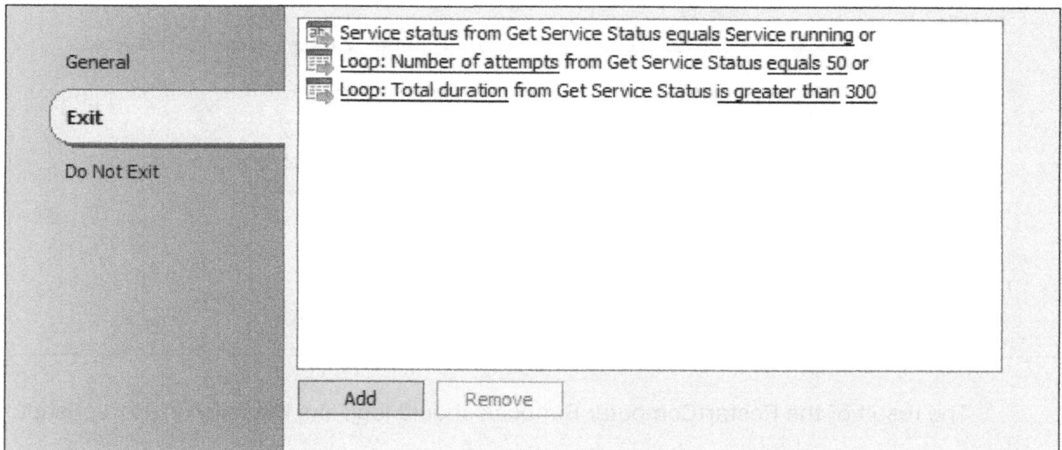

Loop: Number of attempts and **Loop: Total duration** is available if you check **Show common Published Data** in the **Published Data** window.

15. Navigate to the **Activities** section and select **Notification** and drag a **Send Event Log Message** activity into the Runbook next to the **Get Service Status** activity.
16. Link the **Get Service Status** activity to the **Send Event Log Message** activity.

17. Double-click on the **Send Event Log Message** activity and provide the following information:

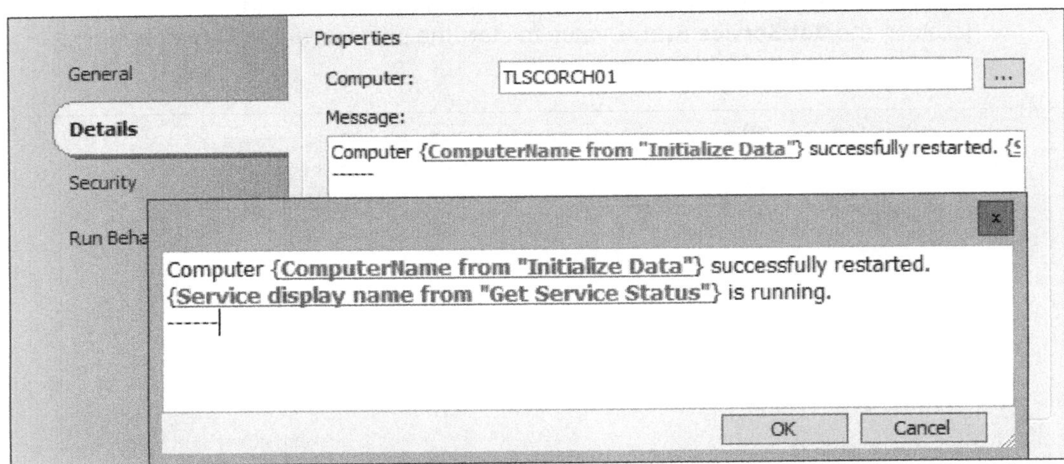

The result of the RestartComputer Runbook should look like the following screenshot:

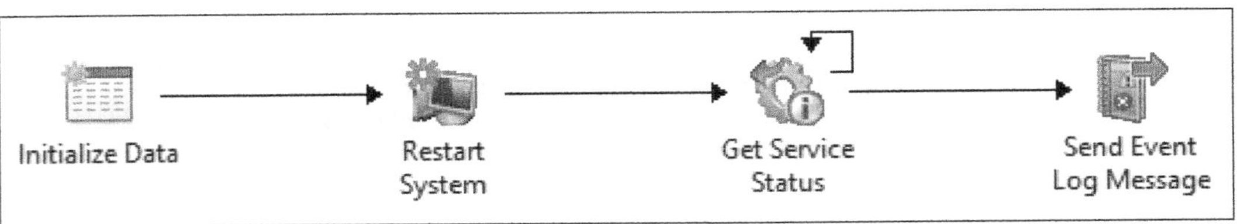

How it works...

When you start the Runbook in the Orchestrator Runbook Tester or on the Orchestration Console website you will be prompted for one parameter `ComputerName`. The `ComputerName` is the NetBIOS computer name of the computer you want to restart (the **Initialize Data** activity).

After providing this information, the next activity will restart the computer (the **Restart System** activity).

As the minimum delay for the reboot is 30 seconds, the next activity needs to wait 40 seconds (trigger delay of 40 seconds on the link between the **Restart System** and **Get Service Status** activities).

The **Get Service Status** activity will check the status of the **Print Spooler** service until one of the defined conditions is meet:

- The **Print Spooler** service status equals **Service running**
- The **Loop: Number of attempts** count reaches **50**
- The **Loop: Total duration** is greater than **300 seconds**

It is recommended to add additional conditions like the **Loop: Number of attempts** and/or **Loop: Total duration**. If you only use the **Print Spooler** service status equals Service running condition, and for some reason the computer failed to restart, the Runbook activity **Get Service Status** will loop **forever**. The Runbook won't end.

The positive result of the **Get Service Status** activity will be logged in the Event-Log after the **Print Spooler** is validated as service is running (**Send Event Log Message** activity).

There's more...

Adding error handling to Looping activities

It is a good practice to add some kind of error handling after a looping activity. In this recipe the restart of the computer might fail. So the **Get Service Status** activity will run out of time (**Loop: Total duration**) or reach the maximum number of attempts (**Loop: Number of attempts**). With error handling, you can cater for this situation. For more information, please take a look at the recipe *Implementing error handling in your Runbooks* in this chapter.

See also

Detailed information for the activities used in this Runbook are available at the following locations:

- Microsoft Technet - Restart System activity: `http://technet.microsoft.com/en-us/library/hh206108.aspx`
- Microsoft Technet - Get Service Status activity: `http://technet.microsoft.com/en-us/library/hh206048.aspx`
- Microsoft Technet - Send Event Log Message activity: `http://technet.microsoft.com/en-us/library/hh206038.aspx`

Useful Websites and Community Resources

Introduction

There is a constant technological advancement and innovation from product developers and professionals in the System Center community. This book is part of the vast pool of information available to readers.

This appendix will list some helpful websites and communities for System Center 2012 Orchestrator.

Our aim at the time of writing was to start or join the reader on their journey of knowledge gathering Orchestrator. The book is complimentary to the vast pool of resources available to you including the list of community websites listed in this appendix.

It is recommended that you mark the sites and follow the blogs to enhance your knowledge with free resources.

Orchestrator partner sites

Orchestration partner sites are as follows:

- Derdack: `www.derdack.com/microsoftsco`
- ITQ End User Portal for System Center Orchestrator (EUPSCO): `http://www.eupsco.com/`
- Kelverion: `http://www.kelverion.com/`

Authors community blogs

The community blogs of authors are as follows:

- Samuel Erskine: `http://www.frameworktorealwork.com/`
- Steve Beaumont: `http://systemscentre.blogspot.co.uk/`
- Andreas Baumgarten (German): `http://startblog.hud.de/`

Other useful community blogs

- System Center: Engineering Blog: `http://blogs.technet.com/b/orchestrator/`
- Kurt van Hoecke (MVP): `http://scug.be/`
- Marcel Zehner (MVP): `http://blog.scsmfaq.ch/`
- Anton Grisenko (MVP): `http://blog.scsmsolutions.com/`
- Patrik Sundqvist (MVP): `http://litware.se/`
- Nathan Lasnosk (MVP): `http://blog.concurrency.com/author/nlasnoski/`
- Anders Bengtsson: `http://contoso.se/blog/`

Frameworks and processes

Official ITIL website: `http://www.itil-officialsite.com/`

Microsoft Operations Framework:`http://technet.microsoft.com/en-us/library/cc506049.aspx`

ISO official website: `http://www.iso.org/iso/home.html`

Valuable community forums and user groups

- TechNet Forums – System Center Orchestrator (EN): `http://social.technet.microsoft.com/Forums/en-US/category/systemcenterorchestrator`
- TechNet Forums - System Center (DE): `http://social.technet.microsoft.com/Forums/de-DE/systemcenterde/threads`
- System Center Central – Orchestrator: `http://www.systemcentercentral.com/forums-archive/forums/orchestrator/`
- System Center Central - Orchestrator Posts: `http://www.systemcentercentral.com/category/blog/orchestrator/`
- SCSM.US: `http://scsm.us/`

- German System Center User Group: `http://scsmug.de/`
- German Private Cloud User Group: `http://www.ms-service-manager.com/index.php/usergroup`

Websites for Orchestrator solutions and extensions

- TechNet Library System Center 2012 Orchestrator: `http://technet.microsoft.com/en-us/library/hh237242.aspx`
- System Center 2012 Orchestrator Community Releases: `http://orchestrator.codeplex.com/`
- System Center Orchestrator Engineering Blog: `http://blogs.technet.com/b/orchestrator/`

Online Wikis

- Microsoft TechNet Wiki: Management Portal: `http://social.technet.microsoft.com/wiki/contents/articles/703.wiki-management-portal.aspx`
- Microsoft TechNet Wiki: Opalis Survival Guide: `http://social.technet.microsoft.com/wiki/contents/articles/768.opalis-survival-guide.aspx`

Social network resources

- System Center on Facebook: `https://www.facebook.com/pages/Microsoft-System-Center-Support/111513322193410`
- System Center on Twitter: `https://twitter.com/system_center`
- Orchestrator on Twitter: `https://twitter.com/SC_Orchestrator`

Index

Symbols

A

B

C

N

O

P

R

S

T

U

V

W

Thank you for buying

Microsoft System Center 2012 Orchestrator Cookbook

About Packt Publishing

Packt, pronounced 'packed', published its first book "*Mastering phpMyAdmin for Effective MySQL Management*" in April 2004 and subsequently continued to specialize in publishing highly focused books on specific technologies and solutions.

Our books and publications share the experiences of your fellow IT professionals in adapting and customizing today's systems, applications, and frameworks. Our solution-based books give you the knowledge and power to customize the software and technologies you're using to get the job done. Packt books are more specific and less general than the IT books you have seen in the past. Our unique business model allows us to bring you more focused information, giving you more of what you need to know, and less of what you don't.

Packt is a modern, yet unique publishing company, which focuses on producing quality, cutting-edge books for communities of developers, administrators, and newbies alike. For more information, please visit our website: `www.PacktPub.com`.

About Packt Enterprise

In 2010, Packt launched two new brands, Packt Enterprise and Packt Open Source, in order to continue its focus on specialization. This book is part of the Packt Enterprise brand, home to books published on enterprise software – software created by major vendors, including (but not limited to) IBM, Microsoft and Oracle, often for use in other corporations. Its titles will offer information relevant to a range of users of this software, including administrators, developers, architects, and end users.

Writing for Packt

We welcome all inquiries from people who are interested in authoring. Book proposals should be sent to `author@packtpub.com`. If your book idea is still at an early stage and you would like to discuss it first before writing a formal book proposal, contact us; one of our commissioning editors will get in touch with you.

We're not just looking for published authors; if you have strong technical skills but no writing experience, our experienced editors can help you develop a writing career, or simply get some

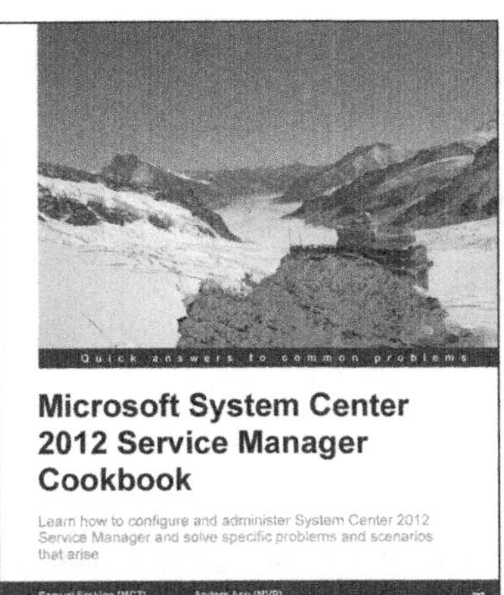

Microsoft System Center 2012 Service Manager Cookbook

ISBN: 978-1-84968-694-5 Paperback: 474 pages

Learn how to configure and administer System Center 2012 Service Manager and solve specific problems and scenarios that arise

1. Practical cookbook with recipes that will help you get the most out of Microsoft System Center 2012 Service Manager
2. Learn the various methods and best practices administrating and using Microsoft System Center 2012 Service Manager

---

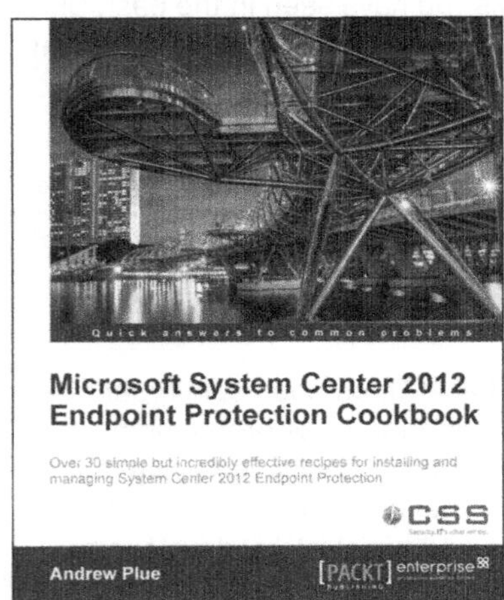

Microsoft System Center 2012 Endpoint Protection Cookbook

ISBN: 978-1-84968-390-6 Paperback: 208 pages

Over 30 simple but incredibly effective recipes for installing and managing System Center 2012 Endpoint Protection

1. Master the most crucial tasks you'll need to implement System Center 2012 Endpoint Protection
2. Provision SCEP administrators with just the right level of privileges, build the best possible SCEP policies for your workstations and servers, discover the hidden potential of command line utilities and much more in this practical book and eBook
3. Quick and easy recipes to ease the pain of migrating from a legacy AV solution to SCEP

Please check **www.PacktPub.com** for information on our titles

additional reward for your expertise.

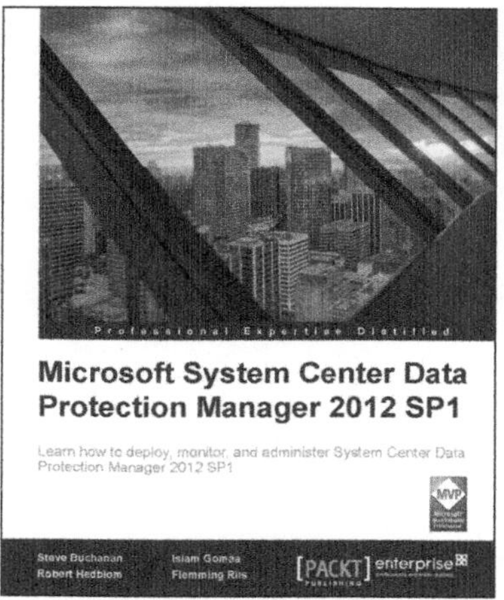

Microsoft System Center Data Protection Manager 2012 SP1

ISBN: 978-1-84968-630-3 Paperback: 328 pages

Learn how to deploy, monitor, and administer System Center Data Protection Manager 2012 SP1

1. Practical guidance that will help you get the most out of Microsoft System Center Data Protection Manager 2012

2. Gain insight into deploying, monitoring, and administering System Center Data Protection Manager 2012 from a team of Microsoft MVPs

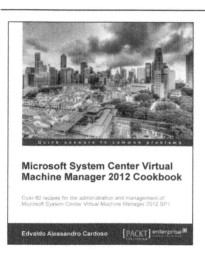

Microsoft System Center Virtual Machine Manager 2012 Cookbook

ISBN: 978-1-84968-632-7 Paperback: 342 pages

Over 60 recipes for the administration and management of Microsoft System Center Virtual Machine Manager 2012 SP1

1. Create, deploy, and manage Datacentres, Private and Hybrid Clouds with hybrid hypervisors by using VMM 2012 SP1, App Controller, and Operations Manager

2. Integrate and manage fabric (compute, storages, gateways, networking) services and resources. Deploy Clusters from bare metal servers

3. Learn how to use VMM 2012 SP1 features such as Windows 2012 and SQL 2012 support, Network Virtualization, Live Migration, Linux VMs, Resource Throttling, and Availability

Please check **www.PacktPub.com** for information on our titles

Lightning Source UK Ltd.
Milton Keynes UK
UKOW06f1039300813

216247UK00005B/54/P

9 781849 688505